PRAIRIE STATE BOOKS

In conjunction with the Illinois Center for the Book, the University of Illinois Press is reissuing in paperback works of fiction and nonfiction that are, by virtue of authorship and/or subject matter, of particular interest to the general reader in the state of Illinois.

*Series Editors*

Michael Anania, University of Illinois at Chicago
Robert Bray, Illinois Wesleyan University
John Hallwas, Western Illinois University
James Hurt, University of Illinois at Urbana-Champaign
Maria Mootry, Grinnell College

*Board of Advisors*

Roger D. Bridges, Illinois Historic Preservation Agency
John Mack Faragher, Mount Holyoke College
George Hendrick, University of Illinois at Urbana-Champaign
Babette Inglehart, Chicago State University
Robert W. Johannsen, University of Illinois at Urbana-Champaign
Bridget L. Lamont, Illinois State Library
Kenneth Nebenzahl, Chicago
Ralph Newman, Chicago
Howard W. Webb, Jr., Southern Illinois University at Carbondale

*A list of books in the series appears at the end of this volume.*

*They Broke the Prairie*

# They Broke the Prairie

*Being some account of the settlement
of the Upper Mississippi Valley by
religious and educational pioneers,
told in terms of one city, Galesburg,
and of one college, Knox*

EARNEST ELMO CALKINS

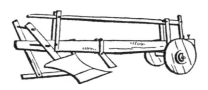

With an Introduction by Rodney O. Davis

UNIVERSITY OF ILLINOIS PRESS
Urbana and Chicago

Publication of this edition of *They Broke the Prairie* was made possible in part by a grant from Knox College. Thanks are also extended to Hugh W. Calkins and Golden Calkins Torgeson; the Admiral Company; Henrietta Bondi Adler; David R. Arnold; the Dick Blick Company; Mary I. Cleaveland; Dr. and Mrs. J. K. Erffmeyer; Mrs. Robert W. Murphy; Rick L. Peterson; Carl and Debbie Strauch; Wagoner Printing Co., Ann Asplund, manager; Howard A. Wilson; and the Walter Alexander Foundation.

P  5  4  3  2  1

*This book is printed on acid-free paper.*

Library of Congress Cataloging-in-Publication Data

Calkins, Earnest Elmo, 1868–1964.
    They broke the prairie : being some account of the settlement of
the Upper Mississippi Valley by religious and educational pioneers,
told in terms of one city, Galesburg, and of one college, Knox /
Earnest Elmo Calkins ; with an introduction by Rodney O. Davis.
        p.   cm. — (Prairie State books)
    Reprint. Originally published: New York : Scribner's, c1937.
    Bibliography: p.
    Includes index.
    ISBN 0-252-06094-6 (alk. paper)
    1. Galesburg (Ill.)—History.   2. Knox College (Galesburg, Ill.)—
History.   I. Title.   II. Series.
F549.G15C3   1989
977.3'49—dc20                                                89-32627
                                                                    CIP

# *Contents*

INTRODUCTION     xi

PREFACE     xxiii

## 1. *Contemporary Portrait*

I    THROUGH THE WINDSHIELD     1

II    DRIVING ABOUT TOWN     5

III    RAILROAD TO MOTOR CAR     7

IV    DOWN TOWN     11

V    AGRICULTURE     14

VI    SOCIAL STRUCTURE     19

VII    ORGANIZED SOCIAL INTERCOURSE     24

VIII    "OLD SIWASH"     28

## 2. *The Founding*

I    FINNEY AND HIS GREAT REVIVAL     35

II    GALE TAKES A HORSEBACK RIDE     37

III    THE "ONION GRUBBERS"     41

IV    CIRCULATING THE PLAN     45

V    THE EXPLORING COMMITTEE     48

VI    ENTER SILVANUS FERRIS     56

VII    "THE MESOPOTAMIA OF THE WEST"     61

VIII    THE THIRD MEETING     66

## 3. *Log City*

I    NEHEMIAH WEST GOES WEST FOR GOOD     71

II    HOOSIERS VS. YANKEES     77

# CONTENTS

III  THE BOAT PARTY                          85
IV   PIONEER ARCHITECTURE                     91
V    FOOD AND CLOTHING                        94
VI   RELIGION                                 97

## 4. *On the Prairie*

I    PAPER CITIES                            101
II   THE PANIC OF 1837                       105
III  KNOX MANUAL LABOR COLLEGE              107
IV   HOUSEHOLD SKILLS                        113
V    COLTON'S STORE                          116
VI   SUBDUING THE LAND                       120

## 5. *The Town Finds Itself*

I    KELLOGG AND THE COLLEGE                 129
II   "WEST BRICKS"                           134
III  JONATHAN BLANCHARD                      137
IV   THE OLD FIRST CHURCH                    141
V    BUSINESS                                145
VI   THE SELF-SCOURING PLOW                  152
VII  THE FERRISES                            155
VIII SOCIAL LIFE                             161
IX   RELIGION                                166

## 6. *Schism*

I    THE ENTERING WEDGE                      169
II   THE MIND OF A ZEALOT                    173
III  EDWARD BEECHER                          178
IV   "OLD MAIN"                              182

# CONTENTS

V  THE BLANCHARD WAR                           184

VI  THE BEECHER CRUSADE                         191

VII  KNOX'S THIRD PRESIDENT                     194


## 7. *Burlington Route*

I  RAILROAD ORGY                                197

II  THE PEORIA & OQUAWKA                        201

III  THE CENTRAL MILITARY TRACT                 206

IV  THE AURORA BRANCH                           210

V  THEY SAVE THE DAY                            213

VI  THE END OF AN ERA                           217


## 8. *The Gay Fifties*

I  UNDERGROUND RAILROAD                         221

II  BISHOP HILL                                 229

III  MORE BUSINESS                              234

IV  AMUSEMENT                                   241

V  CULTURE                                      253

VI  THREE MEN                                   261


## 9. *Lincoln*

I  POLITICS                                     273

II  GALESBURG'S BIG DAY                         277

III  ABRAHAM LINCOLN                            281

IV  STEPHEN A. DOUGLAS                          286

V  THE DEBATE                                   289

VI  "TWINKLE, TWINKLE, LITTLE CARR"             296

VII  WAR                                        300

# CONTENTS

## 10. *County Seat Fight*

I    KNOXVILLE'S LAST BATTLE      309

II    SELDEN GALE'S STRATEGY      315

III    BLANCHARD'S LAST WORD      319

## 11. *The Eighteen Eighties*

I    SOCIAL LIFE      325

II    DOMESTIC LIFE      333

III    MAIN STREET      344

IV    NEWSPAPERS      355

V    PUBLIC AFFAIRS      364

## 12. *Knox College Grows Up*

I    GULLIVER      373

II    NEWTON BATEMAN      383

III    CULTURE      392

IV    BROADER HORIZONS      404

## 13. *The Twentieth Century*

I    CATCHING UP WITH THE PRESENT      417

II    STANDARDIZATION OF AMERICA      422

III    THE HUMAN CONTENT      425

IV    GALESBURG, OF ALL PLACES      430

   BIBLIOGRAPHY      435

   INDEX      443

# *Introduction*

Since its publication in 1937, Earnest Elmo Calkins's *They Broke the Prairie* has been considered a model study of community development in the Middle West. Few towns the size of Galesburg, Illinois, have so good a history; and few local histories can so effectively evoke the development of an entire region. Calkins's broad original vision of his project is reconfirmed in this latest edition published by the University of Illinois Press.

Early in 1934, Mrs. Janet Greig Post, chairwoman of the Centenary of Knox College (1937), approached her long-time friend Earnest Calkins to prepare a history of the college. Calkins hesitated until he could be assured of collaboration by fellow Knox alumnus and Galesburg native Charles Gettemy, whose great-grandfather was college and town co-founder Sylvanus Ferris. He felt from the beginning that the joint founding of the college and the town should be celebrated together and that any book he and Gettemy might write must be a history of both the college and the colony that became Galesburg. Until that proviso was accepted by Mrs. Post, Calkins withheld his commitment.

From the outset, Calkins had been thinking in broader terms than a local history. He had been concerned about what he thought was the unfortunate emphasis by nineteenth-century travel writers on southern Illinois, that portion of the state bounded by the Mississippi River south of St. Louis and the Ohio River, and by the further relative disregard of the prairie region of northern and western Illinois by later writers of a scholarly sort. He hoped to rectify this neglect by writing of Galesburg and Knox College together, as a case study in the development of the prairie region as well as of the entire upper Middle West. Calkins wrote to Gettemy while the project was still in gestation: "I have long speculated about the forces that created the Galesburg that now is, not only the college, but farming, the railroad, the Civil War, the Swedes, Irish and negroes, the coming of industrialization; the same forces of course that were moving the entire Middle West. . . . In telling the story of Galesburg we would be telling then of many other towns and cities."[1] Calkins was also convinced that the book should stand on its own, that it should not be "merely a memorial volume, valuable to the alumni and those in the know," and that he and Gettemy should (as they did) assume sole responsibility for its publication and its contents.[2]

For Calkins, writing *They Broke the Prairie* was both a labor of love and a way out of a retirement that he felt had been premature and forced. His boyhood and early youth had been spent in Galesburg, where his family had moved shortly after his birth in 1868 and where his Knox B.A. was granted in 1891. After working there and in Peoria, plus an earlier false start in New York, Calkins moved permanently to New York in 1897, taking employment with the pioneer advertising firm of Charles Austin Bates. Four years later, he and a Bates colleague, Ralph Holden, struck out on their own, establishing a firm that became instrumental in turning advertising agencies away from the mere placement of ads and toward not only their actual creation but the development of entire campaigns. Calkins and Holden produced advertising of high artistic and imaginative standards for such clients as Sherwin-Williams Paints, Pierce-Arrow, H. J. Heinz, Wesson Oil and Snowdrift, and Arrow Shirts. One of their most famous creations was Phoebe Snow, whose "gown stay[ed] white, from morn till night, upon the Road of Anthracite," the Delaware and Lackawanna Railroad—in fact, the Erie-Lackawanna passenger train named for Phoebe was still in service in the 1960s. Calkins and Holden also published the first textbook on advertising methods, in 1905, and in 1925 Calkins received the Edward Bok Gold

# INTRODUCTION

Medal for his successful efforts in raising the standards of American advertising.

Holden, who was the outside man in the partnership, handled contacts, while Calkins, increasingly affected by the deafness that had plagued him since childhood, concerned himself with the company's internal creative affairs. After Holden's death in 1926, Calkins found it nearly impossible to function in the agency, as sales meetings and conferences were out of the question for him. The growing popularity of radio, and its potential as an advertising medium, also helped to convince him that he should get out, and he reluctantly retired in 1931.[3] As he explained to Knox president Albert Britt in Galesburg, soon after agreeing to write *They Broke the Prairie,* "If I could hear, it would greatly increase the scope of my work here, but on the other hand, if I had my hearing, I would not be here at all, I would be back in New York working on my job."[4]

Though he was obviously not a professional researcher, Calkins's preparation for the project was sound. He was already quite well read in the history of the area, for as he noted, "a deaf man . . . has a lot of time to himself."[5] Much of that time had been spent writing for publication; eventually, Calkins would have a number of books to his credit, including *Business the Civilizer* (1927) and two autobiographical volumes, *Louder, Please* (1924) and *And Hearing Not* (1946), plus some 100 articles in *Atlantic Monthly, Century, Scribner's,* and *Good Housekeeping.* A project suggested by the Atlantic Monthly Press had proved impossible because its completion would have required interviews, which Calkins was simply unable to conduct, and by 1934 he was ready to write a book based on serious research. Calkins took the Galesburg project very seriously and came to consider it "the work of my life, into which I can pour something enduring, the best that I have."[6]

Upon setting to work, Calkins made it his business to become current with scholarship on such subjects as the antislavery movement. He also began a lengthy correspondence with older residents of Galesburg and with descendants of those citizens who had moved elsewhere. One of the latter was George Washington Gale III of California, who remembered a great deal about his grandfather, the founder, and about town co-founder Sylvanus Ferris. Calkins made use of library materials and special collections in New York City, and in the fall of 1934 he spent two months in Galesburg, working mostly with manuscripts and some newspapers in the Knox College Archives and at the Galesburg Public Library. He made subsequent short research trips to Galesburg, and on one occasion, in May 1935, he also traveled to Springfield to deliver at the Illinois State Historical Society a paper that became the basis for the railroad chapters of *They Broke the Prairie*.[7] Most of his writing was done in New York, however, and he depended on the Knox director of publicity, Mrs. Helen Van de Woestyne, and the college's treasurer, Kellogg D. McClelland, to find the answers to later questions that arose. Gettemy's responsibilities at the Federal Reserve Bank of Boston in the end precluded his active collaboration, but he did function as Calkins's editor on the project as it progressed and as a sounding board for various problems and ideas as they came up.

Calkins ultimately came to depend most on reminiscences and correspondence with older citizens and with founders' descendants, official materials from both town and college, manuscripts from the founding period, a miscellany of published items, and newspapers, although he examined the last in a scattered fashion. For the two decades after the Civil War, which the book covers somewhat thoroughly, Calkins relied considerably on his own memory. He professed to consider Knox County's three nineteenth-century and early twentieth-century histories to be tainted sources, but in fact he became rather dependent on them. It did not occur to him to consult such potentially rich materials as the Federal Census manuscripts or the archival material stored in the Knox County Court House (such as assessors' books), on the basis of which useful quantitative inquiries might have been made; such research by historians was in its infancy in the 1930s and would not become important until well after World War II.

# INTRODUCTION

While researching and writing *They Broke the Prairie,* Calkins took on additional responsibilities for the Knox-Galesburg centennial. That he was able to complete so many projects simultaneously is a tribute to his ability and enthusiasm. He prepared and gave an address, "Why They Listened to Lincoln," at the college's Founders' Day observance in February 1937, and later that year, in June, "The Masque of the Prairie Pioneers," a pageant he authored, was performed outdoors on several nights. Calkins advised the Galesburg Chamber of Commerce and downtown merchants about street decorations and window displays for the local celebration, and he designed the centennial logo. An avid hobbyist as well as a reader and writer, he built a detailed scale model of Galesburg in 1857, which was displayed at the celebration, and photographed sections of the model to use as endpaper illustrations for the first two printings of *They Broke the Prairie.* He also helped to arrange a display of nineteenth-century railroad rolling stock at Galesburg's Burlington station. Calkins compiled and published a complete list, with biographical information, of all the first settlers of the Galesburg colony, and he wrote the introduction to and edited *Log City Days,* a volume of two pioneer Galesburg narratives, which was published during the centennial year.[8]

Obviously, Calkins was obliged to work hard and rapidly to successfully meet his self-imposed June 1937 publication deadline for *They Broke the Prairie.* The book, as completed, falls into three major divisions; the founding (parts 2−6) is by far the longest, while shorter sections deal with the coming of the Chicago, Burlington, and Quincy Railroad, the Lincoln-Douglas debate, and the Civil War (parts 7−10), and the postwar era (parts 10−11). Such an emphasis is revealing of Calkins's own priorities, for he never considered the book as a comprehensive history of Galesburg. To that fact can be attributed a certain awkwardness in the book's arrangement, for Mrs. Post and the college's trustees expected a more or less complete history of Knox. Calkins therefore had trouble ending the book because, he confessed to Gettemy, he found the period after 1880 "difficult [due to] its nearness, and the lack of any logical climax on which to end. . . . There is definitely movement to an account of the founding, to the religious controversy, to the fight for the railroad and the county seat. All the factors leading to the Civil War, slave running, abolitionist persecutions, etc. are climaxed in the Lincoln-Douglas debate. After that there is no great issue. The river, having passed rapids and falls, now simply flows on."[9] Accordingly, Calkins's treatment of Galesburg ends, rather abruptly, at a time roughly concurrent with the author's own final departure from the town in the mid-1890s. His introductory and concluding chapters on Galesburg in the 1930s, however, are now valuable descriptions in their own right. Discussion of college affairs continues after the 1880s, to the end of the administration of Albert Britt in 1936, but is rather thin and relies heavily on the recollections and assistance of retired dean William E. Simonds.[10]

Thoughtful contemporary citizens of Galesburg would question Calkins's complaint that after the Civil War the history of the town lacks focus or interest, but he should not, after all, be faulted for not writing about a period that he never intended to write about. For the half century of local history that is the heart of the book, there are a number of grounds for comment. No book is ever free of factual errors; those in *They Broke the Prairie* cannot be considered disabling or even worthy of much note. Calkins does seem to be impatient with dates, as an amateur writing history might be, but the relative paucity of chronological signposts in the book can lead to reader disorientation, especially in Calkins's rendering of the county seat fight with Knoxville. Indeed, chronology rather disappears from the chapter entitled "The Gay Fifties," which is mostly an impressionistic treatment of the decade taken from newspapers and a city directory, so written as to suggest an essential changelessness from the beginning of the period to the end. The 1850s, however, was a period of proportionally the most explosive growth in the town's history, especially after the coming of the railroad, though we get no measure of that expansion, or any adequate sense of how different Galesburg was in 1860 from 1850. Readers in

the late twentieth century will doubtless cringe at Calkins's condescending treatment of Galesburg's black citizens, but on that
subject perhaps nothing better can be expected. Equally noticeable
is his emphasis on the development of Main Street retailing, before
and after the coming of the railroad, seemingly a symptom of a
larger tendency to focus, if not on Galesburg's elite, then definitely
on its entrepreneurial middle class. This is done to the neglect of
the thousands of families supported in the 1850s and after by jobs
on train crews and in the Burlington Railroad shops and yards, and
by the town's growing manufacturing interest. This class-oriented
bias, however inadvertent, can be somewhat corrected, for the
years after the Civil War at least, by a reading of Carl Sandburg's
recollections of the same time in Galesburg, written from a decid-
edly different socioeconomic standpoint.[11]

It must be noted that in the field of social history the priorities of
scholars are now in many instances different from those of Calkins.
A work such as this, if done in the late 1980s, would require more
time to produce; and it would originate, in part, in sources more
refractory than the ones Calkins used and requiring sophisticated
computer techniques, though such sources would also permit inquiry into the impact of the great population changes of the 1850s
and after, as the town became pluralistic and the distribution
of wealth undoubtedly became skewed as never before. Insofar
as Calkins addresses himself to interethnic or class conflict in
post–Civil War Galesburg, for instance, it is briefly in terms of the
local struggle over saloons. He writes on page 331: "Although
there were 30 saloons in town," at a time when Galesburg's population was 18,000, "drinking had no social standing." The matter
cannot now be so easily dismissed, for the saloon issue was deeply
divisive and one of several that separated Galesburg's heavily Yankee
elite and middle class from the Irish, Swedes, and poorer Prot-
estants of British extraction. We are given little insight into the
politics of the community or into group political behavior after the
changes wrought by the coming of the railroad. Neither does
Calkins look into the changing character of the local power struc-

ture; nor into influences that might have mitigated community conflict, countervailing those that stimulated it. The continued attractiveness of Galesburg as a place to live and work over several generations is also something that Calkins merely assumes without investigation, despite powerful evidence to the contrary. He depicts the Burlington Railroad in almost exclusively positive terms, for instance, when in fact its presence was a source of periodic tension as well as prosperity, especially in such crises as the great railroad strike of 1877 or the systemwide strike on the Burlington eleven years later. Calkins would have remembered both confrontations, for each erupted in violence in Galesburg, and bad feelings from the latter lasted for years.

To argue these points, however, is to obscure Calkins's intention. "I am strongly inclined," he told Gettemy once he had started writing, "to treat the book in a broader and freer manner—not argue too long about debated minor points, but to be concerned more with the spirit of the understanding and the more dramatic and illuminating events which can be told with a liveliness that makes them worth reading for their own sake." [12] To take such a position is not necessarily to focus only on the smiling side of life, but it does reveal Calkins's presumption that to write history is to practice a literary art and, perhaps incidentally but significant nonetheless, to do so in a mostly narrative format. The founding and formative years of Galesburg and Knox College were always his primary concerns and certainly amenable to this approach; his treatment of them need never be done again. Indeed, Hermann Muelder implied as much by devoting only an introductory chapter to the years before the Civil War in *Missionaries and Muckrakers*. [13] Calkins had the advantage of writing about a homogeneous colony of like-minded people, much of whose correspondence survives. He could therefore rather carefully detail, for a year or so before departure until the destination was reached and long after, the relocation of a large number of migrants from upstate New York to western Illinois. His descriptions of the settling-in process are evocative and informative, and his portrait of the Galesburg colony as a kind of Yankee exotic on the prairie among earlier-arriving Hoosiers farming the timber is very carefully drawn. And, of course, he does not stint on the nearly disastrous conflict that eventually broke out among the founders and their followers; or on the contentions that existed between the Galesburg Yankees and Yorkers and their Hoosier neighbors. Most midwestern communities went through similar early experiences, and Calkins's goal of writing of Galesburg as a microcosm of the larger region is very satisfactorily realized in these beginning chapters. His achievement was acknowledged at the time of publication, with one reviewer, whose comment was typical, remarking on Calkins's success in lifting local history above antiquarian preoccupations, and "admirably illustrat[ing] the possibilities of the form." [14] It is for this important accomplishment that Calkins continues to deserve recognition.

Calkins's description of the community's involvement in its Lincoln-Douglas debate is the best such account we have for any of the debate sites. Indeed, as he admitted, much of what he wanted to put into the book climaxed with the debate and with the war that followed. Calkins is also very conscious of another benchmark in the town's early history, the significance of which he carefully embellished. This is encompassed in the story of President Blanchard's attempt to stop the Burlington Railroad from operating on Sunday. The story is doubtless exaggerated and has seemed apocryphal to many, but at the least it is symbolic of a considerable truth: that after the coming of the railroad, Galesburg's major activities would increasingly be regulated by an external corporate agenda, not by a local one. [15] The local independence that Galesburg had enjoyed as an insular Yankee settlement would be progressively diminished in the twentieth century, as Calkins was acutely aware. In this sense, again, Galesburg's history replicates that of most small midwestern towns.

Earnest Elmo Calkins lived for twenty-seven years after the publication of *They Broke the Prairie.* Until his death in October 1964, he retained a keen interest in the world and in the affairs of Knox

# INTRODUCTION

College and Galesburg, maintaining high spirits in spite of his handicap. Of his life's work, the remains of which are considerable, the advertising that he created is probably the most ephemeral. His other books, though still occasionally cited, have not remained continuously in print. It seems safe to say that *They Broke the Prairie* will be remembered and read the longest of all, for it set a standard in the writing of community history that continues to be widely aspired to and honored.

—RODNEY O. DAVIS

### NOTES

1. Calkins to Gettemy, February 13, 1934, in Earnest Elmo Calkins Papers, Knox College Archives.

2. Calkins to Gettemy, February 20, 1934, Calkins Papers.

3. Sue Rowe Doe, "Earnest Elmo Calkins: That Remarkable Deaf Man from Galesburg," *Knox Alumnus* (Spring 1987), 8–11; Steven Fox, *The Mirror Makers: A History of Advertising and Its Creators* (New York, 1984), chap. 2; *New York Times,* October 6, 1964.

4. Calkins to Britt, October 8, 1934, Calkins Papers.

5. Calkins to Gettemy, March 6, 1934, Calkins Papers.

6. Calkins to Post, April 15, 1934, Calkins Papers.

7. Earnest Elmo Calkins, "Genesis of a Railroad," *Transactions of the Illinois State Historical Society* (1935), 39–72.

8. Earnest Elmo Calkins, ed., *Log City Days* (Galesburg, 1937).

9. Calkins to Gettemy, August 14, 1936, Calkins Papers.

10. William E. Simonds, "The Four Presidents," ms., Calkins Papers.

11. Carl Sandburg, *Always the Young Strangers* (New York, 1953). Sandburg thought highly of Calkins and admired *They Broke the Prairie* as a "classic portrait of a small town and college in the Midwest" (p. 317). See also Jean C. Lee, *Prairies, Prayers and Promises* (Northridge, Calif., 1987), 44–52.

12. Calkins to Gettemy, January 25, 1935, Calkins Papers.

13. Hermann R. Muelder, *Missionaries and Muckrakers: The First Hundred Years of Knox College* (Urbana, Ill., 1984).

14. Gerald Carson in *New York Herald Tribune,* June 6, 1937.

15. Calkins's informant for the Blanchard story was the daughter of a Burlington employee who might indeed have seen such an event as was depicted. Calkins to Myra Patch, December 11, 1934, Calkins Papers.

# Preface

This book is the fruit of a dream cherished for more than forty years. When in 1894 I wrote for *The University Magazine*, long since perished, a series of papers on the history of Knox College, I promised myself that some day I would compile a more extended account, and link up with it the history of Galesburg, for college and town were the outcome of the same pioneer impulse, and their chronicle is inextricably interwoven. Galesburg is my home town. There I passed the formative and impressionable years of my life. It seemed that a detailed story of the men and influences responsible for its founding might be made a chapter in the history of the Middle West.

I might, however, be still toying with the idea but for the gentle insistence of Janet Greig Post, who felt that such a book would be an appropriate way of marking the end of the first hundred years of the joint lives of the two enterprises. Mrs. Post is an unselfish, devoted friend of Knox College. She was born at a farm near Fonda, N.Y. graduated from the college, was one of its first, and one of its most successful deans of women, and is the only woman member of its board of trustees. At her urgent request I undertook this chronicle. While she is in no way responsible for either fact or opinion, it owes much to her faith and understanding sympathy.

In the beginning I had planned to prepare the work in co-operation with a boyhood friend, a classmate in school and college, a partner in several juvenile amateur publishing ventures, and an earnest student of local history. Charles Ferris Gettemy was born in Galesburg, great-grandson of one of the city's ablest founders, Silvanus Ferris. He is a graduate of the college, and has just completed a memoir of his ancestor that is a model of patient research and painstaking accuracy. His exacting duties as assistant Federal Reserve officer for the Boston district prevented our working together, but I am greatly indebted to him, not only for the carefully sifted data of the Ferris family, but for advice and criticism during the progress of this work, and particularly for a careful reading of the manuscript. He is not responsible, however, for any of the conclusions reached.

Another boyhood friend who should be mentioned is the late Frederic Reuben Jelliff. After fifty-four years in active service on the staff of the local newspaper, now *The Register-Mail,* he died in harness at the age of eighty-two. No man knew better the history of the city where he spent his life. Shortly before his death he compiled from official records a novel and useful municipal history of the town. During the last year of his life he wrote out for me, in that still legible handwriting I had admired as a boy, more than two hundred pages of manuscript in answer to my questionnaires.

A circumstance that has made this research both pleasant and profitable is the Caldwell Collection of books, documents, prints and maps pertaining to the early history of Illinois, collected over a dozen years by Edward Caldwell, of New York, a trustee of Knox College, and given by him to the Henry K. Seymour Library of the college. The collection numbers several thousand items, and in respect to Knox College and Galesburg it is unique. Without it this book could not have been written, and would not have been undertaken. I am further indebted to Mr. Caldwell's wide knowledge of Illinois history for much help, advice and criticism, for a thorough reading of my manuscript, and finally for the preparation of the bibliography, nearly every item of which is found in the Caldwell Collection.

Much of the book, however, rests on reminiscences of old settlers, mainly papers read before the Knox County Historical Society, in the eighties and nineties when many of the original

# PREFACE

pioneers were still living. I have been assisted also by newsy
letters from alumni and former citizens of Galesburg, many of
them over eighty years of age, and some over ninety, who have
recalled for me memories of their youth. One in particular
deserves especial mention, the venerable George Washington
Gale, of Saratoga, California, eighty-nine years old, grandson of
the founder godfather of the town. Handicapped by bodily in-
firmities, he nevertheless writes with vigor and clarity. He is the
only living link with the courageous band who established a
community and "literary institution" on the prairies of Illinois,
the only one who saw them in the flesh.

Space does not permit the mention of other friends who have
contributed valuable information for the purpose of this book,
but I am especially grateful to the following: Mrs. Royal S.
Van de Woestyne, for collating and copying newspaper articles
and old records; Miss Anna Hoover, whose ability has put the
Galesburg Public Library on such a high plane; Doctor William
E. Simonds, until his retirement beloved Dean of Knox College;
Willis E. Terry for his salty anecdotes; Miss Alice Lowrie, descendant of both George W. Gale and Silvanus Ferris; Mrs.
Bertha Chambers Brainard, granddaughter of Matthew Chambers, pioneer merchant; Mrs. Frances Arnold Woods, great-
granddaughter of Silvanus Ferris; Mrs. Mary Lanphere Hayner,
the aging granddaughter of Sarah W. Hitchcock who became
the second wife of the patriarch Silvanus Ferris; Mrs. Hettie
Linsley Thompson, Miss M. Isabel Blood; Miss Myra Patch,
whose father, William W. Patch, was the first conductor on the
C. B. & Q., and whose flair for picturesque anecdotes is remarkable; J. W. Estes, Henry F. Jerauld, John W. Geer and many
others, to all of whom, named and unnamed, I am extremely
grateful.

E. E. C.

New York, March 25, 1937.

[xxv]

# 1

## Contemporary Portrait

### I

#### THROUGH THE WINDSHIELD

A traveller crossing the country through the upper valley of the Mississippi is aware that this broad province of Old Man River differs as greatly from the Atlantic seaboard as it does from the Pacific slope. The old Northwest Territory, Virginia's gift to the nation, ended at the banks of the Mississippi, but Iowa belongs with Illinois, Indiana, and Ohio. They are of the same general character, topographically of one piece, having a common history, the arrival of the pioneers, the breaking of the centuries-old sod, the supreme problem of fencing, the advent of transportation, concentration on the more profitable crops, prosperity, then decline, and now the promise of new birth.

The transcontinental traveller once gathered through the windows of a railroad train impressions of fleeting towns, Elyria, Elkhart, Aurora, Elgin, Moline, Ottumwa, spaced by seeming endless miles of symmetrical and perfectly aligned cornfields, punctuated by upstanding silos and windmills visible for miles on the level prairie. These cities, of approximately the same age, founded as a result of a common westward movement, set on a level prairie lacking the surprise and charm of mountain scenery, seem strangely alike, except where a factory town is sharply differentiated from an agricultural community.

The modern tourist does not sneak in the back way with the railroad, seeing only the selvage. He drives boldly through on Main Street, savoring the town more fully and more slowly, but even to him there appears to be a certain sameness to the monotonous succession of cities.

[ 1 ]

That sameness is but the accident of architecture and physiognomy, for these western towns have individuality in spite of the levelling effect of unending prairie, and the standardization exerted by the one prevailing gainful occupation of farming. Their individuality lies deeper, and is largely the result of their history. More than a passing glance is needed to savor it. To understand the hold, the strange appeal of these prairie towns, let us take a western city and examine it horizontally as well as perpendicularly, and see if we cannot isolate its character, for surely no collection of human beings living in an integrated community can be without human interest.

In western Illinois, midway between the Illinois and the Mississippi rivers, lies Galesburg. It is one hundred sixty miles from Chicago, forty miles from Burlington, and one hundred years from virgin prairie.

Its history is compressed within the limits of a century; one hundred years ago nothing but empty prairie—today thirty thousand souls, living, working, playing, loving, sinning—pursuing the ways of community life. Shops, stores, houses, public buildings, and utilities compose the physical city; the people are the social organization; the manner in which these people make their living constitutes its economic life.

This physical structure and its human content is the result of evolution over five generations, shaped by events from without, the history of the nation of which the town is a unit, but influenced even more by the ferment within. Between them they have made the community something quite different from what its pious founders visioned. It is not the city they intended, nor is it in the hands of their descendants, but much that gives it flavor, its personality, is the result of that initial impetus. Knox College, the main reason for its existence, is not the "literary institution" the founders had in mind, but it has imparted to the town a certain culture more durable than the rigid piety with which the founders sought so earnestly to stiffen it.

From the biography of this town we may learn something of

the history of our country, particularly of that vast domain between the Alleghanies and the Rockies, for the founding of Galesburg as a site for a Christian college was part of the greater movement which settled the upper Mississippi valley, and the struggle of this town with its environment is a page from the history of civilization, and had parallels in other communities of that time and region.

Galesburg may be approached in several ways. The Burlington train from Chicago follows the route of the covered wagons that brought the Yankee pioneers, and lands one at the yellow brick station two blocks from Main Street. The Santa Fé deposits the traveller at its sandstone station the other side of Main Street a block from the public square. Or one can motor over as straight, smooth and level concrete roads as are found anywhere in America and enter the town from any of the four points of the compass, driving past outposts of red and yellow gas pumps and cogged-wheel announcements of Rotary luncheons, direct to the public square, the center, but not the heart of the town.

In its plain prairie way it is an attractive town, for like most agricultural communities it shows few of the rags and scars of the depression. Its boundary is sharply defined; where the prairie ends the town begins, with no slums, no shabby purlieus, to drive through, but rows of neat unaffected houses embowered in trees. The town belongs to the prairie, its setting and its source of sustenance. It rests easily on the land, and gets its beauty from it, and a real beauty it is.

In the public square, grandly known as "City Park," the two principal streets, Main and Broad, bisect. It was intended to be the focus of business, but that tide flowed east, leaving the town a bit off center, just as it shifted from the moral and social core of its founders. The square is a rather forlorn spot. One side is lined with a row of garish repeal taverns, hesitating between restaurant and saloon, huddled together by zoning restrictions. On another facet are garages and filling stations, and some of the humbler shops. But Central Church, marking the site of the pioneer meeting house, also stands on the square, its pretentious architecture characteristic of the end of the century, but somehow falling short of the dignity of the simple wooden temple it displaced.

Main Street goes to the paving brick works at East Galesburg, and west to the old colony cemetery, so near the square its ghosts scared the tide of trade east. Broad Street runs north to what would be "quality hill" (if there were hills in this level town), and south to the college precincts, where it is parked with a triple row of trees. The straggling group of buildings which constitute the high school fills one side of a block; the other has the Carnegie-built public library—one of the best in the state—the old church where Edward Beecher, Henry Ward's brother, preached, now Beecher chapel, and the dormitory for women, once the Female Seminary, now Whiting Hall.

At the end of this shady block the street runs into a park, half of it given over to the courthouse, monument to Galesburg's successful contest with Knoxville—no western town history is complete without its county seat fight—and then comes the college campus, four blocks square, which with that portion of the park not utilized by courthouse allows an open tree-covered space of some thirty-five acres in the middle of the town—a good thing, too, for with the exception of Hope Cemetery this is the only large breathing spot, though there are several tiny parks and two playgrounds, and three country clubs outside the city limits.

In the center of the campus is Old Main, the earliest building, still standing and bearing its years with a sort of dignified beauty in spite of its rather incongruous architecture. Other buildings are scattered over the campus, science hall, gymnasium, men's dormitory, college theatre, but the best of the modern buildings is the library across the street in the row with fraternity houses. In this quarter six hundred young men and women live almost wholly apart from the life of the town around them, a world within a world.

The façade of Main Street is undistinguished, the conventional pattern, banks, chain drug and grocery stores, beauty parlors, clothing and hardware emporiums, department stores, in three-story brick buildings, with lawyers, doctors, dentists and realtors in the offices above. The stores overflow into all the side streets and line the way to the Burlington "depot," near which is the town's chief hostelry, owned by and named for the town's chief magnate, a modern Hotel Red Book house, with shining restaurant, waitresses in bright uniforms, good coffee from silex glass pitchers and "sizzling T-bone steaks a specialty." Over the bar in its modern cocktail lounge smartly dressed barmaids dispense Scotch highballs or pineapple sundaes with equal nonchalance.

It is, to tell the truth, just such a Main Street as Sinclair Lewis describes with such delightful malevolence, but like that Main Street and all Main Streets, behind its commonplace façade life is as varied and colorful as any spot where human beings are gathered, however dull their outward shell may appear to the superficial observer.

## II

### DRIVING ABOUT TOWN

On either side of the brick spine of Main Street lie certain districts or quarters, unofficial but well defined, each with its own character. The north side has been and still is the preferred residential quarter, though its prestige and that of the old families which gave it character has fallen somewhat; but it continues to grow, to creep farther out on to the prairies as the younger generation sets up its homes. It consists of eight long shady streets running north from Main, which as soon as the clusters of stores, churches, clubs and other utilities are cleared, settle down to rows of neat wooden houses with shady lawns, the pattern broken here and there by the more modern brick three-story flats squeezed in between.

East of this, and still north of Main is the Swedish quarter, with its own lares and penates, the most sharply defined ethnic element in the town, descendants of the emigrants who quit Eric Jansson's colony at Bishop Hill in 1857 when that Utopian venture began to break down.

The south side, except for the shady oasis of the college and its dependencies, is occupied by the railroad, meaning the Burlington—the Santa Fé is hardly more than a station and is on the north side—shops, roundhouses, switchyards, steel and tie plants, stockyards, and the homes of those who work for it, once predominantly Irish, that south of Irish stock, Collopys, Garritys, Slatterys, Moloneys; the second generation got education and its cleverer ones graduated into other fields. Edward Hurley, former shipping board head, was one of them.

On the east side north of the railroad territory is Lombard College, once a flourishing Universalist institution, now a group of old red brick buildings scattered over a campus covered with great trees. The Universalists were the first liberal thinkers to modify the tight-laced puritan pattern of the town, but the long rivalry between the two colleges ended when Lombard was merged with Knox, and its plant sold to the city. The main building, an authentic example of scholastic architecture of the Fillmore period—as is also Old Main—is now used as a public school.

West on the south side is the Negro quarter, its grandparents largely the fugitive slaves who found Galesburg a safe asylum in the days of the Underground Railroad. Because of it, the town attracted colored people of an exceptional character, some of whom were successful financially and politically, and many of them respected citizens, while others gave the town its quota of those exponents of darkey philosophy known as "characters." Negroes are not supposed to live north of Main Street or east of Cedar Street, but there is no legal restraint. It is a sort of colored "gentlemen's agreement."

Thus there is a geographic distribution of the only three foreign

[ 6 ]

elements which have seriously modified and diluted the original
New England Yankee Puritan stock of which the primary settlers
wholly consisted. English, Swedish, Irish and African are still the
four principal elements, with a sprinkling of other races, of which
Germans are the most numerous. The Irish and Negroes are
dying out, the Swedes increasing. The latter are excellent citizens,
thrifty and well-behaved. They participate actively in business
life, but socially they are inclined to keep to themselves.

The pioneer town was laid out on generous lines with sixty-four-
foot lots, and few of the first settlers were content with one lot,
thus giving an air of leisurely spaciousness. These roomy lots had
barns, and the family kept a horse, and even a cow. Taking care
of this livestock paid many a student's way through college.

Such is the physical town, the entity known as Galesburg, an
aggregate of buildings, wood and brick, a few stone or stucco,
none distinguished in itself, but somehow blending with the aid
of many trees into a pleasant composition, which in the space of
five generations has evolved from stakes driven into the unbroken
prairie by Samuel Tompkins and Nehemiah West. But houses
do not make a city; its character, its spirit, is expressed by its
people, by their various and interlocking lives, their customs and
habits, which make the texture of the social and economic fabric.

### III

### RAILROAD TO MOTOR CAR

However dismal economics may be as a science, the people of
Galesburg, like the people of all burgs, are more interested in the
way they make their living than in any other topic. The town was
located in this fertile spot because its founders were farmers and
agriculture the principal occupation of the country. It was expected that its wealth would derive from the cultivation of the
land, as it did for many years. The first simple commercial system

was designed to dispose of farm products and receive the necessities of life in return.

Because of its strategic situation, and also because it acted promptly and shrewdly in railroad promotion, the town became the shipping center of a large territory, and shops, roundhouses and switchyards were established. It was a division point, the end of train runs, so that many of the train crews lived there and added to the population, and derived their income from the railroad, and this income was second only to that from farming. The railroad employees, with a smaller number engaged in the few not large factories—nearly all making agricultural machinery —constituted the first industrial population, or labor class. True, some of the railroad engineers received more pay than many professional men, and their standard of living was the same, but they tended to form a separate social class. The officers of the road naturally were part of such aristocracy as the town then afforded.

The Burlington Route, though suffering from conditions which have curtailed all railroad earnings, is Galesburg's largest industry and its chief single source of income, though of course the collective returns from retail trade are greater. Its tie-conditioning plant is said to be the largest in the country. Its switchyard has two hundred and ten miles of track, the greatest mileage of switching in one spot anywhere in the world. Every month the road distributes $275,000 (in 1929 it was $400,000) among its twenty-four hundred employees living in the town, from track-walkers to division superintendent, and they are all customers for the stores on Main Street. The Santa Fé, desirable asset in every way, is a smaller institution, but it employs nevertheless a hundred people. An interesting circumstance in this day of proposed railroad cooperation is the ligature which connects the two roads at Galesburg, so that cars can be switched from one line to the other to facilitate the distribution of freight.

Both roads have suffered from the competition of gasoline and concrete. The many good hard roads radiating from the town have developed motor-borne passenger and freight traffic. The Burlington has responded with its own bus lines. It has done other things to restore its former prestige. "Railroad Week" is a big celebration, with a parade of the twenty-five hundred employees, loud speakers stationed in towers along the route telling the town what it owes to the railroad, and a free train making daily trips around the switchyards with illustrated lectures on the many industries involved. It was the first road to recapture the popular imagination with streamlined stainless steel trains, and the shining, immaculate Zephyrs, on the run from Chicago to Denver, flit through Galesburg morning and evening like silver ghosts.

Local transportation was inaugurated in the town with bob-tailed street cars pulled by mules, succeeded by bigger cars drawn by horses. These gave way to the overhead trolley, and then the whole system was scrapped, the tracks torn up, and the town patrolled by busses. The interurban trolleys which ran to all near-by towns, and as far north as Rock Island and south to Peoria have likewise disappeared, and busses follow their trails.

The loss to Galesburg from the failure of agriculture to hold its place as the chief producer of wealth has been in a measure compensated by the motor car. The town has become a shopping center for a longer radius, trade that in the horse-and-wagon era went to the nearest villages. Transportation was a serious obstacle in the days of dirt roads, which became impassable in wet weather, and the trip a slow one even in dry times. Farmers went no farther than necessary to buy goods or market their crops.

Today they come from fifty miles around over smooth and level concrete, to sell as well as to buy. Galesburg has grain elevators for their corn and wheat, and stockyards for their cattle. The people from the neighboring villages come also, and Saturday night has all the air of a carnival, with people sitting in the closely parked cars, like boxes at a theatre, watching the parade on the sidewalks, partaking of sundaes from the drug stores, and doing the family shopping.

[9]

# CONTEMPORARY PORTRAIT

Thirty years ago Doctor E. V. D. Morris astounded his fellow citizens and scared farm teams hitched in front of the stores by driving down Main Street in the first self-propelled vehicle the town had seen. Within an incredibly short time the physical aspect of the city was altered; its social life transformed. Not only the horses and carriages, the smart surreys of the town, the Studebaker wagons of the country, but the livery stables—those indigenous social centers of small-town life—the tie-barns where the farmers baited their teams, the hitching posts and watering troughs that bordered the streets and the public square, the carriage repository, harness and blacksmith shops, were swept away. In their stead sprang up garages and filling stations, repair shops and salesrooms. On vacant lots oil companies set up their huge galvanized cylinders, and Galesburg became Standard Oil's largest wholesale distributing point in western Illinois.

The streets were ruled off in slanting parking lines, one-way traffic was established, green and red lights hung at intersections, and the police coped with new problems. The different civic picture presented was startling. All the buggies and wagons together never presented such an array as the cars parked on Main Street, overflowing into all adjoining streets for blocks around. This motor age is the third stage of the city's development, the railroad era being the second, and the pioneer years of covered wagon and stage coach the first.

The motor car has brought about a closer relation between town and country, socially as well as economically. Movies, parties, concerts, dinners, dances, a soda at the drug store, the satisfaction of associating more frequently with one's kind, are now as easy to the farm boy and girl as to their city cousins, and they mingle more freely in the same social life. It is ironic that just as the principal bugbear of farm life, isolation, was removed, agriculture should be in the doldrums.

Thus we find this prairie city, founded mainly to foster religious education, expecting to derive its sustenance from the soil, now depending largely for its living on transportation, on its connection with the outside world, a circumstance which as much as any deflected it from the destiny planned for it. The railroad has done more than alter the economic status of the town. It has changed the emotional, social and religious isolation of the community, and drawn it into the current of national ideas, and motor car, cinema and radio have continued and extended the process.

## IV

### DOWN TOWN

The expression "Main Street" implies not only the main artery so named, but at least two parallel streets, and the cross streets leading to them. Here in rows of two- and three-story brick buildings long narrow stores face the street through two plate-glass eyes, the fronts overburdened with signs. At intervals the streets are rubricated with the garish red-and-gold fronts of chain groceries and five-and-tens, a more strident color note than that achieved by the façade of the older and more conservative independents. This is "down town," the business section, the place where retail trade functions and has its being.

Not many of the pioneer concerns, those descended from father to son, or to clerks who bought in and carried on as a second generation, still exist, but there are at least a dozen firm names over the doors that would be recognized by a former inhabitant coming back after half a century. A dry goods store, a men's clothing establishment, a meat market, a grocery, a stationery store, a paint and wall-paper house and several others still carry on the old tradition. But the commercial personnel, the business body of the town, has slowly changed as particle replaced particle, somewhat as the human body is renewed once in seven years.

The front it presents today is neither dazzling nor discouraging. The chains—groceries, drugs, clothing and small knickknacks—have come in to the number of forty, but there are still 300 old-line merchants operating independently. Some of these have joined cooperative buying organizations to enable them to compete with chain prices, but the chains have accelerated the business tempo, and on the whole improved the science of retailing.

The most striking novelty to the returned traveller—and this is true in all cities—is the number of businesses unknown to any Main Street fifty years ago. It is not merely the motor car, and the galaxy of utilities required to service it, but such things as beauty shops, food stores, departmentalized drug stores, dry-cleaning establishments, shops selling electric flatirons, toasters and washing machines, apparel shops, liquor stores, radio shops, all of which add to the heterogeneous variety of Main Street, and give it a modern atmosphere. They would have seemed not only strange, but inexplicable, to a wayfarer of the nineties.

The most unusual wholesale business, and one that gives the town a touch of individuality, is the horse and mule market. Galesburg is the mule capital of the country. More of these useful but obstinate animals are sold there than at any other place. It was the chief source of supply for the government during the World War. Sales are held twice a week. Horses are consigned from Illinois, the Dakotas, Indiana, Kansas, and loaded on the Sante Fé, which has a spur track beside the immense salesbarn, one block long, and are shipped to New England, New York, Ohio, Maryland, Michigan.

Galesburg is not and never has been a manufacturing town. Its first industries were factories making agricultural implements, built around inventions originated by the pioneers themselves when their Yankee ingenuity was first brought up against the problems of a new kind of soil—the self-scouring plow, corn-planter, spiral stalk cutter, check-rower—but these, which never reached larger payrolls than two or three hundred employees, were all gathered up or swept away when farm machinery was merged into a few large concerns such as the Deeres and International Harvester.

There are, however, sixty-four small industries, some of them flourishing, one or two comparatively large, making and selling such things as bread, brooms, artificial ice, candy, coal, overalls. One of these is the paving-brick works at East Galesburg, three miles from the public square, where the clayey shale of the district is burned to a high degree of hardness by roaring flares of crude petroleum. The streets of Galesburg are paved with these brick, and many of the through roads as far as the neighboring towns.

Butter known to housewives everywhere as Meadow Gold is made at Galesburg. Some years ago Louis Nielsen, shrewd and capable Dane—who still speaks English with a strong Scandinavian accent—a dairy farmer by training, arrived in Knox County. Conscious that western Illinois agriculture leaned too heavily on corn and hogs, he started the Pioneer Creamery, and was selling butter as far as New England when Clinton Haskell, who ran a large creamery at Beatrice, Nebraska, began assembling plants in the West to make his company the third largest in the country (National Dairy Products first; Borden's second). Nielsen sold his business for a reputed million and a half, was made vice president in charge of the Galesburg unit, which then became one of five large churning plants of the Beatrice combine, making the nationally known trade-marked brand, Meadow Gold.

Knox County farmers haul their milk to its station, and are paid on the scientific basis of butter-fat content. The creamery takes seventy-five per cent of the milk produced by Knox County cows, and milk is shipped to it from other counties and other states. The butter is of such a rich golden yellow it must be bleached for those who prefer it white, but throughout the Middle West its color is its greatest asset—hence its name. Youthful Galesburg knows the plant best as the source of that delectable confection, Eskimo Pie, for ice cream in all its branches is one of the products.

In recent years fifteen hundred farmers in Knox and adjoining counties organized the Producers Creamery, that made and sold a million pounds of butter the first year. If these two enterprises have the significance of a portent, the picturesque Illinois pig with his black hindquarters and white mess jacket, now contentedly rooting in every field, may have his supremacy as chief

[ 13 ]

agricultural breadwinner challenged by the cow, and cornfields which have produced too abundantly may be transformed into pastures. Already Elgin, butter capital of the midlands, which once made butter prices for the nation, is feeling the sharp edge of competition.

So completely self-contained is the economic system that the town sets its own standard of living, and the cost at which that living may be maintained. Prices are much lower for commodities and services than if the town were overshadowed by the near presence of a large city, where commuters or summer residents introduce standards to which the town must conform. Galesburg is isolated in the center of a farm region with no larger city within fifty miles. It is practically the shire town of the old Military Tract, that triangle between the Illinois and the Mississippi rivers. In this district there are but five towns with more than 3000 population, and but two with more than 4000—Kewanee 17,000, and Monmouth 8000. The vast stretch of prairie, cultivated but empty-looking, especially toward the Mississippi, enhances the isolation, but adds to the sightliness of the environment, and gives the city a position as dominant as one of 100,000 in the more thickly settled East.

## V

### AGRICULTURE

The glorious but melancholy history of American agriculture was enacted on the fertile prairies around Galesburg. Its farm acres have seen the complete cycle. On the level fields surrounding the town, corn is the typical landscape. The corn transmuted into hogs is the county's principal crop. The farms as seen from the road are neat and well-kept. The better houses have telephone, open plumbing, electricity for light and power, central heating, radio, every comfort and convenience of city dwellings. The poorest are able to get their crops to market and do their shopping with less expenditure of time and effort than in the days of horses and wagons and dirt roads.

Although greatly reduced, the farmers' trade—selling him goods and handling his crops—is still an asset to the town, and good roads and the motor car have brought a larger share than in the past—at the expense, it is true, of the smaller villages—but the farms are no longer in the hands of the landed gentry, the wealthy farmers, descendants of the pioneers, who gave Galesburg its prosperity a generation ago.

The farmer who gave the town its pre-eminence in the golden era may be typified by John Wesley George. He was born on his father's farm near Zanesville, Ohio, moved to Illinois with his mother after his father's death, and bought a quarter-section (160 acres) near Galesburg. Corn and potatoes the first year paid half the cost of the farm. He bought a larger farm nearer town, married, brought up six children, all of whom attended Knox College, raised the customary crops of the district—corn, oats, hay, hogs, cattle, horses, feeding most of the grain to the stock—and supplied his own table with vegetables, fruit, beef, pork, poultry and eggs, milk and butter. A cash profit was made nearly every year. He kept one and sometimes two hired men, and a woman to help in the housework. The family lived well, and shared the social life of the town. The farm was a hospitable rendezvous for hosts of friends. None of the children returned to the farm, and so in 1914 he sold out at $250 an acre, and moved to Galesburg with money enough to live on the rest of his life.

Such was the history of the successful farmers who made money from farming in the old days, enriching Galesburg, but leaving no continuing dynasty to carry on the farm. They abandoned farming before it lost its power to create wealth and sank to the status of a mere livelihood. The loss to the countryside was a social as well as economic one. Such families with their wealth, education, leisure, taste, and public spirit, gave farming dignity and enhanced the attractions of country life.

A farm which rounds out the cycle gives a picture of the

situation today. The farmer's grandfather, Scotch-Irish, came from Pennsylvania in 1856, and bought an eighth section too far from the town to enjoy the unearned increment which benefited the George farm. His son, now 80, has retired and lives in the near-by village. The grandson, 53, carries on the farm with a spirit that promises much for the immediate future.

His eighty acres are intensively cultivated, producing more than normal averages, 75 to 80 bushels of corn to the acre, 50 to 75 of oats, against a national average of about 25. His acreage is allotted 27 to corn, 12 to oats, 12 to clover hay, 25 to pasture, orchard and farmstead occupying the remainder. He believes profit lies in the "small farm well tilled" rather than in the large show farm.

The farm is clear of debt, and in the good years in his father's time netted as high as $4000 to $5000 a year. But in 1932 the cash earnings were $600, of which $150 went for taxes. In 1935, what with drouth and chinch bugs, some crops were not even harvested. Hogs fed with poor grain brought little money. With better prices there was nothing to sell. He has been living on his savings.

But he is not downhearted or discouraged. He is looking ahead, experimenting with new crops, working himself out of a predicament which was not his fault. He raises as much of his own food as possible, something the latter-day farmer has neglected. His hobby is fruit, once an important product of Knox County, but allowed to languish in the scramble for corn and hog money. His vineyard has fifty varieties of grapes. He is experimenting with persimmons, also some of the new varieties of nuts, walnut, filbert, hiccan—a cross of hickory and pecan. His land will grow successfully apples, pears, damson plums, grapes, currants, gooseberries, blackberries, strawberries, persimmons—but not peaches and cherries—provided the right varieties for that soil and climate are selected. He cans not only fruit, but pork and chicken.

The whole story is too long to include here, but it is full of promise, both as to possibilities of the land and the spirit of the farmer. Knox County once produced many crops, besides most of the fruits listed above, some of which the settlers found growing wild when they arrived; sorghum, broom corn, maple syrup, honey, buckwheat, rye, millet, flax, wool, and other unusual and now forgotten crops. Perhaps one chance the future offers is return to greater diversity, in which, among other advantages, the farmer raises food for his own table.

Ignoring for the moment outside economic trends, which of course have had their effect, tariff, distribution, freight rates, foreign markets, transportation, a close-up shows us some of the forces which have altered farm life in this neighborhood. The old hierarchy of successful farmers, whose land cost them little and was close to town where it shared in city land values—some of those farms are now suburban additions—the Georges, Sissons, Thirlwells, Clays, Ferrises, Gales, Padens, whose farms received state awards, whose hogs won blue ribbons at agricultural fairs, sold out when profits began to shrink. Their children were educated for other fields. The purchasers lacked the solid backlog of years of prosperity, they paid higher prices for their land which did not continue to appreciate, they perhaps were without experience with local conditions, and so they were ill-prepared to face a long period of agricultural slump, business depression, and a series of natural catastrophes.

One result is a great increase of tenant farmers. The tenant farmer has none of the proprietor's pride and interest. He does not keep up the land, plant trees, prepare for the future. He makes a living—at least some of him do; what the owners get is another matter—but his presence in large numbers does not make for the improvement of agriculture over the long term.

There is also the new spending which takes some of the farmer's income as it does that of his city brother. The children home from college brought new fashions, and the standard of living was raised, or at least varied, in the hope of keeping the boys on the farm. The farm diet has changed. The farmer no longer lives on home-baked bread, meat, potatoes and pie. He buys baker's bread, fresh meat, salads, vegetables and fruits from Florida and California. He lives no better, as far as food is concerned than his forbears, perhaps not as well in some respects, but he too craves variety, or at least novelty, and must pay with the profits of his own labor for baking, mending, repairs and laundry once done by the farm women.

The trip to town, once so arduous, has become a matter of minutes, and drug-store treats absorb some of the farm money, once laid out grimly only on staple necessities in the widely spaced visits of wagon days. Bridge, radio, social intercourse take some of the time once spent in odd jobs that filled the chinks of farm routine. Farm cost of living increased during the years that farm income was falling, not so much from the higher cost of staples, but to satisfy new wants. This is in no sense a criticism. If any one deserves a better social life, it is the farmer. And when agriculture is restored to its proper place in the economic structure, this improvement in social and living conditions will remove one of the greatest handicaps of farm life.

The tractor is displacing the horse, but the question of machinery is a perplexing one. It is as unprofitable to have too much as too little. In a factory machines are used all day every day the year round. Some labor-saving farm implements are used but two to ten days out of the year, and must be sheltered, kept from rusting, and cared for the remainder of the time—hay loaders, grain binders and corn elevators.

The farm rhythm in Knox County runs something like this: spring plowing, two to four weeks, April 15 to May 15, depending on weather; sowing oats may take two weeks, four days or three weeks, according to amount of rainfall; corn cultivation June 1 to 30; haying ten days more or less; harvest and threshing July 12 to August 15. Then follows a season of hauling manure, moving fences because of rotation of crops and pasturage, fall plowing, corn-husking (hardest job of all) three to eight weeks according to rain and the amount of mud. In between on rainy days the farmer repairs his buildings, works with pigs, lambs, poultry, breaks colts, oils harness, trims hedge fences, cuts thistles, docks and plantains, hauls straw for bedding, sees to his roofs (the roofs of an average farm equal in area those of a collection of ten or twelve houses), checks up farm machinery, looks to his tile drains, and vaccinates hogs. On a modern farm they vaccinate for hog cholera, tetanus, contagious abortion, anthrax, and several other ailments, which adds up in the costs. The time actually spent in work in the fields is surprisingly small.

Such is a brief appraisal of the farm conditions near Galesburg, and for the Middle West generally. While western Illinois has managed to make out rather well in spite of the loss of its former income from tributary farms, there is no doubt that re-establishment of agriculture on a sound basis would be of the greatest benefit to it. The history of agriculture shows that farmers have been as resourceful in meeting purely agricultural conditions, in developing their own skills, as bankers and business men. Economic problems have floored them. Such rich farming communities as this are ready to profit by the slightest advance in general conditions.

## VI

### SOCIAL STRUCTURE

Not until the advent of the railroad—to and from which, like the birth of Christ, events seem to date—did anything like social classes appear. The founders of the city were all of one kind, typical Yankees with several New England generations behind them; of English origin as their names showed—Gales, Ferrises, Wests, Farnhams, Roots, Coltons, Churchills, Congers. They were alike in birth, education, religion and means. All they had was their land, their stake in the new city that was to be, and while some had taken up more than others, they were still equal as they labored to produce wealth from the soil. There were storekeepers, college professors, ministers, as well as farmers, blacksmiths, cobblers and millwrights, but all worked with their hands. The few hired men brought from the East were socially equals and ate at the same table. This one class was for years actually a labor class. All that distinguished it from the labor class which developed later was the purpose, the hope that burned brightly in the breast of each pioneer.

When in the early fifties the railroad boom got under way in Illinois, there was insistent demand for laborers to do the rough work. There was no surplus man power in the West. The settlers had put their all in the land and would not leave their farms. It was necessary to import pick-and-shovel workers from the eastern cities, crowded with accumulations of newly arrived immigrants, and they were shipped West in battalions. These immigrants were largely Irish, since the more provident newcomers planned to take up land for themselves. The Irish were natural-born navvies. A large contingent, brought to Galesburg to build the Central Military Tract railroad (which became in time the Burlington Route), remained to share with the negroes the unskilled labor of the community. Their sons with opportunity and education became skilled and supplied the railroad with its locomotive engineers, its yards with switchmen, and its shops and foundries with machinists.

From the beginning the Irish were a separate class, not so easily assimilated—Irish-Catholics in a Protestant community, penniless adventurers among landed proprietors—and they became the nucleus of a labor class, not so much because they labored in a community where manual labor was the rule, but because they were an alien race, set apart by a strange religion and different social habits.

As soon as there was a lower class, there had to be an upper class to look down on it, and one evolved automatically. Some of the original group of pioneers had prospered, particularly those who went into trade. Others held on to their land and added to it, built stores and houses and received rents, and sold to newcomers at the boom prices caused by the railroad. A lot on Main Street which cost $40 in 1837 sold for $7000 in 1857. The railroad opened new doors to wealth. It brought new people to take advantage of the growing city, or to educate their children in one of its two colleges. The railroad connected Galesburg with Chicago and the East, and with the undeveloped fertile prairies· west of the Mississippi; the Civil War left a hectic prosperity in its wake; the county seat was wrested from Knoxville, and the social fabric of the town stratified along class lines, and by 1880 there were the makings of a small-town aristocracy as exclusive as it dared to be in a community so small and interdependent.

It could not afford to be too exclusive where so many depended for livelihood on the good will of fellow-citizens. Storekeepers still waited on their customers in person from behind the counter, even after they attained to the status of employing clerks. Churches were the principal social centers, where in theory at least all were equal before God. The basis of this upper class, as far as it had any other than assumption, was descent from original settlers, residence on the "north side," and a reasonable amount of money, to which might be added, the society instinct.

Its composition was a neat cross-section of the major interests and occupations of the town in the last quarter of the last century; some merchants and bankers, a few manufacturers, its professional men, doctors, lawyers, professors—for the college faculty was still held in high esteem—along with the ministers of the more worldly churches, Presbyterian, Congregational, Universalist, but not Baptists or Methodists. Prosperous farmers whose sons and daughters attended Knox College mingled in the social life of the town, for the old link with the soil was not yet broken. It was still a farming community, its wealth largely represented by fertile farms; its strongest bank the Farmers' and Mechanics' with a directorate composed of real "dirt farmers."

Already in the 1860's the control of the town, economically as well as socially, was shifting from the descendants of the founders to later comers, reared in the same pioneer tradition, but having their roots elsewhere. They beagn to arrive as the town emerged from villagehood and put on the airs of a thriving western city— men who opened larger and more ambitious stores, skilled craftsmen and machinists who established foundries, mills and factories, the advance guard of the new utilities—gas, street railway, electric light, telephone—officers to staff the railroad. By weight of numbers and dominant position in the town's industrial and commercial life, these became the leading citizens as the old strains faded out; their wives became the social leaders, and by another fifty years these newcomers were the old families.

It is curious how completely the descendants of the founders have disappeared from the city their ancestors created on that western prairie. Some of their progeny have gone farther west, the pioneer impulse strong in their blood, and developed new empires. Los Angeles, Riverside, San Francisco, Spokane felt their influence; but the old town has few traces of them, except the physical and social structure they created. It is a melancholy commentary on the dreams and hopes that inspired the Gale colony that today the wife of the manager of the telephone company, the secretary of the Knox Conservatory of Music, a firm of lawyers—two brothers, one of them still owns and operates the farm his ancestor bought in the original colony—the gifted wife of a leading doctor, two expressmen, and a few widows and spinsters are all that is left in the town of its original pioneer stock.

The newcomers who supplanted them were of much the same racial strain. Their English surnames—Sanborns, Prices, Rices, Willards, Mattesons, Carrs, Mathewses, Harringtons, Standishes —struck no new ethnic note. They were spiritual if not physical descendants of the founders. Their forbears had come west in the same general movement that peopled the Mississippi valley, some of them by slow stages, sampling each state on their way to Illinois, with often a generation between successive pilgrimages. Thus an English immigrant settled at Norwich, Connecticut, in 1659; his son moved to Vermont, his grandson to New Hampshire. The fourth generation got as far as Ohio, and the fifth wound up in Illinois. Such were the peregrinations of many of the later accessions, who, like the children of Israel, took a roundabout route to the promised land.

# CONTEMPORARY PORTRAIT

Strong drink has agitated the town since its founding. Almost its first organization was a temperance society. Its founders had three anathemas, irreligion, slavery and intemperance. They thought they had barred alcohol forever by incorporating in all deeds the proviso that if intoxicating drinks were made or sold on the premises, the land would revert to the college. The clause was never legally invoked, and is probably invalid.

The town had forty years of bootlegging—the neighboring villages were uproariously wet—forty years more of the old-time licensed saloon—free lunch, brass rail and sawdust on the floor—nineteen years of comparative aridity, partly under local option and partly under national prohibition, and now operates under the Illinois liquor law, backed by a city ordinance, controlled by the mayor, with the advice of a council of four aldermen. There are fifty-five places where liquor may be bought, and the license fees bring the town $13,640.

Thus, in a town which even in the old license days confined saloons to the side streets, and managed to cast a stigma over all kinds of drinking, there are today smart cocktail lounges with uniformed barmaids, roadhouses beside country lanes, night clubs with floor shows—in one of which "the Music Goes Round and Around" had its birth. The change can be appreciated only by one familiar with the town's century-long fight against the demon rum. In the old days city elections turned on license, the women against the men, but only the men having the vote. The state law in 1914 gave women the vote on local questions, the women voted the town dry, it stayed dry until prohibition, but with repeal it reverted not to its dry status, but to license with a new alignment of the so-called better element. The old stalwarts of the W. C. T. U., once captained by leading women, would be stunned, appalled, if they could see the town today, where their daughters regard modern drinking with tolerance if not with complacency.

## VII

### ORGANIZED SOCIAL INTERCOURSE

One of the curious aspects of Western small-town life is the extraordinary number of organizations apparently required to carry on the process of community living. Because of a pathetic faith in the virtue of associations to accomplish things, even social intercourse, the social structure of the town is so honeycombed with clubs and societies that the local paper has difficulty in keeping abreast of their activities, to allot each its paragraph of praise. There are more than three hundred named organizations in Galesburg, about one for each hundred inhabitants. Almost every human purpose, serious and frivolous, has its appropriate association.

One effect of these clubs is to put a damper on the old-time individual entertaining. With evenings so filled with organized entertainment, there is little time and energy for the dinners and parties which made up the essence of social life forty years ago. Motor cars, movies, radio, play the same large part here they do elsewhere, but the recreational interests of the people seem to center in their numerous societies, leagues and alliances. Even the more serious bodies have their social side.

Of the service clubs, by which name is meant those organizations that make a fetish of hearty good fellowship—Lions, Kiwanis, Eagles, Exchange, Rotary—the town has a complete set. Their peculiar rules, by which only one member of a given profession or trade is admissible, makes this obligatory—something like the selectiveness of college fraternities. The service clubs occupy the important status in social-business life once held by the pompous secret societies, the noonday dinner taking the place of the old-time "lodge night" with its faint aroma of wickedness and deviltry.

The lodges are still represented, Masons, Odd Fellows, Foresters, Maccabees, Woodmen, Redmen, Royal Arcanum, Royal Neighbors, with their female auxiliaries (concession to woman's newly acquired position in business and politics), but Americans seem to be losing their taste for secrecy, rituals, oaths and regalia, and have gone to the other extreme, for the service clubs are the antitheses of the lodges. Their openness, lack of ceremony, cameraderie is in sharp contrast with the stiff, stilted, and carefully tiled mummery of the Mystic Shrines and Knights Templar. In one the emphasis is on dignity and solemnity; in the other on good fellowship and informality—the difference between addressing the presiding officer as "worshipful grand master" and calling him "Bill."

It is an instance of how village habits persist that the noonday luncheon clubs are called "dinner clubs." The city-minded try to establish in name at least the principal meal in the evening, but in practice the majority, especially if they go home at noon, call the midday meal "dinner," and eat supper at night. This meal is even quaintly known as "tea." The church "supper" is still an institution. Formal evening meals, however, are known as dinners. The rural dietary timetable of the farms, where the big meal is always the middle one, influences the practice, or at least the nomenclature of the town.

"Civic service" defines those boards and other bodies which promote and care for institutions and services not provided for by the civil government. Besides the Chamber of Commerce and the so-called dinner clubs, there are the public welfare associations, boards to look after the Public Library, Visiting Nurses, Day Nursery, Free Kindergarten, Hope Cemetery, the Cottage Hospital. There is a Mother's Club and a complete Parent-Teachers Association, with sub-organizations for each of the seven wards. The Catherine Club maintains a home for working girls, and both Boy and Girl Scout organizations condition life for the younger element.

Then there are the patriotic societies, chapters or local branches of the leading national organizations. Galesburg is no worse and no better than other communities in perpetuating memories of old wars. There are both Daughters and Sons of the American Revolution, Veterans of the Spanish War, of Foreign Wars, Sons and Daughters of Union Veterans, and of course the American Legion, which succeeds to the perquisites and technique of the Grand Army of the Republic—once so dominant in Galesburg life, holding all the offices, waving the bloody shirt on Memorial Day, but now extinct.

Occupational associations comprise the professsions, doctors, lawyers, teachers, the college faculty, as well as the Merchants Association, the labor unions, and the railroad brotherhoods, and as fitting in an agricultural community, the Grange and Farm Bureau. Every trade has its labor organization, including letter carriers and railway mail clerks, a total of thirty-one unions. With some 2500 railroad men in the town, every rail brotherhood has a lodge. For years the national headquarters of the Brotherhood of Railroad Trainmen was located at Galesburg. These gainful societies have their social side; the unions have "ladies" auxiliaries to look after their entertainments, and the agricultural organizations have women members, and are a factor in the social intercourse of the countryside.

Spiritual life is ministered to by twenty-one religious bodies, most of which maintain churches. This flowering into so many diverse creeds is significant when the narrow religious intent of the founders is considered. Besides the six standard Protestant denominations—Presbyterian, Congregational, Baptist, Methodist, Episcopalian and Universalist—the large Swedish population supports four, two Lutheran, a Methodist and a Baptist church. The Catholics have two, one quite large, the colored people two, Baptist and Methodist, and there are several nondescript conventicles such as Christian, United Brethren, Pentecostal, and Israel of God. Each church has numerous societies and circles. All the standard associations of young people are represented, Christian Endeavor, Epworth League, Lend a Hand. The "Y" is practically a social club in its own quite complete building. W. C. T. U. belongs here, probably not so formidable as in the old days, nor with the same prestige. Leading women have shifted their allegiance to new causes.

The town is strong for culture. This is primarily the influence of Knox College, and the leavening of social life by some fifty professors and their wives, and especially the college conservatory of music, which has given to Galesburg a peculiar pre-eminence in the Middle West in musical organizations. Two women's clubs, Hawthorne and Mosaic, concentrating on intellectual programs, have had a consistent active existence of more than forty-five years. They have served as models for many others. There are groups studying art, science, literature, music, and current events. Among them, their names indicating their aims, are Home Culture, Clio, Civic Art, Civic Music, Musicians', Household Arts, Sorosis, Round Table, Fortnightly. The Woman's University Club takes in college graduates of that sex living in the town. The Prairie Players is a practical working dramatic club. P. E. O. is a national organization of women, its purpose to help deserving girls secure an education; its only secret the significance of its initials.

But the most illuminating social development is the host of small groups and coteries, each with a name, which dot the social columns of the daily paper with their frequent meetings; actually the parties hostesses normally would give in rotation, reduced to a simple formula of entertainment. Their names, which suggest Pullman sleeping cars, are enough to indicate their scope and importance: Silver Cross, Four G, Palm Leaf, Ossness, Fern Leaf, Priscilla Ladies, Delphian, Cosmos, Tuscarora, Pandora, Double Ten, Sunshine, Mayflower. The Thimble Club and the Fancy Work Club are presumably a bit more serious, and Luther League and Ladies of Viking are evidently Scandinavian.

The ostensible purpose of all these societies is to unite people along the lines of their dominant interests, or to accomplish some needed social duty, but the prime urge back of it all is sociability, amusement, an excuse to get together; though vanity and social ambition may operate in respect to the supposably more exclusive organizations. But with so many clubs in so small a community, the membership is bound to be interlocking, so that social distinctions tend to be weakened or obliterated.

One force at work to keep social life in smaller towns on a more or less equal basis, is the difficulty of living any other life than that which the town endorses. With no large city near by to flee to, with a public opinion which frowns on undue display, it is difficult for the socially ambitious to show off. One does not find liveried chauffeurs or butlers even in homes that elsewhere could afford them. Two maids might be called the peak of domestic ostentation; a fine car, but driven by the owner, the maximum outside. For the rest all are dependent for social recreation on comparatively few people, and can scarcely with peace of mind exceed their standards too greatly, so social rivalry is confined within narrow limits and makes for sensible living.

## VIII

### OLD SIWASH

The old intimate relation between the city and the college has yielded to the complications of modern life. Town and gown do not mix as they once did when college exercises were the town's chief recreations and city affairs were administered or largely guided by the professors and trustees of the college. Both have grown larger and infinitely more complex and self-contained. Each goes its appointed ways, living its own life, busy with its own concerns, so that the college exists as a sort of enclave, completely surrounded by but more or less apart from the town. The only college functions for which the town turns out with real enthusiasm are the athletic contests, and the only criticism on the conduct of the college is when the football eleven fails to win—a long way from the time when a difference of religious opinion within the college divided the town into two bitterly antagonistic camps.

[ 28 ]

# CONTEMPORARY PORTRAIT

George Fitch, a graduate of Knox College, enriched the language with the word "Siwash" in a series of hilarious stories in *The Saturday Evening Post* based remotely on life at Knox College, and the word has become slang for the small western coeducational college at which the salt-water universities are supposed to look down their noses. The part played by such institutions in forming the national character, the contribution they have made in men, in establishing centers of culture in western towns, in fostering a simpler and more virile ideal of education, is beginning to be appreciated more widely. The history of this one shows that they have character and quality, that they are not merely imperfect and incomplete teaching machines, but a distinct species, probably worth as much to the country as its universities.

The old "grad" today, revisiting "dear old Siwash," is surprised and pleased to discover his alma mater apparently being run by, or at least run for, some six hundred appealing young people, to see the college president calmly light a cigarette after lunch in the college commons, to learn there is a smoking room in the sacred precincts of what was once the "Fem. Sem.," or to watch a bevy of vigorous but comely girls in shorts playing hockey on the field where fifty years ago they appeared only as demure spectators. He feels a sense of life, activity, interest, and earnestness which did not seem to prevail when he was a student.

At alumni dinners he no longer hears stories of college pranks that were once the staple reminiscence, how "Squint" Smith put the janitor's cow in the chapel, or "Babe" Murdoch turned the chapel bell up and filled it with water to freeze on a cold night. The modern student seems to despise such amusements. The reason is, beyond doubt, the large measure of self-discipline intrusted to him, and the variety of stimulating interests on which to expend surplus energy. If this is so, then college, Knox or other, has greatly improved, and a moral government proved better than a religious one.

The organization of college life at Knox, duplicating that of most western colleges, consists of numerous specific federations and groups for discipline, mental improvement, sports, social diversions, and reward of merit. There are a student council, a woman's self-government association, a council for each dormitory, and commissions for the sophomore and freshmen classes, all directed toward regulating the deportment of students by the aid of public opinion. The faculty apparently sits back and lets the student body work out the problems which once occupied most of the sessions of its meetings. Students who cannot be kept within bounds by such measures are not wanted.

Sports are more highly organized than any other interests. At the head is a sort of holding company, the athletic board of control; the "K" council is concerned with athletic morale, and there are subsidiary bodies for football, basketball, track, golf, tennis, cross-country running and swimming. Baseball, practically the only sport of the last century, seems to have disappeared. The women have their athletic association, which covers baseball, hockey, archery, tennis, volley ball, riding, golf, basketball and badminton. Finally, there are contests between the fraternities in basketball, volley ball, track, kitten ball, and swimming.

Conscious that a part of the purpose of college is culture, Knox students have a debate club, Spanish, German and French clubs, a theatre group, the Ladies' Mental Improvement Society (sole survivor of the old-time literary societies), the Christian Association, and in the field of music, for the college has a strong conservatory, a college choir, conservatory orchestra, glee club, and military band. There is a general board for publications, with separate organizations for the weekly newspaper, a literary monthly and the college annual.

Seven fraternities and five sororities are guided, directed and controlled by an inter-fraternity council. A striking feature of this interesting set-up is the great number of honorary fraternities, election to which is recognition for excellence in some field of work, at the head of which stands Phi Beta Kappa. But there is also Friars for seniors, Delta Sigma Rho for oratorical proficiency,

CONTEMPORARY PORTRAIT

Mortar Board for women, Key Club for sophomores, Sigma Delta
Psi for athletic winners, and Beta Beta Beta for stars of the
biological laboratory. The theatre group has its Curtain Call,
which rewards not only acting, but management and scene painting; the Reserve Officers Training Corps has both Scabbard and
Blade and its Sponsors, selected from socially prominent co-eds
in the old tradition of woman's smile sending the soldier to the
wars. And the conservatory of music has three fraternities. Add
to these the organization of the four classes, and you have one
aspect of college life contrasting as sharply with that of the eighties
as that period with the simple, excessively pious and primitive
institution which opened its doors on the prairies nearly a hundred
years ago.

To a small city such as Galesburg a college is a distinct asset.
Aside from its contributions to economic and cultural life, both
substantial, it is decorative. The students add life and movement
to the panorama of the streets, as they go about their numerous
activities in their picturesquely informal dress, tremendously concerned with matters remote from the sober business of living and
making a living, which absorb the energies of the town. The
town is not disturbed by the ebullient spirit which finds outlet
for its emotions in parades, bonfires, painting up the streets with
derisive epithets to visiting football teams. It is amused and
sympathetic. It enjoys the presence of so much youth, so carefree
and independent, so remote from the problems of life, as a spectacle on a stage.

There are, of course, closer links. A thousand graduates of the
college live in the town. One fourth of the current attendance
is composed of home boys and girls, and most of the outsiders
come from similar homes in towns and cities of the Middle West,
sharing the same standards and traditions, and these visitors
would fade unobtrusively into the background of town life, except
that the limelight of college life puts them in a class by themselves,
so that socially the town and the college do not often meet, except
through the families of the faculty.

# CONTEMPORARY PORTRAIT

In 1937 Knox College completed ninety-six years of activity. It was on February 15, 1837 that a reluctant state legislature granted it a charter, and that date has been established as Founders' Day, but it was not until 1841 that the college opened its doors to its first freshman class, and those doors have never been closed through wars, panics, internal dissensions, or the vicissitudes of pioneer life. It has gone steadily on, doing its work according to the standards of the time, widening its scope as better ideas of education prevailed, until today it stands on a foundation of history as colorful and disciplinary as that of any similar institution. From those doors, so significant, so pregnant with promise in that sparsely settled prairie land, has poured a stream of young men, and after 1851 of young women, who have received at least some preparation for life, some cultivation of mind and character they would not otherwise have known.

Among them, including those who did not graduate, there are men and women who have made their mark in almost every field of human endeavor. That, of course, is true of all worthwhile colleges, but the measure of usefulness of any institution is the amount it contributes to what we call civilization. It is not maintained that Knox has made a greater contribution in its graduates than other colleges—though that might be argued—or that it is unusual, unique, exceptional, so much as that it has pulled its load, that it belongs to that small group of American colleges engaged in supplying to the nation its quota of desirable citizens, men and women whose viewpoint has been widened, who have some measure of intellectual training.

Knox has had her share of men who have reflected credit on their colleges. The real measure of its usefulness is found in the thousands who have not made the headlines of current history, but who have added something desirable to the spot where they work and live because of contact with the college.

During its ninety-six years the college has had ten presidents. Six were under the domination of the religious concept, by which the presidents were clergymen, and religion more important than any other subject taught. The break with the old tradition came with the election of John Huston Finley, the youngest college president at that time in the country, a graduate of Knox, the only president who had had intimate experience with the great universities of the east. During his administration were begun the changes which have kept the college in step with other institutions of its class, until it has become the modern cultural college you see today. Finley was followed by three men, Thomas McClelland, now dead, James McConaughy, now president of Wesleyan at Middletown, Conn., and Albert Britt, who has recently resigned. Briefly, it might be said that Finley brought prestige, McClelland money, McConaughy scientific management, and Britt sophistication, or the modern point of view.

It is significant that the omniscient Herr Baedeker, in the 1909 edition of his *United States,* the last published, picks this college among the handful selected as examples of higher education. "There are about 400 colleges in the United States," is his laconic note, "in addition to the great universities. Well known colleges are Amherst, Dartmouth, Williams, Hamilton, Oberlin, Lafayette, Rutgers and Knox."

This picture, imperfect, incomplete, of some of the more obvious aspects of a western city, is merely an introduction. It is meant to show the pattern that evolved from one hundred years of history, the goal toward which the town travelled, intentionally or otherwise. The history is composed of several distinct elements like the strands of a cable and like a cable capable of being unravelled and examined separately—religion, social life, business, culture, the college. To understand what happened, how the town became what it is today, what forces produce cities, we must go back more than one hundred years to the real beginning.

# 2

# *The Founding*

## FINNEY AND HIS GREAT REVIVAL

In his little church at Adams, New York, the Reverend George Washington Gale was conducting revival meetings, which he liked much better than plain preaching. The year was 1823. The first faint flames of a religious conflagration that was to sweep the country like prairie fire was just beginning to flicker. Gale, devout, dyspeptic, holding to the grimmer contentions of Calvinism, was not a gifted speaker. Jedediah Burchard, formerly an Albany storekeeper, whose business had failed, who had got religion, and who was a natural-born actor, supplied the fireworks. All things promised a bounteous harvest of souls—but for one circumstance.

The obstacle was a brilliant young lawyer, Charles Grandison Finney, tall, handsome, magnetic, and popular with the young men of the village. He was friendly to Gale and sang in his choir, but the comments he made on his revival methods sent his admirers into stitches of laughter.

"If we can get Finney," said Gale grimly to Burchard, "we can get them all."

Finney's conversion was as spectacular as Saint Paul's. It followed a night of prayer and struggle, and was so sudden Gale could scarcely believe it. He put Finney through a rigorous examination as to his spiritual experience. Convinced at last, he had the satisfaction of baptizing him and most of his satellites.

Finney promptly renounced a promising career at the bar to devote his life to saving souls. He would have none of the theology Gale sought to impart, had no patience with the technical side of religion; he preached a simple ritual of conviction, conversion, salvation—or else, damnation. He was soon in full tilt among the towns along the Erie Canal conducting revivals which reached new highs in religious fervor—the originator of high-pressure evangelicism.

Gale watched his convert with some misgivings, but there were the results—such an outpouring of the spirit as had never been witnessed, and he must have felt some pride in his work, for years later, when report credited the conversion to Burchard, he set down with meticulous care that he alone was responsible.

Finney's fame spread beyond the Mohawk Valley. He was the spiritual ancestor of Dwight Moody and Billy Sunday. He was called to larger cities and became a national figure—about whom Longfellow wrote his humorous poem, "Mr. Finney had a turnip." He ridiculed the old-time theology Gale represented, with its contradictions and inconsistencies, by declaiming to delighted audiences:

> "You can and you can't,
>   You will and you won't;
> You'll be damned if you do;
>   You'll be damned if you don't."

Lyman Beecher, "father of more brains than any man in America"—one of whose brainy offspring was later to stir up a rumpus in Gale's colony on the western prairies—watched Finney's antics from his Boston pulpit, and served notice on him not to invade New England territory, but such was the fame and fervor of Finney that Beecher was compelled to invite him to conduct revivals in Hanover Street Church, and listen to his hectic imagery and impassioned rhetoric with what complacency he could muster.

Finney invented the "protracted" meeting, that method of wearing down obdurate sinners by pounding away for weeks. He organized promising young converts into a flying squad of evangelists and called them his "Holy Band," but Beecher described them as a "host of ardent, inexperienced, impudent young men." Finney was a good showman; under his ministrations· religion became epidemic, and one of the greatest revivals in American history raged in the northern states. It was in this hotbed that Oneida Institute was incubated, and Oneida was the seed of Lane Theological Seminary, Western Reserve University, Oberlin and Knox colleges. For one significant result of Finney's conversion and his subsequent career was its effect on Gale and his dreams.

## II

### GALE TAKES A HORSEBACK RIDE

George Washington Gale was a Presbyterian clergyman who believed in hellfire and had chronic dyspepsia. He was a small man, slight of build, inclined to be thin because his food did not agree with him, but graceful, dignified, and even commanding, with regular features expressing a pensive thoughtfulness when not rendered irritable and querulous by his ailment. He was narrow and intolerant in religion, but gracious in social intercourse, a dreamer, somewhat visionary, but with a canny vein of practicality, though too indifferent to money to handle it carefully or account for it consistently. He lacked the qualities of a leader, but was gifted with powers of persuasion that won converts in his revivals, and raised substantial sums to finance his educational enterprises. His piety and his dyspepsia were the outstanding facts in his life.

He was born at Separate, Dutchess County, New York, December 3, 1789, left an orphan at an early age and brought up by his sisters, of whom he had eight, all married to farmers in the neighborhood. He lived around from farm to farm, doing chores and attending country school. Too sickly for a farmer's life, he decided to become a minister.

At an early age he underwent that peculiar emotional experience known as conversion, accompanied by heart-searchings, agonies, and harrowing dreams. He built himself a little bower in a grove near the home of one of his sisters, and to this he would retire for prayer and meditation, in the true anchorite tradition. Here, despondent over his physical condition, he received a divine message. "I opened my Bible and happened to fall on the 18th Psalm, 17th verse: 'I shall not die, but live, and declare the works of the Lord.' It seemed prophetic of myself. From that time I was more encouraged." From that time, consciously or unconsciously, his sole concern was religion, his sole preoccupation saving souls. He united with the local Presbyterian church, and set about securing an education to enable him to preach.

He walked daily the four miles from his sister's farm to Troy and attended the Latin school there. He spent some months at Middlebury, Vermont, under the instruction of John Frost, head of the Academy. He entered Union College, and in spite of irregular attendance was given his degree in 1814. He studied theology with the third class to enter Princeton Seminary, but ill-health and spells of teaching and preaching to provide funds caused frequent absence and he did not graduate.

In September, 1816, he was licensed to preach by Hudson Presbytery at Fishkill, and after more theology under Professor Yates at Union and a few additional months at Princeton, started his career on the hardest and most gruelling assignment possible, that of itinerant missionary to the settlements along the southern shore of Lake Ontario. It was one of New York's most severe up-state winters. On horseback he rode from village to village, preaching to small groups, converting and baptizing many, holding services three or four times a week with the usual Sunday quota, the rest of the time occupied in getting from place to place. He rode through snow four feet deep, forded half-frozen rivers, sometimes crashing through the ice, was often near death, and frequently arrived at his destination too weak to speak or stand. By spring, though broken by work and exposure, he extended his stay in that inhospitable country to conduct what he believed to be a needed revival. Positive, bigoted, bilious, he was nevertheless of the stuff of which martyrs are made.

Following this drastic apprenticeship, Gale was called to the pastorate of a new church at Adams in New York State. He boarded around with his parishioners, and thus had no place private enough for spiritual conferences with repentant sinners so necessary to his work. He began to think of marriage and a home. He considered this step, as he did everything, in the light of its effect on his religious labors. He reviewed with quaint circumspection the young women of his acquaintance and those recommended for his consideration by friends and parishioners, asking himself whether they had sufficient piety. He must have had some physical attraction, for a young woman of his congregation drowned herself in the canal from unrequited affection for him. He was glad he had taken the precaution to show to one of his deacons some of her indiscreet letters before the tragedy occurred.

His choice finally fell on Harriet Selden, youngest daughter of Charles Selden, of Troy, a man of considerable means, an officer in the Revolutionary War, a graduate of Yale, and a member of the state legislature, but not until he had examined minutely every detail of his future wife's religious history. She was found satisfactory, and they were married September 20, 1820, after some difficulty and delay and misunderstanding caused by selfish and interested relatives. She was twenty-one and he thirty-one. He almost missed his wedding, on account of Joseph Bonaparte, ex-king of Spain, who was making a royal progress from Utica to Troy, and had engaged all the public conveyances.

Harriet was small and very thin, and liable to colds, but her health improved with marriage. She was "plain" in the Quaker sense, objected to the ruffles on her husband's wedding shirts, and removed them. During her twenty years of married life she bore him nine children, six of whom lived to maturity and grew up in her husband's colony of Galesburg. She also brought him a small fortune, with which he financed his share of his educational experiments.

With his wife Gale returned immediately to Adams. In 1823 he conducted the revival which brought Finney into the fold. Ill-health compelled him to abandon preaching for a season. His preferred treatment during one of these spells was a long lonely walk, or a still more extended horseback ride. He resigned his church, persuaded Finney to take charge, left his family with relatives at Troy, and in 1825 set out on his horse for the south, preaching along the way, and suffering horribly from his recalcitrant stomach. He stopped with relatives, friends, or more often strangers, and preached Sundays in local churches. Either because of his ingratiating personality or the unfailing hospitality of those times, he received what seems amazing consideration. He lay ill, sometimes for weeks, in the homes of strangers. There is no evidence that he paid for his accommodation, other than by his services as a minister.

In Washington he heard Clay, Webster and Calhoun speak, and saw Jackson, then a senator, whose policies as President were to give Gale's colony one of its serious setbacks. These men, and all mundane affairs apart from evangelicism, made no impression on him. Becoming too ill to ride, he bought a chaise and continued as far as Charlottesville, where he inspected Jefferson's University of Virginia. He examined its architecture with special interest and made notes for future use, but deplored Jefferson's attempt to conduct a college without religion. "Externally, the arrangements are splendid," he comments, "but it could not prosper on its present plan," and rejoices that after Jefferson's time religious exercises and instructions were instituted. "It is among the appointments of God," he says sagely, "that literature and especially literary institutions cannot flourish except in conjunction with religion, and the more piety the more prosperity in everything." On this singular platform he proposed to found a "literary institution."

But while Gale rode solitary and alone through countries new to him without curiosity as to his surroundings or the men he met, it was because his mind was full of a dream he had, a dream for doing good according to his lights. That dream was nothing less than salvation of the world by proxy, through instruments raised up by his hand, since ill-health barred his own active evangelical work.

He thought of Finney and other young men he had converted. Finney's theology was open to question, but his power was undeniable. Such young men could perform a great missionary work. Could he not prepare them? Could he establish an institution which would afford both material and spiritual education? Poor men's sons made the best ministers. They were prepared for hardship and self-denial. But poor men's sons had not the means to pay for education. The solution was manual labor. The students could sustain themselves while studying, the institution supply the work, the products support the school and pay for board and teaching. Manual labor would also afford the exercise so necessary to one going from farm work to the classroom. Health was essential to a minister's hard life. Gale valued the health he lacked second only to the religion he had. His scheme for a self-supporting college was novel then, though it was to acquire considerable momentum in the Middle West during the next generation, and Gale, who had not heard of the experiments in Switzerland along this line, confidently believed himself to be its originator. He turned the head of his horse toward the north, resolved to put the idea in practice on a small scale.

## III

### THE ONION GRUBBERS

Back from his long ride to Virginia, with his head full of this new vision, he set about realizing it. He bought or rented a farm near the little village of Western in upper New York, and invited seven young men, fruits of his recent revival at Adams, to come and live with him, and till his farm, in return for such theological and other instrucion as he could impart. He would be satisfied, he said, if the enterprise did not cost him over two hundred dollars above what he received for the results of their labors. At the end of the year he was so pleased with the success of his laboratory experiment, he decided to go into large-scale production.

The John Frost who had tutored him at Middlebury had married a rich wife at Whitesboro, a village near Utica, New York, and settled there as a minister. He had taken great interest in the experiment at Western, and was willing to help in the larger plan. Between them they raised some $20,000, to which Arthur and Lewis Tappan, the New York philanthropists, whose money was available for nearly every reform movement, were generous contributors, and began to build the school Gale had conceived.

Joseph White, tutelary genius of Whitesboro, sold them 115 acres for $5639, on which the young theologues were to sweat for their education. The farm bordered the main street of the village, and on this road three buildings were erected from plans drawn by Gale. Some of the contributions were in the form of stone and timber, and the eager students were given a foretaste of manual labor by quarrying the stone and felling the timber. The school was named the Oneida Institute of Science and Industry.

The teaching staff consisted of Gale and Peletiah Rawson, a graduate of Hamilton College, an engineer in the construction of the Erie Canal, and since that work ended, a teacher in the local academy. The system was manual labor, alternate study and work. Besides the usual academic courses, theology was taught. To protect innocent minds from contamination by heathen classics, the New Testament in the original was substituted for the customary Greek, and Hebrew for Latin, which, even if it were not the language spoken in heaven as many believed, afforded as good mental drill as the tongue of Cæsar and Vergil.

Two hours in the early morning the students worked on the farm, or in the carpenter, trunk and harness-making shops. Twenty-seven students cultivated forty acres the first year, but floods destroyed the crops. Next year was better. Then were produced fifty cords of wood, thirty barrels of cider, seven hundred bushels of corn, four hundred of potatoes, one hundred of oats, twenty-five of beans, thirty tons of hay, and eighty bushels of onions—the whole valued at $1000. As this singular school prospered, the number of students increased to 100. The young disciples went about their appointed tasks unmoved by the jeering and heckling of the village boys, who hailed them as "onion grubbers."

Religious fervor was kept at a white heat. Studies were interrupted to hold protracted revival meetings, that there might be no backsliders. The result was a large crop of crusaders and reformers, who were later turned loose to fulminate against drink, slavery, Sabbath breaking, irreligion, some of whom became famous in their proselyting fields. Most of Gale's recruits from the farm at Western followed him to Whitesboro. Finney attended for a year, and when he got into his stride on the road as an evangelist, with rows of repentant sinners kneeling at the mourner's bench every night, he sent a steady stream of students from the more promising of his converts.

Among students thus recruited was colorful, crusading Theodore Dwight Weld, from Hamilton College, who lived in Gale's house and worked for his board. He was one of Finney's Holy Band, and when he left Oneida Institute, he went on to Lane Theological Seminary, where Lyman Beecher was president. There Weld's impassioned anti-slavery harangues disturbed trade with the Kentuckians across the Ohio and irritated the local business men, but so greatly moved and impressed Lyman's young daughter Harriet, who was teaching school in Cincinnati, that years later they inspired, or at least, contributed to *Uncle*

*Tom's Cabin*. Coerced by his trustees, Beecher forbade discussion of slavery in student meetings, and thus precipitated a rebellion. Weld walked out at the head of the rebels, who went over in a body to Oberlin—which swallowed every moral "ism"— and with Arthur Tappan's money, and Finney's moral fervor— he subsequently became president—set that institution on the road to prosperity, and incidentally made it the incubator of practically all the reforms and movements that plagued the Middle West during that turbulent period. These things strengthened an ambition forming in Gale's mind to seek a larger theatre for his uncontrollable urge to grapple with the sin and wickedness of the world, and compel it to accept salvation at his hands, or at the hands of instruments created through his agency.

For he no longer considered Oneida Institute the fulfillment of his dreams. Like the small school at Western, it was one of the steps. In 1834, after seven years with the Institute, "I concluded to resign my place," he says, "and either prosecute a scheme I had for some time cherished of planting an institution on a larger scale in the far West, or do something else, as I might be directed by Providence. I had done enough, expended labor and means enough, to bring the Institute to its maturity and test the practicality of the plan of combining study with labor, and the carrying forward of the enterprise might now devolve on some one else."

It devolved on Beriah Green, summoned from Western Reserve, for whom Gale had nothing but scorn. Through his operations, he notes vaguely but with malicious satisfaction, "the place lost greatly in a religious and moral as well as social view." It lingered on until the sixties, with varying fortunes. Its fiery young graduates managed to stir up excitement wherever they came into conflict with the robust sins of a pioneer generation. Today the remnants of its buildings are used as a Home for Feeble-minded Women. But the institutions its zeal planted on western prairies outlived the causes for which its disciples fought and bled.

# THE FOUNDING

## IV

### CIRCULATING THE PLAN

Gale spent the year after his resignation from Oneida Institute in drawing up the document which was to enlist subscriptions to establish a community and college somewhere in the Middle West, and going about with it among his friends in the Mohawk Valley, getting opinions on it and soliciting money to put it into effect. His circle of acquaintance was wide from his pastoral and other labors in that region, and his custom of roaming about the country when his stomach bothered him.

The prospectus bore the unimaginative title "Circular and Plan," and consisted of a long pious exordium (the Circular), followed by a practical demonstration of ways and means (the Plan). It began rather heavily: "The Indications of Providence and the requisitions of Christ impose on Christians of this day peculiar obligations to devise and execute, so far as in them lies, liberal and efficient plans for spreading the gospel throughout the world."

It continues in the same strain, pointing out the duty of creating ministers to save our political institutions from falling into the hands of "those who are no less enemies of civil liberty than of pure gospel"; demonstrating that the manual-labor system "is peculiarly adapted to qualify men for the self-denying and arduous duties of the gospel ministry, especially in our new settlements and missionary fields abroad," and with a diplomatic touch, mindful of the wives who will read this appeal over their husbands' shoulders, he makes a handsome concession to woman's sphere: "It is beginning to be believed that females are to act a more important part in the conversion of the world than has generally been supposed, not as preachers," he hastens to add, "but as helpmates to those who are."

After disposing of spiritual matters with the customary platitudes of the time, the plan gets down to a clear and business-like

[ 45 ]

presentation of essentials. A subscription is to be opened; when the money subscribed shall amount to $40,000, the subscribers are to meet, organize, elect a board, and send a committee to spy out the land and select a site. A whole township, thirty-six square miles, at the government price ($1.25 an acre) is to be bought, this land to be allotted to subscribers at an average cost of $5 an acre, the profits to be devoted to founding a college, a preparatory school, and a female seminary; with each purchase of eighty acres a scholarship good for twenty-five years is to be given as a bonus, which might be used, rented, or sold at discretion of the owner.

Three square miles, 1920 acres, is to be reserved for the village and college grounds, the remainder of the tract laid out in farms, the profits from the sale of farm lands to go to the college, those from the village to the academy and seminary; the college to be established on the manual-labor system, required labor from two to three hours a day; the Bible in the original to be taught as a textbook, and one of the professors to act as college pastor. These were the only considerations of curriculum important enough to be settled in advance.

It was a sound and workable plan, though, except in detail, not especially novel. Many educational institutions in the West had been established on a similar basis. If completely successful it would yield a handsome nest egg for an infant college. A township at government price would cost $28,800; at $5 an acre bring a profit of $115,200, a tidy sum for those days. And that 300 per cent rise in price was justifiable. It is people that make land valuable. The immediate juxtaposition of forty families with virgin acres could make dollar-and-a-quarter land worth five dollars before a sod had been turned by the breaking plow.

The friends Gale consulted about his plan and the prospectus were practically all clergymen. And more than that, they were clergymen who saw eye to eye with him in every detail of technical doctrine. It was essential that his colonists should be hand picked, that there should be no differences over matters of religious belief. The devout took their religion too hard in those days to risk assembling the seeds of dissent in a small community on a remote and lonely prairie. Moreover, ministers were men of authority a hundred years ago, the arbiters of morals, without whose sanction no important step might be taken, at least in godly communities where the puritan standard still held. They were also the self-appointed custodians of education, which must not be allowed to escape from theological leading strings. They were as much concerned with keeping schools and colleges free from religious heresy as modern business men are to purge them of political heresy.

Of the seven ministers who signed Gale's plan, only two joined him in his western settlement. One of these was John Waters, venerable, white-haired, saintly, a retired minister, famous for his prayers, which his wife, Wealthy, declared were too long. Beyond his money, his prayers, presiding at the early meetings of the colonists and serving as the first president of the first board of trust of the embryo college, he contributed nothing constructive, and soon disappeared from the history of the town.

The other was a man of a more aggressive character. Hiram Huntington Kellogg had considerable business ability. He was born in Clinton, a town not far from Whitesboro, and educated in its Hamilton College, founded by his father's friend, Kirkland, as an Indian school, like Dartmouth, but later becoming a conventional cultural college. There he had been converted, in the same revival wave that swept Weld into the fold, and entered the ministry. He found his métier, however, in conducting a school for girls on a novel plan. This was the Young Ladies' Domestic Seminary, which did not belie its name. Its students were obliged, irrespective of their wealth, to perform all the housework of the institution in addition to their studies. It was actually a woman's manual labor school, probably the first in the world. The housework was divided into four departments, Clothes, House, Cooking and Dishes, with a student in charge of each division, who assigned the work in rotation, with a complete shift at regular periods so that each kind of work was done during the term by all students. Furthermore, the school admitted colored girls on the same basis as white, a practice which made the citizens of Clinton nervous. They did not want slavery, or approve of it, but, like all conservative northerners, they emphatically did not want the matter stirred up. To admit colored girls to a white school roused the South to fury.

Kellogg's odd educational idea (manual labor, that is, not the colored students) inspired an institution more permanent than his Domestic Seminary. In those experimental days a new method was apt to be copied. Mary Lyon heard Kellogg lecture on the merits of his scheme of combining trigonometry with dishwashing, and took an early opportunity of visiting the school at Clinton. What she saw there impressed her so greatly that she established a similar school at South Hadley, Mass., on the same pragmatic plan, which is today Mt. Holyoke, a famous college for women. Practically every college in this country is a set or cutting from some older institution, planted in new soil.

V

THE EXPLORING COMMITTEE

The subscriptions amounted to $21,000 when it was decided to hold a meeting of the subscribers, or the "Society" as they called it among themselves. This to be sure was little more than half the amount set for the goal, but time pressed; the western country was rapidly filling; soon it would be impossible to find so large a tract as their plans called for, combining fertility, healthfulness and desirability of location, subject to government entry. A meeting was held at Rome, N. Y., on the morning of Wednesday, May 6, 1835, in the session room of the First Presbyterian Church. In spite of the recognition in the prospectus of the part "females" might play in the great undertaking, there is no evidence that women were present or invited.

After spending a season in prayer, the white-haired John Waters was made chairman, and Timothy Brewster Jervis acted as secretary. The first move was to appoint a "prudential committee" as a more flexible unit than the rather loose organization of subscribers, to guide the enterprise in its first steps.

The Prudential Committee met immediately at a neighboring house, and recommended sending an exploring committee to "examine" all the important points for effecting the objects of the Society in Indiana and Illinois according to the instructions of the "Society"—these instructions being to confine their attention to that portion of these two states lying between the fortieth and forty-second degrees of north latitude, about half of both states north of an imaginary line running through Crawfordsville, Indiana, and Quincy, Illinois. It also proposed that Gale be appointed a paid agent at a salary of $700 a year and expenses to secure funds and families, one being as much desired as the other, for without settlers the whole thing would fall through, and preference was to be given to those who would both pay and emigrate.

A week later the Prudential Committee met at Gale's house in Whitesboro to select the men who would go west and look for a site. It was difficult to find farmers who would leave their crops at the beginning of the planting season. Nehemiah West, whose interest in the scheme was surpassed only by that of Gale, volunteered to make the sacrifice. Thomas Gilbert, who, as it turned out, was prospecting on his own account and was not averse to having his expenses paid and company along the way, and finally Timothy Jervis, who was at loose ends between an old profession and a new, agreed to join West in the mission.

West was a farmer from near Ira, a village not far from Whitesboro in New York. He was thirty-one years old, patient as Job, willing as a horse, the factotum of the whole colonization scheme, content to be a hewer of wood and a drawer of water. Gilbert was by far the best qualified. West was fortunate in having so good a mentor to introduce him to the prairies, for

Gilbert had already made two trips to the Northwest Territory. As an Indian trader he penetrated to the headwaters of the Mississippi, and again in 1834 travelled over Illinois on horseback, looking for a place to settle on his own account. He had already decided on the country between the Illinois and Mississippi rivers. Now he was going back to take up land in the region of his choice.

Jervis was a young man of twenty-six, a civil engineer, who had subscribed $400 to the fund. Although he made this one trip west he did not in the end join the colony, nor was his participation of much help to the Society. He had been persuaded to complete the committee, possibly without having yet made up his mind about emigrating. He was engaged to be married and had planned to abandon his profession and become a minister. He may have thought the new colony over-supplied with clergymen, as indeed it was, or the failure of his health when exposed to the miasma of the prairies may have discouraged him.

In Thomas Gilbert's pocket was a letter of instructions written by Gale dated May 10, 1835, addressed to the three members of the committee. It was full and explicit. Health was to be the first consideration. They were to examine the water in wells and springs, note whether streams were rapid or sluggish, whether they had their rise in or flowed through swamps or marshes; whether the supply of water, timber and fuel was ample; to note the slope of the land, the depth, variety and character of the soil; to inquire as to facilities of intercourse, roads, canals, navigable streams, the possibility of water power for mills, the state of the population, prospect of increase.

The finger of destiny seemed to point to Illinois, but it was Gale's intention to have both Illinois and Indiana examined. His knowledge of the west was apparently full and accurate. He dismissed Michigan from consideration because of limited prairie areas, realizing that clearing forests took time and labor. He was evidently aware that in Indiana or Illinois there was such land as he had in mind. Either he or his advisers, none of whom had visited the West, must have had access to reliable sources of information on this point.

These sources may well have been the books about the West which were then flooding the country. A steady stream of travels and explorations, as well as gazetteers and emigrants' guides, poured from the press, both here and abroad, beginning as soon as the country had been thrown open to systematic settlement. Before 1835 there were nearly a hundred books by English writers alone, not merely the works of social critics, like Mrs. Trollope, Captain Basil Hall and Harriet Martineau, but careful studies by practical men, often financed by expectant groups at home in the old country, men sent to find out the facts from a prospector's viewpoint, the books of such men as William Cobbett, John Melish, James Stuart, Patrick Shirreff, Isaac Weld, Fearon, Thomas, Darby, Woods, Welby, Faux, filled with firsthand information by "dirt" farmers about soil, expenses, crops, living conditions, the sort of thing indispensable to those about to transfer their destinies to a new country.

Even more interesting than the travellers' books were the emigrants' guides. They were small books, pocket size, containing suprisingly good maps, considering how sketchy the surveys must have been, with descriptions of routes, roads, taverns and wayside cabins where accommodations might be had, advice about conserving health, instructions for building log cabins, suggestions as to crops, methods of cultivation and location of markets, and often detailed accounts of each county in turn, its soil, natural features, water courses, game and trees. They were perfect Baedekers of the prairies. Hardly a covered wagon left the East without one of these guides under its covers, and many a western family still cherishes among its heirlooms the pathfinder which guided great-grandfather into the wilderness.

One of the best and most prolific writers of these guides was John Mason Peck, a Baptist preacher, who conducted an academy at Rock Spring, Illinois, which subsequently moved to Alton and became Shurtleff College. He had lived in that country many years and most of his information was first hand. His *Guide to Emigrants* was published in 1831, and proved so popular a new edition was brought out in 1836. The first edition of his *Gazetteer of Illinois*, 1834, was printed at Jacksonville, Ill., by R. Goudy, in an edition of 4200 copies, an item of early Illinois printing, which was so successful that a new and revised edition was published in Philadelphia in 1837. Gale probably knew these books; he might even have known their author, for in 1814 Peck was pastor of the church at Amenia, New York, less than two miles from Gale's birthplace.

The committee proceeded by canal from Utica to Rochester, and thence to Buffalo. The canal was as yet comparatively new, but there is no reason to think its boats any more comfortable than when Dickens described the accommodations six years later. These consisted of one long, low room, unequally divided by a red curtain, the larger cabin being for men, the other for women. Ranged around these rooms were tiers of hard narrow shelves, three deep, which were the berths. In the morning, the shelves were taken down, and the apartment became the dining room. The passengers washed on deck, dipping up the dirty canal water with a dipper chained in place into a basin also chained, and then went below for a bountiful breakfast of "tea and coffee, and bread and butter, and salmon, and shad, and liver and steak, and potatoes, and pickles, and ham, and pudding, and sausages," washed down by gin, whisky, rum and brandy from the bar at the end of the room. As our three prospectors naturally did not use tobacco, it is to be hoped they were fortunate enough to secure berths in the same section, so as to escape the cross-fire of tobacco-spitting from above and below which so disgusted Dickens. At any rate, they were used to canal-boat travel, and knew what to expect. They were accustomed to the cry of "Low Bridge," at which every one who happened to be on deck automatically ducked.

At Buffalo they embarked on one of those imposing lake steamboats, which excited the admiration of English visitors, with its huge walking beam, bedizened with gilt and plush below, though its internal economy was merely that of the canal boat on a grander scale. It was divided into a large saloon for "gentlemen" which women would enter only at mealtimes, and a much smaller one for "ladies" which it was illegal for any man, even a husband, to enter at any time. Around these saloons the berths were lined, curtained off like Pullman alcoves. By day the men's cabin was used as a dining room, and the fare was even more lavish than that of the canal boat.

The men passengers sat all day in their saloon drinking hard liquor and spitting with an impartiality that missed nothing but the large spittoons stationed at strategic points. At mealtimes they shifted promptly to the table, dispatched the food with a celerity that amazed visitors from the other side, and returned to their places. Our three tourists did not differ greatly from their fellow travellers, aside from such peculiarities as not drinking, smoking, chewing or swearing. They were also part of the great American public, which was still crude in its habits and manners according to our standards today. If their attitude was critical, their judgments were based on morals rather than upon conventional canons of good taste or manners. They were no doubt subjected to the curiosity and catechism which was almost a ritual, "Where are you from?" "Where ye going?" and even more personal questions if the subject was sufficiently responsive.

At Detroit West bought horses, saddles, saddle bags and bridles. Horseback was the best means of transportation, for the roads were bad. The covered wagons were often upset, mired, flooded at the fords, and frequently missed the way altogether. A horse could be sold at the end of the trip, often for as much as was paid for it.

The route from Detroit was the famous Chicago Road, following the equally famous Sauk Trail. It ran through Ann Arbor, Saline, Jonesville, Coldwater, Sturgeon's Prairie, and White Pigeon in Michigan. At Elkhart Prairie they crossed the line into

Indiana, and here made some examination of Indiana lands, but the search was perfunctory; their hearts were set on Illinois. They proceeded through South Bend to La Porte, which the Yankee settlers had quaintly translated as Doorville, the gateway to Illinois, where they left the Sauk Trail and turned north to Chicago, arriving Friday evening, June 12, 1835.

What they saw was a muddy village of one hundred fifty houses on both banks of Chicago River, connected by a bridge. At the mouth of the river, where it emptied into the lake, stood Fort Dearborn, a log blockhouse erected as a defense against the Indians. The few taverns or public houses were small, dirty and crowded. The ground was low, almost a swamp. The mouth of the river was filled with silt. Nevertheless the place was full of land speculators who believed the town would grow, and most of the land was already bought up. For some years the fur trade with the Indians had been its chief commerce, but now the tide of Illinois settlers was giving it a new direction. That somewhat acrimonious English writer, Harriet Martineau, the deaf traveller who collected such a wealth of information about this country in her shining brass ear-trumpet, visited Chicago the very year (1835) that West and his companions passed through it. In her book, *Society in America,* she gives a vivid picture of the hurrah which characterized the feverish speculation in land.

"I never saw a busier place than Chicago was at the time of our arrival," she says. "The streets were crowded with land speculators, hurrying from one sale to another. A Negro, dressed up in scarlet, bearing a scarlet flag, and riding a white horse with housings of scarlet, announced the times of sale. At every street-corner where he stopped, the crowd flocked around him; and it seemed as if some prevalent mania infected the whole people. The rage for speculation might fairly be so regarded."

Gilbert went to Quincy to attend land sales in the Military Tract; Jervis remained in Chicago for a similar purpose, the point being that if they had to buy from speculators, their land would cost more than $1.25 an acre. There was as yet little demand for prairie, but extravagant prices were being paid for timber, ten to twelve dollars an acre.

West, having sold his horse, took the mail stage for Ottawa. He then set out for Knox County in the Military Tract, travelling through the valley of the Illinois, an enchanting prospect even to eyes familiar with the Mohawk, through Hennepin to Princeton, where four years before the Hampshire colony from Northampton, Mass., had established a settlement upon a plan similar to that of the Gale colony; he crossed Spoon River at Fraker's Grove into Knox County, where his colleagues joined him.

Jervis became ill and returned to the East. Gilbert bought a farm near Knoxville, the county seat, and prepared to settle on it. Both he and West were impressed with the obvious advantages of the neighborhood, but found no site they were prepared to recommend to the Society. Gilbert hoped the colony would locate in his neighborhood, and possibly West did also, for later in the year he led a purchasing committee to the same spot, and indeed, he had beheld unwittingly the future site of Galesburg. He returned to New York by the southern route, Illinois, Mississippi, and Ohio Rivers to Pittsburgh, and canal to Philadelphia, crossing the Alleghanies by the rack-and pinion railway, one of the curious transportation devices of those days. He took ship to New York, steamboat to Albany, and Erie canal to his home.

He was the only member of the committee who was present at the meeting of the subscribers held at Whitesboro, August 19. Its main purpose was to act on the urgent suggestion of the exploring committee that an agent be sent out at once to buy as large a tract as possible, but the prospect looked dark. Some subscribers refused to pay because the conditional $40,000 had not been raised. Others could not pay until they sold their farms. "It seemed," says Gale, "as if prudence would dictate that it be relinquished; it was not, however, given up; the enterprise was too important." It was in a spirit of doubt and hesitation that the second meeting was held.

THE FOUNDING

ENTER SILVANUS FERRIS

The second meeting of the subscribers differed in some essentials from the first. There was present, either as a new recruit or because unable to attend the first meeting, Silvanus Ferris, successful dairy farmer and cheese manufacturer from Norway, a small village in Herkimer County, New York. At least, it seems impossible that a man of such initiative and force as he subsequently proved could have been present at the first meeting in Rome and be so completely ignored in the minutes. We do not know how or when he came into the scheme. He was a distant relative of Gale and must have known of his plan. Materially he had nothing to gain by joining the Illinois company. He was sixty-two years old, not an age when a man abandons a secure position for the risks and hardships of pioneer life without strong reasons. But either from belief or friendship he put himself behind the movement, and the outlook took on a different complexion from that moment. "To Mr. Ferris," said George Gale in 1855, "the college owes much of its present prosperity. It could not have been founded without him."

Silvanus Ferris, born in Connecticut in 1773, of English descent with four American generations behind him, married Sally Olmsted, Gale's second cousin, and emigrated to Herkimer County, the young couple making their wedding journey in a "two-wheeled vehicle." The thin rocky soil of his farm was too poor to cultivate profitably, but made good grazing. He bought cattle, made cheese, bought and sold the cheese made by his neighbors, and gave northern New York state its early reputation for good cheddar.

His partner, Robert Nesbit, known as the "old Quaker cheese buyer," scouted for supplies among the farmers of the region and disposed of the product in New York. While both were fair dealers, according to the business ethics of the times, it was considered nothing more than ordinary for Nesbit in making his rounds to cheapen the cheese offered by deprecating its quality, hinting at a bad market, and depart without buying. Later when Ferris arrived in a more optimistic mood, offering a slightly better price, the seller, unaware they were partners, ignorant of the market price, snapped up the offer.

By thrift and hard work, as well as native shrewdness, Silvanus amassed a competency, and had been able to present each of his six sons with a farm in New York State. He was religious, but his religion was tempered and mellowed by a certain amount of practical common sense, and even natural worldliness, which made him both more human and more successful. The company needed such a man, the only business man in the group. He was a link betwen zealots like Gale, Waters, and West, and the business getters who came later, the Coltons, Chambers, and Willards, who gave the community a commercial basis as necessary as its religious foundation. They were all religious men; the difference was that the visionaries were nothing else.

That second meeting was held at Whitesboro, probably in the old church building still standing. Many of the subscribers were members of its congregation. Whether because of the faith of George Gale or the stimulus of Silvanus Ferris' presence, the clouds which had gathered over the project began to be dissipated. Nevertheless it was felt to be a critical moment in the affairs of the prospective colony, for the morning was spent in prayer and other religious exercise.

The proposed purchase of land was cut from thirty-six to twenty sections, amounting to 12,800 acres, partly because the amount of money aimed at had not been raised, but more especially because the chance of finding the larger tract with all the desirable qualities was slim and growing slimmer every day. For, while the committee had failed to find a site to recommend, it was unanimous as to the wisdom of going ahead, even on a less ambitious plan. They decided to dispatch their purchasing committee at once.

Gale, Ferris and Kellogg were chosen for this errand. Kellogg could not leave his Domestic Seminary, and West was persuaded to go in his stead, a wise choice, for West had been over the ground. Thomas Simmons was finally added, making four to share the responsibility of both selecting a site and buying the land. It was impossible to collect all the subscriptions on such short notice. Many found difficulty in disposing of their farms for cash, President Jackson's panic having already begun to have its effect on the money market. The committee took matters into its own hands. It mustered between five and six thousand dollars of the subscriptions, and borrowed ten thousand from the Utica bank, on the committee's joint note, but actually on Ferris' name. This note, which became due January 1, 1836, was several times renewed, and the last instalment, $1200, paid by Ferris out of his own pocket.

Any subscriber who wished was invited to come along and see things for himself, and would have the advantage of choosing his allotments on the ground. Ferris' son, also a Silvanus, but better known by his middle name Western, accompanied him; Simmons invited a friend, Samuel Tompkins, a cobbler of Hamilton, and Waters also went, and was joined later at Detroit by his son James. Gale, Ferris, his son, and West occupied the official wagon. The others travelled independently, to meet at Detroit. They rested Sunday at Batavia, as was their pious custom throughout the journey.

The equinoctial storm was raging furiously when they reached Buffalo, and tied up their steamboat two days. On Wednesday the captain ventured out, but the lake was rough and dangerous; twice they took refuge in port. Gale was taken sick. At Cleveland they were run down while entering the harbor, and a gash cut in their side almost to the waterline. They changed vessels, Gale growing worse, with violent spasms of seasickness aggravated by his weak stomach, and reached Detroit Friday, two days late, where Gale was taken to the house of a friend and put to bed.

It was evident he could go no farther. Consultations were held at his bedside, the ten-thousand-dollar check cashed at a Detroit bank, and the convenient Tompkins added to the committee in Gale's place. Horses and wagons were bought, and the cavalcade set out over the Sauk Trail, still white with "movers" wagons, avoiding Chicago this time and proceeding steadily to Ottawa, down the Illinois River to Hennepin, and arrived in Knox County October 12, where on the previous trip Gilbert had bought a farm, and West had been favorably impressed.

"And here," says Nehemiah West, who shared with Gale the belief that God was guiding the destinies of the enterprise, "we would again recognize a special interposition of Divine Providence. After we thought we had made diligent search for a location and almost despaired of success, the Lord raised up a friend in the person of Doctor Charles Hansford, who conducted us to the spot where it seems God intended we should establish ourselves and where, we truly believe, and earnestly pray, that much may be done for His glory."

They had reached the Promised Land at last.

Doctor Hansford was one of the newly elected commissioners of Knox County. He was living at Knoxville, the county seat even then in the process of building. He was the largest land-owner and was undoubtedly alive to the beneficial effect of the new settlement on his holdings. The site he pointed out was a level stretch lying west of Knoxville and south of Henderson Grove, along the edge of which some southern settlers had taken up farms.

They saw a high prairie, nearly central between the Illinois and the Mississippi, thirty thousand acres of the finest soil lying in one unbroken tract, without a tree or hill or other natural feature, beautifully watered with living springs and streams, with an abundance of coal and building stone, and unquestionably healthful, the whole tract subject to entry on Congress' title at the minimum price of $1.25 an acre. "It is," said George Gale some years later, "the Mesopotamia of the West."

Gale, who had been left in bed at the house of his friend Stuart in Detroit, recovered from his indisposition in about two weeks, and as soon as he was able to travel he set out for home. "Wishing to see some gentlemen in Ohio," he says in a report made for the information of his associates, "and desirous of learning for our benefit respecting the operations at Oberlin, I stopped at Cleveland, and after a few days I was able to get out to the seminary." He made the rough trip to Oberlin to see for himself how that institution, similar in so many ways to his, was getting on, and also no doubt to renew his acquaintance with his obstinate convert, Charles Finney, and his former pupil, Theodore Weld.

He was reassured by what he saw.

"I was pleased with the operations at Oberlin and got some useful hints," he writes. "They are doing great good. It is only two years last spring since the first blow was struck at the forest, and now there is a flourishing village, several large buildings finished, and in progress, and about 300 students, male and female, . . . Their farms had advanced in value even in a wild state covered with forest from 10 to 20 dol. the acre, and their village lots to 200 dol. the acre, and yet they labor under disadvantages of some kinds which we shall not have. . . . Yet any one would be delighted to live there. The society is delightful because it is strictly Christian, and the cause of Christ's kingdom seems to be the absorbing topic, and science and literature and property are made subservient to the great object. The surrounding country feels from this source a strong religious influence . . . among which an occasional encampment of the officers and students with a great tent is not the least."

Gale's somewhat cryptic allusion meant that Finney was in the habit of holding his famous gospel meetings in a big tent, during which college was dismissed, sometimes for days at a time, while both students and residents were subjected to the attacks of his fervid evangelical rhetoric.

# THE FOUNDING

## THE MESOPOTAMIA OF THE WEST

As seen on the map the old Military Tract of Illinois is shaped much like a cornucopia, and to the purchasing committee and other prospective settlers it must have had something the auspice of that ancient symbol, if they had the knowledge and imagination to appreciate it. Today it has about the same geographical significance as the province of Normandy in France. The name was given to the triangle between the Mississippi and Illinois rivers extending as far north as Rock River because Congress had set aside this territory as bounties to the veterans of the War of 1812. Few of them were willing to realize on their holdings by the arduous process of becoming pioneers, and sold their patents to speculators. Lands not thus segregated were thrown open to other settlers.

The titles to these and other western lands had been involved in more or less confusion since the tide of emigration had begun to increase in volume, what with the efforts of the government to collect installments due on land already taken up, and the clamor of the settlers for free land. In 1820 Congress reduced the price and fixed it at $1.25 an acre. Speculators were a disturbing factor, and settlement was retarded by the confusion. Meanwhile squatters pre-empted lands, and were either ousted by the owners, in most cases speculators who had bought the soldiers' patents, or bought off, or, as sometimes happened, when local opinion sided with the squatters, left in possession. Thus there were four kinds of putative owners, the Federal government, veterans, speculators and squatters. To these disturbances were added the tax titles to lands belonging to Eastern owners sold for accumulated taxes.

These were some of the pitfalls faced by the purchasing committee, that had prevented the exploring committee from finding a suitable site at Congress' price. The most satisfactory evidence of ownership was a pristine deed direct from the government, and that is what the committee sought. Moreover, they had been warned by Gale to be secretive about their plans, as the country swarmed with land pirates, and some one might steal a march on them. That is exactly what happened.

Two "improved" farms were bought from southern settlers on the edge of Henderson Grove north of their chosen stretch of prairie, 260 acres, for $1500. The so-called improvements consisted of log cabins, fifty or sixty acres under rude cultivation, about eight acres of wheat in the ground. They had no great opinion of Hoosier agriculture, but the farms connected the tract of prairie they proposed to enter with the timber they planned to buy, so their domain would be all in one piece. The farms would be useful to supply food when the advance guard of their party began to arrive. Back of the farms they bought a quarter section of timber, a fine stand, great oaks, black walnut, butternut, hickory, basswood, all they could secure, the rest being in private hands.

This accomplished, West and Ferris went promptly to Quincy (but not promptly enough), where the United States land office of the Military Tract was located, by way of Oquawka, or Yellow Banks, as it was then known, on the Mississippi, and catching a downriver boat. They found almost the entire township subject to entry, and bought for the Society 10,336 81/100 acres. They got an unpleasant surprise, however. Richard Barrett from Knoxville had heard of their design and sneaked to Quincy ahead of them. He had entered alternate "eighties" in a line through their tract. His object was to sell out either to the colonists or those who came later, at prices made higher by settlement, but he was not so shrewd as he hoped, for his tracts did not strike the site of the village, but in the area set aside for farms. If the Lord raised up a friend from Knoxville, as Nehemiah West piously thought, the devil must have supplied an enemy from the same source. In spite of Barrett's perfidy, the committee were in high spirits over the result of their mission. Before leaving for Quincy, Ferris wrote to Gale: "I will only say we have far exceeded our expectations in almost all respects. The prairie land is very fine, and in a healthy country." They were seeing Illinois at its best time—Indian summer, days of glorious sunshine, punctuated with cool nights, when the air is full of stimulus and it is a pleasure to be alive. Henry Ferris, Silvanus' son, joined his father at Quincy and returned with him to the site of the new city. He had been attending a school in Missouri, and had been driven out when his abolition sentiments became known.

Back at the flower-decked prairie which was to be their home for the rest of their lives, where Waters and his son James and Simmons and his friend Tompkins were awaiting them, their final task was to survey the land they had entered and return to Quincy to file the survey. The survey was made by George A. Charles, of Knoxville, official surveyor for the newly organized county. He little dreamed, as he helped the Yankees lay out their city, that he was raising up an enemy and rival. In the conflicts between Knoxville and the new colony, Charles was to lead the Knoxville forces in the longest and bitterest of the battles between these two prairie towns, so near together, so alike in their aims and ambitions, so different in their human content.

A square mile was reserved for the village itself, and two more sections for the campus and college farm, 1280 acres, in cultivating which students would pay their tuition. The land outside was laid off in eighty-acre tracts, the units with which went the twenty-five-year scholarships. Solemnly they viewed their future city, sketched out with stakes on the level prairie, gay with autumn wild flowers, and christened the town "Galesburg," the "literary institution" "Prairie College." The streets were named for those present at this ceremony, West, Waters, Ferris, Simmons, Tompkins, and one for the absent Kellogg. They knelt beside their stakes, like modern crusaders beside their swords, while white-haired Father Waters prayed for all that should be connected with the institution, to influence or be influenced by its future history.

This strain of consecration which so strongly animated the colonists is further revealed by the words in Nehemiah West's report to the subscribers. After dealing at length with practical matters, he says:

"Thus we have given briefly the outlines of our expedition and success, and relying for the ultimate accomplishment of this benevolent object on the arm of the Almighty, it is ardently hoped that perfect harmony and an entire concert of action and views may prevail in the colony, until the whole valley of the west may be constrained to confess a powerful, happy and salutary influence, resulting from our feeble efforts; and may we all feel that consequences as important as the salvation of immortal souls may attend the success or failure of our enterprise, and that should the blessing of Heaven attend our labor, and we succeed in rearing up a seminary of learning in the great valley, and amidst a mass of moral desolation, and thus be instrumental in sending the bread of life to those that are ready to perish, multitudes in the realms of glory may yet rise up and call us blessed."

Which expresses in the religious metaphor of the times what West must have thought of the hordes of drinking, gambling, tobacco-spitting emigrants, speculators, prospectors, and the illiterate, shiftless, poor whites and "Suckers" he must have encountered on his two trips to Illinois.

It was now October 30. Ferris and West went back to Quincy, leaving Henry busy cutting down trees for the log cabins to be built the following spring when the first of the emigrants would arrive. The survey must be filed at the land office; moreover, Ferris had a private speculation of his own, and one no doubt for his friend Gale. They had bought land for the colony to the limit of the money obtainable, but there were good lands in the neighborhood still untaken. It would be better they should be in the hands of men sympathetic with the aims and purposes of the Society. Also, such lands, bought at government price, would share in the appreciation in value along with the lands sold by the Society.

The Society had acquired a total of 10,746 4/5 acres, including timber and the improved farms, at a cost of $15,094.84. That was roughly seventeen sections. Ferris now invested for himself and Gale, and possibly others, enough to buy nine additional sections, making the total twenty-six, and justifying West in his assertion that they had invested enough to control the township. One section, number 16, was reserved by law for school purposes. Barrett had sneaked in for eighteen "eighties," or two and a quarter sections. All but one and a half sections lay within the boundaries of one township.

West and Ferris returned east from Quincy. They sold their wagon and team at a slight loss, embarked on the *Warrior*, which carried them down the Mississippi and up the Ohio, to Wheeling, from which place they crossed the Alleghanies by stage and railroad to Baltimore, and proceeded by ship from there to New York City, arriving November 23. Their object was to see Stephen B. Munn, who owned thirty quarter sections of timber adjoining their tract. They met with a cordial reception. Munn gave them the refusal of all the timber land they required at $2.50 an acre. More than that he contributed $500 to the enterprise, and promised to see others who owned land in the neighborhood. Such a settlement as they contemplated would boost prices all around.

With this gratifying climax, the two men caught the last Hudson River boat of the season, and reached their respective homes, the one in Norway, the other in Ira, Saturday, November 28, having spent besides the outlay for land $636.20 in travelling, loss on sale of team, cost of survey, etc., and having been away ten weeks and three days.

Some notice should be taken for the benefit of those unfamiliar with it of the peculiar geographical divisions of counties in the prairie states. The counties are divided into townships, six miles square—that is, thirty-six square miles, in rows of six square miles each. The square miles are called sections, and they are numbered beginning in the upper right-hand corner—that is, the northeast corner—and run west to six, then back again in the next row, so that number thirty-six is the section in the southeast corner. A section contains six hundred forty acres, and is subdivided into halves, quarters and eighths. An eighth of a section, eighty acres, was the unit of sale with the Galesburg society which carried a twenty-five-year scholarship. These divisions are not political, but are solely for marking and identifying farm lands. The roads run between the townships, which accounts for the checkerboard road maps of western states, except old roads following the Indian trails developed before the stiff and artificial gridiron pattern came into use. Naturally such a plan would be possible only in a country where the land was practically level.

## VIII

### THE THIRD MEETING

The third and crucial meeting of the subscribers to Gale's plan was held at Whitesboro, Wednesday, January 7, 1836. There had been many changes in the company since the first meeting seven months before. At least once the whole undertaking was near going by the board. Many had dropped out, and new ones had taken their places. Some had gone west and settled in Michigan. To accomplish what progress had been made the prudential committee—or the smaller purchasing committee—or possibly Gale himself—had rather taken matters into their own hands, and while it was not quite the complete and well-rounded project which had been contemplated, still a considerable quantity of land had been bought with money borrowed on the credit of the purchasing committee, and now awaited distribution and sale to those who were ready to go through with it. Gale had been busy with his job as agent, and triumphantly announced there were now forty-six families ready to emigrate.

The group assembled in the session room of the Whitesboro church that Wednesday morning was remarkably homogeneous. These men were like-minded in matters of belief, mainly farmers from the Mohawk valley, in the neighborhood of Utica. They were not indifferent to their own self-interest, were susceptible to the lure of fertile lands in exchange for the thin stony farms they now had, but all accepted implicitly the religious principles upon which the enterprise was founded. In spite of the somewhat reluctant recognition in the prospectus of the role "females" might play in the great undertaking, there is no evidence that women were present or invited.

All were of English descent, with several generations in this country behind them, the stock of the Pilgrim Fathers, with something of Jonathan Edwards' grim theology in their blood. None was very rich, and none very poor. They shared a common tradition, were familiar with the neighborliness engendered by small-town life, the give and take of pioneer communities, and some of them were about to undergo the experience of moving to and settling a new country for the second time in their lives.

In religious belief, they were mainly Presbyterians, with a fair sprinkling of Congregationalists. The line of demarcation was practically indistinguishable in upper New York at that time, for because of scarcity of churches and under a convenient arrangement known as the Plan of Union, the two sects worshipped together. They were accustomed to communities in which the church was the center, not merely of religious but of social and civic life as well. There were also a few trades which some combined with farming—carpentry, cabinetmaking, cobbling, blacksmithery, and other occupations useful in a new country. They lived with a vivid consciousness of God's concern in the affairs of men, ordered their lives in conformity with their beliefs, and were honestly worried over the fate of all who did not share them. To them hell fire was as real as earthquake or tidal wave or any other natural disaster. They were, in short, what we today call fundamentalists.

The important business was the election of trustees for the college, and the assignment of lands to subscribers and purchasers. The college was of course the core of the enterprise, and the college board would control the affairs of the community for some time to come. The board suggested by the nominating committee was accepted, and other names added; the total number of the full board to be twenty-five, of which the president of the college would be one. The tentative or preliminary board agreed upon was Waters, Ferris, Kellogg, Simmons, Smith, Gale, West, Mills. "Colonel Isaac Mills," as Gale explained later, "a farmer of Columbia, Herkimer County, was with his whole family converted to Christ from Universalism in the great rivival of 1825–6," the same revival, by the way, which was indirectly responsible for this movement, and had made most of its participators spiritually eligible.

There were other members of the board, but they are unimportant. They dropped out, and indeed many of these shadowy figures who attended early meetings and took part in the proceedings, served on committees and accepted offices, only to disappear, seem to have been what chemists call catalysts, agents to bring about certain chemical unions in which they have no part.

The names Prairie College and Galesburg were officially confirmed. It was agreed that the village should be subdivided immediately, that land should be set aside for a seminary and an academy, and that the college farm should be fenced and put under cultivation. The fencing was a necessary preliminary, as all stock ran free on the prairie. It was decided to set up a steam sawmill, and arrange for the erection of a boarding house or some sort of tavern or hotel. A committee was appointed to safeguard the morals of the new community.

The farm plots were then assigned, by bid, the highest bidder having first choice, from the plan drawn up by Surveyor Charles, on land none had seen, and few could imagine. So level and uniform was it that this transaction caused little difficulty, there being even less difference between the various "eighties" either as to location or quality of land than between the farmers who cast lots for them. It was promised that any who had cause later for dissatisfaction could arrange for an exchange, but it was noted afterward that none took advantage of this accommodation.

This was the last meeting of the Society in New York, or for that matter anywhere. Some of them were going west as soon as the ice was out of the rivers and lakes and the roads were fit for travel, and when they were established in their new location colony affairs would be administered by the trustees of the college, until such time as it was ready to take on a regular village organization under the laws of Illinois.

The trustees met three times in the East, before their arena was transferred to the prairie. It was arranged to survey the village plot and lay it out, as the subscribers had authorized, as soon as the surveyor could reach the grounds. Some preliminary instructions were formulated. Three lots on the public square were to be reserved for the church, and the corresponding corners of what the planners supposed would be the center of their town were to be withheld from sale until the development of some use worthy of them. Kellogg was instructed to get ready his plans for a female seminary, which was his specialty. As some of the trustees were leaving that summer, it was agreed that members of the board in the West should act as a sort of local executive committee, and that Ferris, Simmons, Gale, Waters and Kellogg look after matters in the East.

During the summer of 1836 Gale visited the land of the dream which had filled his thoughts for ten years, having failed to complete the trip the year before because of his rebellious stomach. It was a flying visit, if that term is permissible. While staying at the temporary camp erected by the first of the emigrants—which will be described later—he was visited by a party from Vermont, consisting of Lusher Gay, Erastus Swift and Matthew Chambers. These men had been prospecting around Illinois on their own account, and having heard about the Galesburg colony, came over to see what was doing there. Gale in his character of agent managed to sell them on his plan, with the result that all bought land and hurried back east to make preparations to move. Gale was impressed with Chambers, and at the next meeting of the board of trust urged and secured his election to that body.

It was an instance of his shrewd judgment of men, for Chambers proved a valuable addition both to the college and the colony, more in a practical, material, economic way than as pious material, though he too was religious.

The substance of what Gale communicated to his associates on the board of trust can be inferred from what he wrote a few years later about the site selected for the town and college.

"Drawing a line from the Mississippi at the mouth of Rock River to the great bend of the Illinois River near Peru, and you have between the rivers a territory larger than the state of Massachusetts, containing in 1840 nearly 100,000 inhabitants, well watered, with for the most part an adequate supply of timber, and abounding in mineral coal. Encircled by navigable waters—almost embosomed by the great Mississippi—almost every inch of the soil arable; yet more rolling, high and healthful than the greater part of Michigan—the whole earth does not contain a spot capable of sustaining a denser population than the region between these rivers. And if there be a soil on the globe where the seeds of salvation ought to be sown with the first breaking of the turf, it is this."

Gale little suspected how short would be the time before the importance of rivers as a means of transportation would cease. He rejoiced that a fifty-mile radius would include one hundred twenty miles of the Mississippi, thirty miles of Rock River, and seventy of the Illinois. He reasoned that commercial towns would grow up along the rivers, and his city, strategically located to avoid the evils of large industrial cities, would draw its students from those towns and escape the contamination of commerce and the vices of river towns. Within a year the Internal Improvements Act was to make Illinois railroad conscious, and in less than twenty the town he founded on the virgin prairie was to become a division point and a railroad center, exceeded in population by only two other cities in the Military Tract.

# 3

# *Log City*

I

## NEHEMIAH WEST GOES WEST FOR GOOD

Thereupon began the epic movement west. The subscribers sold their farms in New York, packed their household goods, hitched their work horses to the farm wagons, and got ready for the toilsome journey to Illinois. Some made a round of farewell visits to relatives they never expected to see again, going miles out of their way to spend a night with parents who shook their heads at so wild an adventure, as age ever does at youth.

Every few months for a period of two years a train of covered wagons left the Mohawk Valley and settled down to a steady plod-plod of twenty miles a day over roads that were bad and became worse as they got farther west. Provisions for the journey, clothes, and some of the less bulky household goods were loaded on the wagons—not the picturesque Conestoga prairie schooners with their rake outboard seen in old prints, but the more sedate Yankee wagons with perpendicular sides, transformed into veritable covered wagons by canvas stretched over hoops. Heavier belongings were sent by water, by sailing vessels to New Orleans and steamboats up the Mississippi to Oquawka, the nearest point on the river, to their destinations. There they would wait until wagons could be sent for them.

Relatives or neighbors banded together to make up a train. The parties must needs be small so as not to overtax the indoor accommodations they hoped to find for at least part of the way, but it was desirable to have enough horses in a train to pull wagons out of mudholes. These "slues" or sloughs were one of the hazards of the prairies, horses and even wagons sometimes disappearing altogether. During the years 1836 and 1837 seven companies averaging twenty to forty persons each, men, women and children, set out from New York and Vermont. The journey was hard, but not especially dangerous, except to health. Two children were buried by the wayside, one woman died, and three men succumbed to the malaria that lurked in the low lands along the western rivers.

As long as their routes lay among the comparatively settled districts of the East, they stopped at taverns. As these became fewer, they looked for settlers' cabins, where the women and children at least could sleep under a roof, and the use of a cook stove be secured to prepare the evening meal. It was also necessary to be on the watch for opportunities to buy food and forage for their horses. Some had cows tied to the tailboard, or drove a small herd ahead of their wagons. Each family looked after its own supplies. There was no common larder. Game was plentiful, and in each wagon was a long rifle. At the stops, the children picked wild fruit and berries. It was for them a perpetual holiday, and most of them, as well as the men and women, walked the entire distance.

None of these pious pilgrims would travel on Sunday, no matter what their necessities. They were taking their uncompromising creed to the rowdy and riotous West, and their every act along the way was mute witness of their disapproval of the morals of the less scrupulous whose trains passed their encampments, desecrating the Lord's day. They boasted in their diaries that they always overtook these Sabbath-breakers before the week was out, proving that God was on their side. Once in Indiana an innkeeper, so fed up with righteousness as to forget his own interest, told a party the Wabash was on the rise, and that they must cross that day if at all, which they did, but mourned to have listened to a son of Belial.

The tide of emigration was setting toward the upper valley of the Mississippi, at an unprecedented rate. In the 1830's the roads leading west were white with covered wagons. From all eastern towns up and down the Atlantic seaboard, and from ships discharging immigrants from Europe at New York, Charleston and New Orleans, by ones, by twos, by families, by colonies, they were pouring into the prairies. It was one of the greatest hegiras in history. And it was determining for all time to come the character of the civilization that was to rise in that land.

Until the opening of the Erie Canal, the high tide of emigration had flowed along the Cumberland Road from Baltimore—the first macadamized highway in the country. At Pittsburgh or Wheeling the emigrants loaded their families and goods on flatboats and floated them down the Ohio. Northern traffic could also reach the Ohio by way of the Ohio canal from Cleveland to Portsmouth, and thus that river remained the most used highway until better facilities in the North, together with growing interest of its people in the West, changed the character of the emigrants in the nick of time to save Illinois from becoming a slave state.

The covered wagons now streamed along the Genesee road in New York, laden with New Yorkers and New Englanders bent on establishing religion and agriculture in the promised land; canal boats and the palatial lake steamers were thronged with emigrants. The Galesburg colony was a wave in this tide. Its different parties did not follow identical roads. There were at least four routes by which such pilgrims could find their way from northeastern New York to western Illinois, and each was followed by at least one of the wagon trains: (1) by land all the way, to Buffalo over the Great Western Turnpike, then south of Lake Erie through Ohio and Indiana into Illinois; (2) by land all the way, crossing Niagara River at Queenston, traversing Canada to Detroit, and thence through Michigan and Indiana; (3) by land and water, loading their wagons on a steamboat at Buffalo, and unloading at Detroit; (4) by water all the way, the Erie Canal to Buffalo, lake steamboat to Cleveland, Ohio Canal to Portsmouth, down the Ohio River, up the Mississippi to

[ 73 ]

Oquawka—or to Copperas Creek on the Illinois River, ten miles farther from their destination than Oquawka. A few of the more prosperous emigrants, Gale, Ferris perhaps, travelled to Chicago by steamboats from Buffalo, the most expeditious as well as the most comfortable means then available. The journey could thus be made in about two weeks.

Those of the wagon trains who made the perilous crossing of Niagara at Lewiston got something of a thrill. The ferry was but five miles below the falls, where the river runs swiftly between high bluffs, with many eddies. The roads down to the water and up the opposite bank are steep and difficult. From the landing on the Lewiston side you can see on Queenston heights the tall monument to General Brock, a gallant British officer who fell at that spot, pierced by a Yankee bullet, in one of the engagements of the War of 1812. The crossing was made by horse-power ferry, which could carry but one wagon at a time. The start was well above the landing to allow for the current, but even then it seemed as if the boat must overshoot the mark and bring up against inaccessible cliffs. The water boiled green and angry around the clumsy craft, but at the critical moment the backwash of the eddy seized it and slowly moved it back. One by one each wagon made the precarious trip, watched anxiously by those waiting for their turn or safely over.

The first of the wagon trains bound for the Gale colony to leave the East was that led by Nehemiah West. It had been arranged he should be on the ground to get things ready, welcome and bestow the later arrivals and set up the machinery of living. He was to be for some years the major domo, the chief factotum of the colony. Gale furnished the idea, Ferris the business head, and West the indispensable working out of a multitude of details. He better than any knew what lay before him. Already he had twice made the difficult trip to Illinois and back; he knew the hardships and discomforts his family and fellow pilgrims must face; what it meant to subdue virgin prairie never before occupied by white men, and provide the means of existing in a country so remote from civilization. But no man, not even Gale, had more faith in the project, a greater conviction of the divine sanctity of their mission. He was of the simple, unquestioning spirit of the first disciples called by Christ.

He set out from Cayuga, New York, in the spring of 1836, as early as roads were passable. There were twenty-one persons in the party, twelve of them children, some of them infants. The route followed was one he knew from his previous trips. The wagons were taken aboard ship at Buffalo, unloaded at Detroit, and from there the Chicago road led them to Illinois. The farther west they fared, the more difficult it was to find lodgings. Even in Chicago there was no place to sleep, until a friend found them accommodations in a house being moved, standing on rollers in the middle of the street. Such sights were common in western towns, the simple structures being mobile, the habits of the settlers restless, and the cheapness of land encouraging change. The men engaged in moving the house were unaware of its temporary occupancy, and when operations started in the morning the heads at the windows were greeted with vigorous profanity. The lodgers for the night were obliged to vacate without preparing breakfast.

They travelled over the prairies of Illinois, "beautiful in the freshness of their May robes," crossed Fox River, went through the village at Peru, saw to their left the famous Starved Rock, "over whose legend as told by their father, the children shed tears." They were now in open, almost empty country, and securing supplies became difficult. Their food was exhausted, and they looked in vain for some settlement. Late at the end of a long day they came to Fraker's Grove, the settlement of a family of southerners, and had their first taste of Hoosier hospitality.

Old Mother Fraker was in one of her moods of hostility to the Yankees who were invading the state in such numbers. She told them sullenly she had neither room nor food—the last undoubtedly true, for the Hoosiers were notoriously poor providers. But Old Man Fraker took pity on them, gave them a rude cabin with a fireplace, directed them to a neighbor a mile distant where they could buy milk, and took corn from his crib and ground it in a primitive mill. A kettle was hung over the fire, and the company dined on mush and milk. Next morning the mothers of the party made hoe-cake for breakfast. The remnants were carefully gathered and carried with them, and their first meal in their new home was cold hoe-cake eaten off a puncheon slab.

Fraker's was but a short distance from the site Nehemiah had selected, bought and staked for the future city. They went immediately to the "improved farms" on the extreme north of their tract, close to the woods known as Henderson Grove. Here there was also a Hoosier settlement, relations with which took on the same mixed character of natural hospitality and sullen suspicion they had already met at the Frakers, a conflict of old established habits and ideals which was to enliven the history of their new town for years to come.

Settling his family in the cabin he had hired from a Hoosier family, West busied himself in installing others in the buildings on the improved farms now belonging to the colony. It was part of the plan to establish a foothold here from which to build their city on the neighboring prairie, for it had been agreed no log cabins would be tolerated in Galesburg. Their town was unique among pioneer settlements in that respect.

In time a group of seventeen log cabins grew up on the edge of Henderson Grove, and was christened Log City. "Grove" was the Illinois word for the patches of timber scattered over the prairie, but Henderson Grove was actually a bit of primeval forest, twelve miles long and six wide. Scattered through it were the settlements of the Hoosiers, for those shivering southerners feared the prairies and sought the protection of the trees from the severe winter winds. They had a large village at Henderson, the first in Knox County, and they took it as evidence of the queerness of the Yankees that they planned to live on the open prairie.

It was in this setting that West and his party dug themselves in, and started the rhythmic round of work, sleep and worship, that was to be the lot of the colony for many years, and prepared to welcome the next arriving train, and initiate it into the life of Log City.

## II

### HOOSIERS VS. YANKEES

The subsequent conflicts between settlers now arriving and the southern immigrants who preceded them will be better understood if some account is given of the latter, of whom the Frakers encountered by West and his party are typical specimens.

If one examines in chronological order the early maps of Illinois, such as were produced almost yearly from the time the state was admitted to the union, it will be obvious that settlement started in the south and gradually flowed north. The lower half of the map is filled with the marks that indicate the occupancy of man while the upper half, except for dots at Chicago, Peoria and Galena, is comparatively empty. Settlements creep up the rivers, Mississippi, Ohio and Wabash, before even counties are laid out in the north.

This immigration was almost wholly southern in origin. The lower half of the state was bordered by slave-owning states. It was itself practically a pro-slavery state. If the mythical boundary between slave territory and free, Mason and Dixon's line, were extended west, it would divide Illinois in half. All of it below Springfield would be geographically in "the South." As far as the sentiment of the population was concerned, that is exactly what it was.

The earliest natural means of transportation were the Ohio and Mississippi rivers. One bordered slave territory; the other flowed through it. This accounts for the predominantly southern character of the early population of Illinois. Not until large and comparatively fast steamboats plied to and fro on the Great Lakes, not until the Erie Canal was opened in 1825, did the upper half of the state begin to fill. The birth date of a surprising number of its cities is found in the years between 1830 and 1840.

The settlements in the southern half antedated them by at least a quarter of a century. Thus the state was on the way to be peopled completely by immigrants of southern origin, when the process was interrupted by the stream from the North, and the complexion of the population diluted down to about half and half, a fact that conditions its history, and that of the city that is the subject of this inquiry.

In order to speak easily and without circumlocution of these two strongly marked divergent peoples, so mutually antagonistic, we will adopt the names they applied to each other, though neither is an exact definition nor a happy designation. Large numbers of the southerners came into the state by way of Indiana, after a preliminary stay in that state, as did the family of Abraham Lincoln. Indiana was the Hoosier state; its inhabitants were Hoosiers, and the northern invaders applied that name indiscriminately to all southern immigrants, irrespective of their origin, though many came directly from Kentucky, Missouri, Virginia and the Carolinas. The term as used in early Illinois characterized specifically the class known in their own states as poor whites, and it is doubtful if southerners of better spirit were thus identified as Hoosiers. In a similar manner the Hoosiers called all northerners Yankees. It was in vain that the Gale colonists expostulated, and explained they were from New York, and therefore not Yankees; the reply was a laconic, "Well, York Yankees is the meanest." The word Yankee as applied to northern soldiers during the Civil War was undoubtedly current in its broader sense long before the war.

A contemporary picture of the two classes, Hoosier and Yankee, may be obtained from the outspoken history of Illinois written by Governor Thomas Ford. Ford was born in Pennsylvania, but was taken to Illinois as a baby, grew up there, mingled with its people, became governor in 1842. He was of both southern and northern descent, and his summary may be taken as fair.

He points out that the southern portion of the state was settled by immigrants from slave-holding states; that they came to

Illinois to escape the odium of living in a locality where even the negroes looked down on any one too poor to own slaves, and called them "po' whites"; that wealthy southerners did not emigrate to free states where they could not take their property, in other words, human chattels, and that on this account the southern population of Illinois did not fairly represent the wealth, enterprise, education, or culture of the South. Those who came were good, kind, hospitable, unambitious people, lovers of ease and social diversion, but indifferent to wealth. On the other hand, northerners, free to bring their property with them, were a different class, wealthy farmers, enterprising merchants, millers and manufacturers. They contributed to the upbuilding of the country, made farms, established mills, built schoolhouses, laid out towns and cities, constructed roads and bridges.

Basic differences occasioned discord between the two peoples. Each harbored unjustified suspicions of the other. The southerners had never seen genuine Yankees. They were familiar with the skinning, trafficking, tricky peddlers from New England who infested the South with tinware, wooden clocks, and other cheap merchandise, and judged all Yankees by those specimens. Consequently, the Hoosiers thought all Yankees close, miserly, selfish, dishonest and inhospitable, lacking all the kindlier feelings of humanity. On the other hand, the Yankees considered their southern neighbors lank, lazy, ignorant animals, but little removed from the savage state, content to squat in a log cabin with a large family of ill-fed, ill-clothed, dirty and idle children.

Both were wrong, Ford concludes. The two people are equally generous, but express it differently. The Hoosier is hospitable to individuals, lavish with his liquor and victuals. The Yankee is liberal toward the community, has more public spirit, works for the common good.

It is desirable to go a little deeper than Ford's cautious account, for he was a politician, trying to distribute praise and blame in equal proportions. We will be seeing these people through the eye of the invading Yankee, to whom the Hoosiers were antipathetic in every way. They deprecated their morals, lack of thrift, untidiness, and garrulous curiosity. The Hoosiers were, in fact, the objectives of the missionary spirit that had brought the Gale colony to the West.

The suspicious attitude of the Hoosiers toward all Yankees was inspired, as Governor Ford intimated, by the Yankee peddlers who toured the South and West and victimized the natives, no match for such wily traders. Connecticut gets its nickname from the supposed practice of palming off wooden nutmegs. Hoosier lawmakers at Vandalia—then the capital of Illinois—had drafted their suspicions into statutes, for while a license to sell liquor cost $2 a year, a license to peddle clocks was fixed at $50.

The Yankees, on the other hand, deplored their neighbors' laxness. They had come west fired with zeal to establish neat, orderly, pious communities, where "the cause of Christ's kingdom" would be "the absorbing topic," as Gale had approved at Oberlin. Instead, they found the Hoosier, far from welcoming their well-meant intentions, quite sure their own ways were infinitely better. The Hoosiers were obstreperously religious, but their preference was for the boisterous exhortations of unlettered but rudely eloquent circuit riders, and the excitements of non-stop camp meetings, which to sedate Presbyterians, who had found even Finney's methods a bit sensational, seemed sacrilegious.

As an example of the easy-going manners of Hoosier preachers, the story is told of a church where it was the young people's weekly duty to clean up the pulpit after each Sunday's services. They rebelled at the amount of chewed tobacco it was necessary to scrape up. A box filled with sand was set beside the pulpit as a hint, strengthened by the admonition in large letters, "Please spit here." Unfortunately the good dominies failed to do so. In the excitement of saving souls they could not hit the target.

It can be imagined that after their own pulpit pyrotechnics the Hoosiers found the Yankee churches dull and boring. They did not care for "high-toned" religion. And there was much more than religion to keep them apart. They clashed on temperance, for whisky was a beverage as natural to the southerners as water to the teetotalers. It was freely distilled from the corn that grew so abundantly in Knox County. They resented that drinking should be considered a moral question, and took it ill that the Yankees did not serve whisky at the corn-huskings, house-raisings and other pioneer merrymakings. And bitterest issue of all was slavery, for the Hoosiers, who owned no slaves, and never had, and never would, and lived in a state technically free, hated an abolitionist like a rattlesnake.

The Yankees expressed their animosity by calling names. Hoosier was a term of contempt. The sobriquet, "Suckers," by which the inhabitants of Illinois were one time known, as Missourians were called "Pukes," may have arisen from an epithet applied originally to the southern immigrants. Governor Ford cites three possible origins of that strange expression, two of them uncomplimentary to the Hoosiers. The more popular version is that the southerners were accustomed to leave their farms to the care of the women folk once a year, and go up the Mississippi to Galena to work in the lead mines, returning in the fall to harvest their crops. Their arrival synchronized with the upstream migration of a fish known as sucker; hence their appearance was greeted with cries of "Here come the Suckers."

Another version is that in tobacco-growing countries from which most of the poor whites came that plant is afflicted with shoots known as suckers, a pest which must be patiently rooted out. By analogy the expression came to be slang for anything objectionable and useless, including worthless members of the community. A more romantic story concerns George Rogers Clark's expedition to drive the English out of Indiana and Illinois. At the capture of Kaskaskia, ancient capital of Illinois, one of his officers discovered a number of settlers sitting in front of a sidewalk café imbibing grenadine through straws. It is appealing to think of expatriated Frenchmen clinging to the apéritif hour in a muddy village on the banks of the Mississippi, like Englishmen dressing for dinner in the jungle. The pathos was lost on the officer, who advanced shouting, "Surrender, you suckers." Whatever its origin, the term was one of reproach, and it is poetic justice that it came in time to apply to all inhabitants of Illinois.

The Hoosiers were humorous, picturesque, colorful, far better literary material than the joyless and long-faced Yankees, but at their worst they were so filthy as to turn the stomachs of many a wayfarer from the northern states. They were not all poor whites, and not all remained so. There was good blood from Virginia and Maryland. Some were ambitious, and attained eminence, and made real contributions to the history of this country. The present-day population of Galesburg and of Knox County is an amalgamation of the two stocks, as is that of most of the state. The mutual misunderstandings and jealousy of the two classes occasioned the more exciting history of the times, until the triumphant Yankees had acquired one after another all the economic, civic and political advantages within their reach.

Thus we have two peoples living side by side in close communion within the area of a single county who differed as widely in essentials, in all that constitutes a philosophy of life, as though they belonged to separate races, which they did not. Both were English strains, one hardened and tightened by sharp New England winters and stony soil, the other relaxed and liberalized by a warm climate and easy cultivation. The deep-seated enmity between them climaxed in the Civil War, to which all these preliminary clashes were but curtain raisers.

So strong was the pro-slavery sentiment in Illinois in the years following its admission to statehood that in 1822 an act was forced through the Hoosier legislature to allow the question of slavery to be submitted to popular vote, notwithstanding the Ordinance of 1787. That compact provided that states carved out of the Northwest territory should be forever free. Governor Ford has intimated that rich slave owners moved to Kentucky and Missouri; that Illinois got the poor whites. The Hoosiers resented the loss of such valuable additions to their population. The law

[ 82 ]

required, however, that the vote on the act must be postponed for two years. In two years northern settlers poured into the state in such numbers that the proposal was defeated by a majority of 1784 votes.

It could be maintained that the North won the Civil War by that same margin. Had Illinois gone for slavery, Indiana would have followed. With both states in the Confederate column, so strategically situated, it is inconceivable that the Union could have triumphed. For thirty years after the coming of the Gale colonists the grim question of slavery was to darken the history of this state, hovering ominously around such settlements as Galesburg, little islands of abolitionism in a sea of pro-slavery.

The country was ripe for settlement, and conditions unusually favorable. Indiana was admitted to the Union in 1816; Illinois in 1818. Both were as yet nearly empty. The last menace from Indians had been removed by the unjust, unprovoked Black Hawk War, reflecting little credit on the authorities, but nevertheless chasing the Indians out of the state. Notwithstanding the spurt of immigration in the 1820's, there were millions of acres still open, particularly prairies. The Hoosiers avoided them, settling instead on the rich but unhealthy river bottoms, where the "shakes" made them sallow, and gave the state an undeserved reputation for insalubrity.

The thought that had been in Gale's mind as he taught belles lettres and moral philosophy at Oneida Institute and pored over his plans for an institution of greater power was that the West was growing faster in population than it was in churches and ministers, that with its great area and potential wealth it would one day be a dominating factor in the nation, and his fear lest the government thus fall under the control of what he considered an untaught, ungodly people.

He was not alone in that idea. It prevailed among many earnest Christian groups animated by missionary zeal, who had already moved or were about to move to set up colonies to leaven the "hell roaring West." There were already three colleges in Illinois and two in Missouri—not counting Catholic foundations at St. Louis, little better than heathen to these zealots—all established in the proselyting spirit of Gale's own scheme. The Yale Band had set up Illinois College at Jacksonville. The Methodists had established McKendree at Lebanon, the Baptists Shurtleff at Alton, and Bishop Chase and the Episcopalians were busy gathering money for Jubilee College at Robin's Nest near Peoria. So prevalent was this form of colonization that a sardonic observer remarked: "A settler could hardly encamp on the prairie, but a college would spring up beside his wagon." Moreover, the state was dotted with communities not so ambitious, such as Princeton and Geneseo, whose hopes did not extend to a college, but did include a church and academy, closely linked and of one faith.

These promotions were not welcomed by the southern population. They opposed the building of the Michigan and Illinois canal lest it bring more Yankees into the state. They contested the establishment of denominational colleges for fear an educated ministry would drive out the circuit riders who catered to their spiritual needs more tolerantly and understandingly. All this was more or less in the minds of the Frakers, when Nehemiah West and his party drove up to their cabin door.

Nehemiah West and his party, the first to arrive, were the first to be brought into contact with the problem of living as neighbors with people so different. At the Grove they found the Gumms, the father a Baptist elder, or itinerant preacher, with four strapping married sons. The Gumms were friendly and helpful. They rented their cabins to the newcomers, though irked by the smugness and complacency of the Yankees, by their evident determination to do them good. Friction was bound to arise. West, whose only book was the Bible, may have thought at times of that other Nehemiah, who also went into a far country and cut timbers in the forest and repaired the gates of Jerusalem, and found himself surrounded by suspicious and hostile neighbors looking for pretexts to wage war.

All the arrangements fell on his sturdy shoulders, and he was

[ 84 ]

qualified. He had a practical mind, good at details. He was unambitious, had no desire to be a leader, but attended to the work at hand, and soon had matters running smoothly at the new settlement. At the end of a summer spent in felling trees, building cabins, and breaking the ground for farms, the community was shocked by the arrival of a young man so weak from malaria he could scarcely sit on his horse. He brought the disastrous tidings that a boatload of fellow colonists was in a desperate situation in the Illinois river bottom at Copperas Creek. Help was earnestly needed to get them to the settlement.

### III

### THE BOAT PARTY

The "boat party," as it was known for years in the annals of the town, usually prefixed by some such adjective as "unfortunate" or "ill-fated," had set out in the spring of 1836 with high hopes. John C. Smith, a canal boat proprietor of Utica in a small way, was active in the deliberations of the subscribers to Gale's plan from the very beginning. Able, energetic, but somewhat visionary, and more familiar with water transport than other methods of progression, he conceived the idea of emigrating to the new settlement in a canal boat by way of the Erie Canal (which he knew thoroughly), Lake Erie, the Erie and Ohio Canal, and the Ohio, Mississippi and Illinois Rivers (of which he was profoundly ignorant); some two thousand miles by water as against one thousand by land (or land and water) adopted by other emigrants.

He organized his company, and a canal boat of the packet type was bought on shares, and fitted up for the voyage. The men's cabin was used for storage of baggage and household goods, leaving only a narrow passageway to get to the bunks. The horses and wagons of the settlers were put on board, the horses to serve as motor power on the tow path. The galley was equipped for cooking, a supply of provisions laid in, and in May the boat started from New London, near Utica, for Buffalo, with Smith as captain, his wife as chief cook, and thirty-seven people on board, seventeen of them small children, one an infant.

On the comparatively quiet trip to Buffalo the passengers of this remarkable ark settled down to some sort of routine. Some were strangers to the others, but with a common purpose and sharing the same discomforts and relaxations, they became as the report says "one large family." Cooking three times a day for thirty-seven people proved too much for Mrs. Smith, and Mrs. Phelps, in spite of six children clinging to her skirts, took charge, and for a time all went smoothly. It was rather close quarters for seventeen lively youngsters, and to give the elders some respite, "Aunt Kitty," as one of the spinsters was affectionately known, organized a sort of school along what would now be known as kindergarten lines, with regular lessons, and the future students of the Prairie College that was to be were thus kept quiet for some hours daily.

As may well be imagined in such a company, religious worship was more important than education, and prayer meetings were held daily. Each Saturday night the boat was tied up, and on Sunday they attended the nearest public service, or if there was none available, they organized their own in a convenient school-house, and invited the neighborhood to join them.

At Buffalo passengers, goods and live stock were transferred to one of the lake steamboats bound for Cleveland; the canal boat was hitched behind. Off Ashtabula a violent storm struck them, so severe the steamboat captain thought his vessel endangered and cut the canal boat adrift. He landed the passengers at Cleveland, dumped their goods on the dock where they lay in the rain and were seriously damaged, while the party anxiously awaited news of their ark.

When the canal boat arrived, the damaged dunnage was loaded into it, the horses again put to work on the tow-path, and the party started to cross Ohio by way of the Ohio and Erie Canal, a winding and tortuous journey. They ascended the valley of the

Cuyahoga, fringed with tulip, walnut and sassafras trees, with a lock every half mile, to Akron, the modern rubber tire city, whose name is Greek, meaning Elevation, now a sort of industrial acropolis. The canal passed through the center of the town by means of twelve locks. Beyond Akron it traversed a lake, with a bridge for the tow horses. Newportage marked the place where the fur traders carried their canoes from the Cuyahoga to the Tuscarawas.

The architecture was now becoming German, big hipped-roof barns with dormer windows, reminiscent of Bavaria, though these travellers probably did not know that. But they must have noted the picturesque village of Zoar with its pretty houses roofed with red tiles, the Moravian settlement of the Wurtemburg Separatists, its Canal Hotel and long wooden bridge spanning both canal and river. They may have caught sight of Swabian shepherds carrying crooks, wearing leather bandoliers ornamented with brass figures, flat-brimmed hats and long gray cloaks.

The mayapple was in full bloom, kingfishers, red-headed woodpeckers and orioles perched on the alder bushes and watched the boat slide slowly by. They gazed in wonder at prehistoric mounds and barrows frequently visible from their boat. They saw corn just springing into leaf, the largest fields they had ever beheld, a foretaste of what was later to become a familiar sight in Illinois. A tourist travelling west in those days beheld the whole cycle of the development of a new country from unbroken prairie to well-tilled farm, but in reverse order, like a movie run backward.

From the high level the canal descends to the valley of the Muskingum and then cuts across to the Sciota, which it follows all the way to the Ohio. On Licking Summit it passes through a cut thirty feet deep; the tow line is lengthened, the horses looking small so high above the boat. They pass Circleville, appropriately named, for the village is surrounded by an Indian mound twelve to twenty feet high like a circular wall. Instead of the conventional public square there is a circular plaza in the center of the village, in which stands a round brick courthouse. After Chillicothe they arrive at Portsmouth where the Sciota and the canal empty into the Ohio, having negotiated fifty-three locks since Licking Summit. They find Portsmouth an inconsiderable town, with broad, unpaved streets, set high on its bank eighty feet above the river. On the trees which border the Ohio they saw curious vegetable growths which must have puzzled them, for it was their first sight of mistletoe. It had no sentimental associations for them, for these New England Christians did not celebrate Christmas.

Southern Ohio was wrought up over the slavery question, and there was much speculation as to the intentions of the boatload of abolitionist Yankees. A deputation of ministers called and warned them they would be mobbed, no idle threat. At Cincinnati the women and children were sent ashore as a precaution, while the men remained on the boat, but no demonstration was made.

Isaac Mills decided to leave rather than face the even worse discomforts and dangers beyond. His announcement caused the utmost consternation. He was the only member of the party with any money left. The others had sunk all they possessed in the venture. The unduly prolonged trip had exhausted their resources. Without him they could not go on, but would be left stranded, their journey half completed. Mills finally yielded to their urgings and remained with the party and defrayed its expenses, a decision that cost him his life.

The long stay in Cincinnati was for the purpose of rigging up some sort of propeller on the stern of the vessel so as to drive it upstream on the Mississippi, worked by a horse in a treadmill on board, and some such contrivance was made, not very efficient, as the sequel proved. Meanwhile the company visited the city, then a town of some 20,000, and saw its sights, which must have included the market, where rows and rows of four-horse Ohio wagons were backed to the curb, permitted to sell every sort of provender but fresh meat.

Cincinnati was then as now the pork city, and its streets were kept comparatively clean by the droves of hogs that roamed at will and ate up the garbage thrown out by housewives. Mills unloaded the horse and buggy which formed part of his cargo on the ark and with his wife and daughter drove about the city. A thill broke, and they sought the shop of William Holyoke, a sturdy wheelwright and forthright abolitionist. While a new thill was being made Mrs. Mills visited with Mrs. Holyoke, and Mills talked with her husband, and what they talked about was Gale's colony in Illinois.

The buggy got a new thill, and the colony gained nine recruits. The following spring Holyoke packed up and moved, with his wife, four sons, one daughter, one adopted daughter, and a woman helper. He bought the first house erected in Galesburg, set up a wagon and carriage shop, and organized the first anti-slavery society in Illinois.

An incident reveals the uncompromising, not to say intolerant, attitude of the Yankee emigrants. Sunday morning a steamboat arrived having on board southern delegates to an ecclesiastical convention. Seeing the canal boat alongside, several went aboard and invited the company to attend the meetings. Up spoke Sophronia Phelps:

"Didn't we see you arrive this morning?"

The puzzled dominie admitted it.

"We do not attend meetings conducted by men who travel on Sunday," was the spirited reply. Thus was visible the thin edge of the wedge that was to split Galesburg in its first great controversy, for what Sophronia meant was that these ministers not only travelled on Sunday, but were from slave-owning states where the church connived at sin.

As the ill-fated bark moved away from the Cincinnati landing and down the Ohio, things grew worse. The river was low, the air foul with miasma, the sun scorching, and the mosquitoes ferocious. They knew as little about malaria and fever and ague as they did about navigating a river full of snags and sandbanks. Often in the middle of the day when the heat became unbearable they tied up to the shore, and the party took refuge in the shade of the trees along the bank. Every one was more or less sick.

The lighter cases nursed the serious ones. It became a grim test of endurance, with no immediate escape from the evils that beset them.

The canal around the rapids at Louisville had just been completed, so they were able to get by where formerly travellers by steamboat had been transferred to another vessel. Between Louisville and the Mississippi lay the bottom lands of Egyptian Illinois with their dreary water-logged deadly towns, Shawneetown, Ft. Massac, Golconda, lawless, disorderly, and inhospitable, hardly safe for such unworldly pilgrims to stop at. In caves along the river lurked bands of pirates who robbed and murdered defenseless travellers by water.

In the Mississippi there was constant delay. Even experienced river pilots are often fooled by this treacherous stream. The propeller refused to work. Parts of it continually dropped off into the river, and Noble Phelps acquired such experience in diving that when Captain Smith lost his watch over the side, he went in and recovered that also. At St. Louis they refused an offer of $1000 for their boat; it would have been wiser to have accepted. Slowly they worked north while the sick lay in their bunks and longed for land.

At length they were forced to make the best arrangements they could for a tow, and were hauled up the Illinois as far as Copperas Creek, about twenty miles below Peoria, and forty from Log City. They had been eleven weeks on the way, and conditions were now desperate. Smith, Mills, and Lyman were seriously ill. They were all big men, over six feet tall. Only one young man had sufficient strength to sit on a horse. He was dispatched to Log City for help.

A rescue party with teams, blankets, and whatever supplies might alleviate the sufferings of the boat load of invalids was quickly assembled. The sight that met its eyes was a sad one. Emaciated, sallow, weak, the company showed the effects of the long strain. The sick and dying were lifted into the wagons for the long, rough, jolting journey back to Log City. Captain Smith died at Knoxville. Mills and Lyman lived only a few weeks. These three were the first martyrs. They lie in Hope Cemetery which the settlers had laid out near the site of their new city. Little Moses Root died the following spring.

In a one-room cabin were installed the worst cases, thirteen in number on beds of poles set in the walls, laced with ropes to support straw-filled ticks. Other beds were made up on the chests that held the clothing, which had to be removed whenever anything was needed. In the center of the room was a huge box stove on which all the cooking was done. In this improvised hospital in the heat of an Illinois summer the survivors slowly recovered. Compared with so lamentable an experience, the minor discomforts and discouragements of the next company, which came all the way by land in covered wagons, were the acme of luxurious travel.

## IV

### PIONEER ARCHITECTURE

The few log cabins that existed when Nehemiah West and his party arrived in the spring of 1836 were augmented by others built during the summer, and by the following spring the earlier arrivals were beginning to move into their new houses on the "prairie," leaving cabins for later comers. Not all arrivals settled in Log City. Some went directly to their farms. The sons of Silvanus Ferris began to erect a sawmill on the bank of Henderson Creek. A creek, in Illinois, was a stream between a brook and a river.

Log City at length comprised a row of seventeen cabins, some double, one or two with lean-tos or additions, and two log barns, a straggly row running east to west and facing south, on the two "improved farms" which joined at the site. The land on the edge of the woods was rougher than the prairie, and the site was cut by two ravines running toward Henderson Creek about a third of a mile south. A good spring in the middle of the settlement furnished water. As a temporary "construction camp" for building a city on an adjacent site, Log City is probably unique in the annals of pioneer settlement.

Here occurred many of the significant events of their lives, births, marriages, and deaths. Here their church was organized. During the one to two years the settlers became acquainted with each other, and lasting friendships were formed. The name had a sentimental interest for years. The children played together in the woods, and formed memories which lasted a lifetime. "There never was," said Sam Holyoke, son of the Cincinnati wheelwright, when eighty-six years old, who lived as a boy in Log City, "another company of people living together for one purpose who lived together so happily and worked with such mighty energy. . . . It will not be possible for those who have no experience with frontier life to realize and appreciate the amount of courage and energy such life demands."

A sketchy community life was set up, education and religion were provided for, and the Galesburg colony had a taste of pioneer life as it was lived by the Hoosiers around them. The cabins were small, generally one room, fourteen by fourteen feet and the families large, and more than one family was the average quota, and this phase of their experience is an interesting interlude to their progress, harsh in the actual experience, but pleasant and romantic in retrospect.

The log cabins, whether bought from the southern settlers or built by themselves, were constructed after the same fashion. From the forest close at hand, where each purchaser of land on the prairie had a timber lot, uniform logs were cut the proper length and pared down on opposite sides to a thickness of nine inches. Timber was also cut for shingles and clapboarding, and joists and spars to be laid across, and the material hauled to the site of the house.

At this point neighbors were called upon, for the "raising." The best axemen were stationed at the corners, as the notching or dovetailing was the more technical operation. The corner man built up the walls of the cabin by fitting the ends of the logs into the corresponding notches square and true. By thus saddling the logs, the walls are raised to a height of about seven feet; the logs are gradually shortened for the gables. After three or four courses, spars are sloped against the sides and the logs rolled up, first by hand, and then with forked sticks. The chinks left between the logs are filled with sticks and daubed with clay, which must be renewed each year.

Poles for the roof are laid from gable to gable and covered with shakes or "Hoosier clapboards," about four feet long, riven from short lengths of log. Weight poles are laid transversely over the shakes to hold them in place, spaced by short bits of timber called "runs." After the house is up and roofed, an opening is cut for a door, usually one on each side to afford air in hot weather, or if a window instead, it is covered with oiled paper. The door is made of spliced clapboards, hung on wooden hinges; the latch is also wood, manipulated by a strap attached, hanging outside through a hole, which is pulled in to lock the door. Sometimes the cabins are double, with a dog-trot between, a pleasant open-air kitchen.

A large perpendicular opening is cut in the gable for the fireplace; the chimney is built outside of sticks laid corncob fashion and heavily coated with clay. The cabin consists of one room, but often poles are laid for a second floor, reached by a ladder through a hole cut in the ceiling. The floor is made by laying sleepers on the ground, to be covered with planks when obtainable. Otherwise puncheons—that is, short lengths of logs split in half, laid flat side up. No nails or other metal are used, wooden pegs or tree nails being employed where necessary.

In this one room the immigrants installed such furniture as they were able to bring on their wagons, eked out by home-made articles improvised on the spot. The fireplace, wide enough to take the biggest log a man can lift, is flanked by a kettle, a long-handled frying pan, and if they were lucky, a Dutch oven—a sheet-iron covered box which could be buried in the coals.

Above the fireplace on the mantel stood a tallow dip thrust into a bottle, or a saucer of lard with a strip of cotton cloth for a wick; on a bench a bucket of water with a gourd dipper. At each of the opposite corners would be a one-legged bed—a pole erected between the floor and ceiling, the width or length of the bed from the walls, with poles running from it to the walls the proper height from the floor. A leather thong or rope laced back and forth on these horizontal poles supported a tick filled with straw, husks, or in some cases feathers. Beneath were pushed the trundle beds on which the children slept.

Most of the shifts and devices employed were learned by the Galesburg colonists from their southern neighbors, who had been on the ground seven years, and who even in the states they came from knew no higher standard of living. The Hoosier housewives, though friendly and curious about their new neighbors, resented what they considered their "quirky" ways, and sniffed when the Yankee women vigorously scrubbed and cleaned the cabins taken over from them.

Tables were rude affairs, sometimes boxes or boards, with three-legged stools and benches; a rough cupboard hanging on the wall made proud display of whatever dishes they boasted. Privacy was insured by hanging muslin curtains around the beds; the attic was sometimes divided into guest rooms in this manner, for there were frequent lodgers, until new arrivals could find accommodations of their own. As the heavier household goods began to arrive by way of the Great Lakes or the Mississippi, the cabins took on a more comfortable and homelike appearance, and under the hands of the tidy housekeepers who had tended better homes in the East, acquired a certain domestic charm.

### V

### FOOD AND CLOTHING

At first the settlement was completely self-contained. Everything they ate, as well as nearly all their clothes, were produced by their own hands. The staples were corn and pork—hog and hominy—the pigs killed and dressed, cured and smoked, the lard rendered by the husband and wife; the corn ground in a hand-mill, generally a hollow stone. Sometimes it was rubbed while still green and soft on a home-made grater—a piece of tin punched with holes (the old-fashioned tin lantern made a good grater). More often it was beaten with a pestle in a mortar made by burning out the inside of a hardwood stump.

Until their own gristmill was set up, all grain had to be carted many miles to be ground—60 miles to Moline, 75 to Rushville, 125 to Aurora. The trip took days, with often long waits because the water was too low to turn the mill, or there were too many already in line.

Although some wheat was raised, the main dependence was corn. It was already known to the Indians, who taught the settlers some of their dishes—succotash, for instance, a savory mixture of corn and beans. The Yankees were not above adopting the Hoosier's recipes, whatever their opinion of their housekeeping. The coarsely ground corn was prepared in several ways. Shortened with lard rendered in the big kettle, it made Johnny-cake; baked in lumps, it was corn-dodgers; the dough raised with yeast —generally "pearl ash" made by burning corncobs—it became corn-pone. Indian pudding, the most delicious of the many corn dishes, was inspired by neither aborigines nor the Hoosiers, but brought by the housewives from New England. It can seldom be met with today in its most appetizing state. The simpler form of cornmeal pudding was the famous hasty pudding. Even good cooks and good etymologists get these two confused.

The baking was done on a flat board or a piece of sheet iron slanted in front of the fire, or in a Dutch oven. Mush and milk was a standard supper dish; also hominy, that is samp, hulled corn, the hard covering peeled off with lye. The horse pail, which served first to water the stock, did duty as a laundry tub, and then scrubbed to a shining whiteness became a mixing bowl for bread, but wheat bread was rare, and coffee and tea great luxuries.

Besides pork and corn, they had milk and butter from their own cows, and chickens and eggs to some extent. There was plenty of game, quail, prairie chickens, wild turkeys, an occasional deer. The rifle and powder horn hung over the door in nearly every cabin. Meat was cooked in the long-handled frying pan, or in the cast-iron spider with legs that could be set down among coals; or was "jerked," that is, hung and dried.

Knox County was rich in bee trees. As much as nine gallons of strained honey and twenty-two pounds of beeswax were taken from a single tree, and John Sanburn of Knoxville, who became trustee of the college and treasurer of the C. B. & Q., shipped honey in barrels made of hollow basswood logs sawed off and the ends stopped. The Indians taught the southern settlers to draw off the syrup from the maple trees, but the Yankees with their New England background must have been familiar with sugaring.

All food reached their kitchens—if they could be said to have had kitchens—in a state of nature. All animals, wild or tame, must be killed, cleaned and dressed. In the bigger operations, such as pig killing, the neighbors joined, and it was made a festival. They were a friendly and homogeneous lot, and such gatherings had social possibilities. There were the customary house raisings, corn huskings and paring bees. In Illinois the lucky finder of a red ear of corn was rewarded by a long pull at the whisky jug instead of the more traditional kiss.

While the Hoosiers had spinning wheels and looms, and spun and wove the wool and cotton, and even flax, all of which they raised sporadically—cotton was once grown in the Military Tract—it is not clear how far back the Galesburg settlers went into the production of cloth. They were but just come from a more advanced district, and the clothing they brought with them may have lasted until new commercial relations could be established with sources of supply, but they spun yarn for knitting, and the women made all the clothes, the men's as well as their own, not merely shirts and underwear, but suits of linsey woolsey and jeans. The manufacture of ready-made clothing had hardly begun yet, even in the East.

As far as dress was concerned, the period was one of transition. The picturesque pioneer costume of leather breeches, deerskin moccasins, and coonskin cap with tail hanging down behind, had begun to disappear, while normal clothes as worn along the Atlantic seaboard would not come until commerce had been established. Men's clothes were made of cloth, generally jeans or full-cloth, bought at the store; women had already begun to abandon the homespun, home-wove, home-dyed vivid red and blue cotton or wool dresses. But the slat-sunbonnet, that perennial symbol of the pioneer woman, was as characteristic as the liberty cap of the French revolutionists. Woman is the real hero of pioneer life. Her adaptability and her self-sacrifice made it possible; her badge was the sunbonnet, which persisted until the women's magazines carried New York fashions to the remotest hamlets of the West.

The skin from butchered animals was tanned and made into leather for shoes. The work was done by a visiting cobbler who stayed until all the family were shod. He was probably Thomas Simmons, who came from New York on foot, who joined the purchasing committee at Detroit, and carried the chain for Nehamiah West at the first surveying of Galesburg, and had a street named for him. He was a deacon of the church and a trustee of the college, and he was also the village shoemaker.

## VI

### RELIGION

With sawmill and timber close at hand, and the site of Galesburg three miles away, the more enterprising built houses at Log City, and in the spring moved these prefabricated structures to their permanent locations on rollers of tree trunks with ox teams as traction, accompanied by much shouting and hurrah. Some were transported in winter on runners. The Log Citizens led a double life, with one home building on the prairie, another at the Grove, going back and forth, felling trees, erecting fences and breaking the land for cultivation. At more or less regular intervals a family left a crowded cabin, to the infinite relief of the other occupants, and set up at the village, or farm near by, and this was repeated until the last family had left, and the log cabins stood empty and forlorn.

While still tenanted, and with the multifarious activities of pioneer life going at full tilt, Log City must have presented something the picturesqueness of New Salem, restored and preserved for our curious eyes with Hearst's money and Paul Angle's research as a memorial to Lincoln. If Log City had been likewise preserved it would be a historic monument of which any city might be proud. But the Galesburgers had no sentiment, no sense of the historic significance of what they did, and no emotion but religion. The trustees sold the site of Log City and 90 acres of land to Peter Groscup for $1000. Peter tore down the cabins and made a brickyard, and paid his debt to the college in brick, used to construct the earliest college building. Even the building built with the brick made from earth beneath Log City no longer stands.

From now on it will be necessary to give a definite consideration from time to time of the course of religion in the lives of these settlers. If the evidence of letters and diaries is to be accepted, it was their chief concern. It is fair to assume they were all sincere, but there is more than a suspicion of coercion by the elders of the church, and much of the talk was a kind of pose or fashion. They must always be "bearing testimony." The records of the church and college are meager because written by tired calloused hands at the end of long days of labor, but whatever else failed to be set down, and the gaps are disconcerting, the prayers that opened and closed every session, religious or secular, were conscientiously mentioned. This ceases to be amusing and becomes irritating when an important meeting, a link in a story, consists of three sentences, one for the business of the meeting, and two for the prayers.

So naturally these first weeks were filled with work and worship, prayer meetings and church, which had never ceased or been neglected even in the covered wagons. Services were held in Hugh Conger's cabin, because having a large family he had most room. The cabin was double, the congregation sat around on stools, boxes, beds; the minister stood in the door between the two rooms. There was a surfeit of preachers, and one was always available; the sermons were long and dull and even the deacons and elders dozed, but they did their duty grimly and uncomplainingly, and spoke of "seasons of grace." The curious Hoosiers gathered round, religion was their big outlet of emotional excitements, but those sedate Yankees put on a poor show.

One such season of grace was the tryout preliminary to organizing the church. It happened there was a professional evangelist in the settlement that winter. John Avery was visiting his sister and two brothers, members of the colony. He had been a pupil of Gale at Oneida Institute, a convert of Finney and member of the "impudent" Holy Band. His presence was perhaps not entirely accidental. Gale mistrusted his own powers when it came to revival meetings. Avery was equal to the occasion, for when in February the church was formally organized, few in the colony had the hardihood to remain out of it. After all, there was no place else to go, no one else to associate with. But one of the youngsters fifty years later testified to the mental agony and spiritual tyranny of the deacons and elders at that time.

For the formal induction a Presbyterian clergyman was imported from Peoria, for Gale had made up his mind as to the denomination, though at least half the company were Congregationalists. Deacon Simmons timidly suggested a vote to determine the sectarian color of the church, but was promptly and bruskly overruled by Gale, who bade the officiating clergyman to proceed. The church was duly organized as fully Presbyterian.

Adults joined by letters from their churches back East; the

young people by confession. The confessions were kept up throughout the winter, even from those with letters, to satisfy Gale as to the orthodoxy of their beliefs. It helped to while away the time until it was warm enough to begin work on their farms.

Having set up the spiritual body of the church, the settlers proceeded to build a place in which to hold it, a double log cabin finished with boards from Ferris' mill. This was also used as a school, and Nehemiah Losey, ultimately to be professor of mathematics in the college, taught it with the help of Lucy Gay. Thus within a year they attained their three objectives, a community, a church, and a school, though all three were temporary, to be transported to the prairie as soon as the majority had moved to their permanent homes. Of more import to the future of the colony, though it did not realize it, was Colton's primitive store in William Lewis' smokehouse, for that was the beginning of "business," a bigger matter than religion, not only to Galesburg, but to the nation at large in the years to come.

One who has vainly sifted the scanty records of this period in search of facts that would throw light on their daily lives may be pardoned a gesture of impatience at the completeness with which the concern with religion blocked out mundane affairs. It crowded their letters and diaries with banal and conventional phrases having no earthly significance, to the exclusion of everything else. One is reminded of the manner in which pictorial art in the Middle Ages presented a similar cul-de-sac. The great artists, who might have been painting the contemporary scene, or portraits of famous men and women, gave all their talent, time, and canvases to madonnas, annunciations, and descents. In both cases, the Catholic world of Italy, the Puritan colonists among the trees of Henderson Grove, it does reveal something of their minds, but the religious expression was artificial and conventional, a sort of stereotyped form, telling nothing of the real men and women behind it.

# 4

# On the Prairie

## I

### PAPER CITIES

The plan on which Galesburg was founded had some peculiar and unusual features. In a general way it was a planned town, actually what was known as a "paper city," but without the odium attached to those words in the first years of the last century, for paper cities were often wildly speculative ventures in which the deluded investor lost his money, such as Cairo, which Dickens satirized in *Martin Chuzzlewit* under the name of Eden. But Galesburg was *planned* in the sense that the site and citizens were not left to chance.

In the ordinary course of events a pioneer settlement grew haphazardly around some nucleus to which settlers gravitated naturally, and there caught and clung—crossroads, ferry, or trading post. Among such spontaneous towns were Galena in the lead country, Dixon at the Rock River ferry, and Chicago on the lake. These towns grew from the center outward. Their population had the mixed character of the typical frontier settlements, gamblers, squatters, speculators, adventurers.

But there was also in those days a disposition to assemble a community in advance, organize a group around some social or political theory, and move to the selected site in a body. Many such towns were socialistic utopias. Rapp's German experiment at New Harmony, Birkbeck's English colony at Albion, the Shakers on the Wabash, the Swiss wine growers on the Ohio, Bishop Chase and his Jubilee College at Robin's Nest, and later the

Swedish Janssonists at Bishop Hill, the Mormons at Nauvoo, all had other purpose than merely settling a new country. Thy saw in those fertile prairies a theater for a better design for living, though none of these enterprises managed to perpetuate their theories, and they are today just towns.

Another class of planned towns contemplated nothing more radical than a Christian community along orthodox lines, adopting the settled pattern of civil government, and concerned more with perfecting the old religious ideal of New England than in establishing a new social order. They meant or at least hoped to avoid the mingled greed and spirit of adventure, the recklessness and impatience of restraint, that attended the casual birth of many pioneer western settlements—which made Chicago a center of unbridled land speculation, Galena a rowdy mining town, and Cairo the instrument of amazing political corruption. There was a sense of going back and starting again from the beginning, shaking off the vices of older towns in the East, shunning the pitfalls of new communities in the West, creating afresh there on the clean prairie a new city, without spot or blemish, a sort of immaculate conception.

Gale's colony belonged in this category. Galesburg sprang complete from his head, like Minerva from Jove's. He had drawn and redrawn the physical map, shaped and reshaped its spiritual policy, selected his disciples with anxious care. The material plan was much too large for immediate needs. It meant that instead of being huddled together into a compact aggregate, the pioneer group was scattered for years over twenty square miles, an outline sketch to be filled in by the growth of future years. In this respect Gale's dream was more than realized, but his religious ideal was far too exalted to become a permanent way of life for human beings, or even for Gale. It began to sag almost as soon as the community began to function.

When the colonists who had spent the severe winter of 1836–7 at Log City began to move out to their proposed village on the prairie, they were at the point of achieving their first objective, the community, for Log City was but a "lodging for the night" and had no permanent place in their plan.

The immediate problem was that which faced every pioneer settlement, whatever its purpose or origin, the need of setting up an economic organization, each home at first a self-contained independent unit; next the exchange of products and services between different members of the community, and finally profitable contact with the world outside, from which they were at present so completely severed. For this purely mundane service they were more indebted to certain merchants, the Swifts, Chamberses, Willards, Coltons, and several inventors, May, Avery, Frost, men who had joined the colony in a less disinterested spirit, perhaps, than to the ghostly councilors occupied primarily with keeping the colony free from sin. And the economic fabric thus created proved more durable, and in the long run more useful, than the more spiritual program on which the town was founded.

The prairie of their choice extended south from the settlements at Henderson Grove, comprising their own Log City and the cabins of the Hoosiers, to Knoxville, the county seat, yet in the making, with its log courthouse and cluster of cabins. It lay on the "divide" between the Illinois and the Mississippi. The highest point was known as "The Mound," and from it a good view could be had, though there was nothing to see, no object natural or otherwise, no tree or shrub, no building or fence, nothing but the prairie grass ablaze with flowers. So naked was it that the cabin of Lusher Gay just outside the Grove stood out with startling distinctness. Its light was the beacon that guided them to Log City after long days of labor on the prairie, and was known for years as "The Lighthouse."

The prairie was skirted in the distance by woods along the watercourses, Henderson River on the north, Court Creek on the east, Brush Creek on the south, and Cherry Grove on the west. Through the center of their tract, washing the northern edge of the plot set aside for the village, meandered Cedar Fork, flowing west to join Henderson River on its way to the Mississippi. To the southeast wound the serpentine convolutions of Spoon River, made famous by the *Anthology* of Edgar Lee Masters, bearing its quota of eroded soil to the Gulf of Mexico. Its name perpetuates the habits of the original inhabitants of the land. Its waters abound with fresh water clams, a sort of mussel, relished by the Indians, who used the shells to scoop up their soup. The Indians called the clams "amaquon." The white men translated it to "spoon." The native word is preserved in Maquon, a village at the crossing of the Indian trail from Peoria Lake to Rock Island.

The tract had been surveyed when it was entered at the land office in Quincy, but now it was laid out in lots and farms by Nehemiah Losey, professor of mathematics of the new college, which did not yet exist. His status was made official when the county surveyor appointed him deputy, and he proceeded to mark the lines which the city of Galesburg was to follow as long as it existed. The village proper was assigned to a rectangle of a little less than a quarter section, 160 acres, in the midst of their holdings, of the conventional checkerboard pattern, six by seven blocks.

Originally it had been six blocks each way, but the first staking brought the crossing of the two principal streets over a small stream. To avoid this, the plan was shifted, a small square was allowed at the crossing, and a tier of blocks added on the east. The farms, quarter sections assigned to the colonists, fringed the village plot; Gale on the north, the numerous Ferrises on the east and south, and many others hemmed the little town. The grounds for the college, seminary, and academy all lay outside the town limits, the college farm extending south from the campus, 1280 acres. All these were to be absorbed into the city within twenty years.

One who has lived in that town wishes the pioneers had possessed some sense of town planning, some premonition of the physical and material needs of a community commensurate with their concern for its spiritual welfare, but the science of town planning was unknown to the world. Baron Hausmann had not yet ploughed his boulevards through the old streets of Paris, from which this modern science dates. New Englanders, fresh from Old England, left wide greens in the centers of their villages, but evidently the tradition perished before reaching New York. Certainly no trace of it can be found on the prairies. There are many early Illinois town maps still in existence of the same stereotyped plan, one small open square the only breathing spot. The Illinois Central used an identical pattern for each community on its long pioneer line.

With the unbounded prairie about them, with land at $1.25 an acre, the village of Galesburg was crowded into forty-two compact, closely set blocks, with a stingy square in the middle. It was a dull, uninspired job, the muffing of a glorious opportunity, this early bit of town planning. Gale should have known better. He had travelled and seen cities, but he was curiously blind to the æsthetic aspects of life. Was it concern with a heavenly city which rendered those pious people so indifferent to beauty in this world? Fortunately the generous acreage set apart for the college, now in the center of the city, makes a green spot and partly repairs that grievous error. Thus the planned cities gained little if any advantage over those which grew haphazardly. Some of those are accidentally prettier because of topographical features which interrupted the rigid plan. A map of Galesburg can be drawn using only a ruler.

## II

### THE PANIC OF 1837

None of the operations necessary to establish a town for forty families was performed easily. Each house, shop, mill, store represented arduous labor, much of it unskilled, with such tools and materials as were available, long hours, much sacrifice, many failures, demanding great patience or great ingenuity. It was not easy to live in a town in the process of building, which had neither the free and easy makeshift character which made the temporary sojourn at Log City a bit of a lark, nor yet the ordered comforts and conveniences of modern towns up to the standard of those they had left in the East. They rested from their labors only for prayer meetings and the services which filled the entire Sabbath.

Everything must go ahead at the same time; one thing was as important as another. But soon a grist mill and a saw mill saved the long trips to supply food and lumber, and a blacksmith shop, a cabinet maker, and a general store furnished other necessities, and life began to fall into its appointed groove, and leave time to consider the mission which had brought them there.

But in the meantime, to add to their difficulties, the year 1837 marked the beginning of the Jackson panic, when the whole country plunged into a depression as severe relatively as that which followed the World War. Money depreciated, banks failed, unemployment reached unprecedented heights. On top of this, Illinois had its own depression as a result of the ill-advised Internal Improvements Act, an orgy of railroad building, with land speculation, public and private, which left the state so deeply in debt repudiation was talked of, and was averted only by the firmness of Governor Ford.

Still a country-wide panic affected this little self-contained isolated community surprisingly little. It was not yet hitched up to the national economic machinery, and its problems were peculiarly its own. There was no unemployment. Every one was busy with his own construction job, which could still go on without check. They did not miss money; they had little in any case. There was no bank, no circulating medium, most of what they needed was produced among themselves, and an ingenious system of barter took care of exchange of goods for services. They reverted for the time being to an even more primitive state of society, such as must have existed before money was invented.

Indeed Galesburg might not have known there was a depression but for two circumstances. The outside market for their corn and hogs disappeared. At best this market was not very profitable. Shipping points were distant, and for a greater part of the year inaccessible, and the expense of moving stock on foot, or hauling grain a hundred or so miles in wagons often resulted in a loss. In fact, they were not yet ready for outside markets until better means of transportation should arrive. In the second and more serious instance, the college which should have got off to a flying start met with a set-back that delayed it for years.

The Galesburg colonists had sold their farms East on time, and when the notes fell due the purchasers were unable to pay them; some had to take their farms back, and the colonists in turn were unable to pay the college for their lands, and the college was forced to grant more time or take the lands back, neither of which brought in any revenue, so that it was unable to proceed with its building program.

But in spite of all this the colonists lived, and lived well as far as food was concerned, and went on building their city, for which they already had material, while the labor was their own. Thus they were busy, while more than half the population of the East was idle. Their credit was good at Colton's store for what supplies they must have. Money was needed only for postage and taxes, but there were nearly always two bits in the town when a letter arrived, and taxes were to some extent a local matter. Thus their very isolation, their detachment from the outside world, proved a blessing at this early crisis in their economic history.

## III

### KNOX MANUAL LABOR COLLEGE

Up till 1838 the college had consisted of nothing more than virgin land and a board of trustees. Steps were taken to give it a concrete existence, but they were taken more slowly than had been anticipated because of unexpected obstacles. It was first necessary that the colonists should be established in their new homes, with some sort of economic machinery functioning to enable them to carry on life, and there was nowhere else to turn, no others who could be called on for either work or money. The trustees were practically doing a real estate business, with Silvanus Ferris as chief salesman, extending time, taking back farms and lots, and selling to newcomers attracted as the fame of the colony became bruited about.

The *ad interim* trustees elected in Whitesboro, or such of them as had now reached the prairie, held their first meeting in the promised land at Gale's one-room cabin at Log City, where seated about on beds and boxes with a roaring fire on the hearth, for it was one of the coldest winters on record, they took two important steps. They elected a new board to take over as soon as the charter was secured, and they changed the name of the institution.

The new board was John Waters, Nehemiah West, George Gale, Nehemiah Losey and Thomas Simmons, from the old board, Matthew Chambers and Erastus Swift, who represented the new element in the colony, men with perhaps more worldly experience and not subscribers to the original plan. To give the college a broader base in that region, four men from neighboring settlements were added: Ralph Hurlburt, a country storekeeper at Mt. Sterling, a small settlement about twenty-five miles south of Galesburg, and George Wright, a doctor at Monmouth, ten miles west. Both these men were immigrants from Oneida County, New York, where they were no doubt known to some of the Galesburg colonists. Two men from Knoxville were also elected, of quite different origin—John Gould Sanburn, born in New England of the same Yankee strain as the other trustees, and Parnach Owen, a Hoosier, from Virginia, an outstanding and picturesque character. Sanburn, who had married Owen's sister, was probably the ablest man in Knoxville, holding nearly all the county offices, and that of postmaster as well. He was simultaneously circuit clerk, recorder, probate judge and notary, and carried the business of all these departments in his tall beaver hat, along with letters for delivery.

Before applying for a charter, it was thought diplomatic to seek the backing of the Hoosier settlers in the immediate neighborhood. They were invited to a meeting, the purpose of the college explained to them, and they were asked to sign the petition for a charter, which most of them did, all who could write, in fact. This was to propitiate a legislature composed of their sort of people, as well as to forestall any counter movement. It was believed, or at least feared, that the Campbellites or Disciples of Christ, a wing of the Baptist denomination strong in that neighborhood, not overly fond of Yankee Presbyterians, might start something of their own, opposition, at least, if not a school, and it seemed best to spike their guns.

It was at the meeting in Gale's cabin that cold December night that the name of the college was changed from Prairie College to Knox Manual Labor College. Why the name was changed, and why Knox was chosen, has puzzled the chroniclers ever since. Perhaps as the time of applying for a charter approached the name Prairie seemed too commonplace, too rural, for such a school as they visioned. But no one knows to this day what particular Knox was honored by the new name—whether it was named "after" Knox County, and thus for General Henry Knox, the first Secretary of War, or for that strong-willed religious reformer and Calvinist, John Knox. Considering the character of these founders, the latter seems more likely.

"Contrary to general belief," says George Candee Gale, great-grandson of Founder Gale, and great-great-grandson of Founder Ferris, "Knox was not named for either General Knox or the Scotch Presbyterian Knox, according to my father. He said his grandfather (Selden Gale) had told him how some of the original founders used to chuckle about the name. Some wanted the college named for one Knox, some for the other; so they compromised on KNOX. Certainly most of them were pious enough to want the churchman and fighters enough to want the soldier as well." The general would have been surprised, no doubt, even if not greatly interested, but the uncompromising theologian would have understood and appreciated and warmly approved what these pious pioneers were trying to do.

The committee *appointed* to go to Vandalia and wangle a charter from a hostile legislature was West, Gale and Sanburn. The committee which *went* was West and James Knox. It was always West when there was a difficult or inconvenient errand to be done. James Knox has not hitherto appeared in Galesburg affairs. He was a rising young man of Knoxville, where his brother kept the store, in which James worked, and which he carried on when his brother died. He was made a trustee some time later, resigned, was re-elected and again resigned. When he died he left a fortune to found an agricultural college in Knox County. The county failing to meet the conditions, the money went to Yale from which Knox had graduated.

James Knox of Knoxville had no doubt been asked to accompany West on his mission because he was a politician, versed in the devious ways of Illinois politics, and better able to deal with the legislature than the simple, pious, straightforward farmer. Both houses were wildly excited that winter over the successful outcome of the plot to move the state capitol to Springfield, and the prospective graft from the infamous Internal Improvements Act (passed February, 1837), and were not in a state of mind to listen patiently to the aims of the Yankee idealists at Galesburg. Joseph Duncan was governor; he was from Jacksonville, a friend of the college there (of which this new institution might be considered a rival) that had just succeeded in erecting its first building, though there is no evidence he placed obstacles in the way of the Knox College petitioners.

West and Knox went to Vandalia, presented their petition and found the legislators peculiarly hostile toward educational institutions with religious proclivities. Charters to colleges thus far granted forbade the establishment of theological departments, or the teaching of theology, and required that no religious test be applied in selecting trustees or admitting students. Further, the amount of land or other property a college could own was strictly limited.

Alton College, a Baptist institution, afterward Shurtleff, had refused the charter granted her under such conditions, and later with McKendree at Lebanon, Illinois at Jacksonville; and Jonesboro (never founded) made common cause in the interests of education, and finally secured through an "omnibus bill" more liberal provisions. This was shortly before the application of Knox. The restrictions struck right at the heart of its scheme, for Knox was founded to impart religious instruction and turn out exactly the brand of ministers the Hoosiers did not want, and its property was entirely land, much in excess of the thousand acres the law allowed.

But on the other hand, the legislators showed an equally illogical and peculiar fondness for manual labor institutions, and had granted charters to three, none of which was ever organized. It may be that the manual labor feature of Knox offset its religious and land-owning shortcomings, for on Thursday, January 19, 1837, the bill entitled "An Act to Incorporate Knox Manual Labor College" was read for the first time and ordered to a second reading, and on motion of Mr. Hardin referred to the committee on corporations. On February 15 it was passed, a long lean legislator from Sangamon, named Abraham Lincoln, then a member of the upper house, among those voting for it. By the terms of the charter the college was allowed a certain number of years in which to dispose of its surplus real estate.

The old board of trustees continued to give its attention to creating a town as a setting for the college, for which they hoped so much, the chief task being to promote the village, and the selling of more land to secure funds to erect a building. They were disposed to give lots to mechanics who would build immediately and practice their needed trades thereon. In this spirit they deeded a lot to Hugh Conger for a blacksmith shop, several lots to a group of men—Gale was one of them—who proposed to erect a sawmill, a lot to another group to set up a flour mill, and a site for a brickyard to Levi Tucker to be paid for in "good merchantable brick" with which the college building could be built. Ten acres were set aside for a burying ground, much too near the center of the town, and donated to the church.

There had been a school at Log City, and when a sufficient number of families had moved to Galesburg—"out on the prairie" as they put it—school was held in a novel building designed and contributed by Chauncey Colton, with a sloping floor like a theatre, so that all pupils could see the teacher, and what was more important, be seen by him. But these were elementary schools, connected with the college only in the sense they were raising up pupils for it.

It was not until 1838 that any building was erected for the use of the college, and this was a plain, inexpensive, even primitive story-and-a-half structure of wood, build not on the college grounds, but on Main Street where it would be more accessible, for they planned to use it for a church and for secular purposes. The first floor was one large schoolroom with built-in benches, occupied by the academy or preparatory school. Access was by two doors, for the sexes entered separately and sat apart, as they did in church, and in fact in all gatherings. On the floor above, reached by a naked outside stairway, were three small rooms. Two of these were occupied respectively by the chairs of science and of languages, presided over by Professors Losey and Grant. The roof sloped to the floor; only in the middle of these rooms was it possible to stand erect.

The third room was a sort of entry where the students hung their wraps and stamped the snow off their feet, but it was the nucleus of a physical laboratory. Here was installed the "philosophical apparatus" which Gale brought back from one of his soliciting visits to the East. He must have regarded this first materialization of his dream with mingled feelings as he recalled his visions at first sight of the University of Virginia.

This humble building was the architectural beginning of Knox

College. It became the social as well as the educational and religious center of the village. In it were held the classes of both "prep" school and college, the three Sunday sessions of the church, the mid-week prayer meeting, the town meetings, the sessions of the college trustees and the elders of the church. Here also were the singing schools, and such decorous entertainments and social gatherings as were countenanced by the theocratic government of the community. For Sunday service it was soon over-crowded, and it was necessary to build an annex where the female half of the congregation worshipped, known as the "court of women."

## IV

### HOUSEHOLD SKILLS

For years the tiny village of Galesburg remained scattered over a plan much too large. The 173 individuals who spent the winter in thirteen cabins at Log City were augmented in the spring by fifty-nine more, but only a few moved into the town. Most of them were farmers; their holdings lay just beyond the village limits, though some for sociability built their homes in the town. And a number remained at Log City until the second summer, or longer.

Upon the clean level prairie they began to build a town of framed wooden houses, and by 1845 there were seventy dwellings, besides stores, mills and shops. Galesburg was distinguished for its white houses, for ordinarily prairie homes were not painted, but Leonard Chappell started an oil mill in the village to grind the flaxseed raised by the farmers, and exchanged oil for seed. There were no sidewalks; paths ran in all directions according to convenience, across lots, cutting corners, and planks were laid for crossing streams. There were no trees, and the neat and tidy white houses stood out against the green prairie like a modern chicken run. It was a village of magnificent distances.

The architecture was without distinction. These people were

not reared in the Georgian tradition which gives dignity to so many New England villages, and they had no taste of their own. They brought their pattern from the towns of central New York. Its only merit was its simplicity. Each man was architect not only of his own fortunes, but of his own domicile.

The first task was to get their little settlement running as a machine for living, houses built, gardens planted, fruit trees set out, and utilities established to supply immediate wants, and on their farms to build not only houses, but barns, outbuildings and fences.

Wood was the only building material. Each buyer of land received one-tenth in timber if he wished. It was comparatively hardwood; there was no pine, but plenty of oak, black walnut, maple and basswood. Magnificent old trees were cut down and ripped up by Henry Ferris in the first sawmill at the Grove. Until they had their own sawmills, the colony had to haul logs ten miles to Knoxville and pay two-thirds of the lumber for toll. These mills supplied planks and boards, but shingles and joists were rived from felled trees. Lumber prepared during the previous winter at Log City had been hauled to the sites over the snow. All the material for building, except glass, builders' hardware, and white lead, was produced in the neighborhood by the settlers' own labors.

A brickyard supplied material for chimneys and foundations, though many made brick on their farms. The clay shale of the neighborhood was admirably adapted, and the manufacture of paving brick ultimately became a leading local industry. There was also stone from the washed-out hollows beside Spoon River. This was used for the foundations of larger buildings. Ready-made sash, doors and blinds were available when Gad Colton got his woodworking shop running.

Each householder was not only his own architect, but his own carpenter, mason and painter, for though primarily farmers, they were handy with tools, as farmers were apt to be in the early years. Skilled mechanics did not come until later.

The houses were framed and enclosed against winter, and finished at leisure as time and material became available. Blankets were hung over the openings, giving the houses a "dubious look," as one chronicler has it, and the whole family helped in the finishing—laying floors, building partitions, plastering and painting, the loving affection for their own home supplying what was lacking in mechanical skill.

Except that the houses were larger and more permanent, though not so picturesque, nor at first so comfortable, domestic economy followed much the same lines as at Log City. But from now on the gradual shift of household industries to store, shop or mill will be observed, as a complete and organized community emerges from pioneer conditions. The houses were better furnished, for household goods began to arrive from New York, and there were craftsmen who could make furniture.

Usually a brick oven was built with the house, and sometimes one outdoors for summer use, but fireplaces were rare. The settlers had had enough of them at Log City, and vastly preferred the less decorative but more efficient stoves, a cookstove at least, and in the larger houses a heating stove. "Stone coal" was mined the first year by Avery Dalton in the southwest part of the county, but many of the settlers had never seen coal, and wood being plentiful, it was the only fuel. There were no matches; when a fire went out a child was dispatched to the nearest neighbor with a copper kettle in which to bring back a live coal. Each housewife made her own soap and candles.

Soap boiling was a regular domestic function. The ashes from wood fires, and all the fats and greases were saved. The ashes were kept in a barrel with holes in the bottom, and leached with water. The lye was mixed with the fat and boiled in a great outdoor kettle for two or three days. The result was "soft soap"— an expression which was slang for flattery in those days. This was used for washing clothes. To make toilet soap, the soft soap was mixed with salt and allowed to harden, and then cut up into cakes.

[ 115 ]

For candles, the tallow from the slaughtered cattle was melted in the washboiler, half full of hot water to keep the tallow near the top. The wicks were tied in rows and dipped in the tallow until of the desired size. Six months' to a year's supply was made at a time.

They bought at the store only what they could not make. Clothes and shoes were made at home. The southerners spun and wove, but the Galesburgers who were working up to the more advanced standard which they had known in the East began with cloth. Henry Ferris sent the wool from his sheep to Peoria or Oquawka, and got back flannel for women's dresses, and full cloth for the men's garments. Then Mary Ann Paden moved in and the family was "sewed up." She was both dressmaker and tailor.

When a horse or cow died, its skin was saved and tanned, and Chris Miner came with his tools and folding bench, and made enough shoes to last the family a year. When Mary Ann and Chris happened to meet at the same house, as often occurred, there was a merry time, for both were good gossips, after the tradition of their crafts, and aware of all the news of the community, and each could sing a song and tell a story, which they did to the great delight of the younger members of the family.

These household industries continued for several years, diminishing as Colton's store, and later Chambers', made manufactured goods available, and better systems of transportation gave the village an export trade. Ready-made shoes could be bought, as well as soap and candles, and then came kerosene, as great an innovation in its way as electricity was later. Less and less was made at home, as the number of stores around the public square increased.

v

COLTON'S STORE

The business life of Galesburg began with a real-estate transaction, the purchase of half a township of government land for a dollar and a quarter an acre and selling it for five dollars an acre. People in conjunction with land produce wealth. The direct means here was agriculture, but the farmers required some organ of distribution to dispose of what they raised, and give them supplies in return, and that was afforded by Chauncey Sill Colton. Trade and industry in this prairie village began with two men— the brothers Colton. Chauncey was a merchant, his brother Gad a mechanic. Retailing and manufacturing stemmed from these two. As a young man seeking opportunity Chauncey went to Illinois. He was not a subscriber to Gale's plan, but roaming about the state he heard of it, and visited Knox County. Before deciding on a location, he surveyed the scene of his venture with a shrewd and appraising eye.

He noted that there was already at Knoxville, the county seat and largest town, a flourishing and well-managed store conducted by Herman Knox sufficient for that neighborhood; that at Henderson, the next choice, was a settlement of Hoosiers who, while sufficiently industrious, made merry over the week-end and spent their Saturdays in outdoor sports, horse races, gander pullings and wrestling bouts—much like the New Salem of Abraham Lincoln's youth—who bet their money on such contests, took frequent pulls at the whisky jug, and on Sundays had little inclination for church; but that over at Log City was a diligent colony of settlers, who planned to establish a village on the prairie near by, who worked all the week preparing their farms for occupancy the coming spring, and spent their Sundays in divine worship, a serious people, who took life seriously; that while he himself was not a church member, or even a professing Christian, and had no pronounced views on temperance, he realized that it would be necessary for many years to do business on long credits, waiting for his money until crops were harvested, and taking his pay in produce, and that he might therefore trade more profitably with the sober, church-going Yankees than with the livelier, pleasure-loving Hoosiers.

He bought a lot on the public square in Galesburg, and returning to the East, advised his brother Gad to follow him to the West as soon as his apprentice time was out, and he himself ordered a bill of such goods as he thought would be in demand in a new country to be shipped to Oquawka. With his wife and son and household goods he returned to Log City, arriving at sundown November 3, 1836.

He secured William Lewis' eight-by-ten smokehouse as a preliminary store, and the New York goods not having arrived, he walked to Oquawka to catch a steamboat to St. Louis to buy stock. There was no boat for two weeks, so Chauncey chopped wood for the landlord to pay for his board. Two merchants waiting on the same errand, one from Monmouth, passed the time in draw poker, but young Chauncey stuck to his wood-chopping. He had $700 for his venture and proposed to hang on to it. At St. Louis he laid out this sum judiciously, informed the wholesaler he would buy more if he could have credit. The wholesaler agreed on condition the man from Monmouth endorse the note. Colton declined (the sporty Monmouth trader went bankrupt the following summer) but told the dealer that having seen his stock, he could safely buy by mail as soon as he had more money. When the goods reached Oquawka they were hauled to Log City, and from his tiny store in the smokehouse Colton supplied the minor wants of the colony until the following spring, when he and the colony moved out on the prairie.

During the winter, while his wife "minded" the store, Colton put in his time getting out lumber for his building in Galesburg, timbers and clapboards of heavy oak carefully worked, and with the help of his brother Gad built his store the following spring, with living quarters above, and stocked it with the goods which had providentially arrived from New York. With a scythe he cut the tall prairie grass on the square in front of his store and proceeded to deflect the Galesburg and Log City trade from Herman Knox at Knoxville, unconsciously adding to the competition that town was beginning to feel and resent, which was to make greater trouble before long.

He engaged in every activity that promised profit, trading goods for the farmers' hogs and corn; he shipped the first consignment of pork and grain down the river. After trying to drive a drove of hogs to Oquawka, and spending the day with all the boys in the colony chasing them over the prairie before getting them corralled in a near-by fenced field, he thereafter slaughtered them first, and at times had all the wagons in the community engaged in hauling merchandise to the river.

Meanwhile Gad Dudley Colton finished his time as apprentice to a house-builder and cabinet-maker, bought with borrowed money a set of tools, pledged them for payment of the last two dollars of his passage money, and arrived in Galesburg the following spring in time to help brother Chauncey build his store. He next put up a small shop of his own, not far from his brother's emporium, and began to function as a wood-worker, principally in the manufacture of furniture, but no doubt turning his hand to any work needed in a community that possessed so few skilled craftsmen. Later he secured wood-working tools, operated at first by foot power, and then by an old blind sorrel horse that walked round and round a creaking capstan, which the college students resented so much they set it up in the public square one night in a position in which it would no longer work. Then came steam power, and the employment of help, and a foundry in which parts were cast for the agricultural machinery that the Mays, Averys and Browns were beginning to make. Thus the community, at first all one caste, began to develop two, the employer and employee—capital and labor.

For three years Colton had no competition in Galesburg, and then Matthew Chambers came back from Knoxville to occupy a store on the opposite side of the public square. Chambers had been given a choice location with the understanding he would build on it, and he did, but finding most of the trade at Knoxville he made his start there, and the building at Galesburg was used for both church and school, until the shedlike wooden academy was built in 1838. He was criticized for failing to join

[ 119 ]

the colony immediately, but besides erecting a building, he bought a farm, planted trees, and otherwise contributed to the town before he moved back to his store on the square and gave Colton a little competition.

## VI

### SUBDUING THE LAND

The first crude beginnings of agriculture on the prairie is of peculiar significance in this chronicle, for not only is agriculture the history of the Middle West, but this town and college were founded on it. The colonists were farmers; their college owned a farm and farmed it. The whole enterprise was linked with the land, and rose and fell with the fortunes of the land. In the history of Galesburg we can almost read the history of American agriculture.

Besides building cabins and getting out sawn lumber for their permanent houses, the inhabitants were busy fencing their farms and preparing the ground for cultivation. Next to transportation, fencing was the most serious prairie problem. Every piece of planted ground had to be enclosed. For years the farmers clamored for legislation forbidding animals to roam at large, but it was not until 1872 that the Illinois Stock Law was passed. Fences were of various kinds, but the cheapest and most generally adopted, where timber was available, was the Virginia rail or zigzag fence, probably introduced by southern immigrants. The twelve hundred acres known as the College Farm was at first enclosed by a sod fence, a strip eight feet wide turned with a breaking plow, a deep ditch with the earth thrown up beside it and covered with the sod, something like the ha-ha on English estates, or wall and moat. Such a fence would turn cattle.

But the rail fence was a distinctive partition in the Knox County landscape for years, characteristic as the stone walls of New England, and when weathered to a soft silver gray, not unsightly. Rail splitting was an accomplishment with the standing of an athletic sport. There were many skilled axemen, of whom Abraham Lincoln was one. The sobriquet "rail splitter" applied in contempt by snobbish Eastern opponents did much to secure him the vote of the Middle West. The Yankee axe which performed such prodigies in the hands of expert choppers was made at Collinsville, Connecticut, and is to this day. A tall tree was felled and "logged" off into ten-foot lengths. The cuts were deftly made to leave one end flat to facilitate splitting. Wedges were introduced, iron at first, then wood; the log halved, quartered, and finally reduced to the desired size for rails. A good tree, of which there were many in Henderson Grove, yielded 150 to 200 rails. Cutting it up was a day's work for a man. For the Virginia fence the rails were laid up zigzag, the ends resting on one another, eight or nine rails high. By driving a stake each side in the corners, crossing them over the top of the fence, and laying a top rail in the crossing, a stake and rider fence is produced, a legal fence against inroads by cattle.

When the thorn hedge craze came, miles of osage orange were planted, and the state was soon covered with these live fences. They invaded Knox County, and the farms around Galesburg soon bristled with the not unattractive edgings. The Virginia rail fence was wasteful, impossible where timber was scarce, and the triangles along the fence could not be cultivated, unimportant while land was plenty, but worth considering as demand for more acreage developed.

The osage orange hedge was developed by Jonathan W. Turner, a professor at Illinois College, Jacksonville, who secured seed from the South, introduced the hedge, and promoted it until it had run its course. Three years after planting it developed a thick, thorny barrier, which in the language of the country was "horse-high, pig-tight, and bull strong." Because of the expense of rail and other wooden fences, it became enormously popular, until in 1871 thirty per cent of the fencing in Illinois was osage orange.

Possibly thorn hedges were not such a novelty to the Galesburg colonists as this narrative might seem to imply, for Olmsted Ferris was so impressed by one he saw in Connecticut, variety not specified, "you couldn't poke a rat through it," that he bought five bushel of the seed and shipped it to his brother Henry at Log City. Olmsted was always on the lookout for novelties. What was done with the seed has not come down to us.

The peak of osage popularity passed. Insect enemies developed; trimming took too much of the farmer's time; Illinois passed its stock law, and barbed wire was invented. Hitherto, wire had been tried and found unsatisfactory. Cattle pushed through it. What was required was a wire fence with thorns. Glidden, who invented barbed wire, was an Illinois farmer, and thus another instance where contact with the land inspired inventions to help solve the problems it created. Between 1874 and 1880 some 80,-000,000 pounds of barbed wire were made and sold.

At the height of the interest in osage orange fences the campus of Illinois College was hedged with it. "Osage Orange Day" is still celebrated there in May, on the anniversary of the day in 1882 when all classes were dismissed so that the students might grub up the hedge plants. Osage orange still lingers in a humble capacity; its trunks are the best posts on which to string the barbed wire.

Until barns could be built the stock was sheltered at night in rude structures consisting of a double fence stuffed with prairie grass hay, and thatched with the same material. These were highly inflammable, and prairie fires were a menace, so several furrows were plowed to isolate them. The fire approached with incredible swiftness when the wind was strong. If not discovered in time to hitch up and plow, it was beaten out with sticks, barrel staves, anything handy, a fatiguing and frequently ineffectual method, as the fire was treacherous, and burned over a long front. Sometimes the alarm came in the night, and the whole family turned out and worked to exhaustion, burned and blackened, sometimes to behold the work of years wiped out in the end.

Travellers across the prairies overtaken by a fire, started one of their own, and walked or rode in its wake, so that when the one behind overtook them, it would die out against the burned tract and go around. It is supposed by some that the frequent burning of the vast tract in the West kept down the trees and made the prairies.

Next to fencing, pioneer farmers were handicapped by lack of markets and transportation, the one involving the other. Wagons and water were the sole means of moving crops. Oquawka on the Mississippi, Peoria on the Illinois, and Chicago on its great lake, were the only points from which produce could be shipped to buyers in the South and East. Nor was there much demand. The whole country was agricultural, and the only advantage the western farmers had was their rich soil which grew bigger crops at less cost, and this advantage was more than lost by the difficulty of reaching the markets.

When taking grain or cattle to market, the farmers encamped along the road, or spent the night at a wayside farm. They unloaded their own grain at the elevators in Chicago, sometimes waiting in a long line when prices were good. Wheat sold from forty cents to a dollar; corn for as little as a quarter. Then as now it was sometimes better to feed the corn to the pigs. Often, in ignorance of prices, the returns did not pay for taking the grain to market. After selling, they bought a load of supplies for the return trip, nearly always including salt, at $1.50 a barrel, worth $3 in Knox County.

Hogs were the principal livestock as they are today. They practically fed themselves, with help from corn, and travelled to market on their own hoofs. Judge Hannamann drove 1300 to Chicago in 1841 with the help of sixteen boys, and lost $5000 on their sale. They were on the road sixteen days, and were hard put for places to stay nights. One stop was at the farm of John Bryant at Princeton, whose brother Cullen back East in Great Barrington had acquired some fame from a poem called "Thanatopsis."

The abundant grass with which the prairies were covered was

not the best fodder for stock, though cattle managed to thrive on it. Cultivated hay was unknown. Olmsted Ferris brought a cupful of timothy seed from New York to Illinois, and raised hay seed. He put nine hundred acres into timothy for the seed alone. With the devices then available, it was impossible to save both hay and seed. He set up a hay press and baled hay for selling. The Gale farm also became a large producer of hay. The cattle improved with the better feed.

Hay, and all similar crops, wheat, oats and barley, were harvested with sickle, scythe and cradle. Grain was threshed with a flail, or trodden out by oxen in the old Biblical manner. Most agricultural processes then in use were almost as old as agriculture. They had sufficed for the small farms of the East, but the West could never attain its greatest empire without farm machinery. And it was produced out of the need for it.

If the industry of dairying had appealed to Galesburg farmers, and if consequently they had left more of their land in a state of pasture, a serious disaster which confronts their fertile acres today would have been avoided. They found the prairie soil protected by a thick blanket of grass roots, the accumulation of centuries. With great labor they broke the ground and turned it over, and once plowed it became friable and easily tilled. Also, it was easily washed or blown away. Thus the soil has suffered greatly from erosion, much of it having been washed into Court and Henderson creeks and carried down the Mississippi into the Gulf of Mexico. If a half or even a third of the farms had been left as grasslands, erosion would have been greatly reduced. As already noted, dairying has become a major interest around Galesburg in recent years, transportation and refrigeration affording a world market. But dairying prospered only in a thickly settled district where there is a ready market for the products of the cow. While a few of the farmers took up stock raising, and most of them kept enough cows to supply their own families the ground was practically all plowed up and sown to grain. In the course of a hundred years much of it has been washed away.

The skill of cheese making was brought by the Ferrises from Herkimer County, famed for its cheese, and its manufacture was attempted at Galesburg, and flourished for a time, but it was not adapted to the labor available, transportation came too late, and it gradually died out, leaving the community poorer in diversity of products. This was the fate of many other such industries, and has a bearing on the plight of farmers today.

As to grain crops, wheat was tried at first, and is still grown to some extent, but the Illinois climate is not so well adapted to wheat as the lands northwest; the snowfall is too light to protect the winter variety, and what might be called the spirit of local agriculture was against it.

The staple crop was corn. Each farmer raised it for his own needs. In 1844 when the Irish famine raised prices at the seaports, Lorentus Conger and two other farmers assembled a large shipload from their own and other farms. It was shelled by trampling it out with horses, hauled to Oquawka, loaded on a flatboat, and shipped down the Mississippi to New Orleans. They returned with its value in groceries and silver dollars. The transaction was not very rewarding on a cost-keeping basis, but it did reveal the need of transportation. By the time the railroad had supplied that, it was found more profitable to feed the corn to hogs, and ship the hogs.

Oats were next to corn in popularity; their feeding value was greater, and their cultivation fitted in well with the rhythm of farm work. Alternately the land was sown to grass or clover. Rye, barley, and millet were also raised, in that order of importance, and these proportions prevailed for years; in fact, to the end of the agricultural golden age.

Other crops, which promised well, were experimented with, and allowed to die out, on account of the instinct to follow the line of least resistance, cultivating that which is easiest to raise and finds the readiest market, leading inevitably to all concentrating on the same few products. Broom corn was at one time produced in large quantities, and the manufacture of brooms became a respectable local industry. This waxed and waned, though some broom corn is raised today, and some brooms still made in the town.

Sorghum was grown for a period, and was profitable both for the home manufacture of molasses and for trade at the store, but as soon as sugar became cheaper, and markets opened for the staple grain crop, the land was put to corn, and the nucleus of another industry languished. Until the splendid native growth of sugar maples was cut down for firewood and fencing, maple sugar was plentiful, affording another example of a natural product allowed to perish. And strangely enough, though wild honey was indigenous to their country, and bee-hunting was a profitable sport for years, domestic bee-keeping was neglected.

The farmers planted vegetables, and raised fruits for their own use. The prairie was crimson with wild strawberries; plums, blackberries and grapes grew abundantly in the woods. Nature pointed emphatically toward market and fruit gardening, but these agriculturists put all their energy and time into grain crops, and allowed their orchards and gardens to die out, until most of them were buying the fresh fruit and vegetables needed for their own tables. A great opportunity was missed, which might have conditioned the melancholy fate that overtook agriculture in the Middle West in the twentieth century.

When cows and pigs were turned loose on the prairie, the ears of the cows were notched, and the marks kept on file at the courthouse to decide disputed ownership. Naturally they overran the streets of the village, and grazed in the city park, and wandered up and down Main Street. While the cattle did not get very fat on the prairie grass, and had to be fed to put them in condition for market, the hogs ate the mast in the woods and the meat was very sweet.

A flock of sheep, possibly the first, was imported from Kentucky in 1842 by Olmsted Ferris, the most adventurous of Silvanus' six sons, and Hiram Kellogg, the first president of Knox College. The following year Calvin Cole took a load of wool from these sheep to Chicago and brought back a load of leather made in Herkimer County, New York, from hides sent there by Olmsted Ferris. The following year Cole took up a second load of wool and brought back cloth also made in Herkimer County from the wool sent the previous year. Wool was about the only product that could be exported from Knox County at a profit.

The children herded sheep and cows on the prairies, a sometimes adventurous experience because of numerous rattlesnakes. Sheep were easy to keep and feed, after the wolves had been exterminated; they furnished both cloth and leather, and were profitable, but they also gave way to the preferred stock—cattle and hogs. The cattle were often sold as they stood on the prairies and driven off and fattened for the market by their purchasers. Horses needed by every one were also raised for home consumption. A good horse was worth $40. Hay brought $3 a ton.

Possibly there is an analogy between mercantile and agricultural history. Retail trade began with the general store which sold practically everything. Then came specialization, hats at hat stores, hardware at hardware stores. Next followed the department stores, the drug stores with diversified lines, the five and tens with goods for all sorts of purposes. Farming began with a wide diversity of crops, then concentrated on a few lines, and has now reached an impasse. The next indicated step seems to be diversity of crops, already foreshadowed in Knox County where milk for the local creameries is competing with corn and hogs as a local product.

# 5

## The Town Finds Itself

### I

#### KELLOGG AND THE COLLEGE

The college, it will be remembered, was getting off to a bad start, its money nearly exhausted, and not much coming in; the only building that wooden academy on Main Street. However, it had a name and a charter, and in 1841 the trustees determined to make a beginning. By extraordinary effort five thousand dollars was raised and a building erected just outside the village on the ground reserved for a "Female Seminary." It was a three-story structure with a cupola of shining tin visible for miles on sunny days. It was not part of Knox College; there was no intention of making the college co-educational; it was merely to provide a secondary school for women in conformity with the promise in the Plan. The idea was that this building could be used temporarily for the men until it was possible to provide a suitable structure on the campus; the women could wait.

Word was sent to the Reverend Hiram Huntington Kellogg at Clinton, N. Y. He loaded his numerous family and household goods in covered wagons and set out for the scene of his new labors. Although it had been agreed before the trustees left New York that Kellogg would take charge of the college, he found it hard to abandon the good beginning he had made. His "Domestic Seminary" had prospered since the days when he and Gale had discussed the prospects of a college on the plains of western Illinois. In spite of his abolitionism, which caused some friction in Clinton, he was popular, and the townspeople took a local pride in his institution.

When Kellogg arrived in Galesburg he found, besides the academy and the new female seminary, a straggly village of five hundred inhabitants, its streets still prairie mud, with a row of one-story buildings around the public square, and small white houses scattered over a half-mile rectangle. The college campus was a bare strip of prairie without a building, flanked by the college farm on which the experiment of manual labor was to be tried.

There was little for him to do in his official capacity. He had some money, the profit from the sale of his Domestic Seminary, which he proceeded to invest in Galesburg. He built the first hotel, the Galesburg House, and hired Levi Sanderson, who had come West with Eli Farnham, to manage it. He built a house for himself on North Prairie Street, and proceeded to consider the materials available for a college.

Plans were made for opening with such students as were ready. The college year was divided into two terms of twenty weeks each, with two weeks vacation in February, and ten weeks in summer. This brought commencement in July—they were yet to learn how hot Illinois summers could be—and eliminated Christmas, in which, for years, the colonists took no stock. Tuition was $24 a year, room rent extra. The faculty, besides President Kellogg, were Innes Grant, modern languages, Nehemiah Losey, mathematics, both from Oneida Institute, and George Gale, moral philosophy and belles-lettres, which was the genteel word for English literature.

All the young men of the village of the proper age and sufficient knowledge to meet the easy requirements made up the first freshman class. They had been preparing in the academy. For entrance they were supposed to know English grammar, arithmetic, algebra through simple equations, the four gospels in Greek, Graeca Minora, or its equivalent in Jacob's Greek Reader, and six books of Vergil.

In the freshman year the studies were geometry, Cicero's orations, part of Graeca Majora, Acts and Romans in Greek,

Blair's Rhetoric, evidences of Christianity and political economy; sophomore: Horace, Graeca Majora, Greek Testament, Day's Mathematics, Bridge's Conic Sections, Paley's Natural Theology and natural history; composition and declamation weekly.

The scholarships given so freely to purchasers of farms were a serious handicap to the college revenue. As the students were all from Galesburg, and as their parents owned scholarships, no money was paid for tuition. When the college opened its doors there were outstanding 2050 years of free tuition, equivalent to a four years' course for 512 students. The college consisted of freshmen only the first year, though the academy was well attended. As the time was not yet ripe for the women's school, there was no opportunity for Kellogg to apply the system in which he was a specialist, that of making the girls do the housework.

Before the first freshman class had reached the senior year the students organized a literary society, lacking which no American college in that era was complete, with the conventional Greek name, in this case "The Adelphi Lyceum of Knox College," later known as "Adelphi." It flourished down to the time in the present century when fraternities and a multiplication of more specialized organizations quietly eliminated it.

The Adelphi had weekly meetings with long dry programs of essays, debates, declamations and orations, listened to for hours by those tough pioneer students. They were no duller than the endless sermons poured into their ears on Sunday. It soon began to justify its name as a lyceum, and Theodore Parker and Ralph Waldo Emerson were the first of a long procession of lecturers to whom the pioneer audiences gravely listened.

Soon Adelphi had a rival, as was natural, for such organizations flourish only on competition. Some of the Adelphians became disgruntled and formed Gnothautii. For fifty years the male student body owed allegiance to one or the other, and the rivalry gave a healthy stimulus to both. Each started a small publication, "Knoxiana" by the Adelphians, "Oak Leaf" by the

Gnothautians, and each began to form a library. What books constituted a library in those days, one wonders. Before long they attempted to compete in lecture courses, but this proved disastrous to both houses. The town was not equal to absorbing so much culture, so they compromised on alternate years. These courses, which persisted to the end of the lyceum movement in this country, covered the whole gamut from Matthew Arnold to Benjamin P. Shillabar (Mrs. Partington).

Beyond their not too exacting studies, the literary society, hustling around selling tickets to their lectures, countless prayer meetings and endless church attendance, there was little to occupy these early Illinois students. No athletics, no social life, none of the pleasant extra-curricular activities which fill so large a place in the modern college. Religion entered into everything; compulsory prayers daily in each class; church twice on Sunday. Monitors were appointed to check up and report; later each student answered for himself at roll call Monday morning. It makes a rather bleak picture, but, human nature being what it is, probably not so. unrelieved as it sounds.

In 1843 the seminary building burned. There was no insurance; it was a total loss. The blow almost paralyzed the community. The board of trustees did not meet for eighteen months. College was held in the attic of the academy building. Money was sorely needed. At the end of this period of inaction, Gale was sent, at his own suggestion, to New York to secure contributions. Kellogg went to Europe, primarily to attend a meeting of the international anti-slavery society, but with a commission to solicit funds in England for Knox. They secured some money, evidently not much, and began the first building on the campus.

When Kellogg returned from England, he found that a coolness had arisen between himself and the trustees, which meant, reduced to its lowest terms, that Gale was dissatisfied with the man he had picked to be president of his college. The board had discussed him when he was abroad, and early in 1845 a letter was written at Gale's instigation which resulted in his resignation.

Outwardly the break was an amicable one. As nearly as can be ascertained, the criticism made was that the college had not flourished under Kellogg's administration. But Gale was restive over Kellogg's Congregationalism and his anti-slavery activities. Theoretically Gale was as much opposed to slavery as any of his colleagues, but he was far more interested in the college, in its source of supplies. Slavery was a controversial question, and slavery agitation made the college unpopular with some who might contribute. Gale was shrewd, and he already saw that slavery might disrupt the two denominations on which Knox chiefly depended.

None of this appeared as yet. The relations between Kellogg and the board were such that he was allowed to name his successor. At the London anti-slavery convention he had met a man from Cincinnati, who was delegate from Ohio as Kellogg was from Illinois. This man was Jonathan Blanchard. He impressed Kellogg as he impressed everybody. He had already made a name in Cincinnati as a dominant and forceful person. His prominence would add prestige to the college. Kellogg saw in Blanchard his own zeal for moral reform, but carried further, backed by more courage, more force. If Kellogg had possessed Blanchard's pugnacity he would have remained president of Knox College, as Blanchard did under similar circumstances. He recommended Blanchard, and his recommendation was adopted. A call was sent to Blanchard and accepted.

Kellogg remained in Galesburg a year or two as pastor of the church. He agreed to represent the college as "agent" and solicit funds. He returned to the East, and his subsequent career is melancholy. He bought back from the Free Will Baptists his old school at Clinton, but his efforts to restore it to its pristine prosperity were vain. He returned to Illinois and endeavored to realize on his property there, but he lost almost the whole of it. He sold out just before the railroad boom boosted values. He sought without success to persuade the trustees to pay him the year's salary he had relinquished. He engaged in religious and educational work, died in Illinois, and was buried there.

He had inaugurated the college, presided until the first class had completed the four-year course, but did not conduct a commencement or preach a baccalaureate. By reason of the confusion attending his resignation, the uncertainty about money, the lack of a suitable building, there was no commencement in 1845. That class left without degrees. The first commencement, in 1846, was the brilliant induction to the able but stormy regime of President Blanchard.

## II

### "WEST BRICKS"

The burning of the seminary building was a crushing blow, but the trustees ultimately recovered their courage, and with money collected by Gale and Kellogg, and a larger amount contributed by Blanchard's friend John Payson Williston, the first building was erected on the campus and named Williston Hall.

It was a curious building, faintly reminiscent of the dormitories Gale had seen at Jefferson's college in Virginia, a two-and-a-half story structure in front; a row of one-story rooms attached, the first unit of a larger plan. When a year later the corresponding building was erected, the plan began to emerge, but it was carried no further. The taller buildings were occupied by classrooms; the literary societies used the attics for their meetings; the one-story dormitories opened directly on the campus. To many college generations the two buildings were known as "East and West Bricks." The bricks came from Farmer Groscup, who had bought the site of Log City and paid for it with brick made where the colonists had once lived.

The colonnade which gives character to the Virginia buildings was never added, though it was contemplated, as can be seen by the letter Gale wrote Silvanus Ferris, the financial agent of the college: "In regard to the student buildings," he says, "you can finish them without the piazza or colonnade. . . . I have thought best . . . to have the rooms (that is, the students' quarters) six feet square including walls, and make recesses for single beds, before which a curtain could be drawn to hide the bed and keep it clean. The place for hanging the clothes might be at the foot of each bed. . . . In this case there would be no closets, the wall at the foot of the bed and the trunks answering. We must make these rooms pleasant and inviting."

Fortunately more space, but not much more, was allowed in the final plan, though by no stretch of imagination could the rooms be considered "pleasant and inviting." The two buildings confronted each other across an open space about four hundred feet wide, each containing eight dormitories. Just beyond the end of "West Bricks" was the old-fashioned noisome latrine, which was promptly dubbed "Number Seventeen," a name it bore, even officially, until the advent of plumbing.

In these rooms, twelve feet square, many students lived for four years, carrying water from the pump in the yard, coal from a pile outside the door. They paid six dollars a year, furnishing their rooms with articles brought from home on the farm wagon. The poorer students—they were all poor—frequently kept house in these cubicles, cooking on the tiny soft-coal stoves, helped out by generous baskets brought back from week-end visits. Stories are told of determined seekers for knowledge who managed to subsist on eleven cents a day. Other outsiders lived in homes in the village, where board and laundry cost as little as a dollar a week.

The out-of-town students were mainly drawn from the immediate vicinity, sons of the pioneer Galesburg farmers, but a few came from greater distances. One was from Fountain Green, a hundred miles away. He was already twenty-four, and had served as sheriff of Hancock County. He arrived riding a horse named Mike, his sole asset. Mike was fed up and curried to fetch as high a price as possible and sold to pay college expenses.

With students living where they could go and come so easily, there was the usual amount of college deviltry, such as tampering with Gad Colton's mill. When Professor Grant, a solemn and dour Scotchman, who stood on his dignity, refused a holiday to attend the county fair, he found a row of hog's heads from the slaughterhouse, ranged neatly on his desk. "Number Seventeen" was burned down to call out the volunteer fire department. Several boys were involved in an outburst of lawlessness described by the faculty as "card playing, ale drinking, singing, and making horrid noises." One of the perpetrators became subsequently a valued member of the board of trustees.

Punishments were expulsion, suspension, public apology, and "rustication," which meant vacating the college rooms and moving to quarters in town. This did not relieve the culprit of surveillance, however, as no householder was permitted to take student boarders who did not agree to report all infractions of college regulations. One rule forbade a student to leave his room after nightfall without permission, except to attend prayer meeting and the session of his literary society, and that must adjourn before ten o'clock. Naturally these childish restrictions set a premium on evasion, and it is a satisfaction to know that boys educated in such a stifling moral atmosphere had enough red blood to raise a rumpus now and then.

Early in Blanchard's incumbency there was added a Female Collegiate three-years' course for women, entirely separate from that of the men, but taught by the same professors. The first class entered in 1847 and graduated in 1850. Commencement was in mid-winter, to keep it wholly apart from the men's baccalaureate. Three women finished in the first class, Gale's daughter Harriet, who married the Hitchcock who became professor of mathematics, Ann Dunn, who as wife of Henry Sanderson, son of Levi the innkeeper, entertained Abraham Lincoln in 1858, and Sarah Fisk, whose father, a minister and a newspaper man, had a "fracas" with Selden Gale that filled several pages of the church session book with the efforts of the elders to fix the blame.

# THE TOWN FINDS ITSELF

The college was at first closely identified with the town, bone of its bone, flesh of its flesh. The men of affairs were professors and trustees of the college. When in 1841 the settlement was incorporated as a village, the college people assumed most of the offices by divine right. This prevailed until enough new settlers arrived to dispute the dominance of the college, which meant the dominance of Gale, and the town began to live its own life independently, though for many years whatever affected the town for good or ill was reflected in the fortunes of the college, and vice versa.

## III

### JONATHAN BLANCHARD

When Blanchard arrived the "Bricks" were ready, likewise the second academy building on the square. He was the ablest man to be connected with the college in any capacity for many years. He was not a man to be cowed by boards of trustees. He loved a fight, and his strong convictions on moral questions, amounting to intolerance, gave him plenty of opportunity. Since he is the most powerful influence yet brought to bear on the history of the town, it is essential to know something about his antecedents.

Jonathan Blanchard was born in a large red farmhouse among the Green Mountains, near Rockingham, Vermont, January 19, 1811. When three years and seven months old he climbed on the fence of his father's farm and heard the British guns booming at Plattsburg in the War of 1812. When his brother told him men were killing one another, he imbibed the first of his convictions, a deep-seated hatred of war. He went to district school at four, began English grammar at seven, Latin at twelve, and was teaching school himself at fourteen-and-a-half. At seventeen he entered Middlebury College, and on graduation taught in the Academy at Plattsburg. He grew up in that period of easy morals, which had its tremendous reaction in the religious revivals of the twenties. Drinking, card-playing and gambling were common. Whisky was free at house-raisings and on training days. The best Christian in town distilled cider brandy. Young Blanchard smashed the jug of liquor intended for his father's harvest hands, and became a foe of rum. His first published writing was a temperance lecture, printed in a local paper. Thus early he tasted reform and publicity.

He was formally converted to religion in the great revival that seems to have furnished most of the characters in this saga of colonization, and added cards and dancing to his list of prohibited sins. He prepared for the ministry at Andover and under Lyman Beecher at Lane Theological Seminary at Cincinnati, where he came under the influence of Theodore Weld and joined his antislavery cause, a hazardous enterprise in a city as rabidly proslavery as Cincinnati.

Blanchard married Mary Bent, a woman of great beauty and charm, was ordained pastor of the Sixth Presbyterian Church of Cincinnati, and was soon attracting more than local attention. His outspoken denunciations of slavery brought proscription and persecution even from brother ministers of the gospel. He saw three anti-slavery printing presses destroyed with sledge hammers and thrown into the Ohio, and narrowly escaped being chucked in himself. At Cincinnati he began his public debates on the sinfulness of slavery, his first opponent being Nathan Lewis, a Presbyterian minister of Kentucky pastorates. The debate was printed and widely circulated. He was known and greatly admired at Oberlin, where he delivered the commencement address in 1839 in Finney's big tent before three thousand people, on "The Perfect State," and praised that hamlet as the nearest thing to paradise he had found on this earth.

A woman in his church told him that the Masons' lodge in Cincinnati had refused to bury her husband although he had paid dues to the lodge for twenty-five years. He published the fact, preached against secret societies, and a band of Masons from Covington, Kentucky, attacked him; again he narrowly escaped with his life. Thus he added Masonry to his index expurgatorius, and the crusade against lodges aroused by the murder of Morgan was spurred by his sermons.

When the call to Knox College came, he accepted, because, as he told his wife, "Knox College is founded and Galesburg settled by anti-Masons from the vicinity of Morgan's murder." Thus he arrived in the town, tall, commanding, strikingly handsome, faultlessly dressed in silk hat and frock coat, a dynamic reformer, ready on short notice to excoriate any malefactors guilty of what he considered the seven deadly sins—card playing, dancing, blasphemy, Sabbath breaking, intemperance, slavery and failing to walk with the church.

That lively chronicler of early life in Galesburg, Erastus Willcox, who came as a boy with his parents in 1837 and grew up with the village, tells how the new president put sinners "on the spot." "The most important thing," says Erastus, "the chief end of man in those days in Galesburg, was to get converted and join the church." A conspicuous and lonely exception from the general conformity was David Edgerton, architect of the Old First Church. During a revival "all the guns and prayers were turned on him, but he would not be persuaded to come forward and make a profession of religion." Catching him alone on the street, Blanchard "began laboring with him, threatening him with the awful and sure fate awaiting him in the next world if he did not join while mercy was freely offered and the lamp held out to burn."

Edgerton stoutly resisted, and told the dominie he was as good without conversion as Blanchard was, sending a "shudder of pious horror" through young Willcox's soul at his temerity, "for we were taught that the more moral and upright a man might be, the more awful his fate if he were not one of the elect." Even Erastus' father did not escape the inquisition. At prayer meeting Blanchard pointed an accusing finger at him for being too long silent, and cried: "And there is Brother Willcox; I have not seen a green leaf on him."

Blanchard's truculence on the street was matched by his long-windedness in the pulpit. Even in a day of long sermons he must have been something of a marvel. Hiram Mars, later a lumber dealer of Galesburg, attended Illinois College at Jacksonville. While he was there Blanchard came to deliver the address before the state Congregational association. Young Mars and another student dutifully attended the session. The sermon began at eight. Mars remained until ten, when memories of unprepared lessons sent him to his room. At half past eleven his friend dropped in.

"How did you like the address?" he was asked.

"I was well pleased with the small part I heard, but he had just announced 'thirdly' in his discourse. From indications when I left he should finish by about four o'clock tomorrow morning."

Blanchard gave the college a vigorous administration. The attendance increased. He brought in additional money, and championed the building program which resulted in two remarkably complete and adequate buildings for the times. Had he been as keen about education as he was for various moral reforms, with his energy and courage the college might easily have led the country. As it was, Knox was one of the best as well as one of the wealthiest of that period.

For a season all went admirably. The real ability of the man won the respect of the townspeople. The practical, hard-headed business men of the board of trustees who cared nothing about fine-spun theological distinctions were pleased to get action. They supported him, and plans were vigorously pushed. But so forthright and outspoken a man was bound to make enemies in any case, even in such an amiable and Christian community as Galesburg was supposed to be. And with the makings of a quarrel already smoking on the controversial hearth, it was only a question of time before Blanchard joined in and helped fan the flames. Unfortunately when the issue was finally joined, he was on the opposite side from Gale.

## IV

### THE OLD FIRST CHURCH

In a community where the first duty of a good citizen was to "support the Gospel" and "walk with the church," the old academy building had become too small for its Sunday congregations, and a meeting house was insistently demanded. In 1841 they set about it. As was the case with the college building, it was a matter of money and labor, the latter drafted from the husky and able-bodied farmers who made up most of its membership, for it must be built with what materials and skill existed in the community, like the cathedrals of old. The few skilled workmen in the village would contribute their facility, along with muscles of expert axemen and the teams of the farmers.

The site for the church, the most conspicuous in the town, a commanding corner on the public square, had been reserved for the purpose when the town was laid out. Money contributions were asked, for some of the material must be bought. The lumber, however, was cut from the noble groves where each settler had his tithe of timber land. The dimensions were on a grand scale, the largest structure but one yet attempted in Illinois, eighty feet long, sixty feet wide, and twenty-four feet to the break of the eaves.

Four great timbers, a foot square and sixty feet long, were required for the frame, to avoid lapping or scarfing. It did not seem possible to find them in the neighborhood, until Olmsted Ferris pointed out one on his lot sixty-three feet to the first branch, a magnificent white oak. Thus inspired, Western Ferris found one, not quite so straight, Sam Holyoke another, and John West the fourth. They were felled, squared with axes, and hauled to the ground.

Thus the lumber was assembled. It was all hardwood, the frame of oak, finished inside and out from baseboard to spire with black walnut. Basswood was the softest material which grew in Henderson Grove. There was no pine in Illinois, and to bring it from the north would have been beyond their means, not to speak of lack of transportation.

After a year of labor the corner of the square was piled high with timber, and the building partly framed, a difficult job with the primitive apparatus available. Then came a lull. Funds were exhausted, but more than that, there was a crisis among the workers. The work was interrupted by a theological argument, like the tower of Babel, and half the church refused to contribute further until the matter was adjusted to their satisfaction. This was accomplished, temporarily at least, as will be told in the next chapter, but more than a year elapsed, the partly built church suffered from the ravages of an Illinois winter, beams had become warped, boards were blown down. Then like a warning from heaven came a terrific thunderstorm; a bolt of lightning struck the building and partially demolished it, splintering many of the beams, scattering the débris about the grounds. At this evidence of heaven's displeasure, the factions patched up their differences, and work was resumed.

The need of money also dogged the progress of the building, but Chauncey Colton came to the rescue, as he did many times in the town's history. He gave credit at his store for the unpaid subscriptions, supplied their value in cash toward the building, and waited for his pay until crops were harvested. It was years before all those debts were paid.

In 1846 the first commencement was held in the new church edifice, which, though incomplete, was by the providence of God sufficiently far along to serve so auspicious and appropriate an occasion. Dresses were washed and furbished. Unless Colton's store had reached the proud eminence of store clothes, the graduates' costumes were home made; certainly their shirts and collars were, and laundered by home talent. They wore boots, over which their pants set badly, and possibly the brocaded or fancy double-breasted vests which were the genteel thing at that period according to old daguerreotypes.

The people came for miles in their slow, springless wagons, dressed in their best, a motley array. They had been up since dawn; a substantial dinner must be prepared and packed, for the exercises lasted all day, and for many the trip was long over rough roads behind horses which had worked all the week.

The church had been equipped with seats of planks laid on short lengths of logs, and chairs borrowed from neighboring houses. The windows were unglazed, and the walls open to the weather, all the better, for it was no doubt excessively hot. They sat on hard, rude, backless seats from nine to twelve, and then ate their dinner in the shadeless public square, and visited with one another until time to go back and sit through an unbelievably long baccalaureate sermon. The sermon was preached by Gale, for no one would think of robbing him of his supreme moment.

Levi Sanderson, landlord of the Galesburg House, bustling, alert, a little peppery, was marshal, his small snapping eyes on every one, ushering the procession, seating the audience, with the same energy he displayed at funerals. The trustees marched up the broad aisle, to the music of the band in the gallery, led by Blanchard and Gale, Blanchard large, strong, dignified, with his leonine locks and great beard, wearing the first academic gown ever seen in Galesburg, Gale small, dapper, smooth-shaven, immaculate, like a steel engraving of some old scholarly New England divine, followed by the members of the board, farmers, storekeepers, ministers, schoolmasters, stiff and awkward in their Sunday blacks, to sit on the stage behind the gentlemen of the graduating class. It was not much of a spectacle beside college processions of today with their gowns and colorful hoods, but it was all they had, and they made a field day of it.

Nine men were graduated and received their degrees. Four became ministers of the Gospel, as was natural considering the purpose of the college. Of the remaining five, one became a professor of mathematics at Knox, one was editor of three successive Galesburg newspapers, the third a doctor, and the fourth a lawyer, and partner of Robert G. Ingersoll, then a rising young lawyer, later the famous Peoria infidel. Of the fifth nothing is now known.

What the intellectual status of the college was those first five years, what the character of the teaching, can be only inferred. It probably compared favorably with any newly started school, remote from educational centers. Four of the faculty were experienced teachers, and two were college graduates. Their instruction, despite lack of books and apparatus, was beneficial to the capacity of teacher and pupil. It is fair to assume that it did a good job. Counting the six men who did not graduate the year before, on account of the difficulty over President Kellogg, but who completed the course, and the six who belonged to this class but did not graduate, there were twenty-one young men who had probably received more education than the majority of their countrymen possessed, in a small badly equipped school on a prairie which ten years before had scarcely known the print of a white man's foot.

The Old First Church, four square in the center of the town, with its steeple towering ninety feet above the level prairie, became the symbol.of the town, its center. Here was held every form of religious exercise, church morning and afternoon, town meetings, lectures, concerts, anti-slavery gatherings, the college commencements and other public entertainments, everything secular that was decorous and fitting. The whole settlement presented its babies to be baptized with all the punctuality of a Catholic parish, and the church records are the only vital statistics that exist. It was well built and possessed a certain dignified simplicity, for the proportions were good. Seen from the prairie it loomed above the surrounding scattered houses and young trees like the parish church of a medieval city.

It resembled the parish church in other ways, for it was upheld, in theory at least, by the entire community. It was the arbiter of all their differences. Not only were offenders against religious discipline cited before the elders for such sins as failing "to support the Gospel" (which means in our language, staying away from service), for blasphemy, drunkenness, heresy (going to the Campbellite church), but civil cases, such as a dispute over a boundary line, non-payment of a debt, breach of contract, or that popular crime, "hooking timber" from government land or that of absentee owners, were tried and adjudicated before the church tribunal. This practice held even after the village was incorporated and a simple machinery of justice set up. The guilty ones either showed signs of repentance and made restitution, or they were suspended, and in some cases "excommunicated," as the clerk of the church, Nehemiah West, with a sense of drama, wrote across their names in the church book.

It was finally dedicated July 25, 1848, five years after the ground was broken for it, with great rejoicings and apparent harmony, though unfortunately there were beneath its roof the seeds of discord that were to grow into the mightiest internal conflict the town was ever to know.

## V

### BUSINESS

Meanwhile the economic machine began to function and expand. The business activities might be classified as stores, services, and factories. Colton's store, forerunner of the modern department store, sold everything the people could not make in their own homes, from combs to buckets, from nails to fullcloth. Service was rendered by such utilities as the grist mill, the linseed oil mill, the blacksmith shop, the cobbler and the tailor. The workshops made products for sale—brooms, furniture, coffins, agricultural machinery. For many years the home market was the only one, and thus we have a small working model of a self-contained industrial community.

These beginnings of commerce collectively constituted the business of the town. All over the Middle West were similar beginnings, the seeds, the nuclei, of our modern industrial system. From just such small enterprises as "Colton's Store" and "Colton's Foundry" the great businesses of America have grown.

Business centered in the public square, an open unshaded space, kneedeep with mud in wet weather, where the farmers tied their teams when they came to market. In it were the town pump, and in front of Colton's the public scales. The mail was brought from Knoxville for a few years by whoever happened to be going to the county seat, and left at Gale's house on the edge of the village where the villagers called for it, paying two-bits postage on all letters from the East. A post office, however, was soon secured, and established in Colton's store, with Professor Losey, the town surveyor, as postmaster. The store became the focus of village opinion, its unofficial chamber of commerce, where were laid the plots and plans by which the town snatched supremacy from her neighbors and competitors.

The sidewalk in front of the store, and all stores, was covered with a sort of wooden arcade or awning to temper the fierce Illinois sun, a distinctive feature of prairie towns, for there was no other shade until trees were planted. Some of these arcades can still be seen in the smaller towns of the state. The newer stores crept around the square. Next to Colton's, Matteson's drug store; on the north the new academy building, then Bartlett & Judson's, which manufactured furniture and made coffins to measure, a hide and leather house, a grocery, a clothing store, and then Matthew Chambers', who moved his business from Knoxville and occupied the store he had built on his arrival in the colony. On the south stood the church, now completed, dwarfing everything in the neighborhood. Gradually, the vacant lots in between were filled, and the tide of trade turned and flowed east on Main Street, where the Galesburg House stood, a block above the square.

New stores were added by fission, like the amoeba. A line split off from the general store and became a specialty. Colton's sold boots and shoes, but Samuel Tompkins or Chris Miner, or whoever was the official cobbler at this time, went to customers and made boots and shoes from their own leathers. As business grew he took a shop and customers came to him. Gradually he put in a line of ready-made footwear, and a shoe store was created.

That evolution still goes on. A generation ago the repair shop was an adjunct of every shoe store. Today it is a separate business, combined with hat cleaning and shoe polishing. Such changes in the routine and habit of business that are making over Main Street today began with the first cluster of shops in pioneer villages.

The variety of footwear offered in those early days is amazing. There was more individuality in dress, and less of what we call fashion. The American man had not then adopted a costume which is almost a uniform. A list advertised in one of the earliest Galesburg papers offered: Men's common, thick, regular, and extra-sized boots; long leg, welt, and double-soled unlined California boots (for the gold seekers); Philadelphia fine dress imitation of stitch-and-sewed calf boots; pump sole, kip, imitation goat, calf and morocco Oxford ties; foxed last and foxed cloth Congress gaiters (those elastic-gored shoes once peculiar to legislators). For women there were polka boots, high buskins, silk lasting gaiters, Jenny Lind buskins and Excelsiors, enamelled village ties and El Dorado slippers.

Hats likewise were offered in infinite variety: moleskin and angola hats; drab pearl beaver, fur, seal, and muskrat hats; Jenny Lind, Kossuth and Hungarian hats; Cerro Gordo wool, Ashland sporting, union hats; palm leaf, leghorn, Rutland, pedal, bird's eye, and China pearl straw hats; Lutton, Dunstable, pedal flats; Grenada hats, Florence bonnets.

Among the goods sold in the dry goods stores were such old-fashioned fabrics as broadcloths, cassimeres, vestings, silk and wool bombazine, jaconet, merino, flannel and fullcloth. Melodeons were sold in Len Miller's music store. The cigar store carried snuff. Colton's sign read "Dry Goods, Groceries, Hardware, Queensware, Iron, Glass, and General Produce Merchants." With such a variety to choose from, the gatherings of the townspeople, at commencements and other festivities, must have presented a varied and colorful picture.

[ 147 ]

THE TOWN FINDS ITSELF

The meat trade underwent the same transformation as other home skills. When the farmer no longer killed his cattle and hogs, they were driven to the village slaughter house, on the bank of Cedar Fork, for nearly a century the town sewer, and the local meat market secured its supply there. Then later Chicago packers took over the whole industry, the farmers' stock was sent to Swift, Armour or other dressed beef companies, the local butcher bought from a wholesale meat house, until last change of all, we have frozen packaged meats sold in food stores, and the local butcher, beloved for the lagnappe of bologna sausage which was your perquisite when you went to market for the family roast, is fading out of the Main Street picture.

Thus one by one, individual lines split off from the general stores and became distinct enterprises, and trade began to diversify, while the general store itself went in more and more for heavier lines, dry goods and clothing. The village started with practically every family its own factory, making at home clothing, cloth, soap, candles, furniture, and preparing its food from raw materials. With prosperity, ready money, the increasing demands of the main job—in most cases farming—it turned to those who could supply it, and slowly but steadily abandoned household skills in favor of articles bought or service rendered for pay by another. Thus the village changed from a community of Jacks-of-all-trades to one of specialists. The specialists again divided. A machine shop, a foundry, or a wagon factory sprang from the blacksmith shop. A carpenter became a woodworker, making trim, or sash and doors, or a cabinet maker producing furniture. The business of money and credit was distributed among banks, insurance brokers, building and loan associations and investment houses.

Among the things manufactured in Galesburg in the second decade of its existence were wagons, plows, cornplanters, castings for other manufactures and for the railroad, furniture, harness, shoes, brick, rope, baskets, marble, brooms, pumps and windmills, candy, sorghum, soap, clothing, millinery, daguerreotypes.

A picturesque craft now extinct, which rose, flourished and died. in this little town under the influence of changing mercantile habits, was the manufacture of custom-made account books. Originally, "Kuhn, Boishell & Colville, blank books, stationery, maps, prints, music, books—with special attention to the publications of the Bible Society, Tract Society and the Sabbath School Union, this firm has now two wagons on the road," says an admiring write-up in 1857, "that travel regularly over the adjoining counties."

Robert Colville, a bookbinder from Scotland, settled in Galesburg in the fifties, and opened a shop on the west side of the square. Books were "kept" in huge volumes specially printed and ruled to fit the nature of the business. Daybook, journal and ledger were required by each merchant. Some stores employed bookkeepers—another trade to be added to the list of gainful occupations—but small proprietors kept their own books.

Robert Colville cut sheets of calendered paper the required size, printed the proper headings for each page, and ruled them according to specifications, blue lines for the items, red lines crossing them vertically to keep the items in their columns. The ruling machine was a large device, reaching to the ceiling, something like a loom, through which the sheets travelled, being fed into it as one feeds a printing press. Quill pens, attached to a movable rod at the proper distances, and inked with the proper color, came into contact with the paper as it travelled through.

The ruled paper was next paged, then bound in book form, with heavy rawhide thongs holding the back together, making deep indentations on the spine. Each volume was about twelve by twenty inches, three, four or more inches thick, the covers half an inch of pasted-up board. For some peculiar reason known only to the trade, business books must be "marbled." For this operation, powdered colors, red and blue usually, were dropped on the surface of a square basin of water, and the spots of color thus made coaxed with a coarse comb into wavy patterns. A sheet laid gently on top of the water received a brilliant impression. This paper was for the covers, the corners being bound in red morocco to match the back. Before putting on the covers the fore edges of the book were also marbled by dipping them lightly in the pool. The backs were stamped in gold with the name of the firm and the title of the book.

As the town grew, demand increased; mercantile houses and banks, the city and county offices required special books for their records. Finally in the twentieth century came the typewriter, the loose-leaf filing system and the adding machine, and this peculiar local industry dried up and disappeared. The shop in the hands of Robert's sons continued doing job printing and binding up sets of magazines until it ended with the death of the last son. The hand-ruling machine disappeared from modern business, as thoroughly as the scythe and sickle from the wheat harvest.

Business letters were written by hand and copied into a letter book. The pages of this book were made of thin paper. The letter was laid in the book, a page dampened with a broad brush was turned over the letter, and a sheet of blotting laid on. The brush when not in use stood in a covered china dish with a slit in the top the width of the brush. The book was then put in the press—something like a wine press—and the wheel screwed down. The pressure printed a copy of the letter reversed on the back of the sheet, but it could be read right-end-to on the other side. This laborious method was used even after the introduction of the typewriter, until some one thought of carbon paper.

Change through inventions, new habits, improved methods of work, has gone on in every community, so that the business directory, the list of occupations by which the town gets its living, is quite different from that which lined Main Street three quarters of a century ago; the garage has replaced the livery stable, the auto repair shop the blacksmith shop, and the plumber the well digger.

It was common in the west when business was simpler for men

of affairs to carry on many occupations at the same time, making a little money on each. Gale's oldest son Selden was a farmer on a large scale, but he also practiced law, bought and sold real estate, was postmaster, edited a newspaper, and held numerous elective offices.

Such men seldom had a place of business, or seldom used it, most of the transactions being completed at various spots in the county where the other parties happened to be, and the business man carried his office with him, frequently in his tall beaver hat. Matthew Chambers had a leather roll, indexed, for holding papers, the ancestor of the brief case, with a loop for hanging over the pommel of the saddle. He travelled about the country, collecting notes, foreclosing mortgages, buying and selling land. Some of the transactions were painfully small. Notes were given for amounts such as three dollars and fifty cents. The documents were narrow slips of paper, folded to a width of two inches for banding together in a neat package, the title written on the end like an endorsement on a check, so that they could be run through quickly to find a required transaction.

The various lines of interest, the church, the college, the shop or store or farm, social life, apparently each a separate stream, were unified by the fact that they were pursued by the same people. Colton and Chambers were trustees of the college. The storekeepers and farmers were elders of the church. All were concerned in such matters as the resignation of Kellogg, the appointment of Blanchard, in the citation of William Ferris before the session. They followed their different interests simultaneously, buying, selling, collecting a bill, serving notice of a citation, or laboring with a recalcitrant brother, as part of the same day's work. Each line of a village's activity follows its own bent, a separate historical trail, but the men who are the actors in each scene are the same men, now drawing together for some benefit to the town or its institutions, now arrayed against one another in some local antagonism. Thus for years this narrative is concerned with one small group, struggling to build a successful growing town after the only model they know, and make a contribution to the public good in the way of a church and a college.

## VI

### THE SELF-SCOURING PLOW

No sooner had the proverbial ingenuity of the Yankee mind been brought into contact with an entirely new type of soil and the problems it presented, than inventions sprang up to cope with them. The evolution from rail fence to thorn hedge to barbed wire has already been noted. Plowing virgin prairie was a new experience for New York farmers. The slight plows brought from the East crumpled like matchwood before the thick prairie turf, with its accumulation of grass roots, the growth of centuries. The land had to be "broken" with a barshare plow, a heavy implement eight feet long, cutting a sixteen-inch furrow. The share was a four-foot bar of iron with a coulter in front. The mold board was split out of winding timber with the proper curve or hewn into shape to turn the soil over. To drag this plow through the root mass required three or four span of oxen.

Once broken, however, the soil became fallow, easily cultivated with an ordinary plow, and was amazingly fertile. The first crop sown was sod corn, dropped on the plowed ground without further cultivation, and brushed in with a small tree dragged over the ground as a harrow. The operation of breaking never had to be repeated, and the barshare plow is no longer used, as every acre of fertile soil in Illinois has long since been cultivated.

Next season when the settlers began to till their fields they encountered another difficulty. The cast-iron plow, the only kind known until then, would not scour bright in the rich prairie loam. Every ten rods or so the plowman had to stop and scrape the soil from the mold board, which wasted time. The invention of the steel self-scouring plow was one of the triumphs of this little band of pioneers.

Harvey Henry May, born in New York but of New England stock, came to Galesburg with his family in 1837, at the age of thirty-three, after a preliminary visit of inspection the year before. He brought to that company of farmers and divines one thing it sorely needed, the technological mind. May was already an inventor. In the East he had perfected a reaper for grain eight years before Cyrus McCormick, but inexperience, lack of money, various obstacles, delayed his securing a patent until one sad day his brother read to him from the pages of the *Scientific American*—he was too overcome to read it himself—the specifications for McCormick's invention, and he realized that they were the same as his own. He was destined to have a similar experience with his next invention.

As soon as he reached Illinois, he began experiments which lasted four years. Skeptics jeered at him, and called him a fool, but others with more faith or more vision cheered him on, promising a hundred dollars, or his choice of a fine horse, for the first successful plow. When he at last realized how much smoother steel was than cast iron, and what a difference it made in the adherence of the soil, he fashioned his mold board from a fine steel blade obtained from William Nowland's sawmill, and in 1842 produced the first successful self-scouring plow.

It worked like a charm. The plowman's output was doubled. It revolutionized agriculture in the Mississippi valley, and added millions to its potential wealth. But the ignorance of two successive patent commissioners, too stupid to grasp the point to the invention, delayed a patent until the idea had been pirated by numerous manufacturers.

May made his own plow, and sold numbers of them, and fought infringements, but long-continued ill-health compelled him to relinquish the fight for complete control. In 1871, as a result of litigation between the Deeres and the Moline Plow Company,

Judge Sidney Breese presiding, it was definitely established that the steel self-scouring plow was the invention of Harvey May.*

May was more of an inventor than a business man, but he manufactured his own contrivances with profit, and when his sons entered the business they carried on by inventing the windmill which was a landmark on the prairies for years, drawing the water from the subsoil for the cattle. But as May sadly remarked:

"The cupidity of man has repeatedly prevented me from being the almoner of the bounties of my own brain."

When the Ferrises started the combination steam saw and grist mill at Henderson Grove, they were helped by a young man named Joseph P. Frost, who had a turn for mechanics. Frost took a small space in Ferris' mill and set up a machine shop. He moved it to the village with the crowd, and later took in Andrew Harrington, a machinist from Chicopee, Mass., and W. S. Bellows, a foundryman, as partners, and the shop grew into a "works," making many of the castings for the agricultural machinery which Galesburg began to produce from inventions of its ingenious citizens. One of these was the spiral stalk cutter, devised by Robert and Cyrus Avery, nephews of John T. Avery, whose moving revival had swept the entire population of Log City into the church. The Averys later produced a cornplanter and made it the nucleus of a factory of their own. There were also Thirlwell's two-horse cultivator for corn and Bassett's steam plow.

Another industrial romance of the prairie was Brown's cornplanter. He was a mechanically minded farmer, not one of the original pioneers, but his story belongs here. It irked him to make

*It should be noted, perhaps, that the invention of the self-scouring steel plow is also claimed for John Deere by the company he founded, The John Deere Company of Moline, Ill. Its story is being told this year—1937—in the agricultural press, with circumstantial detail, even to the incident that Deere, like May, made his first share from a sawmill blade. That the credit belongs to May and not Deere is supported, not only by the reports of the Illinois Supreme Court cited above, but by the testimony of May's contemporaries, Selden Gale, in his History of Knox County and Galesburg (in *Historical Encyclopedia of Illinois*, edited by Newton Bateman and Paul Selby), and by Chapman's *History of Knox County*, published in 1878, when many of the witnesses were still living.

three operations for getting corn into the ground, plowing furrows, dropping the seed by hand, and covering it up, usually by dragging a small tree over the ground as a harrow. He constructed a crude machine that plowed, planted, and covered as it moved along, mounted on the rear wheels of a wagon. From this developed Galesburg's largest industry, and made George W. Brown a local magnate, who later built for the Methodists an impressive church across the street from his big plant.

Thus we have the farmers raising corn and hogs on their farms roundabout, while in the village there were stores that would take their crops in pay for supplies, and factories making the implements they required for their work, at first one-man shops, the proprietor doing all the labor. A sort of industrial rhythm was established.

But there were also minor industries, needful and picturesque, as the town swung slowly from individualism to division of services and labor, and among the contributors to this field was that amazing family, the Ferrises.

## VII

### THE FERRISES

The major difficulty in getting a picture of life a hundred years ago in an obscure Western settlement is the meagerness of the information found in the letters they wrote and the diaries they kept. These yield surprisingly little of what might be called facts, but much of their concern with religion. There is scant information about their daily lives, what they ate, wore, did, but exhaustive accounts of sermons, eulogies of the dominies, and descriptions of deathbeds. It was as you might say a sort of fashion to exchange such lugubrious missives, but it is baffling and exasperating to one seeking information.

The letters the Ferris family wrote to one another are refreshingly different. There are no pious apostrophes, but full accounts of their own worldly affairs, and as such they are revealing—true historical documents. From them we get a glimpse of the machinery by which a colony is set up and started on its way, but unfortunately this family with such a healthy attitude toward its new life was not particularly articulate, and wrote comparatively few letters that have come down to us.

Twenty-five Ferrises went West, a little colony in itself, and the number was augmented in the course of nature to fifty-four in three generations, at the head of which stood old Silvanus, sixty-four years old, something of a patriarch. But it was more than mere numbers that he added. They all brought a little wholesome freedom of action and independence of thought into a community that tended to be a bit too strait-laced and pious for human endurance. The Ferrises did not consider this world, or even the Galesburg colony, solely as an antechamber to heaven, which was a good thing; it leavened the whole lump.

The oldest son, also a Silvanus, but known by his second name, Western (after the village where Gale made his first essay in manual labor), apparently farmed his land in the orthodox manner, and did not figure greatly in the social and business affairs of the village. But that humdrum life did not appeal to the active and restless mind of his brother, Olmsted. He had never been merely a farmer, even in New York, but followed the wider path set by his father in dairying and selling cheese. He experimented with fruit culture, cut fine timber, spruce for ship-building, bird's eye maple for pianos, and shipped it to New York. He was one of those temperamental Jacks-of-all-trades which once diversified the economic pattern of the small towns of the country.

When he learned that glass, builders' hardware, and white lead were the only materials used in construction that the colony could not produce, he bought a supply and shipped it out. He also took workmen with him, a carpenter and a helper, who likewise became colonists and added a technical personnel much needed at the beginning. Having foreseen as far as possible all his needs, he set out with his wife, who bore the piquant name of Concurrance Ann, and his three children, carrying a teacupful of timothy hayseed, and proceeded to add a few colorful chapters to the history of the town.

Arrived at the colony, he helped his brothers set up the sawmill his father had brought from New York, built his own house, and planted his land to timothy. He also tried canary bird seed, and mustard, threshing them by methods of his own invention, and sending them to market, but neither enterprise paid. We have already learned with what success he helped to introduce the first sheep. But his high romantic adventure was popcorn.

When Olmsted learned that this popular American delicacy was unknown in England, he planted sixty acres, and took twenty barrels to London, when he went abroad with a load of fine cattle to sell. He gave a demonstration in the metropolis and popped his corn before the eyes of the astonished Britishers like a second Walter Raleigh smoking the first pipe. The stir attracted the attention of the Prince Consort, which resulted in an invitation to Windsor Castle to pop corn for Queen Victoria.

Olmsted was duly coached by officious friends in what to wear and how to approach a queen—in dress and address. He had boasted in London that everything he wore except the linen in his shirt had been raised on his Illinois farm, and the shirt might have been included if he, like some of his neighbors, had raised flax. History has failed to preserve an account of his court dress, but when he was ushered into Victoria's presence he forgot his carefully studied lessons in court etiquette, and greeted her majesty with Western simplicity and heartiness. The Queen forgave him—she was evidently "amused"—and was soon absorbed in his demonstration of the corn that turned to snow on the application of heat. When the Prince asked how such corn might be raised in England, Olmsted replied:

"By importing a shipload of Illinois soil."

The outcome of this visit was one of the fairy tales of Galesburg for half a century. The Queen asked about his family, and when she learned he had a daughter, and that he would accept no gift for himself, she sent him for the little girl at home the most magnificent French wax doll with real hair that any child in Illinois had ever beheld. Imagine the sensation of such a toy on the prairies. It was cherished for years so solicitously that it seems actually to have mouldered away. The moths ate its hair, its arms and legs came off, and were divided among descendants of the original owner. Some of its fragments are still cherished in a California home.

Back in Galesburg, Olmsted could not subdue his restless, adventurous spirit to farming, and at the outbreak of the gold rush joined the Forty-Niners, and died of an accident in California. His son Silvanus, true to the pioneer tradition in the blood, was one of the founders and promoters of Riverside, California, that earthly paradise to which so many good Galesburgers go before they die.

William did not settle on the farm his father deeded to him, but upon his "ten acre" lot, adjoining the village across the road from the cemetery. Here he lived a variegated existence. He kept cows, sold milk, and followed the ancestral skill of cheese making. The barn he built was the largest in the region, a landmark down to the days of the motor car. He dammed Cedar Fork—not without some protest from settlers below him—and cut ice and sold it. The pond was the young people's skating rink, the only body of water in the town. He was not only the town's first milkman, but its first iceman, and this conjunction of the necessary ingredients led to ice cream, then unknown in the Middle West.

There was one undertaking which ran so counter to the avowed principles of the community that it is significant of the independent character of the Ferrises, or at least of William, and that was the wine press. He planted much of his land to grapes, and made port, which was mellowed in huge casks stored in the cheese house. No intoxicating liquor could be legally made or sold in Galesburg. Every deed contained a restriction to that effect. William's deed originally contained this clause, but shortly after passage of the law it was repealed for lands outside the village limits, which let William out technically, if not morally. His wine was used by the churches for communion ceremonies, which may have atoned in the eyes of the deacons and elders, for strange to say, although William was cited before the session for various delinquencies, his wine making is not mentioned in the church records. When the Ferris sawmill was "raised" Paris Richardson got drunk, not, it was proved, on liquor furnished by the hosts, and was expelled from the church.

Corn whisky could be bought at the groceries of Knoxville and Hendersonville for two bits a pint (legal price) and no doubt was bootlegged into Galesburg at an early date, and probably William's port was drunk as a beverage by his fellow colonists. At any rate, William drank it, with a few of his boon companions, accompanied by raw oysters imported in square tins from Maryland. One gets a glimpse of the affectionate esteem in which William was held from his popular name of Uncle Billy. He used it himself in advertising "Uncle Billy's Ice Cream."

Henry Ferris had some of the versatility of his brother Olmsted, but he was more of a craftsman, with a light touch on a fruit scion or a tool. He started on his 640-acre farm—the only Galesburg farm still in the hands of descendants of an original settler—built his house with his own hands, making brick on the place. He raised sheep, no doubt from the stock introduced by brother Olmsted, and stored wool in his house in a room with a hole in the ceiling through which the wool was tramped down. Soon he moved to town, sent his children to the college, and became with his long beard a sort of Galesburg worthy, popular, easy-going, respected, grafting fruit on his children's orchards, raising grapes and drying them in the attic to make raisins. He loved to sit beside the furnace in the cellar and whittle out axe helves. He was expert with leather, had a cobbler's bench, and made harness. When his foot was mangled by the tumbling-rod of a threshing-machine, he made the special-shaped shoe to fit it.

He never became rich, but was always well-to-do, putting money in an organ factory and losing it, investing in insurance companies which were bankrupted by the Chicago fire. He was one of the first stockholders in the Burlington Route, but sold before the road began to pay dividends. It was his habit to give each of his sons a gold watch with his name engraved on it, and each daughter-in-law a piano.

Old Silvanus took up his residence in the village at the beginning, built a comfortable house which became the rallying place of the clan, particularly on Sundays, in the recess between the two church services, when cold luncheon was served, in two sessions, the children waiting, to all the Ferrises, town and country. The faithful Sally, matriarch of the Ferrises, who had accompanied Silvanus on two migrations, died, and the patriarch married the most distinguished widow in town, mother of the Hitchcocks, one a professor, another the wife of a professor. The grandchildren married until, as Professor Churchill once remarked, it wasn't safe to repeat a bit of gossip about them to any one in town as more than half the community was related to the Ferrises.

The truth is the Ferrises were not keen about church and the counsel of perfection at which the more devout among the colonists aimed. George Washington Gale Ferris, the youngest son, joined the church along with the whole body of colonists that spring morning at Log City, and apparently remained quietly within its portals until he took his letter and moved to Nevada where his son invented the Ferris Wheel first operated at the Chicago World's Fair; his brother Henry did not unite until 1838, and was finally expelled for not walking with the church. Silvanus, the father, was two years in the colony before he joined, and William became a member only after a year, doubtless through stress of public opinion. Neither Western nor Olmsted became members, and none of the wives except Mrs. Henry. No Ferris served as deacon or elder, as men of such prominence naturally would had they been active in the church. They were in fact moderns, more advanced than their fellow colonists, taking much the attitude of most church members today, that church

was a good thing and should be supported, but reserving the right
to decide matters of personal conduct as they saw fit.

## VIII

### SOCIAL LIFE

It must not be thought that life in Galesburg was all religion,
however hard the puritan element sought to make it so. Human
nature is about the same everywhere, and at all times, and no
godly fascism has ever succeeded in permanently squeezing it
into one pious mold. Practically every one joined the church,
such was the strength of public opinion, and theoretically at least
subscribed to its rather bleak conception of life, but as time went
on independent souls, such as the Ferrises, refused to have their
lives ordered by elders, and shook themselves free, or when they
failed to satisfy the church authorities, were dismissed.

Then there were the young people, always a step ahead of their
elders, the children who came with their parents in the covered
wagons, and those born later, growing up in the village and
beginning to think for themselves. The strictness of the original
regime relaxed with each successive generation, chiefly in what
constituted legitimate entertainment. Opportunities for amusement were few, not only because of the strait-laced attitude of the
village fathers, but also because of the primitive, unorganized
state of the little commonwealth itself, remote from the ordinary
diversions of civilization. But they found their amusements, as
youth always will, some legitimate, others natural, though it was
one failing of the puritan church that it recognized so niggardly
the inborn need for recreation.

One of the younger set has left a lively record of his boyhood,
in which he says the only amusements were pitching horseshoes,
hunting prairie chickens, and watching the stage come in from

Peoria. Games played with apparatus were particularly forbidden because of association with gambling. There was not a deck of cards in the colony. The billiard "parlor," honorable competitor of the livery stable as the men's club of country towns, was successfully suppressed for years. A law forbidding ninepins was evaded by adding one pin to the set-up, and thus the game of tenpins was invented. One irate father, when he found his sons playing checkers with red and yellow grains of corn, smashed the home-made board crying, "You may go straight to hell if you must, but not with my connivance." Honest horseshoes, however, apparently escaped the inquisition.

Hunting, like war, has always enjoyed the sanction of religion. Game was plentiful on the prairie; prairie chickens, wild turkey, even deer, often gave variety to the menu. A popular sport was "snipe bagging," snaring quails by means of a net shaped like a long funnel on a frame of hoops, with spreading wings extended a hundred feet, one end centering in a trap. Taking advantage of the bird's habit of running along the ground when driven quietly, great quantities of quail were herded into the net. They sold for a penny a bird ready to cook.

The wolf drive was another form of sport having a utilitarian end. Wolves were so numerous the state placed a bounty on their scalps. For the drive elaborate organization was required. The area was sometimes two townships. Captains were appointed for each facet of the territory to be beaten, about five miles. Each captain manned his line closely to prevent a wolf slipping through. The lines, with a total length of fifty or sixty miles, gradually approached an agreed-upon center, marked by a pole with a flag, and the wolves dispatched at the focal point by another crew.

A dramatic event on Main Street—to Galesburg what changing the guard at Buckingham Palace is to London—was the arrival of Frink & Walker's four-horse stage from Peoria. Thrice a week at three o'clock, when it arrived at the junction of the Knoxville road with Main Street, Clarendon Palmer leaned down, inspected the "insides," and uttered his stereotyped warning, "You better put away them cards, and hide your flasks, and keep from swearing if you kin; this is Galesburg, the pious teetotal abolition town."

The guard wet his lips preparatory to a merry taratantara on his long horn, Palmer gathered up the reins, and horses that had jogged all the way from Knoxville were whipped to a spirited gallop for the grand entrance; the pupils of the brick school on Main Street lined up in front to watch a scene which never palled, and the coach dashed lickity-split down the street, splashing the black prairie mud right and left, scattering the cattle, pigs, and chickens in the road, right past Kellogg's Galesburg House to the post office in the square, where the mail was dropped, then around the square and back to the hotel, before which it drew up with a mighty "whoa," and the passengers descended for supper.

The Galesburgers did not travel much, they had work to do and little money to spend, and lack of transportation made travel no pleasure trip. In compensation a panorama of the world came to their doors. Across the prairie which stretched from the little town in every direction there streamed for years long lines of covered wagons, the prairie schooners on their billowy green ocean, "ten, fifty, a hundred in sight at a time, followed by herds of cows; while women and children, their hair bleached by sun and weather, rode seated on beds, or plodded on foot beside the slowly creeping procession."

They were hopefully on their way to lands farther West across the Mississippi—Iowa, the Dakotas, Kansas and Nebraska—or returning, beaten, bringing stories of the tragedies of the plains, water famines, Indian massacres, cholera, slaughtering cattle for food, burning wagons for fuel. In 1849 the caravans took on a new character; these were the gold seekers, with "California or Bust" lettered on the wagon tops. They camped beside the town, and the hungry were fed, the sick cared for by villagers who had made their own trek so short a time before.

It brought to the sequestered Galesburgers, particularly to the children who had known no other life, a breath of the great world outside.

"The impression upon our life of this great stream of foreign humanity flowing by our door day after day, month after month, was inexpressible," says one who played as a girl beside the trail from the East to the West. "An animated scene surely, not without its solemnizing influence. . . . Here were hundreds of strangers daily passing our door, favoring us with the most novel and picturesque colloquialisms from Pennsylvania, Ohio, and especially choice expressions from Posey County, Indiana. We became expert philologists and ethnologists, young as we were, able to tell at a glance, or certainly after hearing the peculiar tones and pronunciation of certain stock phrases, just what locality our travellers hailed from, and any one of us could have written a very readable book on the manners, customs and dialects of the peoples inhabiting the region of the Illinois River, without having ever stepped out of our own township."

Of theatrical spectacles there was none. Stern parents bitterly opposed the stage along with the circus and other diversions of more sinful communities. People flocked to the public exhibitions of the college, particularly the "open meetings" of the two literary societies, like all public exhibitions held in the Old First Church. There they filled the gallery and sat on the high window sills, through long, dull, amateur orations and debates for the sake of the final "colloquy," as it was called to avoid contamination of association with the drama. These were skits written and acted by the students, most of whom had never seen a play or read one.

For these mild forms of theatrical entertainment, a cambric curtain was hung on wires stretched across the stage, and here were given the strictly moral entertainments by visiting talent, such as the Hutchinson family, the Riley Sisters, the Swiss Bell Ringers, and lectures. When the young Adelina Patti made her appearance in a concert with Ole Bull, those in the gallery were treated to an extra. After each song, as Patti left the stage, the old violinist, waiting in the wings, greeted her with a hearty kiss, supposing himself out of sight of the audience. But the primitive lights threw the artists' shadows on the backwall, and those in the gallery saw the scene in gigantic silhouette.

The three gala days of summer were training day in the spring, Fourth of July in mid-summer, and election day in the fall. These holidays in which the whole community and the countryside participated were interspersed with smaller outings, church picnics in Gale's Grove, berrying parties—the prairies were carpeted with strawberries and the woods teemed with blackberries—raisings, quilting bees, and the gatherings that cornhusking and other harvest duties entailed.

It is doubtful if they read much. Both Gale and Kellogg brought back from their soliciting trips to New York collections of books for the college libraries, five hundred and seven hundred respectively, but what they were cannot be ascertained, though in all probability they were collections of orthodox sermons, dull and unreadable. Among the papers subscribed for were *The Independent, The New York Observer, The Evangelist,* and *The New York Express,* all religious weeklies, and Horace Greeley's *New York Tribune,* but as soon as the town had its own paper, the news from the East, three weeks old, was served up in its columns with appropriate comment.

One diversion they had was music, which flourished at an early date under the tutelage of Leonard Bacon, who came twice a week from Geneseo to conduct a singing class. He later moved to Galesburg and became the leader of the choir. The choir sat in the gallery, and rather surprisingly was accompanied by melodeon, bass viol and violin. The congregation rose and turned around to face the choir, and with fascination watched the near-sighted Bacon lead the singing, play the violin and sing the tenor part at the same time.

There were of course the simple hospitalities of a small community, visits exchanged, "company" to supper, even when dishes and furniture were lacking. There was no standard of living to maintain; they were all in the same boat; if chairs failed the company sat on the bed, boxes or trunks. But abundant meals were always in evidence, though Eastern luxuries were hard to come by. It took five bushels of corn to buy a pound of sugar, and the same quantity of wheat to pay for a pound of tea.

The Hoosiers followed their quaint custom of coming over in the morning with all their children and spending the day, examining everything with frank curiosity, fingering it and asking the cost, and expected the same curiosity in return. When they found the Yankees did not reciprocate, they ceased the only form of hospitality they knew. A Hoosier philosopher remarked that as long as settlers lived on bear meat and corn bread they were all equals, but when a family rose to home-raised meat and flour bread, it became proud and put on airs.

## IX

### RELIGION

One of the group which was young in the forties has left a picture of the harrowing experience of those religious blights which the elders describe in their sanctimonious phrase as a "season of abounding grace."

Says Erastus Willcox:

"Outside the stern necessity of making a living by daily labor and the primal object of giving their children a good education, three vital questions dominated their lives—the questions of temperance, abolitionism and conversion of lost souls, this last first and foremost. . . .

"We had in those days revivals every winter, as part of a regular winter's course, prayer meetings before breakfast, at noon, after school, and sermons served to us hot every night; everybody on hand, everybody expected to stand up and give testimony."

The first teacher of the village school was a pious young ascetic named Van Meter. He succeeded in persuading his little charges, not without threats of future fire and brimstone, to devote their noon hours to prayer meetings. For some weeks, all the time not occupied with gulping down their lunches those boys spent on their knees confessing their sins. The teacher managed to convince them that indulgence in play or sport of any kind was unchristian, and the Gospel-scared little prigs stood around at recess in conscious virtue with their hands in their pockets to keep them out of mischief, until one day the sight of a haystack in Deacon Holyoke's yard next door was too much for them. One made a rush and turned a somersault; others followed, and soon the haystack was demolished and the spell was broken. There were no more school prayer meetings and immolations. They managed to act more like normal boys.

"I would not again go through the terror, the torment of soul I suffered for four or five years after I began to pay attention to sermons, not even to save my own—well, not for anything, for anything," he adds with feling.

It would seem that in so chaste a community, an organization to preserve the purity of morals was the last thing needed, but a number of the young women, eager for some sort of self-expression, organized the Galesburg Female Reform Society in 1842 for combatting licentiousness and the violation of the seventh Commandment. It at least gave them an opportunity to talk about such topics. This society was national, probably a circulation scheme of *The Moral Advocate,* a newspaper devoted to case histories of fallen women, which was read at the meetings, and money raised to subscribe for extra copies to distribute where they would do the most good. At one meeting, the minutes testify, "The confession of Lucretia Cannon, an abandoned woman, was read, which produced a thrilling effect."

The secretary observes (rather regretfully) in reviewing the work of the past year (1845) "Though we have not been called upon to mourn the fall of any members of our society, yet some circumstances lead us to apprehend that there have been recent outrages upon the cause of moral purity within the bounds of our congregation."

[ 167 ]

The boys spoofed at their earnest sisters; one of them wondered how much anxiety there was in the moral reform society over the *good* boys like "Sel" Gale, "By" West (stern Nehemiah's son), "Hank" Sanderson (whose father was the innkeeper), John Colton (offspring of Chauncey) and "Nels" Finch, nephew of the Reverend George Gale, who was what a later generation would call a bit sporty, and who successfully foiled the attempt of the session to discipline him by proving he never joined the church. The Moral Reform Society lingered until 1847, with steadily diminished attendance, and finally lapsed, its purpose no doubt achieved, or else its field grown beyond its powers.

Most people have heard of the Gideons, whose ambition it is to place a Bible beside the bed on top of the telephone directory in the rooms of all hotels which are not persuaded their guests had rather have the morning paper. It would seem that the Galesburg colonists anticipated this mild propaganda by fifty years. In 1840 John Leonard, secretary of the Knox County Bible Society, reported that a copy of the Scriptures had been placed in every room of the taverns of the county.

# 6

## *Schism*

### I

### THE ENTERING WEDGE

On that fateful Friday morning, fateful so far as the religious peace of the colony was concerned, when the church was organized in Hugh Conger's log cabin at Henderson Grove, the gathered company contained almost as many Congregationalists as Presbyterians. Because of that peculiar arrangement known as the Plan of Union, by which the two denominations shared a church and pastor back in York state, it was difficult to differentiate them by their Eastern connection. It was this which led Deacon Simmons (who was "born a deacon," his daughter said) to suggest a similar compromise in the about-to-be-organized conventicle. But no, said Gale, Presbyterians were more numerous, better organized, in better odor, and therefore in a better position to help a struggling college. It was, he decided, expedient to organize the church fully as Presbyterian. And it was so done.

That was a tactical error on Gale's part, and cost him many bitter hours in the years to come. The difference between the two denominations was so slight as to be indistinguishable to the naked eye. Substantially, Congregationalists were independent units, while Presbyterian churches were bossed by Presbytery, which in turn was bossed by Assembly. Also Congregationalists heard causes and examined new members in the presence of the church, while among Presbyterians these things were attended to by the elders. On such slight technical matters of opinion a church and college were nearly wrecked.

For a season all went well. There was plenty of preaching, long, solid sermons—which was what the colonists wanted—by Gale, Waters, Kellogg, Blanchard, and a succession of pastors. The joint arrangement was a practical solution as long as no issue arose to divide the membership. But such an issue did arise, and the members took sides according to their convictions.

The issue was slavery. It was already a moral as well as political issue throughout the North, but warmer in the states bordering the South with an admixture of Southern sympathizers, such as Illinois. The disposition among conservative Northerners, even when opposed to slavery on political or economic grounds, was to keep quiet and not stir up what all realized was a question that might easily disrupt the Union. But those who saw it as a moral issue would not keep silent; they kept the issue fresh. And the Galesburg people were among these. They were fanatically abolitionist.

The Congregationalists were more outspoken than the Presbyterians, for the latter were linked by their Assembly with Southern churches whose members were slave owners, and whose preachers defended the institution of slavery. To the Congregationalists such a situation was intolerable. They insisted the Presbyterians cut loose from their Southern brethren and disavow their sinful co-religionists. But the Presbyterians were not prepared in the 40's and 50's to go so far. And the friction in the Galesburg church was a constant source of irritation, aggravated by the further fact that there was too much Presbyterianism in the church government for Congregational stomachs.

The Congregationalists felt that the promises made them at the organization had not been kept. Lucius Parker, the pastor while the new church was being erected, leaned toward the Congregational side, and led his faction in the revolt already mentioned, which stopped all building for nearly two years. These rebels refused to go on with the work, or pay their subscriptions unless concessions were made. The demand was granted, a compromise arrived at, and in 1845 the church was re-organized along the lines of the Plan of Union.

This action was but a partial cure. The slavery question kept bobbing up. Norman Churchill was clerk of the church, a forth-right outspoken chap with no patience for compromises. His son, much like him, was for fifty years a professor in the college, where his pungent comments were a delight to his students. The elder Churchill, knowing that it was the custom of the Presbytery to review the church books, inserted this dig: "Should Presbytery examine the church records, and such is their usual procedure, it is reminded that this church is rampant Congregational—it claims the privilege of dotting its own *i*'s and crossing its own *t*'s, and will submit to no Presbyterian domination in the matter."

It was much too rampant for the Presbyterian half. In 1851 they withdrew and formed the First Presbyterian Church of Gales-burg, with Gale as pastor. The rump, now almost wholly Con-gregational, did not immediately alter its allegiance or change its form of government. Instead, it continued to pester Presbytery about slavery. After much back talk, it asked to be dismissed from the denomination. Presbytery refused. The church then voted itself out, reorganized with all the Congregational church paraphernalia and called itself the First Church of Christ, but known as long as it lasted as the "Old First Church."

The seceding Presbyterians made capital of the fact that the old church hung on to the property, the building, the site—which had been deeded by the college to the "Presbyterian" church—and the cemetery. The old church got around this by calling its legal organization "the Presbyterian Society," and stood pat. This was not the end, but the beginning of the war between the denominations. It involved the whole village, as it naturally would, its population being members of one or the other of the two sects, and religion a live topic. It spread to the college, just beginning to get on its feet, but with great promise in the near future, for a railroad was already under way.

The men who led the fight in the church were the men who were trustees and professors in the college. The division there was along the same lines. Was Knox College a Presbyterian or a Congregationalist institution, or was it a union of both? Gale was the forefront of the Presbyterian claim. Hadn't he founded the town, the church, and the college? Surely he ought to know what form of religion was to run them. And then arrived the man who was to give the schism national publicity and Gale his most formidable opponent, a man as intolerant and dominating as he, but abler, more energetic and with more moral courage. This man was Jonathan Blanchard, the new president.

In Cincinnati Blanchard had been a Presbyterian. It was this as much as his eminence and influence that made Gale so eager to have him as president of the college. He counted on Blanchard's support in keeping down the Congregational quota. But when Blanchard reached Galesburg he sided with the Congregationalists. He was always more concerned with moral causes than denominational differences. He sympathized with the zealous anti-slavery attitude of the Congregational party. He was pastor of the Old First Church when the Presbyterians quit and formed their own church. He found himself opposed to Gale not only in the church but in the college. It was not that Blanchard wished, as was charged, to make the college exclusively Congregational, but that he was opposed to making it exclusively Presbyterian. The issue was fought on all fronts, in the church, in the college, in the home, at Colton's store, wherever the townspeople met, for fifteen years.

The open break came two years after Blanchard's arrival. In 1848 at a meeting of the college board, Gale tried to strengthen the Presbyterian side of the house by the election to the board of his son Selden and his friend Orville H. Browning, a lawyer of Quincy, later Senator from Illinois and Andrew Johnson's Secretary of the Interior. On their election, because of its implications or from the discussion which accompanied it, Blanchard resigned. The resignation was first accepted; then after considerable wrangling, withdrawn. Instead, the legality of the meeting was successfully attacked on the ground that all members had not been properly notified. The election of Selden Gale and Browning was thus annulled.

At the next meeting of the board, Gale and his following finding themselves in the minority, bolted, leaving the board without a quorum. When two of the seceders cautiously returned to see what would be done, the moderator counted them present, declared a quorum, and proceeded to elect trustees favorable to the Congregational side, one of whom was that Norman Churchill who had "sassed" the Presbytery. This new board passed resolutions endorsing Blanchard's administration, which evoked written commendations from a large number of citizens, and expressions of approval from the student body.

This meeting was followed by one in the fall, which Gale and his party refused to attend. Resolutions were passed declaring it inexpedient for a man to be a member of both faculty and board. It was further resolved that Gale had never been elected a professor, that he had never given satisfaction, that he had brought suit against the trustees, was hostile to the president, and wound up with an uncompromising demand that Gale resign from the faculty of Knox College. This Gale declined to do. He had in mind a more drastic answer. The trustees did not convene again for seven months.

II

THE MIND OF A ZEALOT

Credit must be given Gale for his sincerity. His errors were of the head, not of the heart. Outside of religion he was a kind man. He believed he was fighting a holy war. He believed his faith the only true one. He had lost control of the church, but he was determined that in the college religion should take precedence over all considerations, and that the religion should be Presbyterianism.

Already the town he had founded, which he had visioned as united in one form of worship, was being broken up into sects. Surrounded by Campbellites and Methodists, and other "heretical superstitions," new religions were also boring from within, recruited from the very people he had selected.

Just before the final explosion in the college board a group of Baptists asked for the donation of a lot on which to build a church. It was a natural request; a lot had been given the original church. But the request was refused, and the Baptists even had difficulty in buying a lot, and obtained one by the ruse of negotiating through an unsuspected third party, who deeded the land to the church.

Worse than that, from Gale's point of view, there were in the colony, and among the original settlers, in spite of Gale's watchfulness, a number of Universalists, particularly in the Conger and West families, that he himself had enlisted, and these people had not only organized a church in Galesburg but were building a college.

His was the sort of mind that is intolerant of all forms of Christianity except its own. He once described Congregationalism as "that peculiar religion." Universalists were particularly obnoxious, as well they might be, for they knocked the corner-stone right out from under his beliefs. His whole scheme of salvation rested on a realistic hell. In his missionary days he spoke of converts from rival religions as being "saved."

Toward Methodists and Baptists he was condescending rather than intolerant. He tells of "converting" two Baptists while still preaching in New York. They were sisters, and in deference to the prejudices of their parents he agreed to baptize them by immersion, the critical tenet of the Baptist creed. "Accordingly a convenient place in the creek where there was no ice was found, and I immersed two of the daughters in January. No evil ensued, no colds were taken by them or myself, but we do not consider that any miracle was wrought." There is a touch of grim humor about that last phrase which is rare in Gale's writings.

# SCHISM

When Gale was sixty-six, he began to write his memoirs, though from the circumstantial details much of it must have been originally written at the time it happened. The autobiography was "for the benefit of children, or rather for their satisfaction in time to come." This was in 1855, after the controversy with the Congregationalists had got under way, but the manuscript— it was never published—ends abruptly in 1834, just as his plan for a Western colony was maturing. There is every indication that he meant to complete it—in fact, it may have been undertaken solely to justify his course in the events here narrated—and its abrupt termination suggests two alternatives: it was never finished, or his account of the most exciting episode in his life was suppressed by his hand or another's. Thus we are deprived of his own version of the difficulty which darkened the closing years of his life, and which might have put him in a better light than the record, largely prepared by opponents, seems to do.

To see Gale only in the throes of a religious controversy is to get a one-sided impression of the man. He could be genial and even humorous, and many anecdotes of his kindness and amiability linger, which seem utterly to belie his truculence and bitterness over matters of belief. His house was surrounded by a large apple orchard. Two mischievous small boys, Asa Matteson, later a leading banker, and Miron Rhodes, who became one of the principal merchants of the town, crawled through the hedge and filled their pockets with apples. To their horror they saw the old gentleman coming slowly down the path carrying his habitual long cane. They both climbed a tree. Gale stopped beneath it, waved his stick threateningly, and said:

"Boys, come down."

They came down.

"Follow me." He led them up the path to the woodshed, where he confronted them sternly.

"Empty your pockets of those apples." They did so.

"Now, boys," he said, "those are not the best apples. The best apples are on this tree near the house. Whenever you want apples, you come to me and I will give you all you want. Now, fill your pockets with these, and go home."

There is an anecdote told by John P. Gulliver, fifth president of Knox College, which credits Gale with real wit:

"It is related that Professor Gale putting up at an early tavern was inquired of by the landlord thus: 'Stranger, I perceive you are a clergyman; please let me know whether you are a Presbyterian or a Methodist.'

" 'Why do you inquire this?' said the traveller.

" 'Because I wish to please my guests, and I have observed that a Presbyterian minister is very particular about his own food and bed, and a Methodist about the feed and care of his horse.' "

" 'Very well,' said the professor, 'I am a Presbyterian, but my horse is a Methodist.' "

It is not apparent that Gale had much interest in literature. In the autobiography mentioned only twice does he speak of books. Once, that as a boy he read the *Catechism, New England Primer,* Bunyan's *Pilgrim's Progress, Robinson Crusoe,* Goldsmith's *History of England,* and Campbell's *Overland Journey to England.* The other instance is more illuminating. While Gale was living at Western, after his southern trip, teaching theology in return for farm work, the spiritual welfare of the village was in his opinion imperilled by a wealthy distinguished infidel, General William Floyd, one of the signers of the Declaration of Independence. Floyd was a man of good principles and habits when he came to Western, says Gale, but on his trips back and forth to look after his property on Long Island, he discovered among some books left on the Hudson River sloop a copy of Thomas Paine's *Age of Reason.* He remonstrated with the captain for allowing such a dangerous book on board. The captain defended himself, insisting that the book had been left without his knowledge. Floyd said that he would take charge of it and see it was properly destroyed. Instead, his curiosity got the better of him. He read it, and his faith vanished; he became a convert to its errors:

"That the profane jests and ribaldry of such a man as Paine should have such an effect upon the mind of a man trained to believe in the Gospel . . . a man of education and refinement . . . regarded as fit for a place in the . . . Congress . . . that declared our Independence, is a remarkable circumstance and one which exemplifies the dangerous tendency of infidel books and the danger of tampering with such publications. . . ."

Note the sequel: General Floyd's widow became blind, and was at length converted through Gale's ministrations. She told him her blindness was a blessing in disguise, for otherwise she might have read the book so fatal to her husband, and likewise lost hope of eternal life!

The board's anti-Gale resolution charged that Gale was self-appointed to the faculty of the college, which was true. He was no doubt disappointed that there was no insistence that he be president. He assumed one of the professorships, though he had little qualification for it, and even less liking, except for the inculcation of moral precepts. He selected moral philosophy as being along the lines of his interest, and belles-lettres, negligible from the point of view which prevailed in those days.

The point is that Gale was not an educator, not interested in education in any real sense, nor in young men except as possible instruments for the spread of the Gospel. He was founding a college to create ministers, not to educate youth. His attitude toward his own children was singularly detached and lacking in warmth, as may be learned from his own words.

Although he devotes dozens of pages to his sensational conversions, such as Burchard's and Finney's, he dismisses the birth of each child with a line. On one occasion he writes, "being detained downtown I returned home to find my wife had been prematurely confined; the child, if living at birth, died soon after." Only once does he allude at length to any of his children, and this seemingly to point a moral. Young Josiah had the croup and nearly choked to death. The doctor advised bleeding, which strangely enough relieved the little sufferer. "He was but just saved," dryly remarks the father; "whether this will prove a mercy I cannot say. If he comes to Christ that he may live forever, it will; if not, better have gone then, for of such, said Christ, is the kingdom of heaven."

All his life Gale had been a sufferer from his dyspepsia and this undoubtedly colored his outlook. His attacks of illness frequently interrupted his class work, so much so that recommendation was made in faculty meeting that he provide a substitute. All these things were mounting up against him, as the conflict in the college board grew in bitterness, and were used and exaggerated by his enemies. Nevertheless he clung tightly to his position on the teaching staff, and paid no attention to the request that he resign. Instead, he started legal measures which set the clock back.

### III

#### EDWARD BEECHER

During the seven months before the board again met, Gale and his party entered suit attacking the legality of all meetings held since April 27, 1849. Whether this suit resulted in a court decision, or whether its mere threat of the disastrous consequence to the college was sufficient to produce action, the contending parties came to some sort of a working agreement.

This agreement was substantially that all action of the board since and including the meeting of April 27 should be declared null and void. Such action would cancel elections of trustees by means of which the Congregational element had been running things to suit themselves. It would likewise wash out the reproof coupled with request for resignation directed at Gale. The meeting was outwardly amicable; no votes were recorded against any of the names, which included trustees friendly to both sides of the controversy. Blanchard was re-elected president, Gale voting for him; he also voted for the executive committee, which for the first time since the college was founded did not include his own name. Although he acquiesced in the actions of this meeting, Gale evidently took it hard.

Blanchard was now pastor of the church as well as president of the college. He was a good executive. The college flourished under him as it had not yet done. His peculiarities, his outspoken invectives, his narrow and bigoted views did not disturb the elders. They were merely a more vigorous expression of their own attitude. The students recognized his real ability, and tolerated his truculence, as students do. One of them testified that "Blanchard has done more towards building up, establishing the reputation of, and procuring suitable buildings and instructors for the college than any other member of the board."

With Gale absent from board meetings, and performing his professorial duties perfunctorily, and with frequent absences because of ill-health, Blanchard's stock rose as Gale's fell. While on the face of it, all was going well, it was evident that the personal quarrel between the two principals was growing more bitter, and that Blanchard was steadily increasing the Congregational majority in both board and faculty. Blanchard was the better fighter, more courageous and more open, and he was in the best position, young, able, and successful, while his opponent was sick and aging, and the prestige rightfully his as the founder and originator of the entire project was crumbling in the sight of his fellow men.

At this juncture another personality was injected into the situation, to add to the interest and drama of the schism. In 1855 forty-seven persons were dismissed from the Old First Church to form a second Congregational church, later known as the "Brick Church."

This second Congregational church called Edward Beecher— "the most level-headed and sane member of the famous Beecher family," says John Burgess—and the call was accepted. No Beecher could possibly keep out of a theological row anywhere in his vicinity, and Edward was soon in the thick of this one.

Edward was the son of Lyman Beecher, brother of Henry Ward and Harriet Beecher Stowe. Before his father took hold of Lane Seminary at Cincinnati, where Finney and Weld, as well as Blanchard, were students, Edward had gone to Illinois to take charge of the college at Jacksonville, a hundred miles from Galesburg. There he lived in what is now Beecher Hall, and went through a three-year struggle to get a proper charter from a hostile legislature, one of whose members boasted "I was born in a brier thicket, rocked in a hog trough, and have never had my genius cramped by the pestilential air of a college." Four years later the petitioners for Knox encountered similar hostility.

There were other parallels. Illinois was also founded as a manual labor school. There were farms and shops where the students worked for their board and tuition. Illinois had gone through just such a struggle as was now jeopardizing Knox, and between the same two denominations.

Besides the college difficulties, there was the slavery question. Beecher was an ardent abolitionist, a friend of Elijah Lovejoy. He attended the convention, the call for which was signed by many Galesburg men. He was at Alton later to help his friend install his third press on which to print *The Observer* that so inflamed the Alton citizenry. Lovejoy was shot defending the building in which the press was installed, after Beecher, thinking the riot over, had gone back to Jacksonville. Otherwise, hated almost as thoroughly as Lovejoy, he might have been murdered too.

Among the students was his younger brother Charles, who came out in 1833, to add to Edward's troubles in characteristic Beecher fashion, asking to be excused from Saturday evening prayers to go hunting, and being suspended for "repeated disorders tending to disturb the worship of God in the chapel." When Edward went to the church at Galesburg, he persuaded Charles, who had been expelled from his ministerial association for attacking slavery under the title, "The Duty of Disobedience to Wicked Laws," to become professor of rhetoric at Knox—or possibly persuaded the trustees to accept him. Rhetoric meant elocution.

One of Charles' classmates was Newton Bateman, the "little schoolmaster friend" of Lincoln, who revolutionized education in the state of Illinois as minister of public instruction, and served as president of Knox for twenty years.

Beecher went East in 1844 to raise funds for Illinois College. There he received a letter signed by friends of the college who deprecated his abolition activities and advised him not to return. He promptly resigned and went back to the quiet and peace of Boston. He was preaching at the Salem Street Church when called to build up the new "Brick Church" at Galesburg. So now he was back again on the prairies only to find Galesburg at least as strenuous as Jacksonville had been.

Of Beecher's stay in Galesburg there are many legends. His house on Beecher Avenue was a station on the Underground Railroad, that secret system by which runaway slaves were spirited from below Mason and Dixon's line to a haven in Canada. The house joined at the back that of William Patch, an old friend of Brooklyn days, the first Galesburg conductor on the infant steam railroad. Beecher liked his dry conversation, and used to stroll over there Sunday afternoons, to the scandal of the puritans of a community where ministers do not visit on the Sabbath.

Hs was as absent-minded and unconventional as his great father. He drove to church from his house on the outskirts of the village, and more than once stalked up the aisle to his pulpit with his hat on and his buggy whip in his hand. When Gad Colton, proprietor of the Novelty Works and a local magnate, appeared in church with his third wife, not long after the death of his second, Beecher found in his pulpit Bible an old notice which he thought fresh. He carefully adjusted his glasses and read out with solemn emphasis, "The funeral of the late Mrs. G. D. Colton will be held at the family residence at three o'clock Monday afternoon."

One Sunday after reading his text, he pushed his spectacles

up on top of his head with a characteristic gesture. Forgetting them, he took another pair out of his pocket, and later pushed them up, and then a third, until his head was covered with them, like a Roman helmet. He could not preach without a handkerchief; when he found he had forgotten it, his wife got up and laid hers on the pulpit. His persistent roguishness was always cropping out. Finding a hole in the handkerchief, he held it up before his face and peeked at the congregation through the hole.

Such things endeared him to the younger members, but he had plenty of seriousness, and he could be indignant and even vindictive on occasion. He was 53 years old when he came to Galesburg. He had married Isabella Porter Jones, who bore him eleven children. Four of his sons attended Knox College, and one of them, Eugene, afterwards taught there.

Sociable, unconventional, Edward Beecher added much to the life of the little town, where he was a favorite topic for conversation. A fighter, a Congregationalist and a militant abolitionist, he soon was in the thick of a controversy that had its beginning in Congregational opposition to slavery. Meanwhile the college, over the destiny of which the two parties fought, had become more of a prize than ever because of economic development in which its holdings were still large.

## IV

### "OLD MAIN"

In 1854 the first train on the new railroad rolled into Galesburg, bringing prosperity in its wake. The college lands boomed, and out of the profits of more sales, higher rents, and rapidly increasing population, the college erected two important buildings, which for the time were magnificent. One was the main college for the men students; the other the seminary for women.

The main building was placed in the center of the north half of the campus, so that it was flanked by the two long, low dormitories already erected. The sentinel-like towers were crenelated in a manner faintly suggesting a fortified castle. Incongruous as this may seem, it was highly acceptable scholastic architecture, and the building had a quaint charm which has persisted and increased through the years. Although this time a professional architect was employed—in fact, several—it was still the achievement of the entire community, and the village was as innocently proud of it as of the church it had built with its own hands. It was the brick and mortar symbol of their cherished dreams. In that tiny town, with its two hundred white houses scattered over the prairie, the group made an imposing appearance.

The building had four doors, one in the center of each side, connected by broad halls, which crossed in the middle and divided each floor into eight classrooms, a large one and a small one in each quarter. One half the second floor, extending up into the third, was the chapel. On top was a Greek temple which housed the bell.

The labor of keeping it warm was great. In the center of each lecture room was a huge barrel stove, with a coalbox the size of a small piano standing beside it. Each morning the janitor filled these boxes, eighteen or twenty in all, and in the five-minute recess between the classes each professor stoked his fire. Water was drawn from the pump in the college yard, with a rusty cup attached to it by a chain.

The seminary building at a discreet distance the other side the college park was planned as both dormitory and school. The central part was five stories, with two wings of four stories each. There were bedrooms for forty, with classrooms, a chapel, and all the equipment of a complete institution. The main entrance was in the second story, and a massive flight of steps with bulky balusters led up to it. These were the edifices which the sale of college lands at increased prices made possible. For the first time since its founding the college was prosperous, and equipped with buildings ample for its material needs.

The corner stone of the college was laid in May, 1856, and on

SCHISM

July 7, 1857, Charles Ulrichson, of Peoria, the architect and builder, turned over to the trustees the completed building. The seminary was finished the same year, and both were highly praised in the *Illinois Teacher,* though Editor Sherman of the *Galesburg Free Democrat* took exception to the architectural fitness of the belfry.

The assets of the college were now $400,000. There were four hundred students. The senior class, adding the women from the female department, totaled forty-nine, of whom twenty-three completed their courses. Everything was set for a prosperous future. With all things favorable, its progress was now imperilled by the absurd controversy as to whether its destinies were in the care of one denomination or another.

V

THE BLANCHARD WAR

It was referred to afterward as "the Blanchard War," though with more justice it might be called the Gale War. The crisis between the Congregationalists and the Presbyterians had now reached the critical stage, aggravated by the personal quarrel between the two leaders.

Blanchard had the backing of the solid business men in the board, as well as the moral support of the minister of the Brick Church, the irrepressible Edward Beecher, who, while he had no connection with the college, mixed in as if he had. Gale was supported by his personal friends, Browning and Knox, both lawyers and both from outside of the city; Silvanus Ferris, who had ably seconded his work of founding the college; and Doctor Bunce, Ferris' son-in-law.

The older settlers had great sympathy for Gale, remembering what he had been. They saw in him the founder of their village and college, aging and broken in health, carrying on a losing fight for the sake of a shadowy issue, clinging desperately to his power and importance and prestige. But they knew that

Blanchard was an able man, in his prime, building up the college, which had never been so flourishing. The town cared little for the nominal basis of difference, whether the college was Congregational or Presbyterian, even less for the animosity between Gale and Blanchard, and everything for the success of the institution. It deprecated the disastrous effect of the publicity on the reputation of the college, but revelled in the excitement and scandal and gossip of the fight, which was discussed in all its bearings at all gatherings for years.

On Wednesday, June 27, 1857, the day before commencement in the quaint brick building known as Williston Hall, the trustees assembled for their annual meeting. The sittings were evidently open to the four winds of heaven, for some of the students were interested and critical spectators. Townspeople were there also, among them the Reverend Edward Beecher. "Beecher," says the indignant Browning, "walked into the meeting armed with Jefferson's Manual and acted as counsel for Blanchard during the meeting."

A full board was present. Blanchard was in the chair. The air was charged with suppressed excitement, as if something were about to happen. The customary prayer was offered, and God must have smiled as he noted the passion and hatred in the breasts of some of the trustees. After a few preliminaries, the real purpose of the meeting burst forth. It was suggested as a solution to end the trouble that both disturbing parties resign for the good of the college. A committee was appointed to pass on the proposal consisting of Browning, Knox, Withrow, Colton and Bascom, three for Gale and two for Blanchard. Browning presented the majority report in the following resolution:

"Resolved, that in the opinion of this board the dissension and want of confidence existing between President Blanchard and Professor Gale are exerting a malign influence upon the interests of the college, and that the prosperity and efficiency of the institution require that their connection with it should be dissolved and their places supplied by other persons. Therefore, be it further resolved, that President Blanchard and Professor Gale be and are hereby respectfully requested to resign their places in the faculty of Knox College."

The Machiavellian duplicity of this resolution does credit to Browning's skill as a lawyer, for it should be borne in mind that resignation from the faculty, where he was already discredited and under fire, did not impair Gale's position on the board, but it severed Blanchard's entire connection with the college.

The minority report by the propitiatory Bascom begged for a separate consideration of each man, deprecated linking the resignations in this manner, insisted that the circumstances of the two were utterly different, one strong, able and competent, the other aging and infirm, and appealed to Gale's better nature, pointing out the debt and respect the community already owed him as the founder of the institution, and urging him to increase that debt and respect by resigning spontaneously and alone.

Flavel Bascom, who had considerable influence on Knox College and the Old First Church at Galesburg, was one of that "Yale Band" which breathed the breath of life into Illinois College at Jacksonville. He was born in Cincinnati, 1804, graduated from Yale, ordained in Lincoln's Sangamon County, and came to the Galesburg church in 1850, just in time to be plunged in the denominational controversy which set two groups of Christians by the ears.

The debate that followed coruscated with fireworks. Blanchard defended himself with the eloquence and skill of a man trained in verbal warfare. He pointed out the "heads-you-win, tails-I-lose" nature of the resolution. He criticized Gale's shortcomings as a teacher, said he had not met his classes ten weeks in the past two years; charged him with influencing students to stay away from Knox in order to discredit his, Blanchard's, administration. He told how he had been approached by Bunce before the meeting and offered a year's salary to resign quietly, and that he spurned the offer. He intimated that Knox College had not been founded by Gale, that the idea had originated with Gale's protégé and pupil, Theodore Dwight Weld. He hinted at Gale's well-known carelessness in regard to money matters, and explained why he would not agree to Selden Gale as treasurer of the college, as Gale had once suggested.

Gale retorted that Blanchard's unpopularity kept students away, that Blanchard was a "scheming politician," that he, himself, had paid for substitutes for his classes out of his own pocket though not required to do so; that he was the founder of the institution, and "stood in the same relation to it as the inventor to the invention, that his right was as clear as that of Mr. Morse to the telegraph; "he would rather see the college in ruins than Blanchard the head of it; he would accomplish his ends if thereby he dragged down the whole college, because he could build a better upon the ruins." He charged Blanchard with lying by the hour, as guilty of things he would not pollute their ears by reciting. Thus it went back and forth to the edification of the students present. Some perhaps were reminded of their Vergil, "are the wraths of celestial minds then so great?"

Some suggested that the seniors would refuse to appear at commencement if Blanchard were deposed. "Then they will not receive their diplomas," shouted a Gale partisan. "They already have them," Colton informed them. Bunce, whose son was a senior, dryly observed that *one* student would graduate. It was all intemperate and pitiful, and revealed little of the moral philosophy that Gale had been teaching all these years.

After an entire day spent in wrangling, with the cooler heads pouring oil on the waters, the resolution was adopted, eleven to ten, two of the trustees declining to vote—one of them poor Nehemiah Losey, one of Gale's earliest disciples, torn between two loyalties. In accordance with the decision, Gale and Blanchard resigned from the faculty. Gale had at length attained the end for which he had labored and schemed relentlessly for ten years.

The effect on the student body was galvanic. The two "literary" societies, Adelphi and Gnothautii, met in ten-hour sessions, formally approved the action of the senior class in refusing to graduate, wound up their affairs, turned their property over to the care of trustees, and "resigned from the college." The senior class refused to appear on the commencement platform—with one exception. As his father had prophesied, Charles Bunce was compelled to deliver his oration, which he did to the accompaniment of mild heckling from his classmates among the audience. The rest of the commencement program was filled in with an address by Beecher, who had two sons in the recalcitrant senior class.

"Beecher, who had made himself very unbecomingly officious in the matter," as Browning recorded with vindictive fury in his diary, "gave some twaddle on behalf of the others."

In August, 1857, appeared a memorial from the alumni of the college, urging the restoration of Blanchard on the ground of his competency, the injustice of his removal, and the detriment to the college, signed by twenty-three graduates of the college. This was followed by a protest that the memorial did not correctly represent alumni sentiment, signed by four graduates, to which Southwick Davis tartly replied that only seventeen out of eighty-eight alumni were opposed to Blanchard.

During the following summer appeared a strange bit of literature, a pamphlet or magazine, *The Students' Farewell,* issued by former members of Old Knox, 1857 (printed by J. H. Sherman at the Galesburg book and job print). It opened innocently enough with two essays, one a dissertation on "The Earthly Triumphs of Christianity." Like the scorpion, its sting was in its tail. This was a long diatribe, simply headed "Editorial," commenting acidly on the recent upheaval, signed with the names of nine students, led by Francis Bruner, who later became president of a neighboring college. The little book was for sale all over town at ten cents a copy.

The writers had evidently been present at the board meeting. Their accounts were set down more in sorrow than in anger, though patently biased in Blanchard's behalf. Their narrative has been drawn on for some of the light and shade in the foregoing account of the meeting. In fact, most of this narrative is taken from the heated words, colored by antagonism of partisanship on both sides, for we are more concerned to give the spirit of the controversy than to arrive at the truth about its cause, which is trivial and unimportant to a degree.

Of the strictures on Gale, the most damning was a charge of dishonesty in the conduct of his classes. It was asserted that he issued examination papers consisting of what might be called leading questions—some of the questions answered; answers to others implied in the questions—the object being to enable his classes to make a creditable showing, and thus refute Blanchard's charges of incompetency as a teacher. Extracts from the examination papers were printed in confirmation.

The article contrasted the characters of the two principals. Blanchard was fearless and outspoken. Every one knew where he stood. He was against slavery, intemperance, circuses, horse races and billiards; no one knew how Gale stood on these questions. It quoted the venerable John Waters, one of Gale's earliest adherents, now turned against him, asserting that Gale never paid any real money into the college, but always managed to trade out his share; that Gale had brought about the resignation of Kellogg. It hinted at irregularities in the handling of college funds, and explained that this was why Blanchard had opposed Gale's son as treasurer of the college.

It was a partisan document and even libelous, but whether it was considered a mere students' prank like burning down an outhouse or putting the janitor's cow in the chapel, or whether it was overlooked in the general uproar, there is no record that legal action was taken, or even that those responsible for it were disciplined when they returned to the college, as they did, though at this time they must have believed they had left for good.

So great was the outcry raised over the forced resignation of Blanchard that some of the trustees tried to induce the opposition to agree to retaining him one more year, to win back as many students as possible. The executive committee, its majority anti-Gale, realizing fully that the welfare of the college was at stake, used to the full its executive power and made a private arrangement with Blanchard to remain one year (it is not mentioned in the trustees' records) and in a circular to the striking students, dated August 21, 1857, was able to announce:

"We are happy to inform you that the causes which led many of you to withdraw from this institution are now so far removed as to present no serious obstacle to your return. President Blanchard has consented to resume his former place in the faculty, by invitation of the executive committee, and the place of Professor Gale will be filled by an experienced and successful teacher."

The trustees provided against a repetition of any such independent action as Colton had taken in retaining Blanchard without authority from the board by electing an executive committee entirely Presbyterian. Further, smarting under student criticism and resentful of Beecher's intrusion, it voted to hold all future meetings with closed doors.

Blanchard resigned, as he had agreed to do, when his year was up. He moved to Wheaton, Illinois, and organized Wheaton College, over which he presided until his death. On his eightieth birthday, at a celebration in his honor, a paper written by him was read, in which he summed up his estimate of his contribution to Knox:

"I found the college in debt $5000, and running behind five dollars a day. I credited the treasury with more than $6000 given me . . . by J. W. Williston. I received from Judge Charles Phelps . . . eighteen quarter-sections of land, which sold for $30,000, and by rigid economy saved the college lands, . . . from being sacrificed. I wrote the college diploma, procured the college seal (established) a library; graduated thirteen classes, and left Knox College free from debt, and worth $400,000. When I resigned . . . the board employed me at an advanced salary, to teach another year, and graduate the next class, which I did."

# SCHISM

## VI

### THE BEECHER CRUSADE

The search for a new president prolonged the struggle. Presbyterians now had the whip hand, and were bound to have a president of their sectarian stripe, but the other faction managed to block action by the same tactics their opponents had inaugurated, refusing to attend the meetings, depriving them of a quorum.

Five men, all ministers, were proposed and all rejected. Bascom sadly called attention to the compromise for which they had all voted, agreeing to ignore denominational lines, but now that the Presbyterians were in the saddle, they no longer needed it. Sanburn made the wisest suggestion, which was to secure a college man for their president, and proposed Professor Haven of Amherst, a scholar experienced in college ways and the science of teaching. It would allay some of the rampant sectarianism which had been their chief concern for fifteen years, but this too was rejected. Gale and his party were determined to have the Reverend Harvey Curtis, a Presbyterian minister of Chicago.

Meanwhile Beecher was requested by a committee of forty-one influential Galesburg citizens to make a public statement of the troubles in Knox College. Beecher responded with a two-hour address in his church before a thousand people, exalting Blanchard with all the silver-tongued Beecher eloquence, excoriating Gale and his allies with a virulence only Blanchard himself could have equalled. The expulsion of Blanchard was "moral assassination"; "could no more be defended than if they had poisoned or stabbed him," the proceedings which disbarred him were "atrocious acts of dishonesty and injustice," "deserving of disgrace and infamy"; "I leave Mr. Gale to the just judgment of God."

At the conclusion of this impassioned address a motion for a vote of thanks was received in silence. But when Selden Gale rose, gave Beecher the lie, rebuked him for his intemperate statements, and denied his assertions, the audience burst forth in long continued applause. Nevertheless, the address was printed in the *Free Democrat* and widely circulated.

Shortly after a manifesto appeared in the paper signed by sixteen reputable college students and citizens of Galesburg, testifying that they had been present at the session of the college board at which Blanchard was deposed, that they also had heard Beecher's address, and that the latter's description of what took place in the board meeting was not only strictly true, but characterized by fairness and moderation, though "moderation" seems hardly the right word for it.

Beecher took his address and delivered it in Chicago, where *The Northwestern Christian Advocate* found it "painful." Beecher called on J. W. Patterson, a Presbyterian tycoon, and proposed arbitration of the mooted question, and later reported that Patterson claimed Knox College belonged to the Presbyterians. Patterson flatly contradicted him, of course in appropriate Christian language. Beecher's statements, he said, "were utterly untrue," although Patterson's elaborate explanation did not altogether support that unqualified statement. What Patterson said he said was that if the college belonged to any denomination, it should by rights be Presbyterian.

Beecher visited other towns and spoke at length on the "moral assassination of Blanchard," and the untrustworthy character of Gale and his adherents, particularly Browning, Knox, and Bunce. He invaded Quincy, Browning's city, and spoke in the church of Horatio Foote, a Presbyterian minister, a Knox trustee and a Blanchardite. At the conclusion Browning asked permission to reply. Foote refused to allow his church to be used for such a purpose.

Thereupon Browning wrote a long refutation for the Quincy *Daily Republican,* which showed him as expert a master of invective as Beecher. Beecher's address, he said, "was distinguished for blasphemy and a fiendlike malignity"; his statements "wholly fabrication containing not one word of truth"; he was a "sanctimonious hypocrite," "disgorging venomous scurrility," with the

"sneaking cowardice inherent in the character of a slanderer."
His address was "sixteen columns of coarse vituperation." The
writer had heard that Beecher intended to usurp the presidency
of the college; if attempted "legal aid will be invoked to protect
the college from the degradation of the Reverend Edward
Beecher, D.D." Browning later replied to a charge of scurrility,
that he wasn't any more so than Beecher, who left him hardly
any epithets to use.

The Peoria Presbytery met at Galesburg, at the end of this
hectic summer. They spent two days going over the alleged facts
of the great controversy. The deliberation resulted in a scathing
denunciation of Beecher "as unworthy of our confidence and
Christian courtesy as a minister of the gospel." Beecher, of course,
was a Congregationalist, and not amenable to the Presbytery,
but he complained loudly of the action as tending to damage his
Christian standing.

Next came the battle of the books. The Congregational body
in the state, the General Association of Illinois, made an investigation. Its committee approached the trustees for information, and
were told in polite diplomatic language to mind their own business. None the less, they continued their work, going over the
history of the founding of the college with a fine-toothed comb,
searching out the denominational source of every dollar that had
been contributed, conning the papers and documents to ascertain
the intent of the founders, and while it is utterly unimportant at
this late day, it seems probable that the original purpose was a
"non-sectarian institution under Presbyterian control." The neat
and readable little pamphlet put out by the Association was entitled, *The Rights of Congregationalists in Knox College.*

The Presbyterians countered with their broadside, also a neat
pamphlet, more readable because better written, not any more
convincing—it is astonishing how many sides truth seems to have,
even in the hands of devout Christians—entitled, *Knox College,
by whom Founded and Endowed,* denying most of the contentions of the previous one and putting the figures in a new light.

Its author was John W. Bailey, pastor of the Galesburg Presbyterian Church, and Gale's successor on Knox faculty as professor of moral philosophy and belles-lettres.

The Congregationlists came back with still another pamphlet, *Report on Knox College,* not so well printed nor so entertaining, which put the matter back about where it was in the beginning. This exchange of broadsides might have continued indefinitely, had not the Civil War intervened and turned all men's thoughts into more serious and important channels.

The greatest value of these three pamphlets is that between them they give the most complete and detailed history of the founding of the college in existence. They quoted from documents that have since perished, and thus serve a useful purpose wholly beside the inconsequential one for which they were issued.

Beecher's popularity in Galesburg does not seem to have been impaired a whit by his mixing in on the college fight, or the hard words he used. He remained for some years, until the conflagration was extinguished, in fact. In 1866 he became a member of the Knox board, taking the seat left vacant by the resignation of Matthew Chambers. During the progress of the controversy his people were building a new structure, "the Brick Church," which was no sooner completed than it was blown down by a hurricane —Gale must have thought it the act of an outraged God—and rebuilding was started at once. Beecher's brother, Henry Ward, came out to help, and delivered a course of lectures about the State which netted some $3000. The new church still stands. When in 1895 the two Congregational bodies reunited, tore down the Old First Church building, and erected a more pretentious structure, the Brick Church was acquired by the college and became Beecher Chapel.

## VII

### KNOX'S THIRD PRESIDENT

The search for a new president went on under difficulties. Gale went East on a hunt for a man; Beecher sent a letter to *The Inde-*

*pendent,* which that paper printed, warning the public not to place confidence in Mr. Gale, whose conduct in removing Mr. Blanchard was "unwise, dishonorable and unjust." But Gale had no expectation of finding his president in the East. He was already impressed with Harvey Curtis. He knew exactly how Curtis stood. Gale's son Selden had received a letter which left no room for misunderstanding.

"I have known Mr. Blanchard since our college days," the reverend gentleman said among other things. "I used to think highly of him. . . . But at later periods . . . he has developed traits of character which have sunk him lower in my estimation than any other minister I ever knew. . . . Under cover of professions of eminent piety and zeal for God and truth and righteousness, I have seen and heard more vindictive malice and slander and demagogic plotting to carry personal ends than from all . . . other ministers I was ever acquainted with. . . . I have heard from him statements and insinuations and charges directed against old Doctor Lyman Beecher and Henry Ward Beecher which would make Doctor Edward Beecher's ears tingle were he to hear them. . . ."

On Gale's return the board convened and elected Curtis, 13 to 11. At his installation the following commencement (1858) Curtis referred at length to the denominational difficulties, championing the cause of Gale, which brought Beecher to his feet with a reply that gave to an otherwise dull ceremony an unexpected liveliness.

Curtis' administration was so colorless that little about him has gotten on the record. He was succeeded by another dominie, also a Curtis, but no kin to his predecessor, the Reverened William Staunton Curtis. These two men carried on the college for ten years.

These were the war years. Most of the students went to the front; the war on the home sector occupied the thoughts and labors of all, including those so recently at each other's spiritual throats, for the war between the States came home more closely to Illinois than to any other northern commonwealth.

Thus ended Galesburg's first, greatest and, it can be said, practically its only family quarrel. The point at issue was unimportant,
has no significance today, and the account of it could be omitted
without garbling the history of the college, as has been done generally in the past. It is valuable as a picture of the seriousness with
which sensible men took mere matters of technical doctrine, and
the passions aroused in even Christian breasts over a sectarian difference, which has caused many bloody wars in world history.

September 21, 1861, the Reverend George W. Gale died sud-
denly of a stroke. At the next meeting of trustees, "Doctor
Bunce moved that a committee of three be appointed to report a
memorial in regard to the death of the Reverend George W. Gale;
objections being made, the motion was withdrawn." The founder
of the college was the first trustee whose death was not recognized
by the customary "resolutions of respect." However, the board
elected William Selden Gale, his son, who had been elected and
unseated during the height of the controversy, the action which
had precipitated the crisis, to fill the vacancy caused by the death
of his father.

George Washington Gale lies in Hope Cemetery, the burying
ground given to the Presbyterian church he founded by the college he founded, and retained by the Congregational church when
he marched out with his Presbyterians to establish a church of
their own. On his tombstone in the peaceful village of the dead
lying two blocks from the public square one can read his epitaph:

*Si requiris monumentum—circumspice.*

# 7

## Burlington Route

### RAILROAD ORGY

No chapter in the history of the Northwest Territory is more significant than the railroad chapter. Until the advent of transportation, the wealth of its productive soil was locked up. The settlers who had been lured by the pioneer spirit, the perennial hope of bettering themselves, or dreaming of a new kind of civilization minus the evils of the older towns, found themselves for twenty years marooned on their fertile acres with no means of moving their produce except rivers remote from their farms, and at best roundabout ways to profitable markets. One need consider the history of but one railroad, and its effect on but one small town to get an inkling of the transformation wrought on the prairies by the advent of adequate transportation.

Some intimation of the bounty showered on Galesburg, in quadrupled population and the boom that provided two substantial buildings for the college, has already been given, but the means by which the railroad was procured, why it is where it is, is a saga in the history of this indomitable prairie town which must be told. For just as they solved the problems of cultivating a new kind of soil by inventing the necessary implements, so by their own initiative they obtained the means of shipping the fruits of that soil to Eastern markets. But before they had reached the point of thus working out their destiny, they were given an impressive object lesson in the wrong kind of railroad promotion. The State itself embarked upon a blundering and disastrous move to provide transportation on a scale so ambitious it fell by its own weight. This foolhardy attempt, born of ignorance and graft, delayed constructive development for twenty years.

In 1830, twelve years after receiving the accolade of statehood by padding its census returns a bit, the Illinois legislature at Vandalia was pondering the subject, and weighing the comparative merits of water and rails, with the triumphant success of the Erie Canal and the problematic workings of the crude railroad experiments on the Atlantic seaboard as its inspiration and guide.

The growth of the State thus far had been conditioned by its physical geography. Almost surrounded by navigable streams, with a great lake touching its upper left-hand corner, settlement had naturally clung to its margins, principally in the south and west, leaving the better interior land unpeopled and virgin to the plow. The aim at the outset was to connect the interior with the rivers, which in their minds would always be the chief means of transportation. Confiding settlers believed the towns strung along the Ohio and Mississippi—Shawneetown, Golconda, Metropolis, Cairo, Cahokia, Kaskaskia (the first capital of Illinois), Alton, Oquawka, Galena—were destined to be great cities.

Cairo was as big as Chicago, and many expected the village at the junction of the Ohio and the Mississippi had a better chance of becoming the metropolis of the West than the village on Lake Michigan. Boom followed boom in Cairo, but nothing could raise it from its swamp. Rumor says Dickens invested some of the money poured out so lavishly to hear him read his books in its alleged possibilities, and lambasted it in *Martin Chuzzlewit* because it failed to live up to its prospectus. There were many such boom towns; Oquawka was one; speculation in land was prevalent in all settlements, and the hope of realizing some of these dreams spurred the legislative move to cover the State with railways.

The roads the earliest settlers found were the Indian trails such as the Sauk Trail by which the Galesburg colonists had come from Detroit to Illinois, considerably older than white civilization.

The Military Tract, in fact, all Illinois and the whole Northwest Territory, was criss-crossed with these trails, engineered originally by buffalo moving in herds with irresistible force, finding the best way with uncanny instinct. The Indians appropriated these traces, usually running between convenient fords at the watercourses, and by constant use made them fixtures in the landscape.

One such trail ran diagonally across the high prairie between the Illinois and the Mississippi rivers. It started at the Indian village on Peoria Lake and crossed the Spoon at Amaquon, a village of some importance where burial mounds still exist. Over this road a service by stage was set up between Peoria and Galesburg, with extensions to Fort Armstrong (Rock Island) and Oquawka, the spirited arrival of which contributed to Galesburg's early entertainment. So crooked was it that a wag who made the trip insisted it had been laid out by two men, two horses, a plow and a jug of whisky. Some of the early wagon roads were paved with planks, and there was a mild speculation in wooden turnpikes, which answered fairly well and proved profitable to their promoters. On the completion of one in Fulton, the county adjoining Knox, the joy of the inhabitants expressed itself in a gala celebration with speeches and fireworks.

But the people were clamoring for something better. They knew little about canals and nothing at all about railroads (nor did any one else at that time), but they did know that their deep black soil became deep black mud in wet weather, incapable of supporting anything on wheels, and that hard roads of some description must be provided to move settlers in and produce out. They were right in believing that transportation was the supreme need of the hour, but they made a disastrous mistake in trying to do the whole job at once.

No one foresaw how completely railroads would alter lines of travel, what they would do to water-borne traffic, how they would snatch wealth and growth from river towns and create new centers in the midst of prairies remote from watercourses. The famous Erie Canal, which did so much to people this country, believed to be the last word in transportation, has in our time become extinct and decently buried. Railroads were still looked upon as little more than substitutes for rivers, to supplement and connect them, and it was still an open question whether even for that a canal was not better.

The legislature had already authorized a canal to connect Lake Michigan with the Illinois River, but in Baltimore there was a primitive railroad in actual operation, and James Bucklin, engineer of the canal, went East to look at it. When he came back he was a railroad man. He advised accordingly, and estimated a railroad could be built for $25,000 a mile, while a canal would cost $100,000.

But this was a water era. Governor Duncan stood back of the canal, and clinched his position with the argument that even if the canal was closed by ice in winter, so was the lake, and thus no harm would be done. The canal was built, but it came too late. Its greatest service was in settling the lands along its right of way; it did that before it was completed. But long before it was ready for traffic, the legislature launched a plan of railroad promotion that would have gridded the State from end to end with iron roads having more mileage than in all the rest of the country combined.

This fantastic scheme, known as the Internal Improvement Act, provided for more than 1300 miles of railroad construction. A north and south line was to connect Cairo with Galena—where the earliest settlers found lead and Lincoln found Grant—with a branch to the terminus of the Illinois and Michigan Canal, and four east and west lines at strategic points, the whole to cost twenty million dollars, or $268 for every family then living in the State. Nearly every county would get a piece of railroad, and a bonus was to be divided among counties omitted in this comprehensive program. As it turned out, these were the only counties benefited. Work was to be pushed with the greatest dispatch; construction to begin at both ends of each section and at the crossing of all streams. Among the legislators who voted for this pioneer pork barrel was the representative from Sangamon County, Abraham Lincoln.

In 1841 the bubble burst, saddling the State with a debt of fourteen millions, with nothing to show for it but a stretch of completed railway from Jacksonville to Meredosia twenty-four miles long, of wooden rails strapped with iron, known as the Northern Cross. The rails were sixteen feet long, 5/8 of an inch thick, and 2½ inches wide. The ends were bevelled, which made them sharp. They often curled up and penetrated the car, sometimes killing a passenger. These sinister hazards that rose startlingly through the floor were known as "snake heads." The cars had long slippery seats on each side, like a street car, along which the passengers slid back and forth. Bump-producing link-and-pin couplings were used. In winter the hose connecting the water tank with the boiler sometimes froze, and was thawed by starting a fire beneath it with wood from the tender.

Over this line in 1838 passed the first engine and train to move on rails in Illinois. Engines, like ships and canal boats, had names in those days, and this historic locomotive was called "Rogers." A previous one built in the East and shipped by water was lost in transit and never heard of again. "Rogers" gave so much trouble the company often wished it also had been lost. It was finally sold, and mules installed as motive power, thus getting back again to first principles.

## II

### THE PEORIA AND OQUAWKA

By 1850 the upper Mississippi valley was ripe for transportation. Iowa had become a state; gold had been discovered in California; labor-saving farm machinery had been produced in answer to the demand from the prairies; nothing was needed but railroads to carry the grain and live stock of the West to the markets of the East. The cornucopia of the Military Tract was ready to become a horn of plenty. The good burghers of Galesburg, who had lost neither their vision nor their courage, were among those who realized the time had come for the West to fulfill its destiny.

Transportation was as essential to Galesburg as any place in the State, but during the time that Illinois was going through the throes of its premature railroad boom the colony had been too greatly occupied in establishing itself on the land to take much interest. None of the railroads contemplated by the Internal Improvement Act was planned to enter Knox County. Colonel William McMurtry of Henderson, its representative at Springfield, had wisely chosen the cash, and with it the county had thriftily built the new courthouse that still stands at Knoxville, an engaging example of the Greek revival in the architecture of public buildings which prevailed at that period.

As an instance of the difficulty of even ordinary travel, there is a story in the diary of Orville H. Browning, who completed Stephen A. Douglas' unexpired term as United States senator, and to whose wife Lincoln wrote the famous letter humorously describing his love affair with the fair but fat Mary Owens. Browning will be recalled as one of Gale's most active adherents in the religious controversy over the control of Knox College. In order to attend a meeting of the trustees he left Quincy at eleven in the morning on the river steamboat *Westerner* and arrived at Keokuk at four. Next morning he drove around the rapids to Montrose by coach; at ten took another packet to Burlington, and arrived at four o'clock in the morning. There he remained all day, and the following night until one A.M., when the *Jenny Lind* carried him to Oquawka by daybreak. From there he took the stage coach to Galesburg, and arrived at ten o'clock that night, the itinerary occupying three and a half days, now covered by train in two hours and fifteen minutes.

With railroad speculation in the air, Galesburg was bound to think of it as a solution, though what stirred it to action was a movement elsewhere accompanied by an unfriendly gesture from Knoxville. In 1849 the legislature granted a charter to the Peoria and Oquawka Railroad for a line connecting the Illinois with the Mississippi. Peoria was a village that had grown up where the Illinois widened into Peoria Lake, the site of Fort Creve Coeur and of a large Indian settlement. Oquawka lies on the Illinois side of the Mississippi just where the river makes a great bend to the east above Burlington. It is hardly bigger today than when the farmers of the Military Tract hauled corn and pork to its wharf to catch the New Orleans steamboats.

It had once indulged a dream of pioneer grandeur. Among the early lithographs bearing the magic signature of N. Currier is one seldom sought by collectors. It is an ambitious plot of the city of Oquawka, extending sixteen blocks down the river and ten inland, with quays, fish market, public square, churches and schools. The town showed signs of becoming a place of importance. An immense traffic left its wharf for shipment down the river. All steamboats stopped there. Governor Duncan invested $50,000 in its prospects. But the boom never materialized. Now once again opportunity knocked at its door, but Oquawka failed to respond. Otherwise railroad history would have been different, and its quaint Indian name might have become the nationally-known sobriquet of a proud railroad system, as is that of its nearest neighbor, Burlington.

A bee flying from Peoria to Oquawka would pass but a few miles south of Knoxville and Galesburg. By modern standards both towns were on the line. Galesburg was incensed, though possibly not surprised, that Knoxville devoted her energies not to securing the road for herself, but to keeping Galesburg off. She had influence with the legislators at Springfield, while Galesburg was still a Whig abolitionist pariah among the prairie towns of Illinois. The Quincy *Herald* referred to "the little nigger-stealing town of Galesburg." The contest was bitter; all the old animosity flared up. To the moral, social and political differences between the inhabitants of the two villages was added the economic, for Knoxville was shrewd enough to guess what would happen once those energetic Yankees got a railroad. That town would outgrow her, and her hold on the county seat be put in jeopardy. She would almost rather have no railroad than have Galesburg share it.

The Peoria and Oquawka was capitalized at half a million dollars, and its promoters were unsophisticated enough to believe it could be built for $8000 a mile. Considerable money was raised, and construction planned to begin at both ends, after the example set by the Internal Improvement fiasco, but both ends were slow in getting started. The delay was at the western terminus, for Oquawka failed to raise its contribution of $40,000.

Lest she have no railroad at all, Peoria started still another venture, to be known as the Peoria and Mississippi, designed to go through Farmington and strike the river at Warsaw, another shipping port on the river. This venture got as far as Farmington, when the original group got the kinks in its charter ironed out, and built as far as Elmwood before its money was exhausted.

Burlington was a small settlement on the Iowa side of the Mississippi with no connection but an uncertain ferry. Nevertheless, taking advantage of Oquawka's defection the town raised a substantial guarantee and became a contender for the western terminal. The controversy between the towns lasted a year or more, and was conducted with all the clumsy sarcasm of prairie journalism of the time, when newspapers contained little more than personalities. The Burlington *Telegraph* spoke of the "main line" to Burlington; the Oquawka *Spectator* explained that Burlington "was opposite the end of the eight-mile branch." However, grading was actually begun at a point on the bank across the river from Burlington, and the road, or a road, actually constructed as far as Little America.

You will look in vain on the map for Little America; it is now known by the commonplace name of Kirkwood. In poking about in early Illinois history one finds that many names bestowed light-heartedly by the pioneers were changed later by smug busybodies unable to appreciate the humor and raciness and sometimes significance of the original appellations. Thus Yellow Banks became

Oquawka, in this case a change for the better; the Indian name, an Algonquin word, meaning "yellow earth," is far more distinctive. But Warsaw once rejoiced in the delightful cognomen, Spunky Point. John Hay—it was his birthplace—tells with amusing spleen how some idiots read Jane Porter's *Thaddeus of Warsaw,* a book that had great vogue in the fifties, and decided Warsaw was more genteel than Spunky Point. Hay hopes that every man concerned with the outrage is called Smith in heaven.

Meanwhile another line bobbed up to add to the confusion and increase the excitement. In Quincy the old charter of the Northern Cross Railroad, relic of the Internal Improvement, under which had been built the pioneer line from Merodosia to Jacksonville, since then extended to Springfield, was submitted to the legislature for amendment and came back equipped with a peculiar roving commission popular in those days. The company was given authority "to build a lateral branch from some point in Adams County and running thence on the most eligible, beneficial, expedient, and practicable route through the Military Bounty Tract, and terminating at or near . . . the southern termination of the Chicago Canal, *provided* the said company shall not locate or construct the said branch upon any line east of the town of Knoxville in Knox County." Stripped of legal verbosity it meant that the road was to go to Knoxville before turning east, and leave Galesburg five miles off the line.

John Denny, whose family later founded the city of Seattle in the State of Washington, was the Knox County representative at Springfield. He owed no allegiance to the troublesome Whigs at Galesburg, who had voted against him almost in a body. He was quite willing to do whatever Knoxville wanted. He managed to have the Peoria and Oquawka charter amended to establish the line through Knoxville and Monmouth—Galesburg's rival on the west, missing Galesburg by three miles.

Thus three prospective railroad lines hung dangling in the air, one from Peoria, one from Quincy, and one from the river bank

opposite Burlington, all headed in the general direction of Knoxville and Galesburg, with no money to go farther, while the two
villages wrangled and schemed and pulled wires to join their
loose ends in their respective communities. Knoxville had the advantage. The charters gave her both roads; she had the backing
of the Hoosier legislature, and the sympathy of nearly the whole
of Knox County. But she underestimated the resourcefulness of
those Yankees. The Galesburg men were spurred to an action
that determined the territory and route of one of the country's
great railroad systems.

### III

#### THE CENTRAL MILITARY TRACT

In 1850 Galesburg, a mere hamlet of 882 souls, was spoken of
in the college catalogue as being on the "main stage line between
Peoria and Oquawka." "Hendersonville and Galesboro are small
villages a few miles from Knoxville," says *The Emigrants Guide.*
Twelve years before, the ground on which it stood had been
unbroken prairie. The men who founded the town were still
alive and active in the conduct of its affairs. They were not
captains of industry or financiers or promoters, but simple, pious
pioneers who had learned to work together for a common object
by assembling at log-raisings to help rear each other's houses.
Every one of Galesburg's 882 inhabitants was greatly excited over
the possible advent of a railroad, but among the more active were
a few who took the lead and brought the enterprise to a triumphant conclusion.

Among these were George W. Gale, now grown old, touchy
and irritable, harassed by the religious controversy at the college;
his son Selden Gale, a much better business man than his father,
who had married Silvanus Ferris' daughter, adding another link
to the tie that bound the Gale and Ferris families. Silvanus
himself, now 75, was keenly interested. His activity in the

promotion was represented by his sons, Olmsted, William and Henry, and his son-in-law James Bunce, the pioneer doctor. President Blanchard as head of the college, largest land-owner in the community, in a position to receive the greatest benefit, was on guard lest the sanctity of the Sabbath and the cause of temperance should suffer by this proposed incursion from the outer world.

But the two who did most, contributed most, were probably the town's leading merchants, Chauncey Colton and Silas Willard. Colton we already know. He perhaps more than any other understood what improved transportation would mean to the town. He had struggled for years with primitive shipping facilities, and had been the first to establish commerce with the outside world. He was now aligned with his business rival in a movement of the greatest import to the town.

Silas Willard was a newcomer—he had come the previous year —but connected with the town by marriage to the daughter of Matthew Chambers. He was born in Vermont, and came to Illinois in 1834. He was a harness maker, and practiced his trade in Tazewell County, and later opened a general store there. He moved this business to Galesburg, combined it with that of his father-in-law, and became immediately prosperous.

Such were the men who were about to engage in what has nowadays become a major operation of high finance, railroad promotion; a group of small-town farmers, college professors and country storekeepers, few of whom had yet seen a railroad, but who had had the gumption to create a city and a college on the virgin prairie.

These men and their neighbors were incensed at the tactics of Knoxville; they dropped the struggle to persuade the Peoria and Oquawka line to swing its road three miles farther north; they refused to become excited over the Northern Cross slowly approaching their territory from the direction of Quincy; they decided to go in for railroad promotion on their own hook, build their own line, build in the direction of Chicago, or connect with a line leading to Chicago—there were myriads on paper—and thus not only have a road beyond gainsay, but an irresistible magnet for any road coming east or north.

It was rumored that a road known as the La Salle and Rock Island was planning to pass somewhere north of Galesburg. Overtures were made, and received with open arms. Marcus Osborne, one of its directors, told Selden Gale the proposed road would probably follow the old stage route through Henry County, which would bring it within thirty miles of Galesburg, either at Cambridge or Wethersfield (now Kewanee). Osborne further volunteered the information that a firm of contractors, Sheffield & Farnham, now constructing the Michigan Central, had agreed to build the La Salle road for $22,000 a mile, and take its pay one-half in bonds, one-third in stock, and the remainder in municipal bonds. He was quite sure the Galesburg road could make the same favorable arrangement.

The full story of this interview was published in the *Galesburg Newsletter;* it became the only topic of discussion at the blacksmith shop, at Colton's store, at meetings of college trustees, and around every fireside. The village board in an excess of zeal offered the public square as a site for a railroad station and Broad Street, the principal thoroughfare of the town, as a right of way, but fortunately the offer was not accepted, the final route of the railway demanding entrance on the other side of the village. George Lanphere, the only Democrat on the board, was sent to Springfield with instructions to get the Peoria and Oquawka charter changed if he could; if not, then a charter for a new road. This he got, but the unfriendly legislators slipped a joker in it to the effect that they would regulate the rates, a provision that caused trouble later.

Nevertheless, just five days after the Peoria and Oquawka had thumbed its nose at Galesburg, Galesburg had organized and chartered the Central Military Tract Railroad Company, with authority to connect with the La Salle and Rock Island in either Henry or Bureau County. William McMurtry, from the near-by village of Henderson, now lieutenant-governor, was made president, and Colton, Willard, George W. Gale and Selden Gale, with men from the villages along the new right of way, were elected directors. The La Salle and Rock Island was the germ of what is today the Chicago, Rock Island and Pacific.

The Galesburg promoters were somewhat disturbed when the Rock Island survey finally located the nearest point fifty-four instead of thirty miles away, and along a route more difficult of access and expensive to construct on account of the grades, the high prairie descending to the river valleys in the neighborhood. The junction was to be at what subsequently became the town of Sheffield, originally no doubt a construction camp named for one of the members of the contracting firm. But money was raised and a survey started in the direction of Sheffield, canvassers collecting funds throughout the neighborhood and barely keeping pace with the payrolls; young George Churchill, later a professor at Knox College, was one of the surveyors. Farmers along the right of way opened their homes to the engineers, supplying shelter, hot coffee, and frequently meals and beds, for it was winter, the country was sparsely settled, and there was no place for them to go. It was a neighborhood undertaking, like the bees and raisings.

"I have labored all day and many a day," says Clark M. Carr, "driven in my buggy several miles to obtain as much money as would keep the engineering corps that day. So we labored and toiled several seasons until we finally established a survey to Sheffield on the Rock Island road. The enterprise then flagged for a while, until our engineers' stakes were nearly obscured, and in the meantime some of our people made overtures again to the Peoria and Oquawka interests. But our enterprise had now too far advanced, and the advantages of a direct route to Chicago, over the beautiful country now occupied by the road, were too apparent for many of us to be diverted from the enterprise which was soon so successful."

IV

### THE AURORA BRANCH

About this time Chauncey Colton was in Boston buying goods for his Galesburg store and there he met two men; it was a critical encounter, for great things hung upon it. One of the men was J. W. Grimes, a promising young lawyer from Burlington (later to be governor of Iowa) deeply interested in the Peoria and Oquawka, but even more interested in any railroad that would connect Iowa with the eastern world, for there was not yet a mile of track west of the Mississippi.

The other was named Wadsworth—history unfortunately has not preserved his prenomen—in Boston on a mission similar to Colton's; namely, to buy goods for his general store in Aurora. He also was concerned with a short but ambitious paper railroad called the Aurora Branch, extending from what was known as the Galena Junction (now West Chicago) to Wadsworth's town of Aurora, thus connecting the town with Chicago by the Galena and Chicago Union. The Aurora Branch was a product of the Internal Improvement Act, and was the second railroad in Illinois actually to operate. In 1869 it was consolidated with and made part of the Chicago and Northwestern.

These three men, each with a bit of railroad promotion in his hat, met at the old American House apparently by chance, but they must have been guided by a benevolent fate, for they soon discovered they had much in common. Excitedly they compared notes and exchanged views. Wadsworth explained that the Aurora Branch meant to push on to Mendota, where it would connect with the Illinois Central. He hinted at financial help from eastern capitalists interested in the Michigan Central, and mentioned such well-known names as Forbes and Joy. Grimes thought Burlington could be depended on to co-operate. Finally Colton said:

"Here we are representing three different projects, each having the same end in view; each road by itself is worth nothing. Combined in a single line the roads will prove a great venture."

He showed how a slight change in route would enable the Military Tract road to strike the Aurora Railroad at Mendota; how the Burlington end of the Peoria and Oquawka might build to Galesburg and secure a direct line to Chicago, and how thus would be laid the foundation of a magnificent railroad, a highway for the products of Iowa and the region west as the country developed. As for the Northern Cross, which we have left moving vaguely northeast from Quincy, it would, if connected at Galesburg, serve as a gateway to Missouri and the Southwest.

When Colton got home bursting with this new prospect for Galesburg, he found that Sheffield & Farnham had arrived with their picks and shovels ready to connect the town with the Rock Island. At this point Galesburg dared neither stop nor go ahead. To gain time it was suggested that the Northern Cross people at Quincy be interviewed to find out how the new setup affected them. Quincy listened with its mouth open to the prospect of connection with a line direct to Chicago. They were going that way anyhow under their new charter, and they might much better go over the rails and at the expense of the Military Tract. So, while Sheffield & Farnham cooled their heels, the hands of Galesburg were strengthened.

James F. Joy was one of the earliest of a new profession destined to fill a large and exciting chapter in American financial history, the railroad builders. He represented the interests in railroad promotion of John Murray Forbes, a Boston capitalist. Through Forbes and others associated with him, the wealth won by tea clippers on the China run was being invested in new channels of trade. The pioneer spirit of American commerce had mastered and dominated the high seas; it now turned to the prairies. Forbes was financing Wadsworth's Aurora Branch. He had also bought for two million dollars the bankrupt Michigan Central, a state enterprise, and was reorganizing it under a charter drawn by Daniel Webster.

The Michigan Central was racing with the Michigan Southern —another state enterprise also bankrupt and sold to private promoters—for a terminal at Chicago, and each was concerned not only with a right of way into that city, but also a possible western connection with the fertile prairies of Illinois and Iowa. The Michigan Central hoped to get into Chicago over the Illinois Central's tracks, and the possibilities of the Aurora Branch, especially if it could be linked up with the other railroad fragments, was a further bid for consideration.

Joy has left an account of the negotiations which led to stringing together the Peoria and Oquawka from Burlington to Galesburg, the Central Military Tract from Galesburg to Mendota, and the Aurora Branch from Mendota to Chicago, which differs somewhat from that already given, for in it Joy seems to be the hero rather than Colton, but it has the same happy ending. At any rate, whether Joy put the idea into Colton's head, or whether, as some think, Colton originated it, the significant thing now is that the embryo railroad was switched from what is now the Chicago, Rock Island and Pacific to what is now the Chicago, Burlington and Quincy.

This was the third critical turning point in the checkered history of the line; the first being Oquawka's failure to come in, which shifted the western terminus; the second the hostility of Knoxville which spurred the Galesburgers to build their own line.

Joy was as good as his word. He secured Forbes' backing, and when he paid his promised visit to Galesburg, he brought with him John M. Brooks, a civil engineer whose railroad experience had been acquired on the road that later became the New York Central. Both were delighted with the prospect. They went to Quincy, and exchanged promise for promise, and left for the East, with Galesburg putting its shoulders into the stupendous job of raising $300,000—for it was $300,000 and not $200,000, as Joy, writing thirty years later, rather remorsefully hoped. Joy evidently felt a little guilty over demanding so large a sum, but assured the Galesburg directors that it was necessary to convince the Boston capitalists that the little prairie village was in earnest, though only fifteen years had elapsed since the colony had with difficulty raised $21,000 with which to buy the land where their town stood.

The appeal of the Galesburg committee to its fellow citizens is graphic evidence of the intimate and personal character of this early enterprise of railroad building:

"Now is the time when energetic, harmonious and united action is necessary if we would secure to ourselves advantages so great. True, we are a young community, and cannot command large sums of money; but though individually we are able to do but little, yet collectively we can accomplish much. Every member of the community can do something, and such as cannot furnish money can supply ties, stone and timber for the work, or perform labor upon it."

## V

### THEY SAVE THE DAY

At the eleventh hour only $250,000 of the local subscription had been raised. Fifty thousand were still needed. Every available cent had been squeezed out of the little town; the settlers along the right of way canvassed, but this territory was thinly settled. Much of the prairie was still government land. The prospect looked decidedly dark. Joy arrived in Galesburg with the disheartening message that his Boston capitalists refused either to reduce the amount or extend the time. A meeting was called, and various devices discussed for raising the additional $50,000. At length Colton, who had come forward at so many crises in the town's history, turned to his friend Silas Willard, and startled the meeting:

"I will subscribe half if you will."

Willard promptly accepted, much to Colton's consternation.

He tried to dissuade him, feeling that Willard could not afford so great a sacrifice. Neither could Colton for that matter. Both men had already subscribed to the limits of their resources. But Willard was game. So they borrowed the money, at ten per cent interest, and the contract was made binding on the Boston capitalists.

James Joy could not restrain his admiration for such colossal financial courage. On their way back to Chicago he and Brooks met the treasurer of the Rock Island Route on his way to Galesburg to close a contract with the Central Military Tract Railroad, and open a subscription for stock. By so narrow a margin did a large and potentially profitable section of Burlington Route territory miss becoming tributary to the Rock Island. It cost the little prairie town of a thousand inhabitants the stupendous sum of $300,000 to secure its first railroad, but thirty years later the city of 20,000 inhabitants got the Sante Fé by raising a mere $60,000.

Joy pointed out before he left Galesburg that it was difficult to interest Eastern capital as long as the rates of the new road were subject to legislative control. Selden Gale wrote a new charter, modelled on that of the Illinois Central, and Colton took it to Springfield and got it passed. Galesburg was in a different position now, with the strong backing of Eastern railroads so necessary to the State; its population had increased 500 per cent at the mere prospect of a railroad, from 800 in 1846 to 4000 in 1856. A boom was under way. The college was in line to be the greatest beneficiary. Two new buildings were erected with the profits, and are still standing.

South of the college campus was the 1200-acre college farm, upon which the unsuccessful experiment of manual labor had been tried. Four acres of this land were deeded to the new railroad for depot, with yards, round house and shops, together with the right of way through the city, provided that none of the land so deeded should ever be used for the manufacture or sale of intoxicating liquors. The remainder of the farm was laid out with streets, and was the first addition to the original forty-two blocks of the village.

There was a strong feeling among the Galesburg directors that the terms should go further and forbid Sunday operation, and no doubt Jonathan Blanchard bore down on this point. On their long slow treks to the colony in their covered wagons the pioneers had at considerable inconvenience and financial loss refrained from travelling on the Sabbath, but a railroad was too big an enterprise to be subject to their strict views; they had given a hostage to progress, and from that day the old puritan traditions began to give way to modern liberal ideas.

The capital of the Central Military Tract Railroad was increased from one hundred thousand to six hundred thousand dollars, Brooks was made president and J. M. Berrien chief engineer—both recalled today in Galesburg by Brooks and Berrien streets crossing the new addition. David Sanborn of Galesburg was elected treasurer and secretary; Colton, Willard, George W. and Selden Gale were included among the directors, as well as John Howard Bryant of Princeton. Orville Browning was appointed attorney.

Now the various pieces of the jigsaw puzzle began to slip easily into their places. In the fall of 1854 cars were running as far as Princeton, and by December the first train, a construction train, was pulled into Galesburg by a combination coal-and-wood-burning locomotive named "Reindeer." The first train on the Illinois Central beat it by only six months. The first Pennsylvania locomotive puffed into Pittsburgh in 1851.

The Northern Cross became the Quincy and Chicago, was sold under foreclosure, and bought by the Chicago, Burlington and Quincy. The Peoria and Oquawka changed its name three times, went bankrupt, was taken over by the Central Military Tract, completed, and at length and with many changes of name and management the four fragments were consolidated as the Chicago, Burlington and Quincy, familiarly known as the Burlington Route, but to us who grew up beside it as the "Q."

[ 215 ]

During the next ten years something like a dozen additional scraps of independent railroads in the State were gathered up and absorbed and attached to the parent stem, until the system began to assume the familiar form seen on its railroad maps today. Among such scraps was one known as the Keithsburg branch, which crept up the east bank of the Mississippi from Gladstone to New Boston (New Boston was surveyed by Abraham Lincoln) and thus at long last Oquawka got its railroad, but a way station on a branch line instead of a stately terminal at a bridgehead. Each short line thus assimilated had in its time been chartered and re-chartered by the legislature, with numerous amendments, and named and renamed, as it groped its way to its final destiny. The Burlington Route has collected and absorbed 203 such fragments in its progress (including the lines west of the Mississippi) each of which in its time has had some such individual and human history as has been narrated.

It is related in the Letters and Recollections of John Murray Forbes that so many promoters came to him with a hundred miles or so of railroad to sell, that he was reminded of the cats at his country place at Naushon on Buzzards Bay. They were so numerous and destroyed so many birds he offered a bounty for each cat's tail turned in, and this bounty being increased to a more liberal amount he found that the natives were raising cats to sell him the tails. He was convinced that speculators and contractors were building roads solely for the purpose of selling them to the Burlington Route, and that the more he bought the more "cats' tails" would be brought to him. This gaining currency, the C. B. & Q. branches came to be known as "cats' tails."

It should be noted that this road, at least in Illinois, received no land grants, no federal aid, no subsidies from the State. The 2,500,000 acres given the Illinois Central, the only land grant railroad in the State, proved a boomerang. The road has paid the State $30,000,000 in taxes, and on account of a provision that land grant roads must carry mails, troops and government material at reduced rates, some $8,000,000 to the Federal Government. The Burlington began as a neighborhood affair, and was helped out by Eastern capital only when it had achieved definite results.

Such were the humble beginnings of one of the country's great transportation lines, which now fans out south and west over the fertile prairies of many States to the western mountains. Illinois now has 12,500 miles of railroad; only Texas has more. The fantastic dream of the Internal Improvement Act has become more than an accomplished fact. The mileage of the Burlington Route is 9,383 (2,812 of it in Illinois) and only four roads, and only two of them western roads operating in similar territory, top that. It carries more livestock than any carrier in the world; more grain than any other railroad in the country, and is the second largest coal carrier in the West. These are a few things the West has done for the Burlington.

The contribution made by the Burlington to the development of the triangle between the Illinois and Mississippi rivers—and indeed of the vaster prairies west of the Mississippi—is almost beyond calculation. It opened the sealed cornucopia, sealed by lack of transportation, and its wealth poured forth on the settlers and on the railroad.

## VI

### THE END OF AN ERA

Few today can understand the fascination which the railroad exerted over us all in those early days. The motor car and airplane have dimmed our capacity for wonder. And no one living in a crowded Eastern city can know what the coming and going of the trains meant to an isolated prairie village sixty years ago. It spelled romance, a link with the unknown outside world. To us boys in particular, those trains had the mystery and charm that the old-time sailing ships had for boys living in seaports. I was one of them; I lived beside the tracks for much of my boyhood life. All of us had moments of aspiring to the career of conductor or engineer. We knew every train and engine. The limited trains, the lightning expresses, were our especial pride. The Fast Mail established in 1884, which dashed by the house every night (and still does), was so regular we set the clock by it.

Galesburg had become a railroad town. It had joined the march of progress which was sweeping over the prairies. The railroad brought new people and new ideas, and Galesburg lost much of the odor of sanctity which had given it its reputation among its neighbors, and became more human. The town grew up around the railroad, and its economic life was conditioned by it. With the establishment of car-shops, fully one-fourth the community drew its support from it. The monthly arrival of the pay car was a gala event. The banks and stores remained open until ten o'clock at night. The economic life of the town ebbed and flowed with the distribution of this comparatively vast sum of money. And from time to time some poor chap would be brought home on a grain door, crushed between bumpers, or otherwise injured, for railroading was an extra hazardous occupation.

There was no telegraph; trains ran "wild cat"; no double tracks; each train waited fifteen minutes at a station; if no train appeared it started for the next. If another train was met between stations, one of them backed to the nearest siding.

There were no air brakes; the trainmen ran from car to car setting the brakes, and again to reverse the process when the train started again. As each line built its own freight cars, they were of different lengths and heights, which made it a precarious job to run along the tops on a dark night. The trainmen became a separate estate with their own mores and social standards. Eugene Field celebrated the life of a freight brakeman in a poem in his "Sharps and Flats" column in the *Chicago News*, "with spring-bottomed pants and braid on his coat, hoping to get to Peru in time for a show."

There was no telephone. The sons of railroad men got jobs as "callers." All night they ran from house to house, rapping on the window. When the summons was answered they cried the time the train would be ready: "Two forty-three, Bill." The old familiar whale-oil lantern, one side red, the other white, with a bail through which he could slip his arm, was the conductor's badge. On anniversaries his friends presented him with a silver-plated one.

Passes were distributed with a liberal hand. Every employee and all his family travelled free, not only on his own line, but on all the railroads in the country. The first division superintendent was Henry Hitchcock, a tall stern New Englander, who had been yardmaster in the Michigan Central yards at Chicago. One year after the consolidation of the roads under one name, the employees of the Quincy branch gave him a family Bible. He wrote an execrable hand, an exception for railroad men, for as a boy I admired the beautiful running script, all the words connected, in which telegraphers, train dispatchers and master mechanics wrote train orders on the yellow tissue that could be wadded into a ball and handed thorugh the window of an engine cab. A letter written by Superintendent Hitchcock to a farmer about a cow the road killed was used by the bereaved owner for years as a pass and without question.

It seemed to be a social function to gather at the "deepow" to watch the trains arrive and depart. Galesburg was from the first a junction point. Its inhabitants never suffered the humiliation of seeing even the fastest trains "go through."

And so it happened one Sunday morning at Galesburg's reddish-brown railway station a little drama was enacted that marked the end of an era. When on the first Sunday the train arrived and departed according to its week-day schedule, those of the citizens who had in their keeping the sanctity of the Puritan Sabbath were too surprised and shocked to do anything about it. But the following Sunday among the goodly crowd assembled at the station was a tall, commanding figure in a long frock coat, distinctly clerical, and otherwise clothed with unmistakable authority, his jet black hair slicked back, his heart filled with high purpose, his supporters in their 1850 costumes, standing by ready for any emergency.

There was the engine with steam up, smoke pouring from its enormous top-heavy stack, its tender full of cordwood, its sweeping cow-catcher—so necessary in a country where livestock ran loose even in the village streets—drawing a string of short, square, flat-topped box-like cars—all as if just steamed out of a Currier & Ives print. Before the conductor could shout his "All aboard," and the engineer grab the bell rope, the tall, commanding figure stepped from the crowd, raised his hand, and bade the engineer take the engine to the roundhouse.

"Who are you to give me such orders?" asked the astonished engineer.

"I am President Blanchard of Knox College, and again I order you to take that engine to the roundhouse and not run this train on Sunday."

"Well, President Blanchard of Knox College, you can go to hell and mind your own business, and I'll take my train out as ordered."

And that is what the engineer did. The town had asked for transportation and it had got it. The railroad was no longer a neighborhood enterprise, controlled by the little group of pious men who had founded Galesburg to be a Christian town after their own ideal. Blanchard had worked for the railroad, and contributed to it from his meager salary, but stern moralist that he was, he would no doubt have foregone all its material benefits rather than yield one jot or tittle of the strict observance of the Sabbath which he and the founders of the town had thus far been able to maintain. But President Blanchard was as powerless to stem the tide of liberal ideas which came rolling in with the advent of the railroad as old King Canute had been to halt the inrolling breakers of the North Sea. Galesburg was never the same again.

# 8

## The Gay Fifties

### I

#### UNDERGROUND RAILROAD

In 1843 a colored woman with three children, two little girls and a half-grown boy, were lodged in the county jail at Knoxville on suspicion they were runaway slaves. The suspicion was correct. The woman was known as Susan Richardson. She belonged to Andrew Border who lived in Randolph County in the southern part of the State. Slavery was of course illegal in Illinois, but Border had brought in his slaves while the State was yet a territory, and under cover of strong pro-slavery sentiment, was not interfered with.

Susan had been goaded to flight by the punishment of her children and the threat of flogging for herself, but behind that was the constant fear that her children would be sold down the river to the dreaded rice and sugar plantations of the deep South. She had fled, in her words, "betwixt two suns," made her way to Cairo and there found one of those groups actively engaged in flouting State and Federal laws by aiding slaves to escape. She was started North, and passed from hand to hand until she arrived one cold winter morning at the farm of John Cross in Knox County. It was already after daybreak, and as the fugitives crept out from the bottom of the wagon, officers burst from the underbrush; the Negroes were arrested and taken to jail to await the arrival of a claimant.

Such seizures were common. There was no proof that the Negroes were slaves, but no proof was needed. John Cross was under suspicion and his house was being watched on general principles, as they watched the houses of all suspected "nigger stealers." Cross himself had been arrested several times, and finally brought to trial in Galesburg, where an abolition judge and jury acquitted him. The county, largely of Southern origin, was pro-slavery, but the Galesburg colony in the midst of it was abolition to the core and leading citizens regularly engaged in giving aid and comfort to Negro fugitives. Between them and the authorities at Knoxville there was continual conflict over this issue.

Some humane people in Knoxville bailed Susan out of jail and she obtained work in the village washing for various families, and her son got a job on a near-by farm. The two little girls were left at the hotel, a far too conspicuous place, as it happened. The authorities had prepared a notice of the arrest with a description of the woman and her children, which was circulated widely, and in due course Border came to Knoxville to recover his property. Susan got word at Mrs. Cole's where she was working; her first thought was to rush to the defense of her children. But Border had already recognized the girls at the hotel, and soon gathered in the boy also.

Susan was dissuaded from a hopeless undertaking and urged to save herself, which she did in disguise furnished by Mrs. Cole, who dressed her in her own clothes and gave her a veil to hide her face. Thomas Gilbert, one of the members of the exploring committee which had come to Knox County seeking a site for Galesburg a few years before, chanced to drive up in a sleigh and was persuaded to carry the woman to Galesburg, where she found safe asylum.

Border departed with the children, cynically remarking that the old one would surely follow. When she did not, he returned and began suit for her recovery. In spite of able attorneys and the law on his side, in that stronghold of abolition sentiment he failed of his suit. Volunteer lawyers stood ready at all times in abolition centers to defend both fugitives from slavery and their abettors. Upon just what point Susan was freed is not known, but it might well be that on which Lincoln won the freedom of the slave girl Nance in Tazewell county—that she was free under both the ordinance of 1787 and the Illinois constitution. At any rate, Susan was freed, and was probably the first passenger to reach Galesburg on what was afterwards known as the Underground Railroad, although this peculiar system of transportation had been operating in the older States since the Revolutionary War.

Susan was welcome in Galesburg, found work and did well, bought and paid for a home of her own, joined the Old First Church where she had her own pew and was vastly proud to be a member of the white folks' congregation. As "Aunt Sukey" she was affectionately known to two generations. Her skill as cook, laundress and nurse was much in demand; she was a constant resource in family crises, and was one of a number of colored people of unusual character who found freedom and homes in Galesburg and became unique members of that community. They were on the whole of a rather high average of intelligence and attainment, and some of them became well-to-do.

One Saturday night, some years later, a Negro in a pitiable plight knocked at Susan Richardson's door. He was barefooted, almost naked, starving and exhausted. As soon as he had been revived with food and drink, he told his story; he could not have had a more understanding hearer. He had escaped from a plantation in Missouri, dodging along by night, hiding by day, not daring to beg for food. Five other men had started with him; two were shot, the others recaptured.

Aunt Sukey put him to bed, locked the door of her house on him, and hunted up Jonathan Blanchard and Nehemiah West. Every Negro in Galesburg knew the right place to apply. Blanchard was already known throughout the West for his uncompromising anti-slavery principles. These two men and others made preparations to send Bill Casey to safety. Clothes were secured, but shoes were a problem, his feet were so big naturally, and so swollen from his long hike, it seemed impossible to find in that little town a pair large enough. But he was fitted out at last, hidden in the bottom of a farm wagon and started under the care of a trustworthy conductor toward the next station.

He got through safely, but two years later he came back; they often did; Canada was a strange place, Negroes not naturally pioneers, and the friendly attitude of Galesburg people lingered in his mind. No outcry had been raised, no further pursuit developed, he felt safe, and secured work in the timber northwest of the town. But there were always spies on the watch in that pro-slavery county.

Charley Love, a diminutive darkey, was sweeping the steps of the Galesburg House when two men rode up. Charley recognized "nigger hunters" at a glance.

"Hi, you there, where can we find Bill Casey?"

"Dunno, suh; never heard tell of that feller."

The two riders turned down Main Street in the direction of the public square. Charley darted out the back door, scuttled across lots to the right man, who quickly mounted his horse and dashed off to Henderson Grove. Bill was found, warned, and sent on his way, and so far as any one knows, was never caught.

Such happenings were of frequent occurrence. From the time William Holyoke organized the first anti-slavery society in Illinois eleven days before Elijah Lovejoy was murdered at Alton for running an abolition newspaper, a thin stream of blacks trickled through Galesburg, and through Illinois, and other Northern states. Conveyance was usually the innocent looking farm wagon, not unnaturally on the roads at night when all grain had to be hauled long distances to market. In the bottoms of those wagons the Negroes lay, one, five, even more, covered with grain sacks or hay, driven by a citizen of such irreproachable character one hesitated to challenge him. Arriving with elaborate caution at some remote farmhouse, the driver exchanged signals which disclosed no officers of the law lurking near, and discharged his human cargo, to be welcomed, fed and hid until the following night, when the process was repeated. Thus by slow stages a lake port was reached, where there were steamship captains who would see the contraband landed on Canadian soil before touching at an American port.

One old settler describes a jail delivery at Quincy, from which "black abolition hole" (as Missourians called it) many fugitives reached Galesburg. It is typical of what was happening all over the State, and could be duplicated among the legends of Knoxville.

"One night a captured runaway slave was brought to the jail in Quincy. The news spread among members of the Underground organization, a consultation was held to devise some way to free that slave. About 10 o'clock that night three prominent ladies . . . well acquainted with the unsuspecting old jailer, asked the privilege of giving the Negro his supper . . . he consented, and admitted them to the prisoner's cell, which was some distance up the corridor. . . . Soon the ladies were ready to go. The jailer proceeded to unlock the outside doors. The three came out of the cell, closed the grated door, shutting the prisoner in, blew out their candle and walked out by the dim light of the jailer's lantern. Next morning when he went to the cell he was greeted . . . by one of the ladies. . . . The old jailer . . . dumbfounded, . . . harshly called out, 'What art you doing here?' 'You locked me in last night,' replied his prisoner. 'Where is that nigger?' 'On the road to Canada, Mr. Burrell.' The . . . jailer let her out. When the sheriff demanded how he came to be outwitted he explained that when he went to lock the door of the cell he looked through the grating, saw the old coat and hat of the Negro hanging on the chair, and supposed he had gone to bed. That afternoon Mrs. Turner . . . told . . . how she and the other ladies . . . wore sunbonnets and shawls, took an extra dress with them, had the Negro remove his cowhide shoes, hat and coat, put the dress on him, veil and sunbonnet, wrapped a shawl around him and in the dim light he walked out of the jail unsuspected."

Canada was sanctuary. In 1841 the young Queen Victoria,

who had reigned but six years, proclaimed that fugitives from American slavery were citizens and free as soon as their feet touched British soil. Thus England, which so inexplicably sided with the Confederacy against the Union, aided to bring on the Civil War by thwarting the South in its efforts to plug the holes through which its capital drained away.

Galesburg was the most important station in Illinois. The galleries of its Old First Church afforded hiding places for slaves. There were houses in the village and farms on the prairie whose occupants were ready to receive fugitives at any hour of the night. Illinois was precarious territory for such traffic. But a short time previous it had been saved for free soil only by a narrow majority. The temper of its inhabitants was evidenced by the drastic "Black laws" its representatives had passed. Yet those mysterious trails which were unsurveyed lines of the Underground Railroad traversed the State from south to north.

Fugitives reached Galesburg from Pekin on the Illinois River, from Alton, Jacksonville, and Quincy, and from the Quaker settlements on the west bank of the Mississippi. These towns had different complexions. Alton's population was mixed, as the many slave riots reveal. Jacksonville was more like Galesburg, a town of Northern settlers who thought alike. Quincy was on the whole friendly to slavery agitators. Its principal agent seems to have been David Nelson, who settled there after he had been driven out of Missouri along with his Marion College—linked with Galesburg in that Henry Ferris, old Silvanus' son, was a student there. His anti-slavery views had brought him some unpleasant attentions at Marion.

A steamer was loading cordwood at one of the lake ports. The work was done by a gang of Negro stevedores. Each shouldered a log, carried it up the gangplank, deposited it below, and returned for another, forming a continuous procession. Watching the operation was a posse of Federal officers who had for days trailed five fugitive slaves, traced to this point and lost in the town. The officers were there to see that no attempt was made to put the slaves on the boat. Meanwhile the objects of their search were cowering among the huge piles of wood on the wharf. As the old song had it, "all coons look alike." From time to time one of the fugitives would shoulder a log, join the procession of legitimate stevedores, and march up the plank before the watchful eyes of the officers, inwardly stiff with fear but concealing it with the natural dramatic art of his race. When the boat had been fuelled, and pulled away from the landing, all five of the contrabands were safely hidden among the wood below deck. The phrase, "nigger in the woodpile" originated from this incident.

The slaves received were sent on in the general direction of Chicago, north, northeast, or east, to Henry or Bureau County; sometimes to one station, sometimes to another, zigzagging to baffle pursuers; to Princeton, where there were the Bryants, brothers of the poet, and Owen Lovejoy, who had sworn over the body of his murdered brother to do everything in his power to oppose slavery. Thus for years the dangerous exciting traffic went on, with its conflicts between enthusiast and authority, its midnight alarms, its daylight arrests, slaves rescued, and retaken, and rescued again, a struggle going on in hundreds of towns on lines leading from Mason and Dixon's line to Canada. And the growing breach between Galesburg and Knoxville widened.

One result to Galesburg and other cities similarly involved was to give them a colored population above the average in quality. As has been seen, some of the runaways remained, and others came back, and with the beginning of the Civil War the accession increased. The "house niggers" made excellent servants —"help" they called them—and there are many references to the "contrabands" in old letters from Galesburg to friends in the East.

The Underground Railroad existed in every State from Maine to Iowa, but mainly in Ohio and Illinois. It functioned without formal organization, officers, rules or maps. It was altogether spontaneous. The slaves fled across the border, appealed for help, found it, sent back word; others found the way, and soon scores of men were helping them, how many no one knows.

Each group worked in ignorance of the size of the movement or its ramifications. All they knew were the stations nearest and the men who went to and fro. There were no records, no statistics. The less they knew the better when it came to testifying in court. Passwords were arranged between those dealing with each other. The routes were frequently changed. It was the simplest organization imaginable and in its simplicity lay its success.

The name by which it is known to history was not given it at first. The story is that a discomfited Kentucky planter, having followed a warm trail into Ohio, was baffled by the complete disappearance of his quarry. "He must have gone down an underground road." When railroads became more common it became known as the Underground Railroad, with a whole set of terms taken over from this new method of transportation. The places where slaves were cared for and hidden were "stations"; the owners "agents"; the men who escorted the fugitives from one station to another "conductors"; and the slaves "passengers," though "freight" would have been more accurate, as they were actually shipped, sometimes in crates or cases. The railroad offered a new means of transportation, and companies of Negroes were sent through in freight cars, which eased the burden of the agents, and made pursuit even more difficult.

In 1850 the national law, already severe, was jacked up at the insistent demand of the Southern Congressmen. The fine was increased from $500 to $1000; imprisonment for six months added to the penalty, and those who aided the escape of a slave became liable for damages for the value of the slave. No other testimony as to ownership was required than that of the claimant; the slave was not allowed to testify in his own behalf. Citizens were required to aid in the arrest of fugitives. Not satisfied with this, it was provided that cases should be heard by commissioners instead of local justices, and these commissioners received a fee of ten dollars if they found for the claimant; if not, the fee was five dollars. The Federal laws were defied in some Northern states, which passed laws forbidding their officers to obey them, but Illinois passed laws upholding them in every particular.

Instead of dampening the efforts of fanatical abolitionists, the new law spurred them to greater efforts. This widespread nullification bore a curious resemblance to the flouting of the Prohibition Act of recent memory. Both were examples of unpopular laws which a large proportion of the people deliberately disobeyed, though from quite different motives. The bootlegger received enormous profits, his customers got their liquor, but the operators of the Underground Railroad incurred dislike, expense and personal danger, for no profit whatever except satisfaction of their consciences. It was their protest against slavery, and it roused the South to greater fury than almost any other manifestation. Indeed it was a principal cause of the Civil War. While no calculation has been made, or could have been made, the financial loss to the South was undoubtedly great.

Thus because of conscientious scruples the little town of Galesburg did not pick out the easiest civic road on which to travel. It made itself obnoxious to its neighbors in such matters as Sunday observance, temperance and slavery, on all of which it took an extreme position. It could have got on with less friction if it had not set itself up as a moral example. There is no doubt that Knoxville was delighted to harry a town otherwise so unpopular, or that the Underground Railroad was one of the causes of the breach which was widened by the controversy over the steam railroad and the courthouse fight, all of which were in progress at this time.

## II

### BISHOP HILL

In 1847 there were only six Swedes in Galesburg; in the next dozen years their number increased to between two and three thousand. The explanation is Bishop Hill.

[ 229 ]

In the early 1840's Eric Jansson got into trouble with the Swedish church authorities, not so much by starting a new religion, as for making a public bonfire of the books of the faith he had spurned. He was not especially persecuted, Sweden is a tolerant country, and Jansson not a serious symptom, but he determined to make the time-honored gesture of emigrating to a country where "he could worship God according to the dictates of his own conscience"; his followers, of course, being expected to permit their leader's conscience to do all the dictating, also according to formula. He sent Jonas Olson to America to find a spot where the colony might locate, and Olson picked a beautiful one in Henry County on the bank of Edwards River, about twenty-five miles from Galesburg.

In 1846 Jansson and his proselytes left Sweden with some difficulty and made their way to the chosen spot. Before leaving, each member of the party sold his worldly possessions and put the money into a common fund, for the colony was to be conducted on the communist principles laid down by Christ and his disciples, who had anticipated Carl Marx in some particulars and many years.

Before Sweden was left behind, the sect numbered about 1100, but only 400 joined Olson in Illinois; some turned back, some settled elsewhere, and some died by the way. With later accessions the colony grew to 655. They built a remarkable village and named it Bishop Hill, an English version of the name of the town where Jansson was born.

They established the colony on an economic base of agriculture and small manufacture, largely handcrafts. Their farming technique was peculiar. The fields were cultivated by small squads working in a sort of military formation, moving across the terrain and performing all operations in unison; a row of ox teams breaking the prairie, each team one length to the rear, a row of women broadcasting wheat from bags slung at their girdles; a row of men harvesting the crop, swinging their scythes and cradles rhythmically in exact time with each other, emphasizing in this humble way the cooperative principles of their undertaking.

They built their village around a green, which in time with trees became a sightly spot, church, community house, town hall, workshops, with a grist mill on the river near by, using kiln dried brick which they made themselves, laid with lime extracted from stone carted from Spoon River a few miles away.

A stranger visiting Bishop Hill today for the first time would be aware of its exotic origin with one glance at its architecture. No such buildings were ever erected by Yankee or Hoosier settlers. It is strikingly foreign, with touches of craftsmanship by which the older countries mark the work of their hands. The community house, known as "the Big Brick," perhaps the most novel and arresting of the buildings, where the entire colony lived, was destroyed by fire in 1928. What a pity there was no commission to preserve such things in this country! The church repays inspection, however. It is big, with a hip roof of unusual lines. The pews have open backs with spindles like a chair. In the low basement is an art collection which gives a vivid idea of the colony in its green and palmy days. The pictures are the work of a peasant artist untaught, unskilled, but with a convincing realism which more than atones for lack of artistic qualities. There are about a hundred portraits of Bishop Hill worthies, rugged old peasants with seamed faces full of individuality and character. They form the most surprising collection of designs in whiskers ever beheld.

But the instructive part of the exhibit is the graphic illustration of primitive agricultural methods, showing how the operations of farming were performed by coordinated groups. With their stiff and rhythmical positions, their gay and foreign costumes, they might be scenes from some agricultural musical comedy. Surely, but for the grim purpose on their faces, they must have "come on" singing a chorus. One is strongly reminded of the primitive art in some historic monastery.

The town hall, still used by the modern village, has a clock in its tower, the work of an ingenious emigrant named Blomberg, the huge weights of which rise and descend in chutes extending into the basement. The village is an authentic specimen of Swedish domestic architecture, looking strangely out of place on the Western prairie, despite the interpolation of modern and characteristic buildings by later hands.

They even attempted to convert the countryside, sending out twelve apostles in pairs, but their efforts were unsuccessful. Instead the converts they brought from Sweden backslid and began to drift away. But at first all was prosperous. After some experiment to ascertain what the best crop might be from the money viewpoint, they went in for broom corn, which they introduced into Illinois, and with such success that in one year the colony made a profit of $30,000. The possession of so much money went to their heads. Olson, as business manager, speculated with the funds, in the interest of the community, of course, but with bad judgment, and then disaster followed disaster.

In 1849 the Asiatic cholera ravaged Bishop Hill and destroyed 145 lives. Olson was bitten by the gold bug and left for California. A racketeer by the name of Roof joined the colony, married Carlotta, Jansson's sister, and proved so objectionable he was expelled, his wife and son remaining with the organization. Roof made many attempts to regain the custody of his family, some legal, others unscrupulous, and at length shot Jansson dead in the Henry County Courthouse at Cambridge.

Jansson's murder brought Olson back from California, but the experiment was already on the down grade. It had bought land and built the town of Galva (the name a corruption of Giflé, the place in Helsingsland, Sweden, from which most of the colony came) in order to be on the new railroad. Here a large cooperative store was opened. When that ill-starred project, the American Central Railway was inaugurated, Bishop Hill undertook the Illinois section of the grading contract, and had done considerable work, for which it was paid a million dollars in worthless stock, before the enterprise fell through.

Olson speculated in "wildcat currency," the colony issuing its own bills, beautifully engraved (they were instinctive craftsmen, as all their works showed). The financial crisis of 1857 crushed them completely. In 1860 the colony was dissolved, what property remained being divided up among the surviving members. The financial difficulties occupied the Henry County courts for twenty years. The original religion was abandoned for Methodism, to be followed later by the sect of Second Day Adventists.

Early in 1850, when cholera decimated the colony, the survivors began to leave, large numbers moving to Galesburg; there were continuous accessions from Bishop Hill, and also from the old country, as relatives and friends joined them. In a few years the population of Galesburg was one-sixth Swedish, and it has remained about that proportion ever since. Being a clannish race, there has not been much intermarriage, so that the integrity of the colony has persisted almost as distinctly as that of the Negroes.

Swedes are desirable citizens. They are sober and industrious. The record of their country in recent troubled years is a lesson to all mankind. The Galesburg Swedes established a sort of village by itself within the town, with its own churches, lodges, social life, but they penetrated most gainful occupations, working for the railroad, the cornplanter works, running well-tilled farms, and opening stores and shops, and even a bank of their own nationality.

The pastor of the First Lutheran Church, T. N. Hesselquist, established the first Swedish newspaper in America, *Hemlandet* (Homeland), an organ of Americanization, for while it kept its people informed of what took place in the old country, it interpreted the ways and institutions of the new. It had acquired a circulation of 1000 when in 1859 it moved to Chicago and was consolidated with *Svenska Amerikanaren*, which achieved 80,000 copies weekly.

Other papers followed in Galesburg, but as the second generation learned the language and began to live American, the old tongue died out, was discontinued in the churches, and there was no demand for a foreign language newspaper. The children attended the public schools, when these were after much tribulation established, and were known to the little Yankees as "Snorkies," as the Irish children were "Micks." The Swedes were good at their studies, as they were at most things, and there were few high school commencements after that in which the salutatorian or valedictorian, or both, was not some one whose name ended in "son," "berg," or "quist."

When the Swedes began to arrive in Galesburg in large numbers, a new problem was presented to the post office. Swedish nomenclature, coupled with Swedish handwriting, was so strange to the clerks that it was difficult, in fact impossible, to sort out the mail for general delivery, and these letters arrived in bundles from the old country, which the immigrants had so recently left. Clark Carr, the postmaster, invented the "Swedish roll," a revolving barrel, similar to the device from which picture post cards are retailed today, and set it up in the window, where it could be seen from outside. Upon this roll all general delivery letters for Swedes were posted. The roll could be seen and revolved from outside, though to receive the letters they must be asked for inside. This device persisted until the flood of foreign letters began to wane as home ties weakened, and the post office employees became familiar with Swedish names.

### III

#### MORE BUSINESS

The town has grown since we last glanced at Main Street. The stores extend all around the square, except where interrupted by the academy and the church. The editor of the *Free Democrat* notes with complacency three hundred farmers' teams tied there, but complains that the square is a "mud puddle" and a "duck pond" in wet weather. The clerks in near-by stores obligingly clean the mud off the crossings for their customers.

The square has neither grass nor trees. The town pump stands in one corner with a trough in front; there are other such pumps on Main Street. A tall "liberty" pole rises in the center for displaying a flag on gala days. The stores begin to creep up Main Street, drawn by the pull toward the depot, a new center of business that did not exist before. Thus the tides of trade ebb and flow and eddy, and change the physiognomy of the town.

There are now in 1857 sixty-four retail businesses: among them five boots and shoes, three clothing, one glassware, three drug, four dry goods, two hardware, two lumber, four "butcher shops" (meat markets), one paint, four nurseries (the prairie was being planted), four tailors, five jewelers, six Yankee notion stores. The general store was fading out. The kinds of goods sold in many of these stores, the sort of business done in some of them, are in 1936 practically extinct.

Dunn & Cheesboro announce they have just received a large consignment of candles, ten barrels of alcohol, fifty barrels of molasses, twenty hogsheads of sugar, and seventeen barrels of "burning fluid." This burning fluid was some crude form of paraffin, for petroleum had been discovered and was being commercialized, and candles though still sold were on their way out —"out, brief candle." Burning fluid was dangerous stuff, and many accidents are recorded in the papers. The history of civilization could be written in the progress of lighting. Perhaps no innovation wrought a greater change in the life of the town than lamps.

The Colville firm, which made the gorgeous account books, advertises that "Webster is triumphant"; it has "received forty dozen of his spellers" to fortify youth against the ordeal of the spelling bees. At Len Miller's store there is for sale a melopaean, whatever that may be. Photographers are taking pictures by the methods then in vogue, their products being known as ambrotypes, ambiographs, and melainotypes.

We are reminded by an advertisement of a gentleman's shawl inadvertently left at the shaving and hair-dressing saloon of the Galesburg House that gentlemen wore shawls, and that barber shops were called saloons; also that the word "gentleman" was euphemism for "man." Many families still boiled soft soap, and the stores offered "saponifier, or concentrated lye, the ready family soap maker." The new suction pumps, just put on the market, were known as "water drawers."

Numerous small factories made the town remarkably independent and self-contained. In this little city of less than five thousand there were manufactured in the fifties, machinery, agricultural implements, furniture, coffins, harness, boots and shoes, wagons, carriages, brick, pumps, candy, molasses, soap, "gent's" clothing, sash, doors and blinds, millinery, picture frames, and brooms, to the value it is stated of more than a million dollars.

The brooms used by the housewives were originally homemade, a besom, or bundle of twigs, like those seen in old prints. In 1844 Lucius Nutting came to Knox College, and as he was by trade a broom maker, he swept his way through, working in connection with the manual labor department. The corn was grown on the College Farm, scraped and cut by hand, and fashioned into brooms which sold for a dollar a dozen. A. Boyer, a blind man, developed the industry in the town, having at one time in his warehouse hundreds of tons of corn, raised by neighboring farmers, with improved machinery and fifteen workmen, making 125 dozen brooms a week. In spite of his handicap, Boyer was adept, inventing several devices, and making for those days a financial success.

There were several what might be called perpendicular industries such as Ford has established in the automobile field. P. P. Hemstreet could build in his carriage shop a complete and luxurious custom-made surrey or phaeton, from lumber cut in Henderson Grove, every part made by hand. Gustavus Geyer could buy his leather from Adams & Johnson, wholesale and retail leather merchants—the leather from cattle killed at the slaughter house on the edge of the town, processed by the local tannery—and fashion a smart double harness, which might then be put on a pair of likely colts raised on Thirwell's or Sisson's farm to turn out a "rig" that was a home product in every particular.

And every boy in the town not only knew the name of every strap in that harness, but could "hitch up" as soon as he was tall enough to put the bit in the horse's mouth. And there is not a city in the United States today where either of these remarkable things could happen!

The horse and buggy occupied a place in the social scheme more significant than the motor car today. It was the ambition of every substantial citizen to have a smart turnout, a team, if possible. It conferred more prestige than a motor car, even a Lincoln, now. All the farmers raised colts. Blooded stallions were advertised in bills posted on the barns. In summer, the horses in their shining harness, stamping from the flies in front of Colton's store, wore coquettish head nets, with fitted ears, ending in gay tassels. Sporty drivers, like Jim McKenzie or Forrey Moshier, drove two horses in a narrow side-bar buggy, one foot always resting on the step outside. They all turned out Friday nights when the band played on the square—a band stand having been built in due course—the stores remaining open until nine, the sidewalks filled with citizens shopping or taking their pleasure.

From the home-raised, home-tanned leather saddles were also made, and boots and shoes. There was also a hemp conditioning plant, and a rope walk. Another industry, that has disappeared not only from Galesburg but everywhere, was a factory for the manufacture of hoop skirts. As the locomotives on the railroad switched their fuel from wood to coal, mining of soft coal took on a serious commercial complexion.

Frost's Foundry made pumps, grist mills, saw mills, hay presses, cider presses, sugar mills, and evaporators, with the steam engines to run them. They were primarily for local use, though a market was sought wherever one might be found.

Baled hay carried on an interesting tradition. It will be

remembered that Olmsted Ferris brought a teacup of timothy seed from New York, and raised hayseed. It started the cultivation of "tame" hay, as it was called to distinguish it from the "wild" hay that grew on the prairies. Farmers bought presses, and baled hay became an industry. Just before the Civil War, the hay barn of Watkins & Brother was the largest structure of its kind in the entire West, possibly in the United States. They took in, pressed and shipped fifty tons of hay a day.

Sugar making followed a like course. The mills and evaporators were for crushing and drying the cane. Sorghum was raised on many farms; Illinois soil and weather conditions are admirably adapted to this crop, as they are to the broom corn—the plants are relatives—and the mills produced sugar, molasses and candy, while the canes or grasses made excellent fodder for the cattle. The grist mills ground not only wheat flour, but cornmeal, buckwheat, and feed for the cattle. There was also a factory that carded wool, and a mill which ground flaxseed and made linseed oil.

The ice business, it will be recalled, began with Uncle Billy Ferris, who dammed Cedar Fork, to the disgust of farmers below him. He sold out to a firm which disposed of the business to T. C. McChesney, who dug a lake of two and a half acres on the western border of the town, which became in the next generation the main pleasure ground.

Thus we have a picture of this prairie town with a remarkably diversified group of industries, not large nor producing much money, but self-contained and contributing to its commercial life a pleasing variety of occupations. Factories which started in the forties were beginning to acquire momentum in the fifties, stimulated by the railroad which opened new markets. The men who initiated them, journeymen mechanics working in overalls in shop and foundry beside their workmen, began to move into offices and wear white collars every day. Selling had become a part of industry. By the eighteen-eighties the proprietors had become magnates. At the turn of the century the industries began to disappear, as big business swept them up in combines, or discarded those they did not need to starve to death. Little businesses such as these dried up when it was decided to make all the shoes at Lynn, all the machinery at Pittsburgh, and all the flour at Minneapolis.

One of the curiosities of Main Street was a large dry goods establishment with the apparently ominous name "The Plunder Store," but not ominous to those Westerners who understood "plunder" in its original sense of household goods and personal belongings. The landlord of the inn would tell the colored boy to take "the gentleman's plunder to his room."

For years the only bank the town knew was Colton's store, which gave credit to the farmer against his crops. The first real bank was started by James Dunn, who graduated with the first college class, son of that Patrick Dunn who was "saved" from Catholicism by Gale's ministrations. Dunn's bank began in a seven by nine room with a small sheet-iron safe. Dunn was president, cashier, and teller. As it prospered he built a brick "block," as it was called, on the corner of Main and Prairie—"way uptown," two blocks from the square—over which was Dunn's Hall, the only secular auditorium until Caledonia Hall was built. Dunn's was not a bank of issue, but it put out a local scrip, that could not be used for paying freight or bills from wholesalers. Banking was a precarious occupation. President Jackson had suppressed the national bank, and there was no national currency. A rate of exchange prevailed between Eastern and Western money, and New York bills enjoyed a premium. Strangely enough the only paper money accepted at par in Galesburg was that of a bank at Hartford, Connecticut. What little sound money there was in the country was driven out by "wildcat" currency.

Reed's bank was the second, organized under the general law of the state as a bank of issue, but Reed would not accept his own currency even at thirty cents on the dollar, the legal rate as compared with specie. When in the panic of 1857 nearly every bank in the state went under, the paper of these two banks was accepted at par. However, on Thanksgiving Day, 1863, Dunn's bank closed its doors, leaving its depositors little to be thankful for.

The legal profession should not be overlooked in this economic roster, for Galesburg abounded in attorneys and counselors at law. Their "cards"—for lawyers advertised in those days—filled the entire first column on the first page of the earliest newspaper. They did not confine themselves to law. It is astonishing how many occupations could be combined with the practice of law—farming, real estate, journalism, store keeping, insurance, office holding—the law was not a jealous mistress in pioneer towns. Its practice was a comparatively simple matter. A copy of the Illinois statutes and mother wit was sufficient equipment. Practice consisted of those petty cases and disputes which during the first years had occupied the church session and taxed the judicial acumen of the elders.

One reason for the law's popularity is that it was the stepping stone to public office, and politics was a paramount interest with these people. The railroad brought larger opportunities, one of its important officers was its resident attorney, and the town was about to make a supreme effort to snatch the county seat from Knoxville, a matter of interest to lawyers, a contest that was to array the pick of Galesburg's bar in a series of bitterly contested suits.

The business pulse of the town was regulated by the bell of the Old First Church, which rung at seven, noon and six o'clock. It was also the fire bell, and the front door of the church was broken in several times, suggesting the need of a fire alarm. A clock was agitated for the church tower, but nothing came of it, and many years later one was urged for the tower of the new fire house at the head of Boon's Avenue, a good suggestion—every city should have a town clock—but none was set up until the courthouse was built.

With the advent of industry, including the railroad, with steam to spare for the lungs of business, the job of rousing the workers devolved on several whistles. "There was the old depot whistle," recalls one gaffer, "five-thirty in the morning and the first to blow. Seems like the engineer just tied down the throttle and let it blow for fully five minutes. This was to wake up everybody in general, and then at six o'clock all the whistles would blow a long blast as a warning to get to work, and then at seven the general 'all hands.' . . . The depot whistle was boss of them all, deep and coarse in its far-reaching toot. The Frost whistle was a chime, and very well blended."

St. Patrick's Catholic Church was built over by the tracks where most of its constituents lived. Its low-toned slowly tolled bell at six o'clock P.M. was a familiar and melancholy sound. It was probably the Angelus, but the Fifth Ward boys, mostly Irish who ought to know, called it the "dead bell."

Such was the business aspect of the town within twenty years of its founding, a group of small industries of no great import, but there is something epic in the creation of an integrated community in so short a time and so remote from other centers. It furnished the material background for a social life that was varied and picturesque, probably as full as that of more sophisticated communities, for human nature is the same, whatever the machinery with which it amuses itself.

## IV

### AMUSEMENT

Life in Galesburg in the second decade was more joyous than it had been in the first. Amusements which were taboo while the deacons and elders held the whip hand on the morals of the colony had begun to creep in. There was more money as the community prospered, and new people who did not subscribe to that counsel of perfection which the stricter element sought to set up. In spite of the vigilance of Blanchard, whose position made him a sort of unofficial censor, and whose disposition never flinched from fighting all forms of sin as he saw them, such profane entertainments as dancing and circuses had secured a foothold in the recreations of the town.

It was a period of excitement. Anti-slavery sentiment waxed, whetted by frequent conflicts with Knoxville, seat of authority and favorable to slavery—or at least opposed to abolitionism—while the streams of fugitive slaves were spirited through Galesburg in the night. The fervor with which these pioneers took their politics was a spur to frequent rallies and torchlight processions, all of which drew crowds from the surrounding country, and added to the gaiety of life in the village.

It was in this period that the religious schism just described raged at its fiercest, adding the dramatic interest of conflict, for while the sober-minded took it seriously, it was just so much food for gossip to those who believed there were other things in life besides church and religion. Some of the less devout took a malicious satisfaction in the spectacle of saintly Christian men flying at each other's throats and bandying epithets so inconsistent with their professions.

What people do to amuse themselves is an index of their character. It is evident that there were now other things to do besides pitching horse shoes, shooting prairie chickens and watching the stage come in from Peoria, as a sardonic commentator observed of the earlier era. Ready-made entertainment was not available on such a large scale as today, but there were travelling shows and spectacles which visited the town, and like travellers on shipboard the townsfolk became adept at devising shows of their own—fairs, horse shows, celebrations, dialogues in costume (euphemism for plays), concerts, contests of all sorts, from plowing to elocution, and duels between volunteer hose companies.

Theatrical performances were rare, transportation being difficult, and the town having no adequate theatre. Dunn's Hall, with its meager home-made scenery, was the only place available, the church being out of the question. Here was given "the great moral drama of Uncle Tom's Cabin, produced by Yankee Robinson's Atheneum." But numerous small troops of nondescript performers made the town at intervals, the minor ones showing in vacant stores, the more elaborate in Dunn's Hall. Entertainments of the strictest moral character were permitted to use the church, the largest auditorium in that part of the state, but the word "moral" prefixed to the name of every variety of show did not fool the elders.

These nomadic entertainments were such mild amusements as the Swiss Bell Ringers, the "well-known Riley Family in concerts," "Exhibition of Dissolving Views by aid of Magic Lantern, for Lovers of Science and Art"; "Mr. Dempster, Ballad Singer, admission 50 cents; book 15 cents"; "Mrs. Doctor Loomis, Clairvoyant"; "Mary E. Webb, the colored Siddons, will read 'The Christian Slave' by Mrs. Stowe, based on *Uncle Tom's Cabin,* characters impersonated by the reader"; "the Inimitable Winchell, famous for Droll, Quizzical, Mirth-provoking Impersonations at Dunn's Hall"; "Chinese Jugglers, introducing the only Chinese Fiddle in America," and "J. H. Green, Reformed Gambler, with card tricks." Although kerosene lamps had made their appearance, entertainments began, as announced, at "early candle lighting."

Then there were the panoramas, humble precursors of the moving pictures, scenes painted on strips of canvas unrolled across the stage, lighted from behind as well as in front, touched up here and there with a blaze of red fire at the more lurid incidents. Bunyan's Pilgrim's Progress was a favorite, and was still touring the churches as late as the 1880's. One was billed "Panorama and Cyclorama of the Life of Christ, at the Church; pictures painted by the greatest artists of the day, Raphael, Rubens, Velaque" (*sic*).

The keen interest in California in the early fifties was reflected in some of these primitive peepshows. "Johnson's Panorama on the Gold Mines and Touring thereto" was one of them. Also "Wilkins' Panorama of the Overland Route to California," given in the session house, which was a small building beside the Old First Church where the weekly prayer meetings were held.

In 1846 an English painter named Lewis bought a flatboat on the Mississippi, fitted it up as a studio, and floated from St. Anthony's Falls to New Orleans, painting the river scenes on both banks. These pictures, which are surprisingly good, are the earliest records of many of the towns on the Mississippi. The pictures were enlarged on a strip of canvas half a mile long and twelve feet high, mounted on rollers, and toured the country as a "Panorama of the Mississippi." It was tremendously successful. After covering the United States, where it was viewed by the President, members of his Cabinet, and other dignitaries, with appropriate expressions of wonder and admiration, it was taken to England, and duplicated its American success. It was then sold to a panorama impresario from India and exhibited in the Orient, where all trace of it is lost. It may be touring yet. The artist settled in Düsseldorf, with his original sketches, which were made into a book, the pictures lithographed in color, text in both German and English, and has become a rare item of Western Americana. The curious spelling of American names is a feature, J being used for I, as Jowa, Jllinois.

Of entertainments brought to the town from the outside, the circus was the high spot, that distinctively American institution which even in our day exerts some of its pristine fascination. It loomed large before railroad transportation, when it travelled on its own wheels, and brought to remote hamlets the biggest thrills they knew. It arrived with the dawn, to be greeted by the entire juvenile male population, and some of the grown-ups, too, and as it staked its tents in a vacant lot near the town it set numbers of those boys to work "carrying water for the elephant." Its manager visited the office of the newspaper later in the day and handed out a liberal bunch of "comps" in compensation for favors rendered and to come. The clowns performed the service of the musical comedies of a later date, distributing the popular songs. They were singing "Bridget Donahue" and "Whoa, Emma" in the fifties. Main Street was lined with a dense crowd for the circus parade, and afternoon and evening, despite the stern disapproval of deacons and elders, the tents were packed, including the "concert" after the main performance.

# THE GAY FIFTIES

It is hard to fathom the attitude of rigid moralists toward those early circuses, which seem singularly innocuous entertainment. The emphasis was on the menagerie, and looking at elephants and giraffes not forgetting the "blood-sweating Behemoth of Holy Writ" can hardly be considered a sin. They were always billed as "moral entertainments," and even if they did not qualify for that description, they could scarcely be considered immoral. What the deacons and elders feared, perhaps, were the fleshings worn by the few women performers, or possibly the side-shows and confidence games which followed in the wake of the circus, or even the immemorial lure of the sawdust arena for youthful imaginations which tempted boys to run away with the show. It was the occasion of some innocent hypocrisies, such as going to take the children.

Among the early announcements one finds: "Henry Driesbach's Circus and Menagerie—only living giraffe ever exhibited in a western travelling establishment—aerial steamship, steered by pilot (one wonders how that was done), brilliant cortege." "Yankee Robinson's Big Show, Circus, and Collection of living Animals, Museum of Curiosities; Joe Ginger's Minstrels"; "Moxon & Kemp's Great Eastern Circus, Five Nations, and a Steam Calliope drawn by forty horses that can be heard for miles around."

But among them the name Van Amburgh led all the rest. It was a name better known to the boys of the middle years of last century than the names of the twelve apostles. "Van Amburgh & Company's Menagerie. The only moral and instructive exhibition in America. Hannibal, the mammoth Elephant, African Ostriches nine feet high; Polar Bears, Black Alpaca Sheep, Lions and Cubs, Sacred Cow." That name had more potency in those days than all the Forepaughs, Barnums, Baileys, Coles, Coupés, and Ringlings had later. Poems were written about his show.

> "He puts his head in the lion's mouth
> And keeps it there a while,
> And when he takes it out again
> He greets you with a smile."

In entertainments by home talent, music was the major inspiration. The glee and choral singers gave concerts, and also the brass band, which announced it had been taking lessons from that great musician, Professor Reimann, and was in fine fettle. It met for practice at the furniture shop of Bartlett & Judson, which was headquarters for Fourth of July celebrations, for no one knew better than Fred Bartlett how to paste up a hot air balloon, or soak a fire ball.

Contests of many sorts were popular. An exciting competition in music was staged among three groups, Harmonic Society under leadership of Professor Owens, beginners and amateurs under Professor Miller, and the Old Folks under Conductor Bacon, the pioneer choir leader. Also a lively contest in "elocution" between Professor Griffith, a visiting lecturer on elocution, and Professor Hamill, "the resident elocutionist of Knox College." Public spelling bees were held for the school children.

The constant use of "professor" to distinguish any one connected with cultural activities, a common practice in the West, reflects the craze for titles among a people in which military distinction was rare, hence the multiplication of civil designations. Even the officers of the church were invariably known as Deacon Simmons, Elder Farnham; village magnates were addressed as Esquire Ferris. Hence the numerous "professors" meant little.

Among odd entertainments uncommon today were an exhibition by the deaf and dumb pupils of the institution at Jacksonville, phrenologists who examined one's bumps and expatiated on traits of character revealed, a party of Indians on the way to Washington who gave a show to defray expenses, and a horse-tamer who demonstrated Rarey's methods, in front of Hunt's livery stable. Rarey was a well-known name, and his system had many imitators. This chap advertised for a vicious mustang or a wild and savage bull. Whether he got them is not told, but these horse-breakers could take raw colts and render them docile to harness in an incredibly short time.

The number of State reunions is surprising in so small a town.

New York, Maine, New Hampshire, Massachusetts, Rhode Island, Connecticut, Pennsylvania, and even Georgia were represented. The Maine Society served moose meat, cod, smelts, and chowder. The Sons and Daughters of Connecticut gave an elaborate program—three hundred born in that State—with a poem by Mrs. Sigourney, the Hartford poetess, and a huge cake, two feet high in model of the Statehouse at Hartford. About this time appeared in the local newspaper a protest against scheduling wordly amusements on prayer-meeting nights. Another protest signed "Women's Rights" complained that the stores of the town were regular smoking saloons. One imagines the crowd around the stove in Colton's or Chambers' store.

The laying of the Atlantic cable was followed step by step in the local newspaper, and when completed, Galesburg, a thousand miles from salt water, joined the cities of the country in a big celebration, with parade and speeches. The Negroes, who were an unusually orderly and desirable class of those unfortunate people, celebrated the freeing of the slaves in the West Indies, and held a memorial service in honor of John Brown of Ossawattomie, with white speakers at both. Fred Douglas, famous Negro orator, also spoke, and Editor Sherman of the *Free Democrat* remarked that the Black Douglas was far superior to the white one.

The characteristic mores of this colony and life in the West are best seen in the big outdoor gatherings, the political rallies, county fairs, picnics, and firemen's tournaments, successors to the infares, bees, and raisings of earlier years. The Knox County Fair and Agricultural Association held its annual gatherings at the fair grounds in Knoxville, the first in 1839, until Galesburg wrested this also from that long-suffering village.

Being a farm community, the attendance was enormous, 7000 in a day being common. There were competitions in everything, a list of premiums which filled columns in the newspaper, from the farmer's hogs to his wife's preserves, displayed in Floral Hall, along with patchwork quilts. No doubt the famous pattern "Illinois Roads" was among them. That quilt looked like a modern road map, the highways in Illinois following section lines, making a checkered design.

Strips were marked off on the fair grounds, and the young men held plowing matches, judged by a committee of experts as to speed, neatness, and symmetry. Each contestant had his partisans, it was district against district, farm against farm, and the fun was boisterous.

The trotting matches had the intense interest that only purely local races can have. Nothing like them can be seen today. The sulkies were spidery vehicles with six-foot wheels, the driver so close behind his horse he sat on its tail. Goggle-eyed Knox County farmers saw both Dexter and Maud S. trot a mile in less than two minutes, but outside entrants never exerted quite the fascination as did a race between two home-grown colts. The farmers raised the colts, the people knew both horses and owners, and bet accordingly—for there was betting—and no modern fairs furnish so complete a picture of the folkways of an agricultural community.

Fire was such a menace it was ordered that no more wooden buildings should be erected on Main Street, after a disastrous fire that wiped out a whole block. The local agent of the Aetna Fire Insurance Company offered $50 to $100 toward the organization of a fire department. It was not long before Tornado Number 1 was manned and competing with companies from near-by towns.

These firemen's tournaments were sensational affairs. The companies were volunteer, the motive power muscle, the object to see which squad could squirt the highest stream. Companies came from all over the State, especially after the arrival of railroads, each with its battalion of boosters. The costumes were resplendent, brass helmets, red jackets, high boots. After a parade down Main Street, the contest began in the public square, the 175-foot liberty pole serving as a yardstick. The prize was usually a silver trumpet, through which the chief was supposed to bawl his orders, and one hundred dollars contributed by the merchants whose buildings were supposed to be protected by this exhibition of skill. After the show there was a "soiree" in Dunn's Hall, with refreshments and a dance perhaps. The fire "laddies," as they were affectionately called, who received the kudos later lavished on baseball teams, were probably better at tournaments than at fires. The advent of city water and hydrants put an end to this dramatic form of entertainment.

Not sated with such revels Galesburg inaugurated a National Horse Show and Equestrian Fair, which attracted its host of camp followers and side-shows, a "theatrical corps," jugglers, and even three members of the oldest profession, who rented a house on Main Street, and were, as the newspaper remarked when they were arrested and sent to jail, "sufficiently public to be called national." There were attendant scenes of roughness and drunkenness which no doubt justified the sermon Blanchard preached against it the following Sunday under the title "The Morals of Agricultural Fairs," accusing it of misrepresentation, insisting it was not "national," meaning official with the government, that speakers were announced who did not appear, that cows, hogs, and sheep were not admitted as exhibits, and that its award of premiums was a lottery.

There were horse races and prizes for horsemanship, even a premium for "trained elks," feats by Navajo Indians ("nothing," says the scornful newspaper man, "but a couple of well-tanned Knoxvillains"), but the great event was the women's exhibition riding. The entrants ranged from Mrs. Look, mother of grown sons, who wore a close-fitting habit of black velvet and a full skirt, with neat self-trimmings, a riding hat of velvet with plumes, and yellow gauntlets, down to Caroline Bunce, fourteen years old, in a small cap from which peeped a profusion of curls, a skilful and fearless rider. After displaying their horsemanship for an hour, the equestriennes drew up before the judges' stand, and sitting their mounts in the blazing sun, listened to an address an hour long on the subject of "Woman." Then the premiums were awarded, but the spectators were so indignant because Caroline did not receive a prize that they took up a collection then and there, and gave her the $25 thus contributed.

What they ate in the fifties is as revealing as what they did to amuse themselves. There was an abundance of food; nothing is surer than that the pioneers, whatever they lacked in conveniences and luxuries, had plenty to eat. The prairie teemed with food, game and fruits; their fertile fields and herds produced other foodstuffs, and despite the difficulties of transporation, many foreign delicacies found their way to Galesburg kitchens.

There is in existence the menu of a Gargantuan banquet, modestly styled a supper, printed on white silk with gold ink, which is startling both by its size and its variety, especially when it is remembered that this was but a year after the railroad reached Galesburg, that refrigeration was unknown, and freight a slow and uncertain service. The menu is worth reproduction, not only for its amazing list of foods, but for its refreshing absence of French, that fashion not having yet reached the prairies.

Besides the more formal and arranged for recreations, there were the usual country games and sports, outings, and picnics, usually in Gale's Grove, a small forest of locusts he had planted on his farm just outside the city, perpetuated today by the name of Grove Street. Also berrying and nutting parties in summer, coasting and bobsled rides in winter, the inevitable oyster suppers and strawberry festivals at the Church, or churches as they had now become. To these must be added the numerous exhibitions and open meetings furnished by the college students, to which the town repaired en masse. There was no lack of the materials of a lively and complicated social life.

We, of course, must view the whole question of amusement in the light of the sterner code which prevailed at the city's founding, and was being leavened by the lighter side of life as lived by the more liberal. From the frequent investigations by the college faculty and the punishment of students for playing cards, it may be inferred that the townsfolk were even more familiar with what

## TEMPLARS CELEBRATION SUPPER

Given on the occasion of the Presentation of a Bible to LIBERAL
TEMPLE OF HONOR by the Ladies of COUNCIL SOCIAL DEGREE
at the HASKELL HOUSE on Monday evening, Oct. 22, 1855.
P. G. BALLINGALL, PROPRIETOR, Galesburg, Ills.

### BILL OF FARE

*Oysters on a Half Shell; Soup,* Lobster

*Hot Relieves*—Turkey, with Cranberry Sauce, Tame Ducks, brazed with Jelly,
Tame Chickens, roasted and stuffed, Tame Goose, roast, Sage and Onion stuffing,
Surloin of Beef, roast, with Horse Radish, Spare Rib of Pork, Apple Sauce

*Cold and Ornamental Relieves*—Chicken Salad, in form, Lobster Salad on
Pedestral French, Turkey, decorated with Jelly and green herbs, Round of Beef,
a la mode, and form in jelly, Ham, brazed and garnished with jelly, Beef's
Tongues, garnished with Parsley

*Game*—Prairie Chickens, stuffed and baked, Prairie Chickens, boiled, Cran-
berry Jelly, Quails, baked and brazed with Potatoes, Quails, boiled on crust, Wild
Goose, roast, Sour Sauce, Brant, stuffed and baked, Mallard Duck, roast, Prune
Sauce, Teel Duck, Quince Jelly, Loin of Bear, with Peach Sauce

*Entrees*—Porter House Steaks, boiled and trimmed with fried Oysters, Fresh
Mackinaw Trout, fried, with anchovy sauce, Small Patties, filled with Turkey
Hash, Oyster Pie, baked New England style, Salma of Ducks, French, on pedestral

*Relishes*—Pickled Lobsters, Pickled Cucumbers, Pickled Tomatoes, Sardines
with Lemons, Nova Scotia Herring, Cold Slaw, Horse Radish, Cucumbers, Celery

*Pastry*—*Pies,* Mince, Squash, Apple; *Tarts,* Cranberry, Prune; *Puddings,* Jenny
Lind, Cinnamon Sauce; Tapioca, White Sauce

*Ornamentals*—*Representation of Temple of Honor, Beautifully Decorated with
Confectionery, and Inhabited by an Emblematic Goddess of Truth, Love, Purity
and Fidelity*

*Chinese Pagoda, of Sponge and Pound Cakes, Ornamented with Lozenge
Paste, and Surmounted by Goddess of Liberty*

*Pyramid of Apples Trimmed with Raisins and Mottoes and Decorated with
Banners*

*Confectionery*—Peach Ice Cream, Vanilla Ice Cream, Charlotte Russe, Swiss
Meringues, Florintins, Jumbles, Mottoes, Floating Islands, Transparent Jelly,
Lemon Jelly, Cranberry Jelly, Calf's Feet Jelly, Kisses, Whipped Cream with
Jelly, Variegated Blanc Mange, Chocolate Blanc Mange, Delicate Cake, Jelly
Cake, Pound Cake, Sponge Cake, Italian Cream, Variegated Candies

*Fruits*—Apples, New Havana Oranges, Water Melons, Layer Raisins, Prunes,
Figs, Brazil Nuts, Almonds, English Walnuts, Madeira Nuts, Pecan Nuts, Fil-
berts

*Beverages*—*Tea, Coffee and Chocolate*

[ 251 ]

used to be called the devil's picture books. The conventional attitude of the time toward such amusements is expressed by the Philadelphia women quoted by Harriet Martineau who thought it blasphemous to play cards during a thunderstorm.

The idea seemed to prevail that God almighty especially objected to cards and dancing. Early in this decade "Professor" Lee opened a dancing academy, twelve lessons for six dollars, but students were forbidden to attend. So were adults, as far as the church had authority, for a ball given at the Galesburg House occupied the attention of the session for ten months. Parents were cited before the elders to explain why they had allowed their children to attend, and also justify themselves for the sin of looking on. Some confessed and were disciplined and forgiven, but others were defiant, and were dismissed.

It may shock even some of the moderns to list prostitution under amusement, but it is a good place to mention that the police were waging war on houses of ill fame, and a father suspected of living on the wages of sin earned by his daughter was given a coat of tar and feathers, which the newspaper, while regretting the fact, thought was richly merited. What went on outside of legal and commercial limits is past finding out at this late day.

On the Fourth of July previous to the outbreak of the Civil War a celebration was held which was typical of such jollifications. They took such things seriously then. The birth of the nation was nearer, and patriotism burned fiercely. The nation was on the eve of disruption, and many were conscious of the clouds that were gathering. The town had recently been stirred to its depths by a political rally, the famous Lincoln-Douglas debate. And the program in this city was probably duplicated in every hamlet in the land.

Thirteen guns were fired at sunrise. The procession formed at eleven-thirty, led by the Galesburg cornet band, followed by the Galesburg Light Guards, the Free Masons, Scandinavian Rifles, the orator of the day riding in an open barouche from Ben Buckley's livery stable, veterans of the War of 1812, firemen, Good Templars, Galesburg cadets, citizens generally, and the artillery with one piece of ordnance.

At Gale's Grove the program consisted of prayer, music, reading of the Declaration of Independence, music, oration of the day, music, benediction. In the afternoon the firemen and military performed their evolutions in the public square. In little more than a year the amateur soldiers were to be plunged into real war.

Refreshments were served at the Kellogg House by the ladies of the Mt. Vernon Association, which gave in the evening a series of patriotic *tableaux vivants* from the life of Washington, the proceeds to go toward the fund for buying Mt. Vernon as a public monument. At sunset a salute of thirty-three guns was fired, followed by fireworks on the public square.

V

CULTURE

Nor did the town wholly lose its interest in things of the mind among such a plethora of mundane distractions. There was a very sincere interest in letters, art, and music, however strangely manifested. It was a naïve and unself-conscious interest, exercised by listening to lectures, debates, discussions—political, literary, travel, and informative, including humor; in some amazingly crude forms of art, the only sort within their reach, and in rather good music, the first art developed in the town, and to the end the one they practiced best. In music they took a more active part than in any other department of culture. For ideas or pictures, they were merely listeners or spectators, accepting what was offered.

The books they read consisted about equally of works easily recognizable today, and strange productions so utterly lost it is impossible to speculate about their nature. The books are mostly those which the editor of *The Free Democrat* praised, doubtless sent him for that purpose. As he was their only source of news of literature, it is supposable they at least read some of the books he recommended.

Among books thus noted are Bayard Taylor's *Cyclopedia of Modern Travel, Spurgeon's Sermons, Dred* by Harriet Beecher Stowe (naturally a best seller in a town where her brother was a minister and slavery a live issue), Fowler's *How to Write,* Mrs. Stowe's *Journey to Italy, Letters of Madame de Sevigne,* Colton's *American Atlas, Waverley Novels, Little Dorrit;* but there were also received by the newspaper, *Mabel, or Heart Histories, a tale of truth,* by Rosella Rice, *Kate Weston, or To Will or To Do* by Jennie De Witt, *Missionary Heroes and Martyrs* by Henry Starbuck, *The New World* by Henry Howard Brownell, *Gospel Fruits, or Bible Christianity Illustrated,* and *Edith, or the Quaker's Daughter.*

Hastings & French announce that they have for sale *Turkey and the Turks, Boston Common, a Tale of our own Times, Rozella of Laconia,* a splendid tale of New Hampshire, *Peace or the Stolen Will* by Mary Janvrin, *Lilly Bell, or the Lost Child,* by Alice Fay.

Such works as *The Family Doctor* by Henry S. Taylor, *Plain Home Talk and Medical Common Sense, Every Lady's Counselor and Lawyer* by Frank Crosby are easily classified. Among the textbooks sold in the stores and presumably studied in the schools and colleges were Sanders' and McGuffey's readers, Monteith's, Colton & Fitch's, Mitchell's, and Burritt's geographies, Town's and Clark's grammars, Davis' and Ray's arithmetic, Wells and Cutter's philosophy and chemistry, Worder and Wilson's histories, Quackenboss' composition, Webster's spelling book, and Webster's and Worcester's dictionaries. The store offering this array adds that it has "stereopanes, dominoes, and chessmen (?) for children."

The editor of *The Free Democrat* observes there are "legions of magazine readers." Apparently he was right, for among those received are *Putnam's, Ballou's, Peterson's, Frank Leslie's, Knickerbocker,* and T. S. Arthur's *Home Magazine;* also, *Godey's Lady's Book, Great Republic* (merger of *Emerson's* and *Put-*

*nam's*), *Ladies' Home Magazine, Household Words, Yankee Notions, The Little Pilgrim*, edited by Grace Greenwood, and *The Prairie Farmer*.

During these years an earnest group denominated the Young Men's Literary and Library Association was struggling to establish a library. The head of this movement was Albert Hurd, a character in his own right, and the most distinguished member of Knox faculty. The Association sponsored many lectures, and along about 1855 opened a Reading Room over one of the stores on Main Street, which was the nucleus of Galesburg's exceptionally efficient public library.

It is probable, however, that the intellectually inclined townspeople imbibed more sweetness and light through the medium of lectures than from books. Besides the library organization, both college literary societies were instruments for securing platform speakers to bring word of the outer world to the community, no difficult job, for the country teemed with lecturers. This was at the beginning of the lyceum era, later flowering in Chautauqua and Major Pond's organization, which prevails even yet. Galesburg heard most of the noted platform lights in their heydey.

Among them were Ralph Waldo Emerson, Theodore Parker, whose exciting life has just been celebrated with a lively biography; Thomas Hart Benton of St. Louis, father of Jessie Frémont, senator from Missouri, editor of *The Missouri Enterprise;* Cassius Marcellus Clay, fiery, turbulent abolitionist duelist; John P. Hale, crusading anti-slavery senator from New Hampshire; Wendell Phillips, Elihu Burrit, the learned blacksmith, pioneer peace apostle, editor of *The Christian Citizen;* John B. Gough, Horace Mann, president of Antioch College; John G. Saxe, "mirth-provoking punster and poet," who read his celebrated poem on "Love," and appeared often on the Knox commencement platform; Benjamin P. Shillaber, author of "Mrs. Partington," E. L. Youmans, poet, editor of *The New World;* Parke Benjamin, sued for libel by James Fenimore Cooper; Parke Godwin, editor of *New York Evening Post,* who married Bryant's daughter;

Carl Schurz, Mortimer Thompson, parodist, "Doesticks" of *The New York Tribune* and *Detroit Advertiser;* Horace Greeley, H. J. Raymond, T. DeWitt Talmadge, Bayard Taylor, J. G. Holland, George D. Prentice, editor of *The Louisville Journal;* J. G. Wilson, editor *Northwestern Quarterly;* Henry Ward Beecher.

Literature, it seems, could be brought to them, by word of mouth if not by the printed page, music they could make themselves, but painting is the culture that arrives last, and no practitioner of it seemed to have found shelter in this prairie town, which is unfortunate, for a contemporary artist would have given us pictures of the town's worthies, in their habit as they lived, instead of the stiff daguerreotypes taken at the ends of their lives, or genre pictures of the town itself, of which we have no visual records.

It is impossible to learn what art meant to these people. One of the books offered by a local dealer was *Introduction to the Art of Grecian Painting,* whatever that may be. There was an Art Union, which met over Tilden's store. The public was invited to see Dubufe's celebrated paintings, "Temptation" and "Expulsion" of Adam and Eve, on view at the Methodist Church. J. C. Wolfe announced a class in painting and coloring photographs, which he said was "adapted to ladies." N. O. Bond offered twenty-one oil paintings for sale at fifty cents each at his Daguerrean Rooms.

There was one strange use to which the sale of art was put, hitherto unknown, and that was in the conduct of an unusual form of raffle. A local merchant, who wished to dispose of his store and stock, sold 18,000 copies of what was described as an elegant engraving, "Belle of the West," at a dollar apiece. Each print was numbered, and purchasers drew for choice, including the store itself, as well as the contents. There were several such sales and drawings. Bartlett & Judson offered framed engravings of "The Lord's Prayer" and "The Ten Commandments." It may not have been art, but it was evidently what they liked. Currier & Ives popular chromolithographs adorned many sitting-room walls.

[ 256 ]

THE GAY FIFTIES

Music was one art without sinful implications. Did not the angels sing around the throne of grace? At any rate, whether with or without divine permission, there were several organizations devoted to secular music, which at length flowered in an Academy of Music. Indeed, there was a healthy rivalry between the choruses and glee clubs. Among singers from other parts was Isadora Clark, the "celebrated prima donna," who sang "Lost Birdlings" with "exquisite warbling and trilling" and "Ben Bolt" with such "perfect intonation" that an encore was demanded and given with Hehl's "Sweet Home."

Cantatas were put on by local talent, Root's "Flower Queen," "Esther the Beautiful Queen," Schiller's "Song of the Bells" with Romberg's music, Len Miller, leader, and "The Haymakers," a musical description of that essential farm operation, with a back drop by some local artist showing a hayfield.

The songs they sang included such forgotten gems as "The Spot Where I Was Born," "Some Things Love Me," "John Anderson, My Jo," "Lament of the Irish Emigrant," "The Barring of the Door," "The Death of Warren," "The Blind Boy," "I'm Alone, All Alone," "Duncan Grey," "Strike the Cymbals," "Denmark," "Rest, Spirit, Rest," "The Dying Christian," "The Last Rose of Summer," "Star of Bethlehem."

The chorus class of the Galesburg Musical Institute (which may have been the above-mentioned Academy of Music—there were so many organizations it is impossible to disentangle them) gave a concert at which it sang "Angels Ever Bright and Fair," "On the Field of Glory," Glover's "Beautiful Birds" and "The Hebrew Girl's Lament."

There are other incidents which throw light on the intellectual habits and concerns of a small Western city in the fifties. Interest in science seems to have expressed itself only in the Phrenological and Philosophical Society, that met in a room over one of the stores, which the newspaper perhaps flattered in styling Phrenological Hall, or the lectures by members of the college faculty. The word "philosophy" meant to them what we rather vaguely call science today. The equipment for physics at the college was known as "philosophical apparatus."

Blanchard tried to stir up feeling against the lodges which were being organized in large numbers, invading Galesburg and all Western towns. He was mistaken in his supposition that these colonists were opposed to such things. He delivered many lectures, and wrote long letters to the *Free Democrat,* exposing their iniquities, with no result, apparently, except a letter of protest from a bored reader, who said he had no particular friendship for such organizations, but was tired of the tirades against them. The lodges flourished and turned out in full regalia at all celebrations.

Not much can be gleaned from the subjects orated and debated by the college students in their public meetings. They follow conventional lines, but in 1856 Louis Bunce, older brother of the Bunce whose father compelled him to graduate in the Blanchard war, gave a commencement oration with the singularly modern title, "The Moral Influence of Machinery."

There was a debate on the commencement program of the Female Seminary in 1857, the year of the senior class strike, which is significant. The women graduates held their exercises in midwinter, so that ceremony was unaffected by the subversive tactics which marred the men's baccalaureate. Two young women debated the subject "Are the Six Days of Creation Literal Days?" Knowing something of the temper of the college authorities toward such topics, it is nothing short of surprising that such a discussion should be permitted, especially as the negative had by far the better of it.

The negative was maintained by a seventeen-year-old girl, Mary Ellen Ferris, granddaughter of Silvanus Ferris, and was well reasoned and conclusive. It showed a marked advance in liberal thinking. This was two or three years before Darwin roused the religious world to fury with his *Origin of Species.* The founders of the college, the whole of that church-going community, undoubtedly accepted implicitly the literal truth of the first chapter

[ 258 ]

of Genesis, in fact, of the whole Bible. To doubt it was heresy to most of these fundamentalists. It is of additional interest that the author of this paper was of that family which has seemed to bring a little independent thinking into the air-tight theology of the Sanhedrin of the town.

Miss Ferris did not go back of the divine authorship of the Bible, or of this planet. She merely pointed out that the Mosaic account was undoubtedly a figurative description of the slow process by which the earth's crust was formed and life appeared upon its surface; "the deductions of geology may be true, and the six days of creation something else than literal days of twenty-four hours each. . . . God works by secondary agencies . . . the Mosaic and geological records are independent inscriptions written by the same sun of righteousness."

All of which was nothing but heresy to New School Presbyterians.

A few years earlier these would have been fighting words in Galesburg. Perhaps the powers that be were so full of their own sectarian squabble over the control of the college that this outburst of liberal thought passed unnoticed. At any rate, it is a landmark in the slow growth of tolerance in an ultra-religious community, a type which prevailed everywhere in the West the first half of last century, and is found even today in some parts.

Miss Ferris became Mrs. Gettemy, one of the ablest and most inspiring teachers of her native town, principal of the high school for nearly a quarter of a century, the first woman to take a position only a man had hitherto been thought qualified to fill. The writer of these lines owes much to her instruction. But at best she was a lonely peak. The narrow, bigoted attitude of much of the religious element persisted well toward the end of the century, and created the opposition which intolerance and shutting one's mind to reason always do create.

This town, which its founders had visioned as a sort of inner sanctuary consecrated solely to New School Presbyterianism, had in 1857 already ten churches, and eight varieties of religious belief. The Old First Church had split off both a Presbyterian and a Congregational church, and itself become Congregational. There were both old and new schools of the Calvinists. Even the Universalists were represented. Worse than all, in the opinion of the sectarian founders, thanks to the incursion of the Irish to build the railroad, Roman Catholics were already organizing a parish, which was before long to become the largest denomination in the town.

The Hoosiers, who composed the original settlers of Knox County when the Gale colony arrived, were mainly Methodists and Baptists, and Jacob Gumm, who with his sons welcomed them at Log City, was a Baptist elder. There was, as you might say, a frame for a Baptist church in Galesburg, and one was organized. It included some of the leading people, among them Mrs. William Ferris, wife of Uncle Billy of ice-cream fame.

The Baptists were not only refused the gift of a lot by the college trustees, but had difficulty buying one. The site they secured through the duplictiy of Sidney Edgerton was one of the best in town, on Broad Street, opposite the "Female" Seminary. Here they put up a church, but after a few years they too experienced a dissension which split the organization, the dissenters moving out and building a church of their own.

Meanwhile, the city desired the original lot on Broad Street for a school, and a trade was arranged whereby the Baptists got a lot on Cherry Street, and some cash. Their old church was shorn of its steeple, and made into the Central Primary School, where the writer of these lines studied his A B C's. The corner is now occupied by the high school. The First Baptists, with a desirable lot and some extra cash, made overtures of peace to the Second Baptists, with the result that the two congregations reunited and built a church on the new corner, where they are to this day housed in a modern structure no worse, but no better architecturally than those of the other denominations of the town.

Some of the Wests and Congers in the original group of

colonists selected by Gale turned out to be Universalists, who were regarded with almost as much horror as Unitarians. They also established a church in the fifties, and followed it up with a college, its avowed purpose being to afford an education on a more liberal basis than was permitted by the narrow sectarians of Knox College, at that moment engaged in a wrangle over denominational differences.

The new college was named the Illinois Liberal Institute, and a building set up in the southeast section of the city. This building was almost immediately burned. A new one was started with a contribution from Benjamin Lombard, and the institution was named for him, Lombard University, with a divinity school to justify the name "university."

Thus within fifteen years after its founding, Knox College had a rival in its own town, not serious competition, though Lombard was a good school, and had some excellent teachers, one of them David Starr Jordan, afterward of Leland Stanford. In recent years two things happened. Professor Standish, the wealthiest member of the Lombard faculty, left all his property to Knox, including his home opposite Knox campus, which is now the site of the college library. A few years later Lombard merged with Knox, and its attractive grounds, now covered with ancient elms, was sold to the city.

## VI

### THREE MEN

During the years that the college, despite the theological controversy that raged around it, was gaining strength and prestige under Blanchard's able management, there were graduated in the class of 1851 three young men who had become close friends; their names were Churchill, Comstock and Willcox. Two of them were products of the colony, sons of the pioneers, who had come West in the covered wagons when each was about four years old. The third came to Galesburg to secure an education, and remained there the rest of his life.

George Churchill was one of Norman Churchill's six children. He was born in Winfield, New York, and was brought to Galesburg with his family too young to know any other life than that of a pioneer Western town. His father's many-sidedness and outspoken character have been noted. George inherited some of his traits. He was sturdy, honest, unconventional, energetic and musical. The house his father built on West Main Street was his boyhood home, and he joined in the boy life of the town with gusto, skating, swimming, riding, hunting, welcome everywhere for his wit, religious, but with an underlying vein of hard common sense, which gave his piety a practical rather than a speculative theological turn. He attended the academy, entered college in the fall of 1847 and was graduated in 1851.

This was the largest class entering thus far, but its members were reduced by the gold fever so that out of twenty-seven freshmen only seven seniors were graduated.

Milton Lemmon Comstock was born in Ohio, the third of seven children of Joab and Jane Comstock. His father was a farmer and Methodist preacher. Young Comstock led the life of a country boy of the period, education in a log schoolhouse, with puncheons for seats, doing chores on the farm, breaking prairie, splitting rails, running a sawmill, quarrying stone, raising flax, and cultivating fruit trees, the latter a hobby which lasted a lifetime. In spite of limited opportunities for education, he not only taught school, he was for a year principal of the academy at Yellow Springs, Ohio, precursor of that unorthodox and exciting educational experiment of Horace Mann, Antioch College.

He entered Knox in 1847, and made the acquaintance of his classmates, Churchill and Willcox, and laid the basis of a lifelong friendship. He did so well in his studies and attracted such favorable attention from his teachers, that on graduation he was placed in charge of Knox Academy.

Henry and Mary Willcox, from Bridport, Vermont, were among the earliest of the colonists to arrive at Log City. In the family was a four-year-old boy named Erastus Swift Willcox. The Willcoxes and the Churchills were neighbors, and George and Erastus grew up together. Erastus attended the curious school with the sloping floor, went on to the academy, and prepared for college when he was fourteen. He was already enrolled as a freshman when his father interfered, and forbade his undertaking the course at that age. He waited four years, and entered in the class with Churchill and Comstock. His was an active mind with a refreshing point of view. His boyhood reminiscences have furnished some of the saltiest paragraphs to this book, particularly about the sufferings of normal healthy boys under a religious despotism.

The three young men found each other congenial. Comstock was the oldest, and the most conservative. He was drier, quieter, than his boisterous hearty friend Churchill. The intimacy between Churchill and Willcox was perhaps a little closer. They were of an age; they had grown up together; they roomed with each other throughout the course, probably in one of the diminutive dormitories in the "Bricks."

On graduation, Comstock began his work with the academy, Churchill was employed as surveyor for the new railroad, and Willcox went to Peoria and began the study of German. In 1854 he persuaded Churchill to go abroad with him, a tremendous enterprise then, and the two young men made "the grand tour— London, Berlin, Dresden, Prague, Vienna, Venice, Florence, Rome, Genoa, Switzerland, Paris, crossing the Apennines and Alps on foot—the first Illinoisans who ever did it," Willcox boasts. In Germany Churchill was attracted by the school system, and studied it carefully, storing up notes for future use. He was instinctively the educator.

At the end of his three years at the academy, Comstock went to Iowa, where he busied himself with horticulture and edited the *Iowa Farmer,* later returning to his old post at Yellow

Springs. When Churchill and Willcox came back from their jaunt abroad, Churchill abandoned a half-formed plan to study medicine, and both joined the faculty of Knox College, Churchill as teacher of mathematics, Willcox as professor of modern languages. Comstock was recalled from Yellow Springs to be professor of mathematics, Churchill was made principal of the academy, and the three men were reunited in the institution which saw the birth of their friendship.

All three married. Comstock's wife was Cornelia Ann, sister of Churchill. In college they had made a sentimental vow to name their first-born sons after the other two members of the trio. Comstock's oldest son was George Erastus, Churchill's Milton Erastus, and Willcox's George Milton.

It has already been hinted that three men made a major contribution to the intellectual effectiveness of the college in its formative years, but only two of those we have just described were included. Willcox severed his connection with the college in 1863 and moved to Peoria, where he devoted his life to building up the public library. The important third was an importation from the East, the first mind from the outside college world brought to bear on Knox since the first group of professors arrived with the other immigrants from New York.

Middlebury College, Vermont, was Jonathan Blanchard's alma mater, and when a science teacher was needed, he applied there, and was told to take a look at Albert Hurd, a promising young man who had graduated in 1850. And so when Churchill and Comstock became permanent members of Knox faculty, they found a shy young man therein installed, whose quietness masked a dynamic personality.

During the Revolutionary War Albert Hurd's great grandfather, Phineas Hurd, remained a Tory. He took refuge in Canada, his property was confiscated, and he himself disappeared, spirited away and probably murdered by Whigs. His wife never saw him again. The English government rewarded his loyalty by the gift of a magnificent estate on the banks of the St.

[ 264 ]

Lawrence. The family remained in Canada. That is how, in 1823, Albert Hurd happened to be born at Kemptonville, Ontario.

Another picturesque ancestor was a great-grandmother, Barbara Heck, militant leader of Methodism in this country, who organized the first Methodist service, and built the first Methodist church, in John Street, New York City, though the building now standing is not the original.

Despite the royal gift, which was possibly a white elephant, and the return of the confiscated property in the United States, the father of Albert Hurd was not sufficiently wealthy to give his son an education, and Albert worked on the farm, resisting his father's determination to make a farmer of him, and cherishing an ambition to make teaching his profession. With this plan his mother sympathized, and dissuaded the father, who nevertheless insisted his son must pay for his own education and reimburse his father for the loss of his labor.

He attended the public schools of the province, completing his English education at the age of fourteen, and acquiring a beautiful Spencerian hand which he practiced all his life. He was teaching at sixteen, with such success he was asked to take the school in his own neighborhood, "boys I had fought, girls I had kissed."

At eighteen he entered Victoria College at Coburg, Canada, and studied Latin for the first time, a language he was to make pellucid to generations of Knox undergraduates. At the Ogdensburg, New York, Academy he prepared for college. His teacher here was John Bradshaw, whose son later followed Beecher at the Brick Church in Galesburg, by which time Hurd was a member. The Methodist urge strong in his blood, Hurd had determined to go to Wesleyan at Middletown, Connecticut—its present head, James McConaughy, was ten years ago president of Knox—but Bradshaw urged Middlebury, and Middlebury it was. His circumstances demanded a certain amount of earning, and he spent the long winter vacation, which prevailed at the time, in teaching school.

Contact with three outstanding scientists exercised a profound influence on the mind of this young man, Louis Agassiz in geology, Jeffries Wyman in anatomy, and Eben Norton Horsford (inventor of baking powder) in chemistry. For a year after graduation from Middlebury, he taught at the Vermont Literary and Scientific Institute at Brandon [birthplace of Stephen A. Douglas, with his monument on the village green], and got his outdoor exercise in nature study and searching for specimens, and there he was when Blanchard made his inquiry about a science teacher.

With no idea what was before him, he accepted the call, and set out for Galesburg. The steam-cars took him to New Boston, on the east bank of Lake Michigan, from which a steamboat ferried him to Chicago, where he took the canal to Peru on the Illinois River, and connected with a river steamboat to Peoria. There he caught Frink & Walker's stage, no doubt driven by Clarendon Palmer, in which case he heard much gossip about his new home, and so arrived at Galesburg.

He must have been dismayed at the first sight of that little town of 800 people, so crude and raw and unfinished, so different from the kempt and settled villages of New England, treeless in the pitiless Illinois sun, its streets alternately dust and mud, its college two straggly brick buildings on the campus, and a more upstanding academy on the public square. He found a faculty consisting of George W. Gale teaching moral philosophy, Innes Grant modern languages, Nehemiah Losey mathematics, and Henry Hitchcock principal of the academy, and the board of trustees beginning a wrangle over control that was to cloud the first ten years of his incumbency.

Losey was also a graduate of Middlebury. Grant held a degree from Aberdeen University. Gale had both Union College and Princeton Theological Seminary as a background. The blood of many colleges mingled in the scholastic stream of Knox. One could go back thus from college to college to the orgin of the university idea, which had come down like a sort of apostolic succession to this little institution on the prairies of Illinois.

Hurd roomed in the "West Bricks," his roommate being Francis Colton, afterward American consul at Venice, and took his meals at the home of Chauncey Colton, the wealthy merchant. He married Eleanor Amelia Pennock, built a house, and was made a full professor of chemistry and natural science, but also taught Latin, and devoted his life, his means and his vacations to building up a museum for the college.

He gave lectures about the State, thrilling prairie audiences with the newly discovered wonders of science, and turned the proceeds into the college for the purchase of needed equipment. He had no apparatus, but he wrote his own chemistry. Frank Moulton, a graduate, says:

"Had Knox been able to give Professor Hurd the equipment and leisure to devote to research as in the older and wealthier institutions, he would have been known as a great scientist. He was incomparably a great teacher."

He managed, however, to establish an experimental chemical laboratory which he carried on until modern facilities became available for the college.

His outside activities are no less interesting and instructive. Broken in health by dyspepsia, he sold his house, bought a barren lot, created a garden and home by physical labor, and built himself back to health. He founded the Young Men's Literary and Library Association, and nursed it until Galesburg had a public library, serving as librarian himself two evenings a week. He made several trips to Europe, and studied church architecture, making his notes on the backs of old envelopes in his copperplate script, from which he delivered lectures, and found in this more esthetic study an outlet not afforded by the hard facts of chemistry and geology. His ingrained thrift was a noticeable trait.

When Madame Blanc was in Galesburg, she stayed at the Hurd home. Her picture of the simple, unpretentious life is graphic:

"Three or four rooms on the ground floor, with as many above them—no more; but this modest interior at the first glance sug-

gests ideas of order, scrupulous neatness and studious retirement.
On the dining-room wall hangs the Lord's prayer in ornamental
script. The library is adorned with books which overflow into
every room in the house. There are no mirrors in the tiny parlor,
only the simplest furniture, a few good engravings, family photographs, and flowers; a rare dignity prevails. This is the setting
of one of the noblest and most vigorous figures that I ever saw—
that of an old man robust as any youth, an unselfish scholar,
whose well-filled life has been consecrated from beginning to
end, in spite of the counsels of ambition, to this college; he may
well be called one of its pillars.

"Beside him is his wife, delicate and shy, whose face still bears
traces of those ethereal beauties such as we find, exquisitely engraved, in English 'Books of Beauty.' . . . The professor holds
to old-fashioned ways; nowhere else did I find so perfect an
instance of the Puritan family, as I had imagined it. The husband
and father is still master here, and a tyrannical master, too; his
wife submits with a grace and sweetness not especially American;
the daughter is respectful and reserved. And yet she has a high
degree of culture, as proved by her diplomas; she teaches in the
college, and has undertaken—what her parents never did—a
journey to Europe, after which her life of toil and retirement
seemed no harder to her than before. Everything, bread, clothes,
etc., is made in the house; of course the mother must lend a hand.
The fare is plain, but abundant; temperance is not only preached
but literally practiced in regard to fermented liquor. The father
pronounces a benediction upon every meal."

The Knox faculty was given new life by the accession of Hurd,
Comstock and Churchill, and as time went on these three men
were the outstanding personalities of the middle years. They
were utterly unlike physically as well as temperamentally. Hurd
was tall, slightly stooping, smooth-shaven, with a cameo-like
profile, to which his high-bridged Roman nose gave distinction.
He was austere in dress, his long frock coat and black string tie
with a Gladstone collar was his uniform as long as he lived.

Comstock wore a full beard, which became white with years, so that he resembled somewhat the popular caricatures of Father Time. He was thin and wiry, nervous and quick in his motions, absent minded, forgetting his class in the excitement of a difficult problem of calculus, working it out in a cloud of chalk dust, and turning at the end with a beaming smile for sympathy from the class, few of whom had been able to follow his flights into higher mathematics. In the ample grounds of his home in the southwestern part of the city he rode his hobby of horticulture, and kept an accurate record of Illinois weather for fifty years.

Churchill was bluff and breezy, stocky of figure, and wore sack suits or cutaways in place of the sober frocks, his hair brushed fiercely pompadour, his grizzled beard trimmed short. As head of the academy, he was first in contact with most of those who entered college, and his popularity was great. He was a man of many activities. To his school duties he added those of city engineer. He wrote and spoke fully and often on the early history of the colony, was almost its official chronicler. But his greatest contribution to the town was its public school system.

Ironically enough, the public school system of Galesburg was in a discreditable state. There was nothing but a collection of district schools scattered about the city, their buildings, according to one disgusted critic, little better than coal sheds. It would seem at first blush that a colony of pioneers who came West to establish an educational institution, and had actually set up an academy and a college, would have sooner seen the need of primary education. There are several explanations of this anomalous situation.

The truth is that the founders were not interested in education as they were in religion. They had little education themselves, and the idea of mass education was only beginning to gain currency in the country. Just how unessential education in general seemed to them is curiously illustrated by the circumstance that only a small percentage of the children and grandchildren of the founders graduated from the college, despite the scholarships they possessed. Selden, George W. Gale's oldest son, never attended any college, and his young brother, George W., Jr., who was one of the Forty-Niners, wrote a letter from his camp at Cold Spring, California, near Sacramento Valley, where he was prospecting for gold in 1851, which suggests he never attended even a primary school.

Young Gale was then twenty-five. Although son of the Professor of belles-lettres of Knox College, he misspells the commonest words—"anuf," "righting a leter," "the leter you rote," "posiable," "sucesfool," "valey," etc. He is washing out gold, "that pais from to bites (two bits) to one doler to the pan," and thinks he can make from twenty to thirty dollars a day. He mentions other young men from Galesburg working near him—Chauncey Noteware, his cousin Caleb Finch, and David Colton, nephew of Chauncey. Orthography is no criterion of mental ability, but ignorance of it does imply lack of formal training.

Another cause which may have retarded the establishment of graded schools, adequate buildings, and standards of teaching, was the reluctance of the people to pay for them. It was a new idea, and they fought, some bitterly, against the added tax burden. The struggle lasted for years. Further, in the remote background, there was jealousy on the part of the college trustees for their academy, and the paying pupils it drew. So some of the strongest antagonism came from the college contingent.

Meanwhile, there sprang up a number of select schools, taught by elderly maiden ladies or widows with sufficient education, which cost a small weekly sum, and to these those who could afford it sent their children. It is only in recent years that it has been fully realized that the public schools are the feeders of the colleges in the West, where there are few of those costly "prep" schools, each with an underground pipe line to some famous university.

Illinois passed a law authorizing the establishment of graded schools in cities of the State, and levying taxes to support them, but the matter hung fire, and was debated at public meetings, and by long letters to the *Free Democrat*. The leader of the movement to create such schools, who campaigned intelligently and forcibly, who brought Horace Mann, one of the wisest pedagogues in the country, from Antioch College, and who finally saw his idea wholly prevail, was George Churchill. He had studied such schools in Germany; he was practicing teaching every day, and he shamed and argued the town into submission.

When a graded system was established, Churchill served on the Board of Education for fourteen years. The first well-built schoolhouse, and the oldest standing in the town, is the Churchill School. Albert Hurd gave Galesburg its splendid library; George Churchill its efficient public school system.

# 9

## *Lincoln*

### POLITICS

When Clarendon Palmer, the stage driver, cautioned his passengers against flaunting their vices in the face of Galesburg's piety, it was obvious that there was a spirit of dissent in some bosoms against the puritanical rule of the elders. This spirit organized itself into a small revolt, known for years as the "Anti-trustee" party, which manifested itself at local elections. When the village was incorporated as a town in 1841 the college party calmly took possession of all the offices by divine right, and carried on the extremely moral government so far exercised unofficially by the church. This grew irksome to the younger and more liberal element with whom Palmer sympathized, especially those who arrived later and owed no allegiance to the tight little corporation known as the first settlers.

The contest was also known as "Young America" against the "Old Fogies," or as some saw it, the workingmen versus the aristocrats. It gave a little spice to the early town elections, small as they were. The post office followed national fluctuations, and the college contingent managed to install their Professor Losey as the first postmaster, but Palmer was a Democrat, and when Polk came in as President he was appointed postmaster. It is an example of the thoroughness of the spoils system that Washington should concern itself with a job worth a few dollars a year away out there on the prairies. The population in 1840 was 272.

The first national campaign in which the town participated

was that of William Henry Harrison—"hard-cider, log cabin, Tippecanoe and Tyler, too." The county and the State were strongly Democratic. Just before the arrival of the Galesburg colonists, the few Whigs in the county had been told, when they presented themselves at the polls, "We don't allow no abolitionist Whigs to vote." But Galesburg of course had her own polling place.

This campaign was given peculiar significance because it was the first in which the newly formed Liberty Party participated. The Liberty Party was an anti-slavery movement led by James G. Birney, opposed to Garrison's policy of non-political action. Birney was its candidate for President. It was notable in Galesburg history because here was organized one of the first, if not the first, units in Illinois. The organization of an anti-slavery society in 1839 was followed by a meeting at which Matthew Chambers presided and Eli Farnham acted as secretary, at which fifteen men signed the following pledge:

"We, the members of the Knox County Liberty Association, do hereby pledge ourselves that hereafter we will vote for no slave-holder, apologist for slavery, or for any person for any office who will not make the protection of the inalienable right of men his first duty; and we further pledge ourselves to endeavor to influence others to make this ruling principle in the exercise of the elective franchise, and to give to this purpose our money and our time to the extent of our ability."

In the election only one of these men voted for Birney, while 78 of Galesburg's 108 votes were for Harrison, one of whose electors was Abraham Lincoln, swallowing the "hard cider" feature of the campaign in spite of its temperance principles. Lincoln took the stump in behalf of his friend and law partner, John Stuart, who was running against Douglas for Congress, and spoke at many towns in the North. He may have visited Galesburg then, but there is no record of it. The "stump" was often literally that in those days, for the expression originated from the practice of holding political rallies in the groves, where one of the many standing tree trunks furnished a rostrum for the speaker. Other political expressions date from this time and place, such as "log rolling," and "land office business" is a relic of the day when eager settlers were taking up "Congress land."

The Liberty Party ultimately united with the anti-slavery Whigs and Democrats to form the Free Soil Party, and this became the Republican Party shortly before the election of 1856, when Galesburg became a Republican town and remained so. Even in abolition Galesburg, the thirteen men who cast their votes against slavery were looked upon as daring and extreme. Ten of them were Gale's own picked followers in the original colony movement, but Gale did not vote with them, nor was he, in a real sense, a reformer so much as religionist.

On February 14, 1857, the legislature of the State gave to the city its first charter, and in April of the same year the first election was held. In accordance with a clause in the charter, at this first election the people were to vote for or against granting to the Council power to license the sale of intoxicating drinks; 668 votes were cast, 462 for prohibition, 104 for power to license, and 102 did not vote upon the question, thus making prohibition a clause in the fundamental law of the city, and seconding the efforts of its founders who had inserted the temperance clause in the deed to every village lot.

In the town elections the Young Americans soon became identified with the movement to license saloons. It was composed of those who wanted to drink, and those who believed the only way to control the illegal sale of liquor was to make it legal. But temperance sentiment was too strong for such relaxing of standards. Expediency meant nothing beside the sin of compounding an evil, and the sale of liquor, though often voted on, was not licensed in Galesburg until 1872. Meanwhile liquor was bootlegged and sold in all the drug stores, and at the hotel. The local elections were not conducted along national lines; there were always home issues nearer to the people; mainly liquor, but as the town grew it had the local problems—gas, water, schools

—which every city has, and some of them supplied plenty of excitement, particularly the county seat fight. The people entered into national contests with Western enthusiasm, and election day became one of its holidays, with plenty of lively incidents, especially after the Irish came to build and work on the railroad, and greatly to swell the ranks of the Democrats.

No national election seems to have again stirred the town until 1856, though the issues of the day were debated, and listened to with unabated interest by large crowds. Two thousand people heard a discussion of the Nebraska Bill from the steps of the Presbyterian Church. It was not until Frémont was nominated as the first presidential candidate of the newly-organized Republican Party to run against Buchanan that popular excitement flared up again. The third candidate was Fillmore, who had signed the drastic Fugitive Slave Act, which roused the Galesburg supporters of the Underground Railroad to greater efforts at evasion. William Kellogg, the congressional nominee spoke often in Galesburg. Horace Greeley said he was a "fossil Whig, only varnished over with enough Republicanism to get into Congress." Editor Sherman, of the *Free Democrat,* replied, "we know he is a living, breathing Republican, made of Republican bone and muscle, and clothed with Republican thunder."

This campaign was the one in which the Republican candidate's gifted wife was linked with him in the slogan "Frémont and Jessie." She was the daughter of Frémont's backer, Senator Benton, of Missouri, author of the Missouri Compromise of 1820. The campaign was waged with rallies and parades. A huge meeting was held in the College Park. Delegations came from all the near-by towns. The crowd was said to number 20,000. Lincoln was billed as one of the speakers, but did not appear, and Galesburg had to wait two years to hear him. The parade exhibited the usual wagons of pretty girls impersonating the States. There were many brass bands. The procession from Henderson was a mile and a half long. Home-made banners waved in the air, that prepared by the delegation from Dixon being voted the most beautiful and costly.

What is now known as a straw vote was taken on the newly running railroad trains, and in the shops. The vote in Galesburg was 699 for Frémont, 160 for Buchanan, nothing for Fillmore.

## II

### GALESBURG'S BIG DAY

The political high water mark of the little town was set in 1858, when Galesburg was selected as the scene of the fifth of the famous Lincoln-Douglas debates. Ostensibly the two men were running for office, canvassing for votes, discussing the questions of the day, but one question happened to be the extension of slavery to new territory, given sinister significance by Kansas' struggle to be admitted to the Union as free soil in spite of the Missouri Compromise. The nation's battle was being fought in Illinois that fall, and beneath the air of festivity, the readiness of hard-working settlers to take advantage of an opportunity for an outing, it was no mere political rally that drew tens of thousands to hear that oddly matched pair.

The fame of the performances had run on ahead and whetted interest already keen. Both men were rough and ready controversialists, good at the by-play which delighted Western audiences. Galesburg was fanatically abolitionist, had been from the very day of its founding, but the county, settled mainly by "Hoosiers," was pro-slavery. Many a fugitive slave had Galesburg rescued from Knoxville, the seat of the county government, by means of the Underground Railroad, and sent on to Canada and sanctuary. So the audience that day was compounded of adherents to both causes and friendly to both speakers.

Douglas was well and favorably known in the county, while Lincoln was practically a stranger. Douglas had sat as a judge at Knoxville, and won the approval of local lawyers for his ability and fairness. There is no need to go into the political background of the debate, or the history of the principals. But this fifth meeting of the antagonists was Galesburg's big day, in which the people had their part, and that part has an interest aside from that of the central characters.

Thursday, October 7, was as inauspicious as it well could be. It had rained all day Wednesday, a persistent downfall which turned the prairie roads to mire. In the night the temperature dropped; next day was cold and raw, with a bitter northwest wind. At dawn a gun was fired at Galesburg to inaugurate the day, but long before that there was stir in nearly every farmhouse in Knox County, for neither wind nor mud could keep the people from town that day. Horses had been curried, harness washed, wagons scrubbed and polished to shine in the parade; dinners had been packed and were loaded into the wagons; patriotic floats had been prepared and decorated and were filled with their human freight properly costumed.

In the early bleak light of that October morning the roads leading to Galesburg presented a singular and unforgettable sight. For miles in every direction segments of the day's cavalcade descended on the town. Each village was contributing its quota to the crowd, and its best wit in the way of allegorical groups for the procession. From Rio on the north, the rendezvous of the villages in that district, a wagon train defiled, each vehicle drawn by six or eight matched horses, the pick of the barns, with Ben Harvey in command, on horseback in brave array, who testified he was in the saddle at five-thirty, and never got down until one o'clock.

The first car in this triumphal procession was the band wagon, of home manufacture, a superstructure built on a farm wagon truck, bedecked with bunting and flags, in which rode the band, known as the "Bachus Boys," from the patron who paid for the uniforms and brass horns. Following came another large float in which were the thirty-two prettiest girls in the township seated back to back on two long seats down the middle, dressed in white with blue ribbons across their breasts bearing the names of the thirty-two States in large letters of gold. The framework overhead was covered with green branches making a sort of bower, and the States were crowned with wreaths of flowers. On a shelf extending out behind the wagon stood a melancholy figure dressed in black labelled "Kansas," who beat with her hands on the side of the float, while her banner proclaimed, "They won't let me in."

A woodland scene staged on a hayrack came next; on it lay a huge ten-foot log which, as the float later moved down Main Street, would be halved and quartered and split into fence rails by the half dozen bronzed and sturdy young men in linsey-woolsey now standing beside it with axes and wedges—a delicate compliment to Lincoln the Rail-Splitter, or a sneer at his humble origin, according to your sentiments. Then came a barge showing a wheat-threshing scene, and other farm operations, and others filled with people sitting bolt upright on springless seats for the long muddy ride to town.

At every crossroad new sections joined the cavalcade, and each novel float or motto or sentiment lettered on banners and streamers was greeted with shouts and cheers. One showed a good-sized tree, its roots firmly planted in the wagon box, with thirty-two boys clinging to thirty-two limbs, each waving a flag with the name of a State on it. There were goddesses of liberty, plump matronly women in red, white and blue, with golden crowns on their heads, and mottoes and slogans, and war cries of all shades of political belief, mostly Democratic. On all the roads leading to Galesburg, which radiated from the town like spokes from a wheel, as they still do, similar scenes were being enacted, as the greatest crowd in the history of the town gravitated to that common center. Four, six and eight horses carefully matched, and gorgeously decorated (one participant remembers driving a turnout of thirty-six; could it have been thirty-two, one for each State?) drew wagons. There were even spans of oxen.

The few wealthier folk rode in carriages, and hundreds on horseback, thousands on foot, and each section shepherded by a busy, bustling and important-looking captain.

As each division arrived at the town, it was guided to its appointed place by marshals, resplendent in sashes, long-legged California boots and bridle ribbons, Jim Bennet, Charlie Bonney, or Hank Carpenter, on horseback, until the little town was packed with people and horses, girls in red, white and blue dresses, men in the rude but picturesque costume of the time, many tall beaver hats, frock coats and top boots, bands blowing and drumming, militia marching and countermarching. No event could possibly appeal more strongly to such a crowd than one which combined politics with a picnic. But amid all the Fourth-of-July excitement, there was an undercurrent of gravity, of deep feeling and sleeping passions. It was a time when crowds gave vent to their emotions. It would be impossible today to assemble so colorful and picturesque a gathering in that spot.

The new railroad, only three years old, was manfully doing its part to swell the crowd. The little town was already a railroad center, born one, in fact, with four branch lines, and over each came delegations from Avon, Abingdon, Monmouth, Altona, Wataga, and other near-by villages. For many it was their first ride on the cars. Avon brought its band of thirteen brass horns and two drums, and Monmouth its locally famous glee club.

From the Peoria and Oquawka railroad Alva Willcox chartered a special train, at a cost of $400, for excursionists living down Peoria way, Elmwood, Gilson, Yates City and Maquon. The train consisted of two coaches and eighteen flat and box cars, fitted up with rough seats, and three engines, one in front and two behind. But in spite of all that locomotive power, the train stalled on the grades, and the male passengers turned out to push it up hill. It reached the Venetian-red pine "depot" at Galesburg just as Douglas on the college campus a block away finished his speech. No matter; there were people and to spare. The little burg with five thousand inhabitants had absorbed four times its population, topping the figures at the other debates, and setting a bench mark which stood long for measuring other crowds.

### III

#### ABRAHAM LINCOLN

Lincoln arrived at Knoxville Wednesday night, coming by train from Peoria. He was met at the depot by a large delegation and escorted to the Hebard House, where the best room opening on the balcony had been set aside for him. Knoxville, already a bit jealous of Galesburg's growing prestige at her expense, was disposed to make the most of her small part in the celebration. The crowd in front of the hotel called for a speech, and Lincoln spoke briefly from the balcony. As he stood in the shadow of the veranda, some one hoisted a lantern on a pole to "spotlight" him. "My friends," said Lincoln, "the less you see of me, the better you will like me."

Next morning Knoxville escorted Lincoln to the Galesburg city line. The procession was a mile and a half long, composed of much the same elements as those waiting at Galesburg five miles away, with four- and six-horse teams attached to wagons filled with girls representing the States, goddesses of liberty, and numerous citizens in wagons, on horseback and on foot. The town had been scoured to find a fitting equipage for the guest of honor. Finally Benny Hebard's horses were hitched to Bill Holcomb's carriage to produce a turnout worthy of the occasion. In this Lincoln was seated with James Knox, chairman of the day's exercises, beside him; also in the carriage were Benny Hebard (Benny was mayor of Knoxville) and John Winter, editor of the *Knox Republican,* reputed to be one of the first, if not the first, newspapers in the country to suggest Lincoln for President—country weeklies had more weight in those days.

Charlie Parmenter, steward of the Hebard House, held the reins. "I had been chosen to drive the rig because it was at that time the finest rig in Knoxville," said Charlie, "and the team was one of the finest in the country, and Uncle Benny said he wouldn't let any one but me drive them. As we drove along Uncle Benny and Jimmie Knox would point out to Lincoln the homes of the different people along the road, and as we rode Uncle Benny said:

"'There is where Isaac Guliher lives.'

"Lincoln said, 'Old Isaac Guliher?' and Uncle Benny said, 'Yes.'

"Lincoln said, 'I must stop and shake hands with him.'"

Guliher was an old friend from Sangamon County. He had served under Lincoln in the unjustifiable Black Hawk War. He was lined up in front of his house with his wife and eleven children, or as many as had survived the hazardous childhood of those days, to see the parade go by. Lincoln shook hands with Guliher, kissed his wife, and patted the children on the head, the sort of thing which endeared him to multitudes, while the procession waited.

Meanwhile, one of the Galesburg floats coming out to meet the Knoxville parade, fearful lest Lincoln should miss the heroic preparation to do him honor, and incidentally advertise the business, had driven down the road to where Lincoln was chatting with Guliher. This float was the display of the Brown corn-planter works, appropriately the biggest manufacturing industry in that agricultural community. It was a wagon extended to forty feet by lengthening the reach, drawn by twelve superb horses, driven by George W. Brown himself in a high "plug" hat. The wagon was filled with new and shiny specimens of Brown's invention, the corn-planter, a godsend to the settlers for dropping seed for the tall corn. On one end of the wagon was a steam engine tooting away raucously. It was manned by the entire working force of the factory, and when Lincoln came out of Guliher's he found the men lined up each side the gate to give him a rousing cheer, and he dutifully shook hands with each of them.

According to one observer, Lincoln left his carriage at intervals on the ride from Knoxville and climbed up on the wagons behind, visiting with the people in them. Long before the procession reached the Galesburg cohorts parked beside the fairgrounds he had shaken hands with most of his entourage.

In 1908, on the fiftieth anniversary of the occasion, the editor of the Galesburg newspaper collected reminiscences from several hundred old settlers who attended the original debate, and these letters and interviews contain a wealth of detail as to what happened on that eventful day. Unfortunately there is as much discrepancy between these stories as there is between the four Gospels, and as great difficulty in harmonizing them. Several eye-witnesses assert that the vehicle which awaited Lincoln at the outskirts of the city was a wagon loaded with fence rails. He was expected to make his entry riding on this undignified vehicle, and complied with his wonted good nature. The legend has spawned the usual anecdote, for it is related that a Democrat sourly observed, "Lincoln needs a load of rails to ride him in to town, but one would be enough to ride him out." Others, equally creditable, deny the story emphatically, and insist that a proper carriage was provided, fully equal to the smart rig turned out by Knoxville.

At the fair grounds the Galesburg contingent took charge of Lincoln to escort him to the home of his host, Henry (Hank) Sanderson, whose father, Levi Sanderson, had helped to found the town which that day was but twenty years removed from virgin prairie. The two parades, Galesburg and Knoxville, fell in behind, and the procession moved slowly down Main Street, where the flags and bunting hung disconsolately, soaked by yesterday's rain, and whipped to tatters by today's wind, around the square into Broad Street, where stood the Sanderson mansion, a large square house with a "captain's walk" on top, an unusual adornment in the Middle West where a tower was the preferred mark of gentility.

Another mooted point on which the synoptists disagree is where Lincoln ate dinner on that eventful day, which brings up the question as to what the word "dinner" means. Mrs. Sanderson, his hostess, was quite sure Lincoln ate his midday meal at her house at high noon. She did not recall the names of any of the other guests except James Knox, though she remembers a doctor who talked too much and embarrassed Lincoln by his reminiscences, the man, she said, who had "trained" Lincoln for a duel which was never fought. On the other hand, Mrs. Roy Guild is equally certain Lincoln ate "dinner" with her mother, Mrs. Abram S. Bergen, known to a generation of Galesburgers as "Mother" Bergen.

Twice widowed, she supported herself and family, which included her husband's children by a previous marriage, by taking students to board (terms: one dollar and a bit if paid in cash; one dollar and two shillings if paid in truck). She mothered the boys who occupied her rooms, and ultimately mothered the whole town. With a natural talent for nursing, supplemented by skill learned from her doctor husband, she was an angel of mercy to the sick without pay, a faithful ally to Doctor Bunce during the cholera epidemic.

Before coming to Galesburg Mother Bergen lived in Springfield, where Lincoln was a close friend of her husband and herself. She sent her son to bring him to her house for dinner, and according to her daughter Lincoln came. It seems improbable that two such estimable women should be mistaken about so noteworthy a guest. The explanation may lie in the fact that noon was official dinner time in Galesburg, that Lincoln ate dinner at the Sandersons', and what he had at Mother Bergen's was technically supper, however elaborate the feast, after the exercises were over, and before the beginning of the reception at the Sanderson house which filled the evening until a late hour. No doubt Mrs. Sanderson was glad to have her guest taken care of for one meal, domestic service being what it was in a prairie town in the fifties.

Carl Sandburg, himself a Galesburg product and one of its ornaments, says in his *Abraham Lincoln: the Prairie Years,* that

Lincoln had a bath at the Sandersons', and tells how Sanderson brought hot water and towels and admired the "lean, hard organization of the muscles that sheathed the bony framework." There is no reason to doubt it; it was entirely within the character of the man. The difficulty is to find a place for it in the time-table. Lincoln came from Knoxville in the morning (though one lone witness deposes that he arrived at Galesburg the evening before, and spent the night there); he received an address of welcome and two silk banners after reaching the Sanderson home. Dinner was promptly at twelve. The exercises were at two o'clock. We will have to allow Lincoln his bath after the speaking and before he set out for Mother Bergen's for supper.

Thomas Gold Frost delivered the address of welcome. He was one of the organizers of the new-born Republican Party. His father back in New York, the Reverend John Frost, had been the first man consulted by George W. Gale about his plan for establishing a city and college in the West. Lincoln spoke a few words in reply. Then came an army of young women with banners.

"Mr. Sanderson," inquired Lincoln, "what is the meaning of this?"

"They desire to present a flag to you," was the answer.

"But what am I to do?" inquired Lincoln anxiously.

"O, go out and accept it and make them a little talk, telling them you are obliged to them."

"I don't mind making a speech, but I have no small change."

No sooner was this ceremony disposed of, when another deputation arrived, a cavalcade of young women on horseback, bringing a still more gorgeous banner, the patient needlework of the Republican women of Galesburg—which meant in those pre-woman's suffrage days merely the women whose husbands were Republicans. The presentation was made by Ada Hurd. She became Lady Van Horne when her husband was knighted for building the Canadian Pacific Railway. When Mrs. Sanderson came to put her house to rights next day, she found the banners hanging on the hatrack where Lincoln had left them. One of them is now fittingly enshrined in the State historical museum of Kansas, whose plight furnished inspiration for several of the allegorical floats, and indeed was the main theme of the debate.


## IV

### STEPHEN A. DOUGLAS

Meanwhile Douglas had received such a welcome as the comparatively small body of Democrats in the town could give. He arrived from Oquawka, where he had made a political speech the night before, by the morning train along with a crowd of supporters and opposers, and was met at the train by a delegation headed by George Lanphere, the most prominent Democrat in the town and an old friend of Douglas. Lanphere had been postmaster until thrown out by Buchanan after he and Douglas had parted company.

Across the street from the station stood the Bancroft House, and there a group of Lombard students was waiting to bestow a silk banner on Douglas. The presentation was made by George Elwell, and Douglas remarked, "That young man will make his mark." He did, though not such a shining one as Lady Van Horne, but he did become senator from Missouri.

From the Bancroft House Douglas was taken to a hotel on Main Street conducted by Messrs. Bonney and Haskell and known indifferently to the inhabitants as the Bonney House or the Haskell House, though its official name was Haskell. Here he was assigned a large parlor on the second floor in which to receive his friends, with a balcony from which to view the parade. His ebony walking stick with an old English "D" on a silver band was left behind at the Bancroft House, and it remains in Galesburg to this day.

The parade started about eleven o'clock. We have seen the various elements gathering. These, together with the cortege from

Knoxville, were fused in one line of march, with the inevitable confusions and misunderstandings as the drivers got their long strings of horses entangled and marshals galloped furiously hither and thither. The streets of Galesburg were as innocent of pavement as the prairie roads, and the mud, though partly dried by the wind, made all progress difficult. Nevertheless the procession moved with considerable impressiveness, if not with military smartness, down Main Street into Broad, thence around the park to the college campus, where it disbanded, and the participants scurried to find places in the lee of the buildings to unpack and eat their dinners.

Every inch of space on the line of march was taken. The people stood on the sidewalk, in the windows, on the roofs, and on the arcades or wooden awnings which covered the sidewalks in front of business buildings of prairie towns in the fifties. The street was one vast amphitheater of faces, for twelve blocks. Nearly all the wagons and floats displayed banners or streamers inscribed with slogans voicing the humor and partisanship of the two factions. Among them could be read, "Honest Abe, the Rail Splitter," "Free States and Free Men," "Lincoln, the Giant Killer," while Democratic floats bore such phrases as "The Constitution as It Is," "Popular Sovereignty," "Hurrah for the Little Giant," "No Nigger Inequality," "Down with the Abolitionists." One of the local Democrats had received news shortly before the parade started which he thought would cheer his comrades, so his daughter from her car in the parade displayed a placard on which was lettered the inscription, "Maine Goes Democratic by 3000 Majority." The delegation from Sparta township carried a banner with the splendidly non-committal war cry, "Spartans Never Surrender."

One work of art was a railroad train, the cars labelled with the names of the free States, pulled by an engine marked "Freedom"; on the track ahead was the Douglas cart loaded with cotton and stuck fast, the Negro driver represented as saying, "Fo' God, massa, I believes we's in danger." On one piece of canvas had been rudely sketched a cartoon of Lincoln as a snapping cur and Douglas as a lordly lion, at which the Republicans jeered, "Better a live dog than a dead lion." Most of the wagons carried tall flag-staffs cut from hickory saplings with a tuft of leaves left at the top.

The Avon brass band with its thirteen horns, piqued at not see-ing Douglas on his balcony when passing the Haskell House, stopped and gave vent to a stentorian rendition of "Hail, Colum-bia," which brought the Little Giant smilingly out, whereupon John Terry, perched on the arcade opposite, in a voice like a trumpet, called for three cheers, and the crowd from Prairie Street to the Square responded with a will.

When the parade had finally disappeared around the Square into Broad Street, and the vast crowd dispersed to eat its picnic dinners wherever it could find a place, and the numerous small restaurants of the town did a roaring business, Douglas was car-ried off by his friend Lanphere to eat one of Mrs. Lanphere's famous dinners. Her daughter Ione has left an account of the meal:

"My mother, who was a splendid cook, had called in extra help for the occasion, for she would allow no one to assist her in mak-ing the mince pies, a delicacy which she was famous in preparing. My mother remarked: 'Mr. Douglas used to be very fond of our mince pies in the old days of our friendship, when we lived in Monmouth and he used to stop with us. I think he wanted to stay with us so that he could go out in our peach orchard and rehearse his speches that he had to make before the court. I have heard some of his best efforts from my kitchen window. Then he would go down to the courthouse and make the same grand speech there.'

"When they came to the house and the greetings were passed, with kind reference by Mr. Douglas to the old days when we were small children, etc., they were invited out to dinner. They were hardly seated at the table when Mr. Douglas turned to my mother saying, 'Matilda, have you got a mince pie such as you

used to have in old times?' Mother told him she had made some
especially for him, and had one placed before him, and that pie
with a cup of coffee was all the dinner he partook of. The turkey,
oysters and all that elaborate repast, that had caused Mother so
much anxiety in the preparation for Mr. Douglas especially, was
enjoyed by the other guests at the table, but Mr. Douglas ate the
pie with decided relish, and remarked that that pie and that coffee were worth taking a long trip to enjoy."

## V

### THE DEBATE

The crowd on Knox campus grew denser as the spectators from
the streets began to seek places among those already ensconced
on every available spot. It had been planned to hold the exercises on the south front of the main college building, where space
was ample, but the sharp wind made it necessary to seek a place
where the speakers at least would be sheltered from its blast.
The temporary platform which had been erected the day before
was taken down, and set up against the east end of the building,
which had been completed only the year previous, the most ambitious structure in the town; the college was justly proud of it.

The space in front of the platform was restricted. About fifty
yards east was the dormitory, known as "East Bricks." Into this
space the crowd squeezed, and overflowed laterally, so that hundreds stood in the full force of the winds. The roof of East
Bricks was thickly covered with spectators, and every student who
roomed there had his window filled with relatives. So many old
settlers avowed they stood within ten feet of the platform that
one skeptic insisted they must have stood like acrobats on each
other's shoulders.

A large banner reading "Knox College for Lincoln" had with
considerable difficulty been attached to the finial of the belfry
above the main building, but with the change of location of the

platform it was taken down and draped across the east end of the building. But the wind had torn it, and in rehanging it a part of the lettering was turned to the wall, and thus it hung during the program, putting the pictures of the scene drawn since from imagination in the wrong, as one patriot who skinned his hands putting it up has taken pains to testify.

Chairs for the speakers' platform had been borrowed from the dormitories, and sophomore Charles Mason White was thrilled to see the old yellow chair in which he habitually studied his Aeneid and trigonometry occupied by Stephen A. Douglas. Among the worthies whom various witnesses remember sitting on the platform were George Ford, George Lanphere, Governor McMurtry, James Knox, R. L. Hanneman, William Kellogg, John Winter, Long John Wentworth (of Chicago), Governor Bruington, and Major Yvonett. Until the arrival of the speakers, the crowd was entertained by Editor Reed of Alexis, a dry and witty speaker. There was music by the band, and songs by the glee club. A four-horse carriage brought the orators of the day to the campus, accompanied by a band and three companies of militia, though one account says Lincoln walked, as well he might, the Sanderson house being only two blocks from the scene. The speakers entered the front door of "Old Main," and stepped out on the platform through one of the windows, Lincoln remarking that he had now gone through Knox College. The crowd greeted them with thunders of applause.

Galesburg was one of the towns where it had been agreed beforehand that Douglas should speak first. He spoke for an hour, followed by Lincoln for an hour and a half, with half an hour for rebuttal. George Ford introduced Douglas, and James Knox presented Lincoln, and for three hours the crowd massed densely around the building and standing all the time, listened with unflagging interest, though not in silence, while the entire country waited the accounts of the speeches, reported in shorthand for the first time in newspaper history.

Again are furnished instances of the unreliability of the human memory, which has driven lawyers to despair, in the conflicting reports of what the speakers did and did not say. The formal debates were recorded and printed and exist today in many forms, but the reporter did not, as any newspaper man today would have done, take down the by-play, the exchange of personalities and raillery which so delighted the crowd. Mixed up with what the speakers did say on this occasion are stories recalled from other debates and other speeches, characteristic Lincolnia. The narrator could not remember after fifty years whether he heard them from Lincoln's lips, or from friends in the crowd.

Lincoln wore a long cloak instead of his customary shawl, and as he rose to respond, he stretched to his full height, slipped off the cloak and handed it to a man sitting near, saying:

"Hold this while I stone Stephen."

Or, according to another auditor, as Lincoln rose, Douglas remarked,

"How long, O Lord, how long!" to which Lincoln retorted,

"The days and the years of the wicked are short."

He compared unfavorably with his easier and more accomplished opponent, and everybody noticed it. His arms hung awkwardly; he walked back and forth aimlessly without saying anything, and his admirers groaned inwardly. One staunch adherent said long years after, "When Douglas finished and Lincoln rose, I felt like crying. I was sorry for him and ashamed of my politics, but he hadn't spoken ten minutes until I was shouting with the rest of them, full of joy as a Methodist camp-meeting."

Many recalled the whisky-selling story, though it is not in the official record. "I remember," recalls Ed Russell, "that he (Douglas) told how Abe could always outrun the other boys, and how he could throw and whip them, and how Abe used to keep a grocery store and sell sugar to the women and whisky to the men. I could see Lincoln nod and laugh as Douglas told this. When it came his turn to speak he said it was true he could outrun all the boys and the reason they could not whip him was because they could not catch him. 'I did sell whisky in those days,' said Lincoln, 'and Steve was my best customer.'" Douglas' well-known fondness for drink made this a hit the crowd appreciated.

Sam Brown thought the strongest part of Lincoln's speech was about "a house divided against itself cannot stand, and that this Union must be all slave or all free." Major Clay, one of the leading farmers in a community of leading farmers, is positive that neither the whisky-selling incident nor the house-divided allusion was used at Galesburg. They were all honorable men, but fifty years cloud the memory until what might have been became what was.

James Paden, another of those stalwart farmers with which Knox County abounded, six years county supervisor, gives his recollection of a story Lincoln did tell at Galesburg: He was thirty-one when he heard the debate; at eighty-one he writes: "I was so close to the stand that I could see all those that had seats on it, and hear all that was said. I recall one of the famous stories of Lincoln." (The story Lincoln told to point up his denial of the authorship of fraudulent resolutions which in spite of his denial Douglas kept throwing up at him.) "In the course of his speech Lincoln said that the constant reiteration of this story by Douglas reminded him of the old woman whose husband had been drowned. The man was a fisherman and his body had been found in the water. It had evidently been in the water for some time. The parties on examining it found that the pockets were full of eels. They reported the death to the widow, and also informed her that the pockets were full of eels.

" 'That so?' she said, drying her tears. 'Well, take the eels out of the pockets and set the body again.'"

This anecdote appears in the official stenographic report, but much less wordy. "The fraud having been apparently successful upon the occasion, both Harris and Douglas have more than once been attempting to put it to new uses. As the fisherman's wife, whose drowned husband was brought home with his body full of eels, said when she was asked what was to be done with him, 'take the eels out and set him again,' so Harris and Douglas have shown a disposition to take the eels out of that stale fraud . . . and set the fraud again."

Douglas sat with his familiar white hat on, the stub of a cigar clenched between his teeth, stirring restlessly at times as something Lincoln said aroused him. When his turn came to speak in rebuttal, he rose quickly and spoke excitedly. He began by telling the crowd that the greatest compliment it could pay him was to listen in silence, in reproof of the applause, heckling and cries of disapproval which had punctuated both speeches, but particularly Douglas'.

The speeches no doubt were more effective delivered than they are now in cold type. Douglas' effusion reads better than Lincoln's, which has none of the compact effectiveness of the Gettysburg address. Allowance must be made for the personality of the man, and this can be read in the reactions of many of his listeners, who have recorded their disappointment at Lincoln's unprepossessing appearance, and the awkwardness with which he got under way.

"Douglas' voice was so powerful," said one hearer, "he was heard distinctly to the outskirts of that vast audience." "Douglas was hoarse," says another, "from long speaking in the open air; he could not be heard at a distance. Lincoln's voice rang clear as a bell." This hearer noted that Lincoln pronounced "put" as if it were spelled "putt."

One deep impression was made to the discomfiture of two students who lived in the East Bricks, in front of which the crowd was packed. They had just bought a ton of coal, that had been dumped in front of their door on ground softened by the previous day's heavy rain. Next morning they found it trodden so deeply into the earth by people standing on it, they had to mine it before they could carry it into their room.

The debate ended, the men began to hitch up for the homeward journey, the women to collect their children and gather up the baskets. Many remained in town for receptions in the evening, Douglas at the Haskell House, Lincoln at the Sanderson home. Most of the callers desired to shake hands with both men to tell their grandchildren, for they were dimly aware a significant page of history had been turned that day. A few couples took advantage of being in town and the general excited state in which they were in, to make it their wedding day. Among the heroes who deserve a tribute of praise were the patient and rugged farmers who had risen before daybreak, ridden many of them twenty-five miles in springless wagons, stood for three hours in a bitter wind, and would ride all the way home again over none too good roads, before they slept.

The business of vote-making, that is the receptions of the candidates to their adherents, lasted until a late hour. One incident stands out as illustrating Lincoln's unfailing friendliness and his memory for faces and names.

"Uncle Billy" Camp was justice of the peace of the little Scotch hamlet of Oneida a dozen miles away. He had boasted to his cronies that he knew both Douglas and Lincoln; he didn't know Lincoln as well as he knew Douglas; Lincoln might not recognize him, but Douglas would.

"Then," cried his friends, "you've got to introduce the whole crowd to Douglas and Lincoln."

Uncle Billy agreed. On the evening of the great day he led them to the Haskell House and up to Douglas' room. The Little Giant was exhausted with the exertions of the day—he had none of Lincoln's tremendous vitality, and his drinking habits told on him—he was resting with half-closed eyes, his chin on his bosom, when the delegation entered. Camp addressed him:

"Hello, Judge, I knew you in Springfield."

Douglas opened his eyes, but did not move.

"Probably, but I don't remember you," and closed his eyes again.

The crowd taunted Uncle Billy unmercifully.

"Now, then, Billy; you've made us acquainted with Douglas; take us around to see Lincoln."

Billy's confidence faded. He would not risk another affront. "Maybe Lincoln would not remember him." But the crowd insisted, and dragged him off to the Sanderson mansion, where Lincoln was receiving his Republican friends. As soon as Lincoln saw Camp, he strode toward him, grasped his hand, and greeted him by name in his own hearty manner. Camp introduced his friends, who were thereby transformed into Republicans as far as their votes for Lincoln were concerned. Hundreds of the letters bear testimony to Lincoln's kindly smile of greeting. It was as great a factor in winning votes as his forensic logic.

Edward Beecher was in that great audience which assembled at the east steps of Old Main, and when the debate was over he went home and wrote:

"There was a grandeur in his thoughts, a comprehensiveness in his arguments, a binding force in his conclusions, which were perfectly irresistible. The vast throng was silent as death; every eye was fixed upon the speaker, and all gave him serious attention. He was the tall man eloquent; his countenance glowed with animation, and his eye glistened with an intelligence which made it lustrous. He was no longer awkward and ungainly, but graceful, bold, commanding."

"Old Main will forever remain distinguished," says Ida Tarbell, "because it was the background of one of that series of great debates, but what particularly distinguishes it is that here for the first time in the series Lincoln drove his argument down to the question of the right or wrong of slavery, here for the first time boldly proclaimed that the final and unanswerable reason for opposing the extension of slavery was that it was a wicked institution."

The great day was over. Next morning Mrs. Sanderson, with the aid of Aunt Sukey, one of the first of the contraband slaves to find asylum in Galesburg, set about the job of scraping up the prairie mud tramped into her carpets by Lincoln's admirers.

# LINCOLN

## VI

## "TWINKLE, TWINKLE, LITTLE CARR"

It is unnecessary to remind any one that Lincoln and Douglas were campaigning for the United States Senate, or that Lincoln failed of election but won the presidency by his adroit handling of the ticklish question of State rights in connection with slavery. "Mud elected Douglas," sagely observed *The Free Democrat*. "Two days of fair weather before election would have returned Lincoln to the United States Senate. Majorities in some districts were so light that the turnout of a few fair-weather Republicans would have turned the results."

It was not Lincoln's first visit to Galesburg. Whether or not he came in the course of his campaigning for John Stuart, he was in the town casually not long before this time, for C. A. Hinckley, son of Clarissa Root, met him one day on Main Street coming out of the barber shop, with the familiar shawl draped over his shoulders. Lincoln greeted him, and asked him to walk with him to the railway station, explaining that he was passing through and had been waiting for a train.

The presidential campaign two years later was the most intensely exciting any State has experienced before or since. The cause for which Galesburg had fought, and for which it had defied the laws of the nation and the State, was now at its crisis. Both candidates were from Illinois, and both were known in Galesburg. Lincoln had won his audience that day on Knox Campus, as was shown by the vote at the election. Legend (in this case, Chapman's *History of Knox County*) asserts it was a Knox County man, Rufus Miles, who first suggested him for President. A county normally Democratic returned a handsome majority for Lincoln.

The presidential campaign of 1860 was inaugurated in Knox County in August by a huge rally. The crowd was so large the editor of *The Free Democrat* testified "the numbers present at the

[ 296 ]

great debate will bear no comparison with those present on this occasion." The parade bore so strong a resemblance to that which lent éclat to the debate that there is suspicion the recollections of the two demonstrations became confused in the memories of the participants. There were eighteen brass bands from sixteen communities. There was a parade by night as well as by day, 900 carrying lighted torches. The Wide Awakes participated to the extent of 1200 men.

All the local industries were represented by floats. George W. Brown turned out with the same equipage which had welcomed Lincoln two years before. A tin shop on wheels capitalized the popular meaning of "in a horn" with three large tin horns labelled "Douglas, our next President, in a—," with similar slurs for Breckinridge and Bell. The carriage makers, cabinetmakers, carpenters, stonecutters, masons, printers, shoemakers, and coppersmiths, like the guilds of an ancient English town, had each a characteristic exhibit in the line, displaying their skill at their crafts, the sides of the wagons covered with mottoes and phrases full of weak puns, testifying their allegiance. That of the shoemakers is a fair specimen:

> "Shoemakers for Lincoln pledge their *awl*
> To elect Abe; we take his *measure*.
> Our *soles* we pledge at freedom's call;
> Breck and Bell will *peg* at leisure,
> And *wax* Steve Douglas in the fall."

John Bell was the fourth candidate, the nominee of the Union Constitutional Party.

There was a detachment of railroad employees, a log cabin and a cornfield on wheels, a railsplitter and a flat boat as tribute to Old Abe's early occupations. There were dozens of bandwagons of girls representing the thirty-two States, one composed entirely of unusually pretty Swedish maidens, with the now accepted allegory of Kansas in mourning. The Swedes took an active part in the campaign, and had several units in line. Among the speakers were the Kellogg whom Greeley aspersed, Owen Lovejoy, brother of the martyr, and Governor Grimes of Iowa, who had co-operated with Chauncey Colton in the matter of the railroad.

An incident of the campaign was the speech of Bob Ingersoll at Maquon on Spoon River, ten miles from Galesburg, in which he was reported to have said, "Any man that will vote for Lincoln is a damned dog, and should be kicked out of the State." He told his audience that if they did not think God and the Democratic Party were right, and did not want to vote for them, they might all go to hell, God damn them. The incident made considerable stir, and in corroboration of the above words, a statement was drawn up by eight reputable citizens of Maquon and published in the newspaper over their signatures. Subsequently Ingersoll bolted both God and the Democratic Party.

The jubilant editor of *The Free Democrat* prophesied, "The enthusiasm of the people is unbounded and betokens a glorious triumph in November next. Set down Old Knox as good for over 2000 majority for Lincoln and Hamlin." The estimate was just a bit too optimistic. The Knox County vote was Lincoln 3832, Douglas 2208, and Breckenridge 17, a majority of 1617. In the same election Newton Bateman, Lincoln's "big little schoolmaster," candidate for a third term as Superintendent of Public Instruction, polled three more votes in Knox County than Lincoln, against his two opponents, Roe and Snow. Bateman became president of Knox College fifteen years later.

Rufus Miles, reputed discoverer of Lincoln, sent him a feather from the wing of an eagle shot in Knox County with which to write his inaugural address. The three sons of old George Gale were divided in their allegiance during the campaign, Selden being for Lincoln, George for Douglas, and Josiah for Breckinridge. "Whoever may be elected," said John Winter, in *The Knox Republican,* "the Gale family will get the post office." It did not, however, for Lincoln's appointment was Clark Ezra Carr.

Clark Carr was the beau ideal of the small town statesman. He was for years the biggest politician in Knox County, literally as well as in Republican magnitude, for he was portly, even corpulent, with a certain rolling dignity of manner, and the slightly magniloquent style of talking, especially in his speeches, which marked the public men of the Middle West in the period after the Civil War. His reign was occasionally disputed, and he obtained no elective office, but he had much to say and considerable influence in the councils of the party, and was an unfailing resource when a speech was to be made.

He was brought to Illinois in the conventional covered wagon at an early age, by his family, who settled in near-by Henry County. His father Clark M. came to Galesburg to work for the promotion of the railroad, and Galesburg remained young Carr's home until he died. He was known as "Colonel" Carr, but the title indicated no familiarity with gunpowder. During the war Carr served in an office at Springfield engaged in clerical work in connection with organizing Illinois troops, and emerged with a military title, a desirable asset for a politician in the years following that great conflict.

As has been said, he was appointed postmaster at Galesburg, and held the office for twenty-four Republican years, until the succession was broken by Cleveland. The duties of the office were not onerous. Under our peculiar system, the real postmaster is the chief clerk, in this case an unusually able one, George Colville, of the bookbinding firm which manufactured the daybooks, so that Carr was free to follow many pursuits. He had attended Knox but did not graduate, studied law at Albany, and was admitted to the bar, but the only profession he practiced was politics. For a time he was editor of *The Republican,* and was the target for many of Stephe Smith's darts. His house in late years was the largest and most pretentious in town, the only one with a ball-room, and here prominent visitors were entertained, including three Presidents. His wife was a social leader, and the parties she gave were functions.

When President Harrison appointed Carr Minister to Denmark, he remarked that it was highly appropriate, as Hamlet was his favorite play. On his return to Galesburg with increased prestige, he continued to run the Republican Party, act as chairman at meetings, toastmaster at banquets, and write books. Among these are *The Illini, My Day and Generation, Lincoln at Gettysburg* (he was present on that occasion), and *The Life of Stephen A. Douglas.*

No national campaign achieved such depth of feeling as the one in which Lincoln was elected, at least in this spot in the nation. It was the eve of war, soon to absorb the energies and interests of the town, and from then on the town took its politics as most American cities do. There were rallies, torchlight parades, speeches, and transparencies, but the old fervor died out. The town had been brought to a one-party basis, the outcome never in doubt, with no clearcut issue to enlist feeling and sympathy. The pioneer era ended with the close of the war.

## VII

### WAR

The history of Galesburg includes four wars. The Black Hawk War was over before the colonists arrived, and had swept the Indians from the Military Tract and across the Mississippi, solving one pioneer problem. It was an unjust and uncalled-for war; the government broke faith with the redmen, as it did on most occasions in the conquest of the West, but this conflict did not directly concern our colonists. Such Indians as lingered were vagrants, petty pilferers, and even beggars. The family of Nehemiah West got a fright when Shuannee carried off little Mary playing in the woods, though he brought her back and begged her mother to give the little white papoose to him, but that being out of the question Mary Allen West was preserved to become the famed W. C. T. U. worker, tireless foe of rum and the first woman in Illinois to fill the office of county school superintendent.

The Mexican War, inaugurated on the flimsiest of pretexts by hot-head expansionists at Washington, caused scarcely a ripple in the life of the community. It was not that they were pacifists; piety and militarism have always gone hand in hand. But the village was too new and too isolated; the colonists were too busy getting their town going and their college started to be drawn into the remote currents of national life. There was some excitement at the county seat. Major McKee mustered the militia, and read the call for troops. One hundred nine men volunteered, but the quota was already filled, and Texas was annexed without the help of Knox County.

The Civil War stirred the town to its depths. Feeling in Illinois was perhaps more intense than in other States. The President belonged to Illinois, giving the State a deep personal interest in the problems that faced him. And Grant, rescued from obscurity by the accident of war, also belonged to Illinois. The nation made an idol of him, the State took pride and felt a sense of proprietorship. Illinois stood solidly behind Governor Yates; political differences were buried. She contributed 244,496 men to the carnage, 14,596 in excess of her quota, and lost 34,834, two-thirds from diseases incident to war.

Galesburg's interest was foreordained. It had taken active part in that peculiar nullification of the Fugitive Slave Act, known as the Underground Railroad. Galesburg was one of the best-known slave sanctuaries in the West. Illinois had been the scene of the Lincoln-Douglas debates, arguing the issue on which the war was fought, and one of these debates had been held in Galesburg, where the memory of Lincoln still lingered, and aroused patriotic desire to serve under his leadership. Knox County exceeded her quota of 3842 men, and raised $66,000 as bounties for soldiers and to care for their families while they were at the front.

Fifty dollars was paid at first to men who volunteered. This was later increased to three hundred. The city council in an excess of zeal voted twelve dollars a month to all soldiers' families, and when the mayor refused to sign the ordinance on the ground the town could not pay so much, he was forced to resign his office. The war brought the usual stringency and self denial. Potatoes rose to a dollar a bushel, and onions to two or three times that. The pay of the city officers was cut fifty per cent.

The nearness of the town to the theater of war in the West was another factor in its wholehearted participation. The C. B. & Q. had been completed just in time and made Galesburg a distributing point. Supplies and troops were constantly passing through. Letters contained such passages as the following from Jerusha Farnham:

"No lack of things to talk about nowadays, if ever before, Union and secession, Lincoln & Davis, Scott & Beauregard are on the lips of all every day, and sounds of war and battle are ringing in the ears of the nation. Yesterday a train of 18 or 20 cars came into town under the stars & stripes with the Irish Brigade of 1000 from Chicago. Today another brigade is expected, which will make the third this week all going to Missouri."

That William Patch, whom Doctor Beecher visited on Sunday afternoons to the disapproval of the stricter element, was instrumental in saving the life of General Sherman; otherwise there would have been no march to the sea, and the outcome of the war might have been different. Patch was the first conductor hired by the railroad after it became the C. B. & Q. During the war he was transferred to government service, moving troops and carrying supplies in the South. He was in charge of a train bearing Sherman and his staff from Memphis to Corinth, with a body-guard of fifty-four soldiers. The engineer was a Confederate, in a plot to capture the general. It had been agreed he would stop the train in a densely wooded spot where a detachment of Confederates was ambushed. As soon as the train came to a standstill the Southerners burst from the woods with the rebel yell and began firing, some of them boarding the train. Patch grasped the situation instantly. Climbing over the tender he put his revolver at the engineer's head and ordered him to go ahead at full speed.

The engineer obeyed. The train went on carrying off some of the enemy. Sherman and his staff were in their private car. A desperate struggle ensued between his guards and the invaders. The train drew into Colliersville, Sherman and his staff jumped from one end and raced for the fort, while the Confederates leaped from the other and disappeared in the woods before the Union soldiers swarming from the fort could reach the scene. Years later Sherman visited Galesburg with President Hayes, and singled out Patch in the assembled crowd, and called him up for a reminiscent chat.

The women of the town organized. The Ladies' Aid Society sewed and put up fruits and jellies for boxes sent to the front. The young women formed the Juvenile Soldiers' Aid Society. There was demand for anti-scorbutic foods for the soldiers. As always, disease was a worse enemy than gunfire or bayonets. Hundreds of cans of tomatoes, and thousands of jugs of blackberry cordial, a specialty of Galesburg women, were shipped to the camps and hospitals. A sanitary fair was held on the public square, with a dining-room in Colton's store. The merchants and manufacturers contributed goods to be sold, which netted over $4000.

There was scarcely a home in the town that was not affected. As the war went on and on, and more men were called, every household waited anxiously for news from the front, and scanned the casualty lists with fear and dread, a feeling that will be understood by mothers and wives today who remember the World War. Soon the wounded began to return, cripples were seen on the streets, and mourning appeared on many a wife and mother. The terrible accounts of such prison camps as Andersonville were whispered about, though a few miles north at Rock Island was a Union prison as full of horror as any Southern detention camp. For four years the town lived from day to day on the fluctuating fortunes of the war. The college was almost denuded of students. All other interests were submerged.

Galesburg had its heroine. There was no Red Cross in those days, and nursing of soldiers was by volunteers. Mother Bickerdyke—not even her monument in the courthouse park gives her first name—was a sort of prairie Florence Nightingale. She acted on her own initiative, though connected with the Christian Commission. She rode a mule, accompanied by a fat Negro woman, with her supplies and equipment on another mule, a large brass kettle being the most conspicuous. When there was an engagement the Negro woman made a kettle full of hot soup, and as the wounded were brought back, each was given a cup, and his wounds were dressed. After a sharp skirmish on Missionary Ridge, the soup kettle was full and ready, when a Negro body-servant came up cap in hand with a tin cup. "Capen Smiff presents his compliments to Mrs. Bickerdyke, and requests she send him some of her soup."

"You can present my compliments to Captain Smith, and tell him if there is any soup left after the boys are cared for, he can have some, but not before."

She visited military hospitals and made generals stand round. Her autocratic methods in correcting abuses in the distribution of sanitary supplies irritated the officer in charge. He complained to headquarters, asking to have that woman removed.

"What woman?" inquired General Grant.

"A Mrs. Bickerdyke."

"Oh, well," replied Grant, "she ranks me. You must apply to President Lincoln."

She organized the hospital at Memphis. Milk and eggs were sorely needed. "I know where I can get them," she said, and returning to Galesburg, swept the chairman of the local society and other workers into her train, canvassed Knox County farm by farm, and assembled 200 cows and 1000 hens. She loaded these on a flatboat and towed them down the Mississippi. Grant assigned her President's Island in the river for her live stock, and the camp had eggs and milk until the end of the war, when the animals were distributed to the newly freed Negroes in the neighborhood.

The aftermath of the war, so far as Galesburg was concerned, was the exaltation of the returned soldiers until no civilian could be elected to office against a veteran. Nor did it die out, as with the World War. For years the Grand Army of the Republic dominated the town, turning out at every Memorial Day and Fourth of July celebration in their blue coats and broad-brimmed black hats with gold braid around them, with oratory full of hatred and bitterness toward the South; the war was refought for years. Every county history published in the years following the war gives more space to the roster of volunteers than to any other topic. The sons of the soldiers formed the Sons of Veterans, and the wives the Woman's Relief Corps, both of which marched in the parades, singing "John Brown's Body" and "We'll Hang Jeff Davis on a Sour Apple Tree."

The town escaped the soldiers and sailors monument which disfigures the squares and parks of too many American towns. The council in the midst of the patriotic enthusiasm which followed the surrender of Lee voted $10,000 for the purpose, but the act was held up pending an investigation as to the cost of a memorial and what form it should take, and was never pushed through. The state of public taste following the war, the lowest in our history, being what it was, nothing but a miracle could have given the town a memorial which would not have been an eyesore. They did, however, set up a liberty pole in the square 200 feet high, and this must have been the time when such flagstaffs were erected elsewhere, for the Western prairies bristled with them for a score of years after.

The men brought home war songs and Negro melodies, which became popular at all singings, displacing the college songs and the hymns, until engulfed in a wave of Gospel Hymns and Sacred Songs by Bliss and Sankey. The town heard and sang for the first time the stirring measures of "Tramp, tramp, tramp, the boys are marching," "Rally round the flag," "Tenting on the Old Camp Ground," "We shall meet but we shall miss him," and the lively Negro ditty "The Year of Jubilo":

# LINCOLN

"The massa run, ha-ha, the darkies stay, ho-ho;
  It must be now is the kingdom comin' and the year of Jubilo."

A plaintive air now seldom heard was "Nicodemus":

"Nicodemus the slave was of African birth;
  He was bought for a bag full of gold.
He was reckoned as part of the salt of the earth,
  And he died years ago, very old.
'Twas his last sad request as we laid him away
  In the trunk of an old hollow tree:
'Wake me up,' were his words, at the first break of day;
  'Wake me up for the new Jubilee.'"

and the chorus:

"O, run an' tell Elijah to hurry up Pomp
  An' meet us at the gum-tree down in the swamp
    To wake Nicodemus today."

Another after-effect was the continuing interest in martial affairs. The young men organized a company of the National Guard with swagger dress uniforms, and gave balls and other social functions. While the fervor lasted, the company was composed of the elite of the town, but as the military ardor died down, the more prominent young men no longer joined, and it was made up of men from the shops and foundries, and its uniform was the regulation blue of the regular army, its social affairs without prestige, and its principal service to overawe strikers at the behest of capital. A socialistic cobbler who had been a drum major in the war organized a drum corps of boys from seven to fourteen, in natty uniforms of silver gray, which was the bright and shining feature of Fourth of July parades, and with a handkerchief stuffed under the snares to muffle the beat, of Memorial Day. Some of the juvenile drummers became experts, and appeared on programs at the opera house with imitations of the battle of

Gettysburg, simulating the march, the quickstep, the rattle of musketry, the roll of the cannon, popular as long as most of the audience remembered the war. There was no such disillusion as followed the World War. War records made up a large part of the annals of the town. The Battle of Gettysburg was not described in all its realistic horror until McKinley Cantor's *Long Remember* in 1934.

In the years following the Civil War, the town gathered itself for its supreme struggle, the fight for the county seat, against its ancient enemy, Knoxville, and all other interests were swallowed up in varying fortunes of that long-drawn-out battle.

# 10

# County Seat Fight

I

### KNOXVILLE'S LAST BATTLE

No sooner had Galesburg secured the railroad, than it cast covetous eyes at Knoxville's sole remaining asset, the county seat, and laid plans to wrest it from her grasp. The two towns had grown up side by side, neither having the advantage in population until the final location of the railroad made Galesburg the railroad center not only of Knox County, but of the entire Military Tract. In the boom that followed the railroad, Galesburg's population doubled and quadrupled, and two years after the first locomotive snorted up to its red-painted pine "depot" it began to scheme and plot to move the seat of justice from the village of Knoxville to the city of Galesburg, for on the strength of its population increase it had set up as a city.

The columns of *The Knox Republican* carried predictions of the approaching storm. A citizen signing himself Alpha advises Knoxville to become self-sufficient or face the possibility of becoming a "place which *was,* but *is not."* "You are aware that a great portion of the trade of Galesburg comes from, in and around Knoxville. If we or our wives want anything . . . we go to Galesburg to buy it."

Galesburg's claim was based on size alone, for the railroad had not made it much more accessible to the majority of the townships. Knoxville had the better right. It was almost in the center of the county. It was the older town, had indeed been laid out and built to be the county seat. Its people had bought land and

[ 309 ]

settled there with that understanding. The county had erected a courthouse, a picturesque example of the Greek revival on the Western prairies, good enough for years to come. The other townships stood by Knoxville. They could see little advantage to themselves in the change.

But the Knoxville people were actuated by something deeper than a sense of injustice at this latest outrage on the part of Galesburg. The old hostility, born of different social and political outlooks, added bitterness and acrimony to this contest.

The original bitterness might in the ordinary course of things have died down, what with the mutual give and take and intercourse of pioneer life, but that events combined to keep it alive and add to natural prejudice the pinch of material competition. The stores of Galesburg deflected trade from Knoxville. Abolitionist Galesburg aided fugitive slaves to find sanctuary in Canada, blocking Knoxville's efforts to apprehend them, as it was bound to do under the law of the State. The long contest for the railroad, in which Galesburg came off victor, was but just ended, and the memory of her wrongs kept Knoxville rancor at fever heat. And it was with a sore misgiving that the town watched the preparations of her enemy to snatch one more advantage. They were rivals in everything, on opposite sides of every question. Knoxville had been jealous and suspicious from the beginning, and her suspicions were more than justified.

In 1857 the *Republican,* Knoxville organ, was still confident enough to be courteous and charitable:

"Our neighbors of Galesburg are about to enter upon the duties and labors of City organization. . . . Although we cannot exactly approve of the stealthy march that they attempted to make in reference to a de facto removal of the county seat from us to their great and (in their estimation) all-important place, yet we wish them good success and great prosperity."

A year later Knoxville began to show her teeth:

"Our grasping neighbors of the magnificent city of Galesburg seem determined to carry out their threat of swallowing up all their neighbors in their own magnificent whirlpool. "The article pledges Knoxville to "defend our citadel to the end."

Most of the legal business now originated in Galesburg. It irked the lawyers to be obliged to go five miles, not only to try their cases, but to file papers. Even after the new train made its one trip a day each way, attorneys kept fast horses for emergencies, and there was many a spirited race down the Knoxville road to enter a claim ahead of a rival against some property in litigation. But that was merely a matter of convenience. The county seat was the biggest plum an ambitious prairie town could pluck and Galesburg was determined to pluck it.

She bided her time. Action must originate in the board of supervisors, the governing body of the county, in which Galesburg had but one vote. Its supervisor was Selden Gale. As the eldest son of the Reverend George W., he might be supposed to have a titular interest in the city, but he chose the county as his field of action, and served as supervisor with one interruption for thirty-eight years. Gale was merchant, real estate operator, lawyer, editor, postmaster, college trustee, farmer, his farm so large the trains stopped at it. He got his mercantile experience working for Herman and James Knox of Knoxville; hence the close relation with James in the religious controversy. He was now thirty-six years old, a cold, unemotional logical man, a dogged fighter, a good parliamentarian, well schooled in political tactics and strategy by his long apprenticeship in the railroad fight. In the seventeen-year controversy for the county seat he led the Galesburg forces, and slowly but surely assembled the backing that was needed for his triumph.

He was opposed by George Charles, who as county surveyor had helped the Galesburgers lay out their town. Charles was supervisor from Knox township, a man of forty-six, also a large farmer, with a long term of service on the board; not a Southerner though most of his constituents were—he was born in Pennsylvania and had settled in the county before the Galesburg colonists arrived, and grown up with the township he represented so ably, and whose battle he fought so bitterly, until, shortly after the long contest ended, he died a disappointed man.

Geographically Knox consists of twenty townships (originally twenty-two, until in 1839 two were taken like the rib from Adam's side to help create the adjoining county of Stark). The townships are arranged in a parallelogram, four across and five down. Obviously the center of the county lies between two townships. One of these is Knox in which is the city of Knoxville. Galesburg is in the center of the western rim. Only four townships are nearer Galesburg than they are to Knoxville, and the difference is so slight as to be negligible.

This layout explains why the townships were indifferent to Galesburg's overture; there was nothing in the move to benefit them, and they rather feared to have the county's destiny in Galesburg's hands, lest those ambitious and restless Yankees should push the pace and plunge them in expenses involving more taxes.

The county had been organized in 1830, and named after Washington's Secretary of War, Henry Knox (most of the counties in the Military Tract were named for military leaders). This was five years before George W. Gale and his followers appeared on the scene. The southern settlers decided they had enough inhabitants to justify a political set-up—the legal number was 350, but nobody bothered to count them. A meeting was held in Henderson township, not far from where later the Galesburgers pitched their temporary camp named Log City, at Samuel White's cabin, which served the dual purpose of general store and saloon.

A petition was prepared, and presented to the judge of the fifth judicial district, praying for a county, which was duly granted and the petitioners authorized to go ahead and organize. Three commissioners were selected, one of whom was Charles Hansford, the man who pointed out to the purchasing committee for the Gale colony the best site for their town, little dreaming how much trouble that act would one day cause his people.

The commission met in Jacob Gumm's log cabin and perfected

its organization. Its first official act was to make an honest man of Samuel White by licensing him for two dollars a year to sell at the legal rate of two bits a pint the corn whisky he had been dispensing, and thus providing another point for friction with the new arrivals.

Gumm's cabin continued to be the seat of justice until the following year, when the town of Knoxville was surveyed on the virgin prairie and laid out as the county seat, and a log courthouse built at a cost of $395.43. With memory of the Southern states from which they came, it was at first known as "Knox Court House." In due course the log building was succeeded by the Greek temple of red brick and white stone, and the people of Knoxville settled down to the belief they were fixed for life, as they would have been had their opponents been of the same temper as themselves.

But the Yankees were another sort. They were indefatigable in seeking advantages for their little city. As early as 1856 Selden Gale began his maneuvers to secure the necessary majority in the board of supervisors, a seemingly hopeless task with the whole county arrayed against him. But the law provided that each township was entitled to one representative on the board, and two if it had 800 voters, though not more in any case. Galesburg found that it now had 829 and elected a second supervisor, who, after considerable bickering and a careful check up and count of the voters in Galesburg, was duly seated. The score was now 2 to 19.

From this time on the threat of moving the county seat cast its shadows over every meeting of the board, a menace to Knoxville, a hope to Galesburg, keeping Supervisor Charles on the defensive, and spurring Supervisor Gale to watch for every slight advantage, every entering wedge. Every discussion of improvement or extension of the county's present plant at Knoxville was portentous in its significance, and Galesburg's steady growth was like the writing on the wall in that council chamber in the old red brick courthouse where the supervisors met. During this interval Knoxville scored one small point. It managed to have inserted in the new state constitution a clause forbidding the moving of county seats further from the centers of counties.

Then came the Civil War, which swallowed up the local quarrel. Illinois, which began its statehood with a pro-slavery element so strong that the State was preserved for free soil only by a narrow majority, was solidified for the North by Lincoln and the influx of Northern settlers. It rendered good service to the Union, and as soon as peace was declared and the last man mustered out, the two factions took up their little county seat war where they had dropped it.

In 1866 Selden Gale slipped one over. He presented a petition to divide Galesburg the city from Galesburg the town, taking care to provide 800 voters in each division. The ostensible reason was that Galesburg had too many votes to be handled in one precinct. Strange to relate, the board allowed him to get away with it. However, Knoxville had now passed the 800 mark also, and its right to two supervisors could not be gainsaid—certainly not by Galesburg—and the score stood four to twenty.

Both sides had recourse to the state legislature. This body had been distinctly unfriendly to Galesburg in the past. It had favored Knoxville throughout the railroad controversy. Its members were largely pro-slavery Democrats when Galesburg was abolitionist Whig. Galesburg had gone from Whig to Liberty Party, and thence to the newly born Republican Party; the war had put a different face on state politics. Oglesby was governor, the legislature was Republican—in fact, the situation was exactly reversed. Knoxville was now the unpopular stepchild. Galesburg had a powerful lobby at Springfield, which succeeded in securing the passage of an act permitting the question of moving the county seat to be submitted to the vote of the county. But though Springfield had altered its attitude toward Galesburg, the rest of Knox County had not. The election was held and Galesburg overwhelmingly defeated.

# COUNTY SEAT FIGHT

## II

### SELDEN GALE'S STRATEGY

Gale then prepared for another move. He had a bill drawn up allowing Galesburg township one supervisor, and Galesburg city five. This would increase Galesburg's vote in the board by two. The Knoxville lobby put up a magnificent fight, but the bill was passed, and at the next election Galesburg added her two new supervisors, and the score stood six to twenty. Gale now had a party of his own in the board, men of ability and standing in the county. One was Henry Sanderson, mayor of Galesburg, who had entertained Lincoln at the time of his debate with Douglas, and Charles Lanphere, who had been the emissary of Galesburg to Springfield during the campaign for the railroad. At least two men affiliated with Galesburg had settled in distant townships and been returned as supervisors.

James Holyoke, one of that numerous family which had moved to Galesburg from Cleveland after listening to the glowing accounts by the canal boat party when it stopped there to repair its ark, had settled on a farm in Sparta township. Smith Chambers, whose father Matthew was one of the principal merchants of Galesburg, had established a branch store on the line of the railroad in Walnut Grove. There was no village between Galesburg and Kewanee when construction work began, and this store supplied the needs of the work gangs encamped in the neighborhood, and became the nucleus of the town of Altona. Holyoke and Chambers were elected supervisors and naturally sided with Galesburg. Score eight to eighteen.

Gradually, and with various arguments, Galesburg undermined Knoxville's majority in the board, and won over enough of the more distant and distinterested townships so that opinion was evenly balanced. On all measures remotely affecting the removal of the county seat, such as repairing the jail at Knoxville, the vote stood thirteen to thirteen. The course of public business was

[ 315 ]

often interfered with by this deadlock. Ballotting for chairman at one time lasted three days, and was finally decided by flipping a coin.

The next proposal was to send Gale to the legislature. His election was fought entirely on the county seat issue. Gale was elected by a small margin, went to Springfield, and as soon as practicable introduced a bill permitting the question of county seat removal to be again submitted to a vote of the county. Both lobbies went into action, but again the legislature favored Galesburg as against Knoxville, and the measure passed.

It was now necessary to find out what Galesburg would do to get the county seat, what inducement it would offer, and the board of supervisors appointed a commission to find out. The offer was a handsome one. The city would donate the site for the jail, and contribute $20,000 toward building it; a lot and fireproof building for storing the records; a room for holding court free for ten years, before the end of which time it was confidently believed the new courthouse would be built; and the city would pay all the expenses of moving. When the county should be ready to build Galesburg would provide a suitable site for the courthouse. These offers were printed in the form of broadsheets and the county was literally covered with them. The distribution was followed by canvassing, in which every trick known to politicians was employed by both sides.

The money was raised with ease, and to meet Knoxville's skepticism as to the good faith of the offers, bonds were furnished. The public square, which had been offered the railroad for a station and rejected, was put forward as a site for the courthouse, but fortunately for the town, not so used, though what was done was almost as bad.

The campaign pursued its fevered course, with excitement rising to a high pitch as election day approached. Knoxville's one practical claim was its nearness to the center of the county, but its best argument was its vested right, the sentimental appeal, the good faith with which it had been established, the disappointment and financial loss of those who had settled there. Knoxville had the good will and support of most of the county, geographically, but that meant little with the bulk of population in the city of Galesburg, and the opportunity to use that population to its full weight, as it could not do in the board of supervisors.

Election day came, always something of a holiday in Western prairie towns, reminiscent of the days when it was the chief excuse for getting together. The old machinery of getting out the vote was put in motion. Workers were supplied with horses and buggies and sent after the tardy voters who were plied with cigars and whisky, even in puritan Galesburg. So great was the interest in the dominant issue that the candidates for the county offices got scanty attention; the electorate was divided solely on its attitude toward the removal. Ballots were printed on strips of paper, and shoved into the box in view of everybody. There was nothing secret about it. Electioneering could be carried on right up to the ballot box and there was no opportunity to back-slide. The vote was the largest ever cast in the county hitherto—too large, as the sequel proved.

All night, in crowded smoky rooms packed to the limit with onlookers, the tellers tabulated the returns, while men on horse-back, arrived from other precincts, rode up with figures, and departed with fresh ones. Excitement waxed as hopes were dashed or raised by the fluctuating returns. From Knoxville, however, there was no news. All was mysteriously silent. Not until the returns from the entire county were known did that canny burg reveal her vote, and then it appeared she had won the election by a majority of 247!

Immediately there was uproar and recrimination. Galesburg cried "fraud"; Knoxville retorted "fraud yourself!" Galesburg excitedly pointed out that Knoxville's vote was three times the average vote of that township. Where did it get all those citizens? Knoxville shrugged her shoulders, replied that the town had grown, and wanted to know why Galesburg's vote was at least a fourth larger than normal. It was evident that both sides had "stuffed" the ballot boxes, Knoxville successfully. Knoxville had guessed Galesburg would do that and had prepared to beat her at her own game, arguing that both returns would be thrown out, and she would win on the county vote, which was overwhelmingly in her favor. She guessed right, but argued wrong.

The supervisors met and canvassed the vote, over protests from the Knoxville contingent that such a step was illegal, that supervisors had no authority to take such action. A committee was appointed, three from Galesburg, two from Knoxville, to investigate and report. The report was presented, finding that Knoxville's legal vote was 639 instead of 1520, deducted the 884 illegally cast, and changed the result from a majority of 247 against to 634 in favor of the removal. It whitewashed Galesburg completely, pointing out the growth brought by the railroad, and that rival candidates in the city had watched the polls closely, and that no frauds were possible. It left a small loophole for further purging, if necessary, but insisted nothing could change the result.

Only the Galesburg members of the committee signed the report. The two die-hards from Knoxville not only refused to sign, but refused to vote either for or against its acceptance, still insisting that the committee was illegal, that the board had no right to review the vote. Notwithstanding this protest, the report was adopted by the board of supervisors.

Upon which a summons was served on the entire board to appear at the June term of circuit court to answer to a bill of complaint brought by a taxpayer, really a test case that had been cooked up to settle the matter. The case had to be tried on a change of venue to a neighboring county to secure an unbiased jury. Both sides were represented by their ablest lawyers; the case was vigorously presented and fought, and the decision handed down by the court seems an astounding one in light of the facts.

The court found that while Galesburg had sinned, Knoxville had sinned more; that the election in that township was "illegal, false, fraudulent, and void," that even with the Galesburg illegal

[ 318 ]

votes thrown out Galesburg still had a majority of 200, that while both sides had evidently cheated, Knoxville had cheated most, and that therefore Galesburg had won. The decision contained permission to appeal, and appeal was promptly taken.

The Illinois supreme court, while it reduced the votes of both Knoxville and Galesburg, making the majority 100, confirmed the finding of the lower court. Galesburg went wild with joy. At the next meeting of the board of supervisors, steps were taken to start the removal and begin the building of the jail. They were stopped by an injunction. A long and bitter protest from Knoxville was read to show that the supreme court had reduced Knoxville's vote to 311, whereas it had and could prove a legal vote of 700, which would drown Galesburg's meager 100 allowed by the same court. The protest was spread on the minutes, but that was all that was done about it. The injunction was dissolved.

Knoxville gave up the fight to prove the election illegal, conceded the success of Galesburg, and instead managed to secure a new election, this time to move the county seat from Galesburg back to Knoxville. The second election was held. Watchers from the two towns involved were posted at the opponents' polls to insure integrity. The contest was close, 3785 to 3309, Galesburg winning by 476. Geographically the county was for Knoxville, since of the twenty townships only six sided with Galesburg. Galesburg won solely by her own vote. The closeness of the decision caused friction in the board for many years, during all the time of building the new courthouse, and delayed its commencement for fifteen years after the decision was made.

### III

### BLANCHARD'S LAST WORD

For Galesburg did not, with all the money it spent, wires it pulled, anxiety it suffered, get its courthouse at once. Having obtained the county seat, and clinched its title by the second election, it began to turn over to the county the gifts and bonuses it had promised, all but the site for the courthouse; the fireproof building in which to store the records, also used as offices for the county and circuit courts; the site for the jail and $20,000 toward building it; $4000 to pay for moving, and the new "opera house" for a courtroom.

The opera house—it was a common name for theatre in the Middle West, but never housed anything nearer opera than a musical comedy or a Hoyt farce—was a three-story brick building on the public square built by Charlie Brechwald and his con-frères in the liquor business in anticipation of the breaking of Galesburg's thirty-five year ban on saloons. Court promised as good business as the drama, and already there were several saloons on the first floor. The second floor supplied jury rooms and offices for lawyers. The third floor was the theatre, and here for ten years justice sat, backed up against a drop curtain decorated with a heroic figure of Thalia—which some of the ladies thought indecent—flanked by comic and tragic masks and edged with the advertisements of local merchants. When the drama required the use of the theatre, the paraphernalia of justice was moved out and the orchestra chairs screwed down.

The arrangement was assumed to be temporary, but year after year the defeated bloc in the board of supervisors was still strong enough to hold up any movement toward building. The resolu-tion to start the work was repeatedly introduced by Gale, and repeatedly voted down, and Gale realized that no proposition coming from Galesburg would get over. It must be sponsored by some one else. The Galesburg group worked on and won over Charles Sansbury from the remote township of Victoria. He went home, explained the situation to his constituents, and came back fortified with a resolution in favor of building at once. The burning of the opera house in the fall of 1883, which fortunately occurred when the theatre was empty, the inconvenience of hav-ing jail, records and court in different parts of the city, all con-spired to aid the city fathers in their ambition, and it was finally voted to commence work.

Knox College had been vitally interested from the beginning. Selden Gale was a trustee of the college, as were others concerned in the fight; in fact, the college and town were still in close communion. The college was the largest landowner; increase in values would help it immensely. It made its contribution, in addition to sums subscribed by individual trustees and others identified with it. College Park, the splendid open space between the two groups of buildings, was sold to the city for $21,000, and the eastern half given to the county as a site for the courthouse. That may have been a fair price for it, considered simply as so much land, but its potential value to the college was immensely greater, so its willingness to part with it was essentially a handsome contribution.

On this delightful spot the courthouse was built, a remarkably good looking building still. It cost $150,000, and under Gale's watchful management was built without waste or graft, almost unique for a public building in the West in those days. The old red brick temple at Knoxville together with all the property of the county in that village was presented to that town as a gracious gesture, which did little to console her for the loss of her birthright.

"Galesburg left Knoxville the Court House," said *The Knoxville Journal,* "because it could not move it, and the public square for the same reason."

It was the *coup de grâce;* the town never recovered from the blow, and is today but the small town Galesburg would have been if the course of events had been different. It had become "a place which *was,* but *is not.*"

In 1885 the cornerstone of the new building was laid with great flourish, the Illinois grand lodge of Masons performing their rites with the assistance of delegates from forty-three counties. There was a mighty parade of plumed hats and swords, the ladies of the Baptist Church prepared a banquet, and Judge Alfred Craig pronounced the oration of the day. That redoubtable old fighter, Jonathan Blanchard, who had furnished a dramatic touch to the completion of the railroad by impressively forbidding it to run its trains on Sunday, supplied the climax to this realization of another of Galesburg's dreams. He wrote an open letter to Judge Craig, his old pupil, published it in the local paper, rating him for presiding and giving sanction to such "monkey business," the Baptists for feeding the Masons, and the church for tolerating a Mason for its pastor, and the college a Mason for its president.

"You knew," he thundered, "that the city where you spoke owed its foundations, and the college its existence to the prayers, money, and self-denial of anti-Masonic Christians; that the patriarch Silvanus Ferris, whose business judgment saved the infant college from bankruptcy, was familiar with the Morgan trials, where the Masonic oath defeated the oath of God, and the Judiciary of the State of New York! You knew that Special Justice Wm. L. Marcy, Judge, Governor, U. S. Cabinet Secretary . . . when he saw Masonic church members and church officers . . . commit perjury without stint, obedient to their Masonic oath— . . . exclaimed from the Bench, 'If men will defy heaven and earth, what can human courts do?' No wonder, surrounded as you were by that same lodge which defeated Judge Marcy, and shielded murder most foul and horrible . . . that you should gasp out the feeble fond hope that courts in that Court House may balance the scales of justice with honesty and integrity. But you well know, Hon. Sir, that you were hoping against hope, to hope that the lodge, whose known and avowed principle is partiality to Masons and proscription to outsiders, will administer justice to all alike. To hope that Masons will do as they are sworn by cut-throat oaths not to do, is to profess your belief that Masonry means nothing. . . .

"When sick . . . in a pleasant home between Galesburg and Knoxville, . . . I . . . read an editorial in denunciation of our Union soldiers, then fighting to save popular government, because they obeyed their officers, and disobeyed the signs of rebel Masons, who were fighting to destroy it. *The Voice of Masonry* which thus gave aid and comfort to treason, is still . . . published in Chicago. I have since conversed with the Secretary of Federal Lodge, No. 1, D. C. He told me he left the lodge at the opening of the war because 'the lodges all went for secession.' . . . You were a war Democrat. But the lodge rooms of the south were the council chambers of treason, and inaugurated the war of the rebellion, to strangle free government and eternize human slavery.

"Let that bloody drama pass, curtained by oblivion. But my dear honored sir, now that I am old and gray-headed, nearing heaven's portal, I beg for the wife and sons who love you, for the people who have promoted you, for the Republic which shelters and honors you, for your old President whom you have befriended, and above all for the Savior who died for you, never again lift your voice in honor of a religion which is opposed to Christ . . . the good Col. Chambers . . . on his dying bed, called his family around him and left his testimony against the lodge. Tell your friends and fellow citizens that Freemasonry is an accursed religious imposition and cheat."

# 11

# *The Eighteen Eighties*

## I

### SOCIAL LIFE

By 1875 Galesburg was "sitting pretty." The city might be said to be "headed up" now, like the tall corn which grew so thickly around it. Its early objectives had been obtained; it was in a way complete, with nothing to do but grow. From the eighties on there were no major conflicts, nothing comparable in excitement and wholesale participation to the religious conflict, the struggle for the railroad, the row over public schools, the fight for the county seat, and the long period of slave running culminating in the Lincoln-Douglas debate, the ensuing presidential election and the Civil War. The World War did not penetrate so deeply; it was too remote from their lives. "Making the world safe for democracy" had no such meaning for them as extension of slavery, a question they had lived with daily from the moment William Holyoke arrived at Log City.

The war was over, but the hatreds it engendered had not died down; the G. A. R. still dominated politics, and there were many graves in Hope Cemetery that displayed little flags on Memorial Days. The town had won the county seat, though its new courthouse was not yet built. The railroad was functioning and expanding, pumping a stream of dollars into the economic veins of the town. Stores and factories flourished, drawing trade from the country round, and making a small group of men discreetly rich. The farms were producing as much corn and hogs as their fertile acres were capable of, with no thought of such preposterous obstacles as overproduction and artificial scarcity. It had become the largest city in the county, and for forty miles in all directions.

Perhaps never again would the town, as a town, throw itself so completely into a movement to further the city's material interest as in those formative years when it acted as a unit, when every inhabitant took seriously and felt keenly each step in the town's advancement along the road to cityhood. Life had now become more complex; personal ambition had begun to overshadow community ambition; there were many movements, but none that dominated, none that wholly absorbed its thought and energy.

By hard-headed Yankee faculty and gumption the town, which had plumped itself down in the midst of hostile neighbors, had wrested from its softer and less resourceful opponents everything necessary to its career as a city. To those who remembered the hardships and shortcomings of pioneer days, it was the acme of comfort, and even luxury, though compared with the amazing array of conveniences available today, its standards were unpresuming, and its equipment crude.

It was no longer homogeneous. The Swedes, Irish and Negroes composed substantial segments of its population, and presented ethical and social problems unforeseen by the founders. A few German Jews had established businesses, one a hat and cap factory, one a retail clothing store, and one a tobacco shop, but they were looked upon as desirable citizens, which they were, and accepted without discrimination. One lone representative each of Italy and China gave variety to Main Street, Sing Wah in his laundry, and P. Lagomarcino with his fruit stall. There were a few Indians, of mixed blood, one a student at the college, so it was possible for pupils of the public schools, who were then taught there were five races of man, to see specimens of four of them in the town's dramatis personnae.

In little more than forty years, then, after the first sod had been turned by ox-drawn breaking plows, the city of Galesburg, which began as a remarkably homogeneous one-class community, was composed of four well-defined ethnic units and had stratified into what must be considered distinct upper, middle and lower classes. The upper class, the elite, smart set, aristocracy—there seems to be no word that is not a bit top-heavy for the fifty or so families which arrogated a trifle more of gentility than their neighbors—was not much gayer or more frivolous, nor did its daily life differ greatly from that of the class immediately beneath. It was merely that its social functions caused some heart-burning among those left out, which is one object of all social exclusiveness. Public opinion set a limit to which the wealthier families might go in splurging, and kept life on an unostentatious plane. There was bound to be intercourse along other lines in so small a community, so that Mrs. A. of North Prairie Street had relations with Mrs. Z. of South Academy Street.

Fashions in living spread slowly fifty years ago, and the town was still geared to a primitive and hard-working village routine, the day beginning with breakfast at half past six, or seven, for even professional men and proprietors were in their offices or stores before eight. All went home to a noon dinner; supper was half past six. Entertainments began at eight, or earlier, parties with simple refreshments prepared by the hostess, at which games were played, with occasionally a more elaborate stand-up-and-hold-your-plate reception. To devise original amusements for such gatherings was one of the tests of a hostess in circles where cards and dancing were strictly banned.

For larger affairs the "collation"—chicken salad, ice cream, cake and coffee (duly mentioned in the newspaper accounts)—was sent in from Anderson's restaurant, and folding chairs were rented from Norton's undertaking establishment. Festoons of smilax hung from gas jets and decorated the tables. An ambitious hostess would now and then advance the supper hour to seven, and call it dinner. There were not half a dozen dress suits in town.

The town was emerging from a religious tradition which regarded all amusements with suspicion. Its pious founders had expected the people to spend their time in work or worship. Gale had visioned this ideal when he described Oberlin with such enthusiasm: "The society is delightful because it is strictly Christian, and the cause of Christ's kingdom seems to be the absorbing topic, and science and literature and property are made subservient to the great object." The town had evidently swung back from the freer and gayer life of the fifties; the war had intervened and sobered men's thoughts, and the church people had regained dominance in the town. Cards, dancing and the theatre were regarded with strong disapproval. A décolleté gown was considered shameless and abandoned, worn only by the fancy women from the "John House," a brothel just outside the city—who shocked the town by riding up and down Main Street in open barouches on pleasant afternoons.

But the sinful pleasures of more worldly communities slowly penetrated the town, fought at each step by the church people. Dancing was not fully tolerated until the nineties, by which time even pillars of the more liberal churches were giving dances on platforms laid down on their lawns under trees lit by Chinese lanterns. This of course was in summer. There were also "hops" at the Soangetaha Club on the shores of the artificial lake east of the town. In winter more formal affairs were held at the Galesburg Club, a suite of rooms over stores on Main Street, and at Caledonia Hall. Music was furnished by the Millers, who conducted a music store on the square next to "Sep" Merrick's saloon, and sold pianos, gave music lessons, and furnished an orchestra for any function desiring one—Anna at the piano, Fleet with the bass viol, and Art with his fiddle calling the complicated evolutions of the square dances. They were children of Len Miller, the pioneer music dealer of the community.

Formal balls opened with a grand march, followed by lancers, military schottische, and minuet, alternating with round dances such as waltz, schottische and polka—polka redowa or polka mazurka—ending with a lively gallop to the air "We Won't Go Home Till Morning" and a final waltz to the measures of "Home, Sweet Home." Often the final number was a romping Virginia

Reel. Popular waltzes were "Mysotis," "Kiss Me Again" and the perennial "Blue Danube." Each dancer, male and female, carried a gaudy printed program, with pencil, cord and tassel, on which to keep track of engagements. It was a more stately affair than today, and there was no cutting in.

On more august occasions the ball ended in a german or cotillion, that bizarre mixture of dancing and children's games, with favors distributed at the end of each figure. The variations of these figures taxed the ingenuity of the leader, who was supposed to invent a few surprises for each affair. Of such leaders Will Farrell was undoubtedly the most picturesque. He was a young Irishman who resigned his position in the dress goods department of Murdoch's store to start a dancing class, which became in time practically an academy, and he was the professional organizer of most of the formal balls, and authority on the etiquette of such functions, master of ceremonies and Galesburg's Beau Nash.

Aside from the surreptitious games of draw poker in the back rooms of saloons, euchre and cinque (high five) were the popular card games. In the card-playing set, which gradually grew in spite of ban by the church, progressive parties were given with prizes for the winners, including a booby prize, bought at the 99-cent store, and refreshments, all furnished by the hostess.

After the opera house burned down, while still being used as a court room, the town had no proper theatre, except Caledonia Hall—which was used for every form of public entertainment—until a group of saloon keepers bought the old roller skating rink and transformed it into the Auditorium. Because of its favorable railroad situation, practically every worth-while touring company made the town, and from 1890 until the displacement of the theatre by the moving pictures the people enjoyed an unusual dramatic program. The list of dramas, melodramas, musical comedies, Hamlets, burlesques, spectacles such as those of the inimitable Imre and Bolossy Kiralfy, which appeared at the Auditorium, would duplicate that shown in New York or

Chicago during the same period. The ten-, twenty-, thirty-cent stock companies remained a week and produced their entire repertoire, showing at Calendonia Hall in such perennial standbys as "East Lynne," "Uncle Tom's Cabin," "St. Elmo," and "The Lady of Lyons."

All such amusements, dancing, cards, theatre, as well as billiards, circuses, low-necked dresses and drinking, were classed as sins by the devout, and there was much preaching and praying against them. The churches took rank socially, usually in inverse order to their spiritual fervor. The Presbyterian led for some mysterious reason, probably because it contained so many pioneer families who had acquired wealth, though the Old First Church, which ranked second, was even yet the one closest to the original group. The society churches tolerated, if they could not condone, the rising tide of worldliness manifested in dancing and card playing, since their wealthiest parishioners countenanced them, but Methodists and Baptists stuck to their tenets, and continued to rank lower in the social scale.

One of the folkways of western towns was New Year's calls, made with appropriate ceremony. Congenial groups of women clubbed together, matrons in some groups, misses in others, met at the house of one of the group, with refreshments prepared and contributed to by all, to "receive." The list of such hostesses with the hours and places was printed in the local newspaper. On New Year's Day, parties of men, young and old, sallied forth, with the printed list in their pockets, and fortified with special cards bearing their names and appropriate sentiments—it was a rare opportunity for the wags to display their wit, and the vehicles used were sometimes of the burlesque character—and made the rounds, calling at as many of the houses as they dared.

Refreshments were of the simple innocuous Galesburg character, but there were always a few hostesses who thought the festival deserved wine or a mild punch, and young men started out in their best Sunday suits, their ears ringing with maternal injunctions to "touch not, taste not, handle not the wine." The

knowing ones gravitated to the right places, and some finished
the day considerably uplifted, to the embarrassment of the ladies
where they paid their last respects. The hostesses compared their
respective piles of cards, registering the popularity of the different
groups.

Although there were thirty saloons in the town, drinking had
no social standing. Galesburg drinking was straight drinking,
to get drunk, and getting drunk was as common as you would
expect it to be in a town with 18,000 people and thirty saloons,
the market for farmers for miles around. Drinking was more or
less furtive, the saloons heavily screened, which gave them the
added charm of mystery. The more discreet preferred to get their
drams at the drug store. Wine was not served in any Galesburg
home, except possibly at New Years by a few of the more liberal
families.

Drinking was man's prerogative. The women were against it
almost unanimously. There was a strong W. C. T. U., which
once had considerable social prestige, led by Mary Allen West,
the militant temperance crusader, state president and editor of
the *Union Signal,* whose father was the Nehemiah who contributed so much diligent oversight to the founding of the town.
She organized the infants into a Band of Hope to save them from
drunkards' graves, and taught them to recite the following quaint
pledge:

"Trusting in God to help me keep this pledge, I do solemnly
promise to abstain from the use of intoxicating liquor as a
beverage, wine, beer and cider included, from all profanity, and
from the use of tobacco in all its forms."

Few of those six-year olds knew what "intoxicating" and
"beverage" meant.

Sweeping as this was, some reformers wished to strike out the
words "as a beverage," and there were Spartan mothers who said
they would rather see their offspring laid in their graves than
save their lives with malt extract. The war between the home
and the saloon, as it was regarded, went on for more than forty

years, until shortly before the World War the women got the chance to vote. They closed the saloons, and they stayed closed until repeal opened them so wide in Illinois that towns which had never tolerated them were practically compelled to become wet.

The two unofficial, unrecognized social classes in the town, the strict churchgoing anti-liquor people, and the worldly liberal element, were united, like the houses of Montagu and Capulet, in a wedding that lingered in shocked gossip for many weeks and became one of the legends of the town. The daughter of the leading livery-stable keeper and the son of the leading college professor were married at a big wedding at which wine flowed freely. The bride was beautiful, the groom one of the most popular young men, and the ceremony ended in a riot. The young men, exhilarated by the unaccustomed drink, tried to compel the newly married pair to ride to the railway station on a dray which had been decorated like a Fourth of July float. In the fight that ensued coats were ripped up the back, trousers torn, and the male wedding guests rolled in the dust of the road. The husky young groom was no mean fighter himself, and rescued his bride from the mob and rode off in triumph in his own conveyance, somewhat the worse for wear.

Through all these years the clash between public and private morals and the dying puritan tradition persisted, and as late as fifty years ago it was stock strategy for pious young women to try to convert the men in whom they were interested, and the cause of righteousness received many recruits under false colors. The college still maintained its evangelical attitude, though dancing had crept in there, along with the fraternities, which were also condemned by the college, until new men joined the faculty, already "Greeks" in the institutions from which they came. As the town became liberal more rapidly than the college, it assumed the aspect of a menace to the morals of the students in the eyes of its conservative faculty and president.

One peculiar phase of Galesburg life at this period is that its social leader was a young Jew, son of the owner of the principal and still existing clothing store. He was immensely popular, not only with the socialites, but with all classes, drawing custom to the store by his unfailing good nature and cordiality. Galesburg was too naïve and unsophistocated to be aware of popular prejudice, or else peculiarly fortunate in her quota of Jewish people. No town ever had an abler or more public-spirited citizen than this young man's brother-in-law, Max J. Mack, a partner in the clothing store, who served the town competently and unselfishly for thirty years as councilman, and as mayor gave it the most efficient administration it ever had.

## II

### DOMESTIC LIFE

In so far as the tycoons of the upper class were business and political leaders they influenced the destinies of the town, but its real life, its very essence, was in the middle class, the average people, the thousands of families in between the elite and the proletariat. They constituted the bulk of the population. Their way of life did not differ materially from that of the socially more pretentious, for there was neither extreme wealth nor extreme poverty, and the gap between the richest and the poorest was a small one.

The distinguishing feature of this middle class was that it held more closely to the old pious tradition in which the town was steeped by its founders. Its social life centered in its churches, and it shunned amusements on which the church frowned, and found food for gossip in what it considered the excesses of the smart set. At its simple parties games were played, "Going to California," "Old Dan Tucker." There were Estey organs or square pianos in its parlors around which family and guests gathered to sing Bliss and Sankey's *Gospel Hymns:* "The Ninety and Nine," "Pull for the Shore," "Hold the Fort." It cherished the pioneer tradition of neighborliness emanating from the days of changing work with "bees" and "raisings"—chats over the back fence while hanging out the wash, swapping recipes, exchanging gifts of baking powder biscuit or currant "jell."

It baked and cooked for its sociables, church suppers, and picnics; "took" delegates when the church entertained the district association or conference. It went to camp meetings in summer and wasted weeks in winter at protracted meetings, those high-powered methods of saving souls. These were the homes which had not yet reached the "hired girl" status; the cooking was done by the wife and mother on a wood or soft coal stove with heavy cast iron spiders and kettles, water brought from the pump outdoors.

It was composed of decent, hard-working, self-respecting people, leading lives rich with a common humanity, rearing its children in the fear of the Lord, by keeping them off the streets, out of the billiard parlors; sending them to Sunday-school, scolding them for playing marbles for "keeps"; educating them at the public schools and Knox College. It was the era of family life. The young people brought their friends home, and they had taffy-pulls, coasting and skating parties, straw rides, diversions at least as amusing as the hops and euchres of the gilded set. Such homes fostered memories, and are recalled with wistful affection by many great and near great in faraway large cities. From them have come social, industrial and intellectual leaders. They were the nurseries, the training schools of much that is best in our American life.

The life of the town was lived in its homes, much the same in spite of social distinctions. Even the houses of the well-to-do lacked conveniences taken for granted today in the cheapest four-room bungalow, not missed because not yet known. They believed their homes were comfortable, and they were comfortable in their way, but it required an almost unbelievable amount of physical labor to take care of them. The better houses were larger and more luxuriously—but not necessarily more tastefully—

furnished, but their architecture was substantially the same. The houses were designed by the carpenters who built them—there was no architect until the nineties—and were the spontaneous expression of the people's needs and lives, and while without distinction were not without a certain homely charm. They were principally story and a half, with parlor, sitting room, dining room and kitchen—no serving pantry, but usually a large store room off the kitchen called the buttery—with a porch at the side or across the front; not a large porch, for this was the transition between the porchless houses of pioneers who had no time to sit down and the modern outdoor living rooms of an age with greater leisure.

Central heating was still a novelty; a few houses had hot-air furnaces, but mostly the upstairs rooms were unheated, and dressing in cold rooms was not considered a hardship. Fuel was hard wood and soft coal, but when the railroad began to bring anthracite, the hard coal base burner became the chief heating plant, its isinglass windows affording a pleasant glow, and a drum in the ceiling gave a modicum of heat to the chamber above.

On the floors were carpets, tacked down over straw, large figured, Ingrain or Brussels in the parlor, home-made rag in the common rooms; dining room and kitchen floors or bare wood scrubbed at least once a week. Every fall one of the Herculean labors was taking up the carpets, beating them, and laying them over fresh straw, which until tramped down gave the floor a billowy effect like the rolling prairies which surround the town. At the same time the bed ticks were filled with fresh straw, unless one could afford feathers.

In the chilly, shut-up parlor, opened only for funerals and formal calls, were whatnots with sea shells, hair wreaths, and wax flowers in frames, marble-topped tables covered with drapes on which lay the Bible and photograph albums, Rogers' groups in the windows and Currier & Ives prints on the walls, much of it brought from New York in the covered wagons of their fathers.

As city water did not get under way until the nineties, there were no bathrooms. Soft water was caught in a wooden cistern and brought to a wooden sink in the kitchen by a dwarf iron pump painted green. Well water—so-called to distinguish it from rain water—was obtained from a pump in the back porch with an endless chain turned by a crank. The drip froze in winter, and had to be chopped out to get the bucket under the spout. Hot water was dipped from a reservoir on the back of the stove. In order to be near the water supply the Saturday night bath was taken in the kitchen in one of the heavy wooden washtubs, which had to be carried out to be emptied. Richer people had high back tin tubs shaped like a modern porch chair. The only toilet was a privy in the backyard.

Gas was available in the sixties, but was used principally for street lighting; the mains were slow in penetrating the residence quarters and it was difficult to instal in houses already built. In most homes on a shelf beneath the clock stood a row of kerosene lamps, with red flannel in their glass bowls, to be filled, trimmed, and their chimneys cleaned every day.

Food was brought to the house in a state of nature and manufactured in the kitchen. The steak was pounded on a board with a mallet to make it tender. Oatmeal and beans were soaked overnight. Hash and cabbage slaw were chopped in a huge wooden bowl with a chopping knife. Butter and milk were hung down the well to keep them cool. Chickens must be plucked and cleaned before they could be cooked. Washday was distinguished by a peculiar odor of soap mixed with cabbage, the hot fire required for boiling the clothes being utilized for a boiled dinner. Cothes were washed with soap, water, and elbow grease. Dishes were washed with a rag. Floors were washed with a mop or scrubbing brush, furniture dusted with a cloth or turkey wing. The regular chores included making the beds and emptying the slops, and intervals left over were filled with mending, darning, baking, and religion.

Biscuit was raised with saleratus mixed with vinegar. There was no baking powder, and no granulated or domino sugar. The only kinds were brown and white, both filled with irregular lumps, and loaf sugar in small cubes. Coffee was bought green and roasted in a dripping pan.

The chores stretched out and filled the housewife's waking hours. The labor involved is beyond calculation. The number of foot pounds exerted by our grandmothers in lifting scuttles of coal, buckets of water, iron pots, and kettles would run to fantastic figures. The only difference between the wealthier homes and the more modest ones was that the mistress of the former could have help for the more laborious tasks, and when labor-saving devices began to arrive, they were the first to instal them. The "help" was the daughter of an Irish railroad laborer, a handsome colleen who had to be taught the simplest household routine, or a husky dusky daughter of a former fugitive slave.

The houses were surrounded by lawns covered with shade trees, and when cows and pigs were restrained from roaming the streets, fences were removed, giving a parklike effect to the town. Even in the more aristocratic homes, the son, if he were old enough, did the chores, mowing the lawn, milking the cow, taking care of the horse. If there was no son, a college boy worked for his board. It was all democratic and simple. There was usually a kitchen garden, rather neglected, but seldom a flower garden. The home flower garden in the West is the product of a later age. The garden instinct was not native to the pioneers, whose sense of duty was stronger than their sense of beauty.

These homely details are given because they are a part of the social history of Galesburg, and of all western towns. Some of you no doubt remember those times, but most of you were born into a world where hot and cold water comes from taps as a matter of course into hand basins and bathtubs and kitchen sinks and laundry trays, and empties itself without effort; where the gas range is lighted without striking a match, and lights turned on by pressing a button, and many of the arduous and back-breaking tasks of housekeeping are done in factories and the almost finished results come to you in handy packages. It took more brawn than brains to keep house in those early days and as the demands on brawn lessened the brain was released to engage in other things besides housekeeping.

The amazing changes that have occurred in this super-industry of homemaking have been brought about not so much by ideas as things, devices that cut down drudgery and yield results as good as or better than the old treadmill housekeeping, such things as gas ranges, hot-water heating, electric refrigerators, aluminum cooking utensils, quick-drying lacquers, canned foods of high quality, double boilers, kitchen cabinets, package goods, vegetable shortenings, ready-mixed flours, ready-to-wear clothes. The homes of Galesburg had gone a long way in comfort and convenience from the cabins of Log City in which the town began its life, but the changes of the next fifty years were even more sweeping and had the far-reaching result of bringing woman into the public life of the town.

Mark Sullivan says in *Our Times:* "Is it not tenable to suggest that the perfecting of the vacuum cleaner and the electric flatiron by business may have meant more to the average woman—and been more prized by her—than the bringing of woman suffrage? That making telephone and electric light available, as well as bathtubs and modern plumbing, may have meant more to the average man than, let us say, the sum of all the politics associated with William Jennings Bryan?"

Any boy who in the 1880's struggled with an old-fashioned furnace, who each morning shook down wheelbarrow loads of ashes, scraped out obstinate clinkers from the grate, and filled its insatiable maw with soft coal; who came upstairs with eyes and nose and ears filled with coal dust and ashes, and made a complete toilet before he was in fit condition for school, will agree that the greatest gift of modern invention to man is the oil burner, which practically runs itself. It is one of the tragedies of progress that the new generation is born into its modern world, takes conditions for granted, and is blissfully unaware of the hardships of

[ 338 ]

living the preceding generation underwent. Only those who lived through the eighties and are still living to compare its lack of conveniences with the modern array of labor-savers, can appreciate what ingenuity backed by advertising has done to make the modern home the comfortable place it is.

The change from the outdoor privy to the indoor toilet is one of the epochal events in the history of man, hitherto unchronicled because of prudery. Let any one go back to the old institution, as he still may in some primitive places, and he will agree. When Galesburg celebrated the completion of her gigantic sanitary sewer, one of the addresses was made by an old citizen who had lived the complete cycle from Chic Sale to Standard Sanitary, and he spoke with the plainness of Holy Writ about conditions as he knew them when a boy, which shocked some of his hearers, but left none unconvinced that in this department of homely human life, the progress made is real and definite.

In nearly all the homes, breakfast dispatched, father gone to work, the housewife's next task was getting the children off to school. By eight-thirty the streets were filled with children hurrying to beat the "last" bell at eight forty-five. In each of the seven wards was a two-story brick building, with four rooms, feeders for the high school in Broad Street, near the center of the town. This was a taller brick building, with a tower in which hung the bell that regulated the town's educational life. It was actually a graded school like the others, only three rooms being needed for the high school proper.

On the same block, separated from it by the home of Albert Jacobi, the venerable and much-liked clothing merchant, stood the Central Primary, made out of the Baptists' first church, which they had traded to the city for a new lot on Cherry Street. Here the children of the first ward began their educational careers when they had reached the legal age of six. The large ground around the building was divided by a high tight-board fence into playgrounds for boys and girls. In the corner of each stood an unsanitary privy, one of which, boys being what they are, not all the superficial attention of the overworked and underpaid janitor could keep fit for use.

At the end of two years the Central Primarians who "passed" went over to the high school building, and found life much the same, as it was also in the other wards. These were the school customs of the period, in Galesburg and all Western cities. The more persistent pupils finally reached "high," and of these a small percentage went on to college.

At the opening of the school day there was a brief religious exercise, Bible reading, prayer, and singing, not always hymns. The pupils were expected to join heartily in such hypocritical words as,

> "When bright the day is breaking,
> And school day bells are waking,
> With joy our homes forsaking,
> We hail our pleasant school."

Another gem which lingers in memory was,

> "O come to the church in the wildwood,
> O come to the church in the vale.
> No spot is so dear to my childhood
> As the little brown church in the vale."

The first break in the routine was "recess," which lasted fifteen minutes, when the boys played "hornaway" in their yard, a game that consisted of running safely from one fence to the opposite without being "tagged" by those standing in the center, who were "it." They also played marbles, each having in his pocket a draw-string bag filled with "commies" of vulgar clay painted bright hues which came ten for a penny; "chinas" which cost a cent, "glassies" and "potteries" two cents, and carnelians which showed moons when struck sharply and cost ten cents or more. Teachers joined parents in hounding those who played for "keeps," with no more success than the Puritan element had in weaning their elders from more adult sins.

Marbles were contraband if taken out in school; so also were "rubber guns," crotched sticks fitted with rubber bands and a leather tab to hold the missile. They were deadly weapons, and young marksmen could kill a bullfrog at twenty paces. The frogs' legs were then wrapped in clay and roasted over an open fire—this was ages before Boy Scouts had made camp life respectable—and tasted like chicken. Strange, since thousands of prairie boys had thus eaten frogs' legs with relish, the American Expeditionary Force took it so hard that the French ate them and nicknamed them "Frogs."

Other misdemeanors which earned the penalty of being "kept after school" were whispering and shooting paper wads, small pellets worked up with saliva that would squash on the back of an enemy's neck. The rooms were close, and an odor of chalk dust prevailed. There was no home work. Camouflaged behind geographies girls read *Chatterbox, Little Women, Elsie Dinsmore,* while boys indulged in Jules Verne, Oliver Optic, J. T. Trowbridge, or Harry Castlemon. The more daring had nickel libraries and dime novels, easier to conceal, but carrying a double hazard, once for reading in school, and twice for reading pernicious literature, no more pernicious, of course, than the Harper Story Books, the Franconia Stories, and Rollo Books by Jacob Abbott, father of Lyman, and other namby-pamby works which were permitted, though not during school hours. Today collectors seek and libraries exhibit the celebrated works of Mr. Nick Carter and Mr. Beadle.

Friday afternoons there was speaking, each pupil being required in turn to recite a "piece," agony, even when parents were not there to add to the embarrassment, for all but born exhibitionists. The pieces were those found in the school readers, or in numerous *Public Speakers,* or *Elocutionists,* such time-honored gems as "Excelsior," "Marco Bozzaris," "Spartacus to the Gladiators," "Olea for Castile," and "The Baron's Last Banquet." Elo-

quent orations written by white men were put in the mouths of
taciturn Indians: "White man, thou hast two tongues and two
faces; speak the truth, or thy children shall surely die."

Patriotism was sedulously cultivated. A perennial favorite was
"The Charge of the Light Brigade," glorifying the gallantry of
600 who died because of an officer's error, with only a line and not
a word of criticism for the blundering fool who sent them to their
deaths. The blunders and the glories were repeated on a large
scale in the World War. Most of the selections spouted on Friday
afternoons were martial, "Sheridan's Ride," "How the News Was
Brought," "Paul Revere," "Barbara Frietchie." The moral and
religious lessons inculcated by the textbooks of the Puritan regime
were giving way to patriotic propaganda. "Casabianca" celebrated the triumph of duty over common sense, the blind obedience necessary to army discipline. That generation smiled later
at the modern child's comment. Pressed by her mother as to
whether Casabianca was not "good," she said, "Yes, mamma, I
think he was drefful good, but not the least bit smart."

The fierce hatreds generated by the Civil War still dominated.
No Northern child had a good opinion of a Southerner. They
marched about the playground to the tune of "We'll hang Jeff
Davis on a sour apple tree." They pored over the harrowing
stories of Andersonville and Libby prisons, and learned, not that
war was despicable and made beasts of men, but that war was
glorious and the "secesh" monsters. Their minds were filled with
catchphrases and slogans, "Dulce et decorum," "Don't fire until
you see the whites of the enemies' eyes," "Don't give up the ship,"
"I have not yet begun to fight," "A little more grape, Captain
Bragg," "We'll whip the redcoats or Molly Stark's a widow."

> "We don't want to fight, but by jingo if we do,
> We've got the men, we've got the ships,
> We've got the money, too."

Such was the educational foundation that made it possible to
foment the war fever of 1917.

School books were written and edited with this thought in mind, that it was unthinkable that youth should suspect its country was ever wrong, or any country that opposed it ever right, or that the men who founded it were anything but grand and noble—in short, demigods. Nothing was further from the minds of the patriotic beadles and churchwardens in the good old days than that children were sent to school to learn the truth about anything, least of all history. Even today there are sharp outcries against liberalizing the school books to approximate at least something of the truth.

They studied, when they studied, "numbers," which became arithmetic, and ultimately mathematics, geography, reading, and writing according to the characterless model of Platt R. Spencer. The long reign of William McGuffey was just ending. His primer was used in the Central Primary, but the readers were Monroe's, suave stuff without a spark of life in it, or reflecting any conceivable human interest. The higher numbers, one went from first to second, second to third, were made up of extracts and quotations from the best writers, selected with the same eye to morals and deportment rather than literary quality.

At the end of the month each student received a report card, which shamelessly blazoned his shortcomings abroad, for white was excellent, blue good, red fair, and yellow poor, which he was expected to take home and have signed by a parent. The school houses in the different wards were used as polling places, and though election day was not a holiday for adults, schools were dismissed. It was not seemly that pupils who would soon be taught civil government should witness how that government was maintained or what inducements were offered to bring out and secure the vote.

Presiding over the high school was that able teacher Mrs. Gettemy. She was the Mary Ellen Ferris whose graduating paper was a defense of the thesis that the first chapter of Genesis is an allegory, which showed the intellectual integrity of her mind. In a small room adjoining, Latin was taught by Ida McCall, whose skill as a conversationist and genius for friendship made her not only popular, but something of a character. The remaining room was taught by the daughter of a farmer, who won the position after a battle in the board of education, the majority of which favored a man for so difficult a room. It was one of the early minor victories of feminism.

Comparatively few of the students who graduated from the high school went on to college. There was no understanding between the two, and the high school studies were not preparatory. The college had not then learned the wisdom of close relations with the high school which now prevail. There was, indeed, a faint hostility. The college was short-sighted enough to be jealous of the competition, and preferred that town boys and girls intending to enter college should prepare at the college's own academy. That has all been done away with now. Knox Academy has been abolished, and the college cultivates the good will not only of the local high school but all of first rank in the State, and high school marks are accepted for admission.

III

MAIN STREET

Downtown on Main Street and the adjoining thoroughfares given over to trade, conditions were as different in the 1880's from what they are today as in the households, for storekeeping has undergone as complete a transformation as housekeeping. Physically the buildings present much the same appearance; there is little improvement architecturally; the brick stores are taller and more of them; the red line of business has been slowly extending down residential streets. Open spaces have been built up, and such familiar sights as livery stables and blacksmith shops are nonexistent. The old market lot adjoining the square, with its public scales, where the farmers' wagons laden with wood or hay once stood, is gone. But the greatest change is within the stores, in the kinds of merchandise sold, the arrangement of the goods, and the method of doing business.

Instead of the chain grocery with its garish front now rubricating the business section, its smart package goods ranged in orderly and scientific precision on its brightly painted shelves, there were in 1880 old-fashioned grocery stores, D. C. Raymond, Stone & Leonard, Andy Hoover—long, narrow rooms with counters on both sides; behind the counters wooden bins; in the bins tea, coffee, dried peaches, beans, rice, dried peas, cornmeal, flour, prunes, oatmeal, dried apples, everything sold in bulk. In back were the huge barrel stove and the high desk where the grocer kept his accounts.

On the shelves were the few package goods of that early day, soda (familiarly known as saleratus), Baker's Chocolate, and a few canned goods, tomatoes, peaches, salmon, with fancy names but of unknown origin; a housewife who used canned goods felt disgraced. They were emergency rations—sure sign her larder was empty. In smaller receptacles were salt, pepper, cinnamon, cloves, allspice, nutmegs. Tipped forward in front of the counter was a row of open tubs or kegs, more or less covered by their original tops roughly nailed together as lids. In one was butter, another pickles, a third salt mackerel, and the fourth was apt to be a pail of fine-cut chewing tobacco. On the end of the long counter stood a cage of fine wire netting in which was incarcerated like a rare bird a huge American cheese, no doubt a product of one of the Ferrises who brought the cheese technique from Herkimer County, New York. At the back of the store stood the cracker barrels, loosely covered, into which customers dipped from time to time.

On shelves near the front window were rows of glass canisters with tin covers containing stick candy—white with red stripes flavored with peppermint, gum drops, stick licorice, peppermint mottoes, and chocolate drops coated with bitter chocolate and filled with an almost insoluble fondant.

Each purchase involved five or six distinct operations. The

grocer took a sheet of paper from the counter—where the cat no doubt slept at night—and laid it on the scale pan. With a scoop, the same scoop often, he shovelled beans, tea, rice, sugar, or oatmeal, on to the paper. Then with a dexterity, the result of long practice, he wrapped the ticklish package and tied a string around it. If the commodity happened to be dried peaches, or crackers, or loaf sugar—the dice-shaped loaf-sugar of pre-domino days—he used his hands, grabbing a handful from the bin and dropping them in the pan more and more slowly until the beam kicked. Pickles or butter or any other moist eatable was ladled into a small wooden boat, a piece of thin paper stuck on top, and wrapped like the rest. Molasses and vinegar were drawn from the wood into the customer's own brown jugs, light brown for vinegar, dark for molasses. The two barrels were more easily distinguished by the flies that covered the gallon measure which stood beneath the spigot of the molasses barrel. From the measure the jug was filled and stoppered with a corncob. Not a grocery store had a bottle of olive oil for sale in the eighties; lettuce was eaten dressed with sugar and vinegar.

The meat sold in the meat market was home-killed. The packing houses of Chicago were just beginning to build their nationwide distribution and get a strangle hold on the provision industry. There were no refrigerator cars as yet, and the meat that Galesburg bought came from the slaughter house on the edge of the town, the stench from which was evident for blocks around. The offal was thrown into the creek, which had been for fifty years the main sewer of the town. It was a small matter in the early days, but already it had become such a nuisance there was constant complaint, and injunctions had been obtained by irate citizens to compel the council to do something about it. The situation was serious when city water was inaugurated and plumbing installed in the houses. By 1902 there were 190 miles of sewers emptying into Cedar Fork. It was not until 1932 that a trunk sewer was built in the valley of the creek, with a modern disposal plant in the suburbs.

Animal food then arrived on its own feet from the farms roundabout or through the stockyards, and the sides of beef, pork, and mutton were cut up and dressed by the butcher, who also made his own sausage, and prices were so low that a prime rib roast sold for ten cents a pound. Up to the era of refrigeration, it is doubtful if any stay-at-home Galesburger had ever seen a lobster or an oyster on the half shell. Oysters came in square tin boxes, small but excellent for stews, and were the mainstay of church suppers in winter, as was the strawberry in summer.

The drug stores sold only drugs, patent medicines and toilet articles. In the windows were tall glass bottles filled with red and green liquid, as orthodox a sign for a drug store as the striped pole for a barbershop. Behind the prescription counter were the rows of white medicine jars with their mystical inscriptions, now eagerly sought by collectors. At the front of the store was a short marble-topped counter, the soda bar; from the fountain behind it were dispensed sodas: chocolate, vanilla, and lemon. There were no sandwiches, ice cream, or fruit mixtures. The first innovations were milk shake and egg phosphate, and from this humble beginning emanated the varied repertoire of the modern soda bar reaching nearly the length of the store. Cosmetics were an unimportant line. No doubt rouge could be had, the frail ladies from the John House were customers, but rice powder was the limit for the self-respecting. There were no beauty parlors; Galesburg women brushed their own hair; barbershops in the cellars underneath the stores were exclusively masculine; their waiting literature was *The Police Gazette,* and there were no pants-pressing establishments or dry cleaners. Pants were worn as is, without creases.

In dreary, dusty, meagerly furnished rooms above the stores were the offices of doctors, dentists, and lawyers, with law or medical books piled promiscuously about. The idea of taste in such utilitarian quarters was as little dreamed of in Galesburg as anywhere in the country. A waiting room was the dark space partitioned off behind the office. All store buildings were on one stereotyped plan, a long room, twenty-four feet across the front and sixty feet deep. A double store was two such sections thrown into one.

Such was the curious stage setting of business in Galesburg in the eighties. From then on its history was that of progress in better taste in the selling of goods and services, together with the striking changes brought about by new ways of living, new inventions, and a closer contact with the outside world brought by improved communication and transportation.

Main Street was still the index of the life of the town. To its offices and stores came daily on legitimate errands, or merely to stroll in the center of what little bustle and excitement the town afforded, nearly every inhabitant. It stretched from the public square east to the Burlington tracks, but beyond Chambers Street the stores became fewer, and there were more dwellings.

Here on a pleasant spring morning one is aware of the cool earthy odors from the gratings of the cellars beneath the grocery stores, mingled with the smell of damp dust from the freshly sprinkled street. The little park in the center of the square has been fenced, and farmers' teams are tied to the railings. Grass and a few small trees grow in it, and there are the tall liberty pole and the bandstand. On the south rises the white bulk of the Old First Church; on one side the market lot, with its public scales, removed from the square, where wagons loaded with hay, wood, or coal stand, deep with dust or mud, according to the weather. On the other is the opera house, which, when it burned in 1883, furnished an exciting spectacle, and speeded up the building of a courthouse.

Colton's Store is still on the square, but now grown to a large brick block; it is managed by his son, John B., who came back to Galesburg after an adventurous career in the California gold fields with the Jayhawkers, one of the many Galesburg caravans which sought that El Dorado. Across the square are the Union Hotel and the clothing store of Albert Jacobi and his son-in-law, Max J. Mack, and coming round that angle into Main Street, one passes the offices of *The Republican-Register,* where that oddly matched firm, Beatty and Grubb, make a profitable business out of a country daily. On the angle with Main Street is "E. F. Thomas Corner," the sign painter's omission of the apostrophe leaving a doubt as to whether his name is Thomas or Corner.

Across the street is Trask & Gentry's jewelry store, and upstairs the photograph gallery of Barker & Bulkley, the imprint found on the back of most of the "cabinets" and "cartes de visite" in the plush-covered albums on the marble-topped center tables in the parlors of the homes along Prairie Street.

In front of Stone & Leonard's grocery, vegetables are displayed on a stand, young onions, heads of lettuce, carrots and peas, kept fresh by a miniature fountain tossing a ball in a wire cage. Green vegetables are to be had only when they grow in the gardens around the town. For the remainder of the year canned vegetables are the only resource, mainly corn, tomatoes, and peas, helped out by the root crops in the cellars, potatoes, parsnips, beets, and turnips.

Appropriately over Grose & Stire's bookstore is the public library, fruit of Professor Hurd's unselfish devotion, a long narrow room the size of the store beneath. The ingenious apparatus whereby patrons learned whether the books they sought were in would have astonished Melvil Dewey, the father of modern library methods. A white wooden screen separated the reading public from the storehouse of literature. The screen was punched with thousands of small holes, and in each hole was a plug, one end red, the other blue; and over each hole was the number of a book. When a book was taken out, the librarian reversed its plug, red indicating realization; blue frustration.

On the next corner going up Main is the store of "E. Scharps, the One-Price Clothier." That phrase is no empty flourish. It marks a new era in merchandising, the passing of the old regime of haggling which had prevailed in American retailing since the beginning. The practice had been to charge all the traffic would stand, all the customer could be made to pay—*caveat emptor.*

The new method was to sell at a fixed price, the same to all. In thousands of towns and cities merchants had begun to experiment with an honester and fairer method, and "one-price" had a definite meaning.

These shops were in what was known as the Metropolitan Block, an ambitious three-story structure of red brick in the florid commercial architecture of the time, of which the townspeople were vastly proud. It had replaced the pioneer general store of Matthew Chambers on one corner, and the old hostelry known as the Galesburg House which President Kellogg had built on the other. In the center of this block was Murdoch's, a dry goods store conducted by a canny Scots merchant, who had helped build Caledonia Hall. He was a good Presbyterian, but in his employ was one clerk whose chief mission was to attract the trade of the gay ladies from the John House, and who reciprocated by patronizing the wares they sold. The leading dentist had his office in this block, whose name was an unfailing source of waggishness, for it was Doctor J. A. W. Davis.

Across Cherry Street and on Main one passed Charvet's fur store with its forlorn moth-eaten stuffed bear leaning on a staff as a sign, to O. T. Johnson's, the biggest dry goods store, now a department store and one of the units in a chain. The brothers Johnson, looking enough alike to be twins, mingled with their customers affably, content to let Murdoch's monopolize the trade of the demimonde. Robert Chappell was a partner, afterward sole owner, whose money came from the oil mill where his father ground flaxseed for the white paint that distinguished Galesburg's first frame houses.

Across the way was the gents' furnishing store of Charlie Merrill, chief competitor of Jacobi & Mack on the Square. His failing memory in later years cost him the collection of many an account. An old customer would come in, buy a hat, and say "Charge it." Merrill could not bring himself to say he had forgotten the name. He sadly watched him out of the store, and entered in his daybook, "May 6—Man bought a hat." Such entries finally closed his books for good.

At Boon's Avenue, the short and quick way to destruction, down which nice females never walked because of the saloons on both sides, was Sam Friedberg's hat store. His brother, under the professional name of Ralph Temple, became a star bicycle rider in the days when no county fair program was complete without trick riding, the sort where the rider takes his bicycle to pieces without dismounting, and rides off on the front wheel.

Outpost to the east was Brown's Hotel—built by the corn-planter man, biggest manufacturer in the town, rated second only to the Union on the Square—where the touring theatrical companies got rates, and the second-string drummers put up. Thus the businesses that constituted Galesburg's economic life lined its main street for five blocks, and overflowed in the near-by cross streets, many of them survivals of pioneer enterprises, carried on by the next generation, but still more often by newcomers from elsewhere, drawn to the growing town. Each generation of store-keepers began as clerks and learned their trade of their elders, and no new ideas disturbed their primitive methods until the advent of modern advertising, trained salesmanship, chain stores, and the innovations distributed by manufacturers to help retailers sell their goods.

None of the thirty saloons was on Main Street. Not until re-peal was liquor sold on this thoroughfare. The saloons were con-fined to the Square, Prairie Street, and the one-block lane known as Boon's Avenue, in which stood the White Elephant, a bone of contention in the long struggle between temperance and license. The problem of the city council for years had been to permit sites for so many dram shops and still leave streets clear of saloons to afford passage to college and church. There was always a drunk or two sleeping in odd corners which the police had overlooked the night before.

By half past six on a weekday morning the humblest employee

of each store and office appeared to sweep out, and in winter kindle the fires. By seven all were ready for business. The clerks and proprietors arrived, the latter driven to work by some member of the family in a surrey or side-bar buggy. All had been roused from slumber by the stentorian blasts of the whistle on the Burlington shops at five ante-meridian.

After the workers came the school children, with here and there a Knox cadet in his ill-fitting ready-made uniform, and then the mothers, having gotten the children off and the breakfast dishes washed, appeared with market baskets to purchase the day's supplies, those from the privileged class in the buggies which had taken their husbands to their offices and stores. From twelve to one the street was as dead as a French town for all went home to dinner. In the afternoon the street took on a lighter and more frivolous tone, for instead of marketing, the women were shopping. In the middle of the afternoon the streets again filled with children. The parade of the frails in their open carriages drove up and down the street, and small boys whispered to one another that they knew what they were.

Saturdays the street took on its most festive air. The farmers came with their Studebaker wagons loaded with produce, which they delivered to the mill or stockyards or market lot. They ate Anderson's twenty-five cent dinner, had a nip at the White Elephant, their wives shopped, there was much greeting and gossip before setting out on the long slow dusty drive home. When the C. B. & Q. pay car happened to arrive on a Friday, Saturday's business boomed and zoomed; stores remained open until midnight. Trade was brisk, saloons were crowded, and the police gathered up quite a grist for the justices to sit on Monday morning.

The business pulse of the town beat slowly. In the offices over the stores lawyers waited for clients, and whiled the time away with cards or billiards—one firm had a table in its back room. The clients were often farmers, and the fee a calf or colt. Most lawyers had a little live stock on hand earned in this way, waiting for a sale. The doctors, however, were busy. They drove day and night in their mud-spattered buggies, to wash which there was never time, diagnosing, prescribing and putting up the prescriptions on the spot—Doctor Foote, the homeopath, with his neat case of sugar pills which he saturated with the medicine prescribed; Doctor Chase, of the old school, with his handsome face and patriarchal white whiskers, never too old to respond to an opportunity for gallantry; Doctor Judd, ablest of them all, who would not coddle his patients but told them the brutal truth, and was disliked but always called in desperate cases.

Sunday morning the devout gathered at the churches, and the undevout in the cool front doors of Andy Dow's or Jim O'Connor's livery stables, but both contingents met at the post office at noon, when the one mail for the day was distributed. They went home after Sunday-school for the biggest dinner of the week, after which father took a nap, and the children a walk, generally to the cemetery which had its attraction, or to the depot to see the trains come in, or along Main Street to look in the windows.

The Catholics, mostly the Irish railroad men and their families, were not seen so often on Main Street. St. Patrick's little church was situated beside the railroad tracks far out on Academy Street, with the square brick house of Father Howard, next door, a man of learning and fine understanding, as so many of those country priests were.

Some time between the stern regime of President Blanchard, when college classes were held on December 25 the same as any day, and the Eighteen Eighties the celebration of Christmas became a fixture in the puritan town of Galesburg. The public revolt was in 1871, when the young people of the Old First Church announced they were going to have a tree for the children of the Sunday-school, and did so without breaking any bones. But before that, Christmas was a modest festival in most homes. The observation of the day may have been brought by the Swedes, who shared a hearty participation in the day with the Germans. Stockings were hung up on various projections, or tacked up be-

hind the base burner, for there were no fireplaces to help keep
up the tradition, and an orange was such a novelty it was deemed
a worthy present, along with a striped peppermint cane, a bag of
peanuts, and one or two much needed and useful articles, such as
stockings or mittens, knit by mother or grandmother. The mittens were tethered to one another by a long cord, so that if one
were lost, both must be. By 1880 there were Christmas windows
in the stores and signs reading "Holiday Goods."

In the eighties came the twilight of the sturdy pioneers whose
ambitions and convictions gave the colony its original stamp. At
the beginning of the decade many were still living, gaunt, bearded
men, in old-fashioned garments, familiar landmarks, but no longer
vital in the life of the town. It seemed incredible to the younger
generation that those old men had once been young and had performed the epic task of subduing the virgin prairie and laying
the foundation of the town and the college. Still living in 1880
was Chauncey Colton, the first merchant, rich, trustee of the college, owner of the largest hotel, principal stockholder in the leading bank, director of the Burlington Route, one son carrying on
the old store, another American consul at Venice; Norman
Churchill, the clerk of the church who had sassed the Presbytery
over the slavery question, whose son was one of the most useful
men in the city, and whose grandson was building a successful
hardware business; Eli Farnham, whose wife, Jerusha, had kept a
diary of their overland trek, a simple hardworking farmer, but
trustee of the college; Innes Grant and Nehemiah Losey, the first
professors in the college; Caleb Finch, nephew of George W.
Gale, captain of militia, and political mentor of Colonel Clark E.
Carr; Henry Ferris, the first of that family to go West, who had
been driven from school in Missouri for his anti-slavery leanings
—all these men were dead by 1890. William Ferris, "Uncle Billy,"
who made port in his cheese house on Academy Street, and sold
ice and milk and ice cream to the pioneer village, was the last of
Silvanus' sons to go. He lived until 1905, and was the sole survivor of the original band which immigrated to this prairie in

1837. They were the last links between the colony and the New York from which it sprang.

## IV

### NEWSPAPERS

The newspapers of a small town in the years before the Civil War are a disappointment to one seeking facts about the community because of the dearth of what is technically known as local news. They are made up wholly of digests of world news condensed from city papers, advertisements, miscellaneous reading matter, lengthy contributions on controversial topics, poetry, and the editor's comments on things in general.

The reason is obvious. In a town of 1000 in the days before communication and transportation had developed, local happenings were already known to every inhabitant. They circulated faster than a weekly newspaper. So the editor refrained from repeating what was already known to his readers, and confined himself to occasional comment as one might contribute to a conversation.

The editor was usually a practical printer—the two occupations were almost synonymous in small towns. He not only wrote such original matter as appeared in his paper, he set the type, and ran off the paper, one sheet at a time, on a Washington hand-lever press. Many of those old-time editors put their thoughts into type without bothering to write copy. The pages of the early prints were unusually large, mostly nine columns, but as two pages of advertisements, more or less, were kept standing from issue to issue, the labor was not as great as might appear.

The advertising with which the paper was almost filled consisted of "foreign," that is, business from outside the town, and "local," the cards of the town's business houses. These were squares of one or two inches giving the name, address and line of business. The more enterprising, the Coltons, Willards, Mattesons, Sages and Woods, used larger space, with a long catalogue of goods "just arrived." A column advertisement of *The New York Tribune* paid for a subscription to that paper, from which the editor got most of his news. For the rest he depended on his exchanges and his own inner consciousness.

Numerous patent medicines, together with the "doctor books" mentioned elsewhere, show that our ancestors were as gullible as we are, and that what the profession denounces as self-medication was common. Here are some old-time remedies, a few of which still flourish, and are objects of solicitous attention by the Food and Drug Bill which has been trying for two years to become a law:

Moffet's Life Pills and Phoenix Bitters, Herrick's Sugar-coated Pills and Kidney Strengthening Plasters, Doctor Easterly's Odine and Sarsaparilla, Doctor Sanford's Liver Invigorator, Doctor Baker's Specific for Diseases of the Genital Organs, Doctor Carter's Cough Balsam, Ayer's Cherry Pectoral and Cathartic Pills, Professor Wood's Hair Restorer, all of which might be had at Matteson's or Lanphere's drug store.

There was, however, a personal relation between the editor and his readers which is altogether delightful, savoring as it does of the pioneer spirit, the mutual give and take which makes allowances, and is revealed in the confidential remarks about the editor's personal difficulties. He explains with engaging frankness that "pressure of job and pamphlet work has prevented our giving the usual amount of reading matter in today's issue."

Again: "Our editorial columns are not so full this week as common, but the immense amount of outdoor labor which has devolved upon us must be our excuse for the deficiency of mental labor we are able today to expend."

Even more intriguing is the announcement that the paper is smaller because the state of the roads delayed delivery of paper on which to print it. The roads being impassable by reason of rain, the advertisements are omitted instead of reading matter, as the stores would not do much business anyway, and people compelled to stay home would need their reading matter more than usual.

So it is only by deduction that anything can be learned from files of old newspapers about the inner life of the town. Local happenings are revealed more by the copious advance notices than by any account after the happening, or else by some editorial comment, disappointingly brief and lacking in the details on which the comment is based.

The chief delight of the western editor was a controversy, especially a dispute with a rival newspaper in his own city or elsewhere. As Galesburg had her share of differences, the early papers were not only full of debate, they were established for the purpose of conducting the debate. The first was the religious schism, which was internal, and demanded two local papers to uphold the two sides.

*The Intelligencer* (1848) championed the embattled Presbyterians; *The Northwestern Gazetteer* (1849) defended the Congregationalists in that famous controversy. Neither paper had as much vitality as the quarrel that gave them birth, and both expired before the dispute ended.

The second occasion that demanded an organ was the fight with Knoxville for the railroad. To combat the hostile propaganda of the Knox *Republican* the Gales started *The Newsletter* in 1850. The peculiar fame of this sheet was the frequency with which it changed its owner, name and editorial policy. For in 1852 the name was enlarged to *The Newsletter and Henry County Chronicle,* in the hope of widening its field by adding another county. One year later, in fresh hands as *The Western Freeman,* it became a political organ with anti-slavery as its platform, a popular policy in abolition Galesburg. It could not have flourished greatly, for within two years it had a new owner and a new name, *The Free Democrat,* and changed hands six times under that masthead, becoming a daily in 1857. After the Civil War it was bought by an old soldier who called it *The Free Press,* and its politics, in turn anti-slavery, free soil, and Republican, became

Democratic to support Horace Greeley against General Grant. By 1886 it was known as *The Knox County Chronicle,* a weekly once more, and then it was sold to Gershom Martin, one of those picturesque newspaper characters, half printer, half editor, and wholly individualist, that the prairies seemed to breed fifty years ago.

Martin was born in Pickaway County, Ohio, 1826, son of a farmer, left home when he was twelve, walked to Illinois and became a mule driver on the Illinois and Michigan Canal. He learned to set type at a country printshop, and became that ideally independent rover, the tramp printer, working on small papers, adding a shrewd worldly wisdom to his natural stock of ideas.

He turned up at Galesburg in 1886, managed to raise money to buy *The Chronicle,* named it *The Press and People,* and proceeded to give the town a kind of newspaper it had never known, anticipating the yellow journalism of Pulitzer and Hearst by about three decades. He printed news no other paper would handle, made countless enemies, but built up a large circulation of readers who dared not miss seeing it. It was read in New York newspaper offices, and Charles A. Dana, recognizing an original spirit, reprinted some of its editorials in *The New York Sun,* the last one being "Guided by Tradition," which Martin wrote just before he died in 1894.

The paper contained little news; it was all editorials, comments on happenings in the town and national affairs, written by the editor, who introduced "caps" in the text for emphasis long before Brisbane thought of it. "Gersh" was opposed to the smug moral complacency of the town, wrote up the rich and the righteous when they slipped, as readily as the poor and unfortunate. He was against college, church, temperance, and puritanism, was seldom sober, wore a white felt which by long use had become steepled like a clown's, and wrote with a pen that put vigor and sting into his comments.

His office and printing plant occupied the second floor of a three-story brick building, between a business college above and the W. C. T. U. headquarters below. Local wags said you could get education on the third floor, damnation on the second, and salvation on the first. Gersh anticipated the outspoken frankness of the present day, named names, and called a spade a spade. No respectable citizen would be seen taking *The Press and People* from the post office, but they all read it, and its stinging editorials gave the city a needed tonic.

The things with which Gersh scandalized the good burghers of the town and boosted his circulation were of this order. Mrs. Martin, motherly soul, sought to add to her income by taking college boarders. Mrs. Whiting, matron of the seminary—the old word "female" now disused—warned some prospective tenants that Gersh Martin's house was not a respectable place. Some months later one of the Seminary girls was sent home "in an interesting condition" as the phrase then was. *The Republican-Register* discreetly ignored the happening according to the long-established ethics of country journalism. Not so Gersh. He roared: "Gersh Martin's house not respectable? How about Mrs. Whiting's house?" When the superintendent of the Baptist Sunday-school was found short in his accounts as bookkeeper of the leading department store, *The Republican-Register* wrote more in sorrow than reproof, "another good man gone wrong." "No," paraphrased *The Press and People,* "another bad man found out." And human nature being what it is, no doubt many of his surreptitious readers agreed with him.

Gersh was honest and courageous. His weaknesses were drink and a liking for the sort of stories Lincoln used to tell. He was perhaps a better man than many who deplored him. At any rate, good Doctor Gale's *Newsletter* had reached its apogee. When Gersh died his paper died with him, having lasted from 1850 to 1894, borne six names, and been successfully owned by twelve different sets of proprietors.

Then there was Stephe R. Smith. He was born in Virginia, of a wealthy family, who sent him to an exclusive "prep" school. His roommate was a lovesick amorous youth, and Stephe and his friends hoaxed him by abstracting his ardent letters and answering them, Stephe writing the fictitious replies. The joke climaxed in a mock marriage with a Negro slave girl from Stephe's father's plantation, veiled and disguised, personating the bride. The roommate was furious, and Stephe fled, but the victim pursued him and put a bullet in his head, which he carried until his death, lodged just behind his ear. That, his daughter thought, accounted for all his subsequent eccentricities.

Stephe came to Galesburg in 1866 and started *The Register,* which not long after became a daily. Four years later *The Republican* was launched by a group of men in the interest of Clark E. Carr, postmaster, in training to become a political magnate, who needed an organ. The duties of the post office not being pressing and having a capable chief clerk, Carr became editor of *The Republican.* The two papers exchanged editorial amenities in the unrestrained manner of those times.

> "Twinkle, twinkle, little Carr,
> How I wonder what you are,"

paraphrased Stephe.

> "Guzzle, guzzle, Stephe R,
> No one wonders what you are,"

replied Carr.

*The Republican* and *Register* "scrapped" and blackguarded each other in the unstinted Western style until 1872 or thereabouts when the two papers were merged as *The Republican-Register,* daily and weekly, which flourished for fifty years under that name, and is still the town's principal and only important newspaper, with another change in its title. Its success was owing to two men of great ability and strongly marked idiosyncrasies, Zaccheus Beatty and S. W. Grubb.

Both were printers. Beatty was a taciturn, almost morose man, whose taciturnity extended even to writing. He wrote as little as possible. His editorials consisted almost wholly of reprint clipped from rival papers, with a terse line of comment, which was fortunate for the compositors, as few could read his writing, and only after long practice. The paper was steadily and consistently pledged to the temperance cause, but Beatty liked his dram, which he took at regular intervals at the neighboring drug store, as was the custom of all the more respectable drinkers, being attended with less publicity than patronizing one of the numerous saloons, of which this temperance city now boasted forty.

Grubb was business manager, a printer who once worked on the famous *National Era,* an anti-slavery paper which published "Uncle Tom's Cabin" as a serial. But he was as odd in his way as Beatty, irascible and apoplectic, eloquently profane, very near-sighted with a queer defect which required holding reading matter close to and a little above his forehead, as if reading with his antennæ. He was a shrewd business man, a "go-getter," independent as the traditional hog on ice, and managed to get advertising and get paid for it.

By keeping himself gently pickled and writing as little as possible, but exercising a shrewd newspaper instinct, Beatty managed with the assistance of his partner downstairs in the business office to produce one of the most successful sheets in the whole State of Illinois. It built up an amazingly complete county correspondence, the mainstay of a country weekly, without paying for it except by a few perquisites, and its circulation with no serious competitor was large. For fifty years the gathering of the news was in the hands of Frederick Reuben Jelliff. Jelliff was born in Whitesboro, the place where the Galesburg colony originated. He was graduated from Knox, taught school a bit, and in 1882 joined the staff of *The Republican-Register* as local editor. He also found time to act as Associated Press representative, and as correspondent for a long list of metropolitan newspapers. His career as a newspaper man was creditable, but at heart he was a student, a scholar and a scientist.

His passion was geology. He made himself an authority on the geologic history of Illinois. His collection of specimens was one of the best in the State. He found time in the eighties, when his working day was eighteen hours, Sundays included, to take a company of boys afield armed with hammers and crack open the rocks to learn the history of the past ages, and for some of these boys it was the most of geology they learned. His article on "The Prevention of Pollution of Illinois Streams," read before the Knox County Academy of Science, was widely reprinted, attracted statewide interest, and resulted in the passage of the Ickes Bill—named for the wife of Roosevelt's Secretary of the Interior, a graduate of Knox College—to preserve the watercourses of the State from contamination. He was president of the Illinois Academy of Science and a life member of the American Association for the Advancement of Science. His life was one which shows what may be accomplished in a small town in broadening one's horizon.

The paper exercised for years, with occasional interruptions, what was practically a monopoly, but so cleverly did it steer a middle course, so astute was its non-partisanship, it managed to keep its constituency satisfied with one paper. It was nominally, and occasionally energetically, Republican, but so was the majority of the townsfolk, and for years at a time there was not enough opposition to finance another paper. It welcomed each newcomer, and there were many, fought them cleverly, finally absorbed them, and remained dominating its field as it does today.

One of these competitors was raised up by Colville Brothers, sons of the Robert Colville, the bookbinder, who ran the ruling machine and made day books and ledgers for commercial Galesburg. His sons inherited the business, which included a good-sized printing plant.

But in 1891 the political situation seemed to demand another newspaper. *The Republican-Register* still supported Clark E. Carr, the titular political genius of the town. Philip Sidney Post, also a Republican, was opposing him for Congress in the tenth district. Bennett Barnes, who had sold *The Knox County Chronicle* he inherited from his father to Gersh Martin, joined with the Colvilles to publish *The Evening Mail,* to support the other wing of the Republicans, and the victory of General Post at the polls gave the new sheet a good start.

The Hamptons, father and son, had been giving a statewide reputation to *The Macomb Bystander.* They came to Galesburg and bought *The Mail,* of which the Colvilles were getting a little tired, its mission having been successfully achieved, and Ben Bowles Hampton, afterward founder of *Hampton's Magazine* in New York, rapidly built the paper into a profitable enterprise. The Hamptons sold out, and after a few changes of ownership *The Mail* came into the hands of *The Republican-Register,* was merged with it, and it became *The Register-Mail,* rated with a circulation of 18,616, starred—that is, authenticated, in Ayer's *Newspaper Directory.*

For some years *The Republican-Register* had a competitor in the weekly *Plaindealer.* The firm of Emerich & Biggs would have delighted Charles Dickens. They had that combination of outward peculiarities and inward kindheartedness which that old sentimentalist loved to portray. Henry Emerich, of German extraction, was round, short, bearded and cheerful. Iram Biggs was tall, stoop-shouldered and gloomy. Emerich did the editing, not much more extended than that of Editor Beatty, marched with the G. A. R., attended the political meetings, and lobbied for his fellow veterans. In the years immediately following the war it was impossible for any candidate to be elected, no matter how well qualified, in opposition to a Grand Army man. Biggs ran the job printing, hovering over the imposing stone in his long dingy apron like some bird of evil omen, a disillusioned philosopher, as were so many of those old time printers. His jaundiced views of life and his acid comments on the town, his fellow citizens, the college, church people, and affairs generally, were rarely entertaining, though of course they never saw the light of print. If he had but been a Stephe Smith or Gersh Martin.

Emerich was cursed with a distressing impediment in his speech, which Editor Beatty was unchivalrous enough to caricature in one of their numerous spats:

*"The Plaindealer* says: 'T-t-the Rep-p-publican p-p-party——' "

How Henry did sputter as he wrote his indignant reply to that dig! Such were the printers of Galesburg, as picturesque and likable a group as could be found. It was the articulate ones like Stephe and Gersh who wrote, pouring forth comment, witty, sometimes vitriolic, but always readable; the reticent ones, like Beatty and Emerich, who made money. In the long run, the small town does not want to hear the truth. It is only in retrospect that these incidents are so appealing.

V

### PUBLIC AFFAIRS

The town was slow in providing the facilities now considered necessary to every well-conducted community. From the introduction of gas in 1861 down to the extermination of the last trolley in favor of a bus line, the period was punctuated with struggles to install paving, electricity, transportation, telephone, water and a sewage system. The public did not take kindly to them. Such things meant bond issues, assessments, taxes; aldermen were elected and went down later, as public opinion veered, and the determined ones fought for the improvements the town must eventually have.

The streets were one source of annoyance. Paved by nature with mud in wet weather and dust in dry, the mud stalled the farm wagons which brought trade to the town, the dust ground to powder by the wheels sifted over the housewife's curtains and the merchants' goods. The sidewalks were of wood, with plank crossings, which became impassable from mud piled on them by wheels. Twice a day in dry weather the watering carts made their rounds downtown, wooden tanks on wheels with a perforated spout behind where boys ran to enjoy shower baths in hot weather.

When the wisdom of paving was first agitated, E. D. Matthews, one of the newer business men, owned a block on Main Street, which would naturally be subject to assessment for the improvement, so he fought it bitterly. One Sunday morning when the mire before his store was almost liquid and of unknown depth, the town woke up to find a large sign displayed in the deepest part which read, "Matthews Boulevard." It hung there for days, until Matthews could find some one who for hire would wade out and take it down.

The streets were finally paved with gravel, but when the paving brick industry was developed in the Court Creek valley east of the town, its product was adopted, not only for roads, but for sidewalks, and resisted even the advent of concrete.

The story of any town might be told in terms of light. Illumination has had as much to do with the development of what we call civilization as any other physical factor. Progress is measured by our victory over natural forces, darkness being one, compelling them to our service. We have not yet found a way to curb or control weather, though we have done something about foretelling its vagaries. With heating, refrigeration and air-conditioning we have gone far toward mastering, or at least offsetting, climate. We have certainly annihilated what James Hunecker called "the pathos of distance." But few things have done so much to widen the scope of man's powers and activities as a satisfactory substitute for the light of day.

The cabins of the Galesburg pioneers at Log City were dimly lit. They planned their days to rise with the sun and retire with its setting. For the few hours they endeavored to snatch from the night there was a saucer of lard oil with a cotton flannel wick floating in it, a device almost identical with Roman lamps dug up at Pompeii. As soon as possible the housewives made candles, dipping them or shaping them in molds, producing lights that were not even one candlepower. At the store they were able later to buy better candles, and sticks to hold them, with chimneys to protect the flickering flame. When they fared forth after dark they carried tin lanterns with holes punched in them and candles inside, and this was the only thing in the way of street lighting the little village knew. Study, work, social life were all circumscribed and limited by the short radius of light.

Hardly had they time to go through the phases of candlelight before kerosene arrived and increased and made available the hours taken from the night. Lamps and lamp chimneys improved in design and ingenuity. One of the larger national advertisers in the 1880's was Macbeth who made unbreakable chimneys. Lamps were hung from brackets, and there was a device for the dinner table by which the light could be raised and lowered. Next came the Argand burner with circular wick from which evolved the student lamp that gave a steadier and clearer light. In some towns streets were lit with kerosene, but Galesburg had no public lighting until the age of gas.

In 1865 a few citizens got together and secured permission to set up a gas plant on a block near the center of the town, not far from where it stands today. Its purpose was to light the streets, and for years the company and the council rowed over rates. Meanwhile gas crept into public buildings, stores and houses as the mains branched out. The naked jet which whistled at times was modified and improved by inventions which added to the flexibility of the new light, such as the Welsbach burner, and floor and table lamps with detachable rubber tubes caused many tragedies. It was a better light than kerosene, and was put to new uses. Store windows were illuminated, jets with powerful reflectors lit the churches, and footlights were installed in Caledonia Hall and the Opera House. The street lamps had to be lit at dusk and extinguished at midnight, and the men who made the rounds with short ladders became familiar figures. There was a popular novel in the 1860's entitled *The Lamplighter*. By the time electricity arrived, gas was well established, but the rate was high, $3.25 a thousand cubic feet. In its fight with the gas company the city installed street lamps burning gasoline, but in the midst of its tribulations the new illuminant arrived and turned the history of light in other channels.

In 1880 the Brush Company obtained permission to stage a demonstration of electric lighting in the public square. The whole town turned out to see two large arc lights sputtering at the top of a tall pole, casting a weird radiance over a familiar scene. It was actually believed that the whole town could be lighted by one 2000-candle-power lamp on a pole one hundred fifty feet high. Even in New York there was a pole on Madison Square Garden Tower with a ring of arc lights hung on it.

With the invention of the incandescent lamp, electricity reached its zenith for domestic lighting. Probably no other invention has had greater influence on the destiny of mankind. Light for every purpose, brought to the desired spot, shaded, colored, tempered as needed; light with a sunlight quality that showed the true color of fabrics, shadowless lights for operating rooms, dentists, and barbers, time added to human life. These phases entered and altered existence in Galesburg along with the rest of the world, and the town which in less than a hundred years had run the entire gamut of illumination from the flickering home-made candle to light that springs into being at the touch of a button, found in that first demonstration of the arc light the same wonder with which it viewed the wood-burning locomotive that snorted into the town in 1854.

The local gas company, perceiving the trend, had secured the first franchise for electric lighting, in spite of the Brush Company. The usual arguments over rates resulted in a city-owned plant. Meanwhile the gas company had been bought out by a syndicate —this was the beginning of mergers and holding companies which have proved so disastrous to investors in recent years—and the same company had acquired the local trolley line.

This enterprise was also local in origin. A group of citizens sponsored the first stubby cars, drawn by mules, which was followed by another company on different streets, but electric traction was brought by outsiders, and the systems were consolidated under alien managership. Interurban lines were promoted, and the council was inundated by requests for permission to lay tracks, but were checkmated by property owners who did not want the lines on their streets, and then overruled by merchants covetous of the trade the trolleys would bring from the nearby cities. Then when the town was thoroughly striated with tracks, the motor car arrived. The council was now besieged for permission to remove tracks and poles, and to reorganize transportation on a bus basis.

Today Galesburg is serviced with gas and electrcity by the Illinois Light and Power Company. It is of more than passing interest that the power which turns the dynamos to supply Galesburg's current is generated by the rapids of the Mississippi at Keokuk, and thus Ol' Man River, so closely linked with Galesburg's first shipping of corn and hogs, is still working for it. In spite of the theory that water power is cheapest, the rate is not low, grading from 8 to 4 cents, while gas is $1.45 first 5000 cu. ft. per M. These utility prices are exceptions to the low cost of living which prevails in the prairie towns.

The telephone company had much the same history, but with a happier ending. It also began with a home-promoted undertaking, passed to outside hands, became part of A. T. & T., went through the throes of two competing lines, and wound up in the hands of a local company, where it is today. There are 6500 installations, almost one for every five inhabitants. All wires, both electric and telephone, are underground, and it is the next best thing to municipal ownership.

Water was plentiful on the prairies. The subsoil was full of it; and for fifty years the town depended on wells. But they did not furnish enough water for fire protection, and the multiplication of wells in proximity to outdoor latrines was a menace to health. By 1880 the public began to think of city water. The town fell into the snare of a plausible promoter who built a waterworks supplied by gangwells, and was soon involved in a long and tiresome legal fight over breach of contract. The water proved bad, unfit to drink, and even for washing many witnesses testified they had to wear clothes-pins on their noses because of the odor.

Having shaken off this promoter, the town made other experiments and finally arrived at its municipally owned plant, also supplied by wells, in a different part of the city, which pays a handsome profit into the city treasury.

In 1887 the opportunity came to persuade the Santa Fé, extending its line from the Mississippi to Chicago, to run through Galesburg. The opportunity was seized, a vigorous campaign waged, a bonus of $60,000 raised, and the road secured. "Colonel" Clark Ezra Carr, then Galesburg's leading citizen, was probably the one who did most to attain this end, his close acquaintance with Santa Fé officers being an influential factor. It was a neat and competent job of promotion, and gave the town a place on two great railroad lines, but the work of securing it was done by a few business and political leaders. The movement did not reach down and involve every person in the town as did the gigantic struggle to build its link in what became the Burlington Route.

The saloons were the old-fashioned small-town grog shops, screened from the street, with a back room for cards and billiards. As in most communities they were linked with gambling, prostitution, and other vices. They distressed the Puritan element, the situation being aggravated by the presence of the two colleges. Saloons had the glamour for youth of the forbidden and hidden. The farmers on market day got drunk, spent the night in the calaboose, and were fined Monday morning by Squire Holcomb. Eminent citizens misjudged their capacity and came home late and unsteady—as they did and do everywhere. At Peoria, fifty miles away, the largest distilleries in the country flourished. Bob Ingersoll had written a tribute to corn whisky that was a classic. It was a whisky country.

Mary Allen West spurred the college to act on the famous clause in all its deeds, which, theoretically, should have made the city as dry as a bone. The trustees consulted lawyers and received opinion that the clause was now unenforceable, the statute of limitations acting as a bar. The trustees had been living in a fool's paradise, believing they only had to act to wipe out the whole liquor business, but the original clause had not been drawn with sufficient foresight and worldly wisdom to cope with modern legal shrewdness.

A man named Holmes, none other than the proprietor of the quaintly named "Plunder Store," the emporium beneath Caledonia Hall, besought the trustees to give him a quitclaim deed without the liquor clause for the land on which his property stood. He was about to spend a large sum of money on the building, which he would have to borrow, and his lawyer felt that the old clause constituted a flaw in the title, which must be removed before the bank would lend on the property. The trustees granted the deed, establishing a precedent, and thus the dead hand of old George Gale was unloosed from all the land in the original town of Galesburg, and one of his cherished dreams dissipated into thin air.

For forty years the war between temperance and liberalism raged intermittently. Its arena was the city council, which changed its complexion with every election. From time to time the question was grudgingly submitted to a vote of the people, but license was sustained in every case but one. The liberals maintained—and the law seemed to support them—that the council had no legal right to submit the question to popular vote, and that the result of such a vote was not mandatory, but merely advisory. So when the no-license party secured a slight majority, the liberal council ignored it. Many conscientiously opposed to drinking felt that license gave control, mitigated some of the evils, while the income from the fees was a welcome addition to the city's revenues.

The next time the question came up in an election, the drys hired Billy Sunday, who put on one of his best shows. Mass meetings were held, attended by thousands, and a strong temperance sentiment was whipped up. No-license won by a small majority, but again the liberal majority in the council refused to act on the popular vote.

In 1914 the State legislature passed a law giving women the right to vote on questions of public policy. The result was an overwhelming majority for "no license," 5179 to 2344. The ballot proved more effective than W. C. T. U., Band of Hope, or red, white and blue ribbons. Galesburg became dry, and entered the prohibition era with no saloons, and comparatively little bootlegging.

# 12

## Knox College Grows Up

### I

#### GULLIVER

We left Knox College back there in the sixties under the administration of the two Curtises. Harvey Curtis died in 1863, and was succeeded by William Staunton Curtis. The war years were difficult ones for the college, as all public interest concentrated in the great struggle, and the young men were called or drafted for the army. Of the eighty-seven students who graduated during the war years, only forty-five were men. Those who remained at college gave most of their time to war work on the home sector, and the college made little progress.

A military unit was organized among the students, precursor of the R. O. T. C., and drill was compulsory. The members of the corps served in rotation as officers. The uniform was "a flannel shirt, and a cheap pair of overalls, with suitable cap, the whole to cost not over two or three dollars." A Major Standen, whose status in the town during a war is unexplained, was drill master. Some students were excused for reasons not stated, but there were applications from outside the college for permission to join the unit, which was probably granted.

A decided effort was made to put the Seminary in a position to obtain a large increase in patronage, so that it need not fear the competition of the Galesburg high school. The trustees said that "combining intellectual teaching with moral and religious training would outweigh intellectual training alone." Evidently the high school did not stress the religious idea. The course was extended to four years, and the women students from out of town were required to live at the Seminary to make good the promise that those from abroad were under the supervision of the principal. Another provision was that the inmates attend church twice on Sunday, and learn a Bible lesson for recitation Monday morning. There was perhaps some disagreement between President Curtis and the board over these changes, for Curtis resigned because of "differences over co-education."

There was constant reluctance on the part of the trustees to put boys and girls in the same classes, though the faculty frequently urged it to reduce expenses and save them the double duty of teaching the same lesson twice. At all public mixed gatherings the men and women still sat on different sides of the room.

The administration which followed was one of the most brilliant the college had ever known. In 1868 John Putnam Gulliver was made president. He brought to the faculty young men of such promise and scholarship, and he was himself a man of so many accomplishments, social and intellectual, that the few still living who sat under him speak of him with enthusiasm mingled with regret.

Gulliver had more intellectual breadth than the average minister chosen to head an intellectual institution. Education was a passion with him. At Norwich, Connecticut, he carried on a long and successful fight for the establishment of Norwich Free Academy, which still stands a monument to his ideas. For years he was "Acting Visitor," a position similar to Superintendent of Schools. He knew more about education, and had been more concerned with it than any man who had yet headed Knox College.

Like nearly every one in the North with strong moral convictions, Gulliver was active in the anti-slavery agitation. While still preaching at Norwich, an incident occurred which, while it has no direct bearing on this history, adds one more to the number of those concerned with Galesburg and Knox College, who came into contact with Abraham Lincoln. Lincoln spoke at Norwich during his campaign for President, and Gulliver went up and congratulated him. Lincoln was naïvely surprised at the reception his speech had met in the East, and asked Gulliver to tell him in what its merits lay. Gulliver replied,

"The clearness of your statements, the unanswerable style of your reasoning, and especially your illustrations, which were romance and pathos and fun and logic all welded together."

Gulliver was curious to know how Lincoln acquired his power of putting things. Lincoln said it was true he never went to school more than six months in his life, but that even as a child he was irritated when he heard expressions he did not understand.

"I can remember going to my little bedroom, after hearing the neighbors talk of an evening with my father, and spend no small part of the night walking up and down, and trying to make out what was the meaning of some of their, to me, dark sayings. I could not sleep, though I often tried to, when I got on such a hunt after an idea, until I caught it; and when I thought I had got it, I was not satisfied until I repeated it over and over, until I had put it in language plain enough, as I thought, for any boy I knew to comprehend. This was a kind of passion with me, for I am never easy now, when I am handling a thought, till I have bounded it north and bounded it south and bounded it east and bounded it west. Perhaps that accounts for the characteristics you observe in my speeches, though I never put the two things together before."

Lincoln went on to speak of his preparation for the practice of law:

"In the course of my law reading I constantly came upon the word 'demonstrate.' I thought at first that I understood its meaning, but soon became satisfied that I did not . . . I consulted all the dictionaries and books of reference I could find, but with no better results. You might as well have defined 'blue' to a blind man. At last I said, 'Lincoln, you can never make a lawyer if you do not understand what "demonstrate" means'; and I left my situation in Springfield, and went home to my father's house, and stayed there until I could give any proposition in the six books of Euclid at sight. I then found what 'demonstrate' means, and went back to my law studies."

Gulliver had the instinct of a good reporter. He wrote an account of this interview and it was published in *The New York Independent*. In this account Gulliver records that he said to Lincoln:

" 'You have become by the controversy with Mr. Douglas one of our leaders in this great struggle with slavery, which is undoubtedly the struggle of the nation and the age. What I would like to say is this, and I say it with a full heart: Be true to your principles and we will be true to you, and God will be true to us all.' His homely face lighted up instantly with a beaming expression and taking my hand warmly in both his he said: 'I say amen to that—amen to that.' "

Gulliver was already one of the trustees of the college, having been elected but a short time before he was elevated to the presidency. He was evidently a good bargainer, with a proper appreciation of his own worth, for his salary was $4000 plus one-half the income received from additional tuitions. The gap between this and the pay of the professors was so marked, the trustees were apologetic, and promised that as soon as the results of Gulliver's administration were felt, their salaries would be increased. The pay of a full professor was $1500, but within a year this was advanced to $1800.

Gulliver was a handsome man, and aware of it, a bit of a poser, but with sterling intellectual gifts. One of his students said he would give anything if he could turn over his wrist as elegantly as Doctor Gulliver. His well-trimmed whiskers were a golden brown, exactly matching the gold-rimmed spectacles he wore. He dressed in faultless taste, and soon after his arrival he set up a smart carriage with two horses, which was considered by the strait-laced rather sporty for the President of the college. He was inducted into the presidency with impressive exercises, presided over by Edward Beecher, and proceeded to build up the faculty.

The most colorful addition to the faculty and to the social life of Galesburg was Madame Mary Ives Seymour, teacher of French and music. She had beauty and that indefinable charm sometimes coarsely described as sex appeal. She brought to the town a flavor of cosmopolitanism, for she had studied in Europe, was a pupil of Gottschalk, and must have seemed to those staid burgers a creature from another world.

Madame Seymour introduced the salon to that simple prairie city, and her "at homes" exerted such fascination for susceptible undergraduates the faculty felt called on to intervene. Among her youthful victims were George A. Lawrence, life-long friend of Knox and vice-president of the trustees, and Eugene Field, columnist and poet.

Madame Seymour found the prairie town too unsophisticated for her accomplishments, and the trustees were unable to adjust themselves to so vivid a personality. At the end of the year she left for Vienna to teach the archdukes and archduchesses of the royal Austrian family, and write sprightly sketches of continental life for *Harper's Magazine* under the pen name of "Octavia Hensel."

The most distinguished man added to Knox faculty by President Gulliver was John William Burgess, of Amherst, now well known as the founder of the School of Political Science at Columbia University, and its head until his death. Burgess met Gulliver when the latter came to Amherst seeking a professor of history and political economy. Professor Julius H. Seelye had given Burgess an unqualified recommendation, but Burgess had just been admitted to practice law at the Massachusetts bar and was reluctant to abandon a legal career. He yielded to the united persuasions of Gulliver and Seelye, and went to Galesburg with misgivings, but always felt the decision was an error.

In his book, *Reminiscences of an American Scholar,* which is fascinating reading, Burgess gives his impression of Galesburg as he found it:

"Socially the two years I passed at Knox College were exceedingly agreeable. Educationally, I do not think I accomplished much. I was too young, and my mind was filled with embryonic visions. I made one disciple who has always been to me a joy and a reward. He was William Mackintire Salter, the now famous ethical teacher and writer, one of the loveliest characters and bravest scholars whom the world has ever produced. I remarked his fine intellect and gentle manners from the first moment of our acquaintance, and I have never lost touch with him from that day to this. If I never did anything at Knox College beyond contributing my mite to the education of William Mackintire Salter, I would feel that I have enjoyed full compensation for all my labors there."

Salter was indeed an unusual person, and it is a credit to Burgess' powers of discernment that he recognized his worth. He was born in Burlington, Iowa, 1853, began Latin at ten, Greek at twelve, and entered Knox at fourteen, graduating in 1871. During his college course he became skeptical of some of the religious doctrine so earnestly inculcated at Knox, and his commencement oration on the subject, "Is Orthodox Theology Necessary to the Christian?" caused some consternation, although as long ago as 1857 Ella Ferris had questioned the literal truth of the first chapter of Genesis, without, as far as known, any serious repercussions. Some trustees questioned the propriety of giving Salter his degree, which he had earned by a brilliant performance, but wiser councils prevailed, and the college did not stultify itself.

His subsequent career is interesting. He studied theology at Yale, became a Unitarian, was Parker Fellow of Harvard at Göttingen, where he acquired the predilection for German culture he retained throughout his life; he herded sheep on a Colorado ranch and meditated on spiritual matters, which resulted in several books. He met Felix Adler, joined the Ethical Culture Society, and became one of its most distinguished lecturers. At the outbreak of the World War he was writing his book, *Nietzsche the Thinker,* in the Tyrol. He returned to the United States and finished it in the seclusion of his country home, remaining pro-German throughout the war. Among his books is one on Walt Whitman. He died in 1931.

It was Burgess who was responsible for the attendance at Knox College of Eugene Field, who alluded to it affectionately afterward as one of his numerous *almæ matres*. Field's father, the noted jurist Roswell W. Field, had appointed Burgess educational guardian of his son. Burgess had placed Eugene in Williams College shortly before coming to Knox. During the winter term he received a request from Mark Hopkins, president of Williams, to take Field away, as he was no longer wanted. The burden of Hopkins' complaint was that while Field was low on scholarship, his wit was such the faculty could not cope with it. It made them ridiculous. As a result when Burgess went West he took Eugene with him and placed him in Knox College.

At Knox, Field repeated his tactics at Williams. He was easily the most popular man in the school, a good writer and ready speaker, flirting with the Seminary girls, getting around the women members of the faculty, and exercising all the privileges of an irresponsible but engaging personality. After two years at Knox, when he was approaching his majority, by which time Burgess' responsibility would be ended, Field disappeared from Galesburg, and for two weeks no trace of him could be found. At length a letter informed his harassed guardian that he was at Columbia, Missouri, visiting his brother Roswell, who was at school there. Burgess let him remain, for in a short time Field became of age and received his entire inheritance, about $50,000, from his financial guardian. He at once set out in high spirits for Europe, with a friend whose expenses he paid, spent the whole of his patrimony, and wrote home for more. It may have been on this expedition that he discovered and bought the antique bedstead in Kalvarstraat, Amsterdam, which turned out to have been made by "Berkey & Gay, Grand Rapids, Michigan, U. S. A."

Burgess writes of all this with much patience and forbearance. How unimportant are Field's vagaries beside his achievements.

It is hardly necessary to remind any one today that he was a poet of rare charm, a humorist with a biting irony, that he was one of the first "columnists," conducting the "Sharps and Flats" in *The Chicago Record* (later *Record-Herald*), a collector of rare books and children's toys, and one of the congenial spirits who gathered in the "Saints and Sinners Corner" of McClurg's bookstore in Chicago, along with Francis Wilson, the actor, and Frank Gunsaulus, president of Armour Institute.

In Galesburg Burgess lived at Hi Belden's Union Hotel, on the north side of the public square. One day he stuffed a thousand dollar bond, and five hundred in cash, his entire means, in his pocket, and went for a walk. When he returned the hotel was on fire. He watched it burn to the ground, thinking of his books and papers, congratulating himself on the bond and cash he had unconsciously salvaged. He received five hundred dollars insurance on his books and furniture, and five hundred dollars from John Deere of Moline, the wealthy plow-maker, for some service, and with twenty-five hundred dollars in hand decided to sever his connection with Knox. His resignation was not accepted, but he was given a leave of absence, and when after two years he did not return, his name was dropped from the rolls.

One great change in the college for which Gulliver was responsible was making it completely co-educational. Thus far, though closely connected, and in most instances taught by the same instructors, the college and seminary had been separate institutions. Early in his administration, a six years' course for women was established, for any who cared to undertake it, and when completed carried the same degrees as given to men. In 1872 two sisters, Maud and Helen Tenney, were the first women to receive the degree of bachelor of arts from Knox College, and from then until the modernization of the college, when all courses were open to both sexes equally, women had the choice of a college or seminary course. Oberlin was the first college in the United States to grant degrees to women, but Knox was among the pioneers.

[ 380 ]

Another reform by Gulliver, or perhaps the ripening of public opinion, was the passing of the old regulation requiring students to report at roll-call Monday morning their attendance at church the day previous. One morning an Armenian student, Arvedis Marderosian, who must have viewed with some amazement the religious fervor of this American college, replied to the usual question, "How many times did you attend church yesterday?" with a naïve "That is my own business," which effectually stopped the inquisition for good. A member of the first class to graduate had become a missionary to Armenia, and now a visitor from that benighted region performed a little missionary work at Knox.

Besides the coterie of brilliant teachers Gulliver had installed, the college still had the stalwart trio Hurd, Comstock, and Churchill, and its faculty, headed by Gulliver, was at that time probably the most able and distinguished west of the Alleghanies. Numerous students were attracted, and the college was functioning in its capacity as an educational institution as never before in its history.

But the relations between the president and his board of trustees were strained. The college was running beyond its income, and the trustees insisted that the salaries of the professors be cut. They also adopted the suicidal policy of selling the college lands, at a sacrifice, eating up their endowment. Gulliver believed, and rightly, too, that it was his business to make Knox as good a college as possible, and the trustees' job to find the money. He opposed both measures vigorously, but the retrenchments were made. Salaries were cut, four women teachers dismissed, and their classes turned over to the men professors. The time-honored commencement dinner was abandoned and a simple "sociable" took its place.

Gulliver himself was no financier; his personal affairs were generally more or less involved, he anticipated his salary, and applied to the treasurer for advances. He lived well, his home was the center of a gay, civilized, cultivated social life; his wife one of the most popular hostesses in the town. It was a period of great charm, and might have continued indefinitely had the board taken seriously its duties of providing funds to maintain the intellectual status of the college. But when their salaries were reduced the ambitious young men began to leave, Burgess being the first to go.

There could be only one outcome for a man of Gulliver's temperament and ability. He tendered his resignation in a ringing letter, of such sound sense mingled with such sincere concern for the prospects and opportunities of the college, it should be read at board meetings once a year, as an exposition of the duties of trustees.

"For two reasons," says Gulliver, in the course of this long letter, only a few paragraphs of which can be given here, ". . . I resign completely and finally. The first reason is . . . the failure on the part of the Trustees to provide, or even to attempt to provide an additional endowment. . . . The second . . . is the threatened introduction of a scheme of retrenchment which throws the whole burden of reducing the deficit upon the Faculty . . . and which cannot but seriously affect, if it does not absolutely destroy, the scholarly character of the College, drive away its best students, and break down the reputation which it has with so much difficulty earned in the community. . . . Bear with me a moment while I plead with you for the life of the Institution . . . before you plunge the dagger to its heart. . . . It is simply a question of $5000.00—the income of an endowment of $50,000.00. If, instead of gaining that sum by cutting down the instruction, you will raise the money by subscription, . . . I will engage to maintain the present corps of teachers—bring back Prof. Burgess—supply the new professor for whom he stipulates —push the institution forward in character & reputation more rapidly than ever, and bring you out at the end of the year without a deficit. If the Faculty will unite with me, I would be willing on those terms, to take for our salaries . . . whatever may be left of the income after paying all other expenses except repairs. The only condition I would make would be that I have an

Executive Committee who are not in hostility to the systematic modes of doing business in which I have been trained, and the fruits of which you have seen during the last year. The success of a year or two of such management would render probable a larger endowment, until our loss of capital would soon cease and accumulation begin. So confident am I of some such general results that, if there were not reasons of a private and domestic nature which may compel me to seek another climate, I would be willing to take the College on contract of that sort for ten years and carry it through. . . .

"But what will be the result if you adopt the suicidal policy of extracting this $5000.00 from the life-blood and scholarship of the professors, and from the privileges now enjoyed by the students? You must calculate on losing a large number of your best students, and some of the best members of your Faculty, with no prospect of recruiting it from the ranks of the best scholars in the country. The college will become a *local* institution, both as to its teachers and its pupils—a policy long since abandoned by our best Eastern colleges, where no man has the least chance of a professorship who has not added to the training of his own college, an education in European universities—Your college will dwindle, year by year, under such a policy. . . ."

When Gulliver went a large number of students, three-fourths of the freshman class, finished at Eastern colleges. Of the class of 1875 only five graduated from Knox. Professor Hurd was appointed acting president, and carried on as nobly as was possible under such adverse conditions until, three years later, a new president was elected.

## II

### NEWTON BATEMAN

In 1875 there came to the presidency of the college a man who was to hold that office longer than any other incumbent, who brought to the college no innovations, no new educational methods, but who won the affection of his students as none of his predecessors had done, and who carried on the old regime with distinction and prestige. All his life he had been prominent in educational work. The warm personal friend of Lincoln and other prominent men, he was so popular with the people of Illinois that he was elected Superintendent of Public Instruction by the largest Republican majority the State ever gave. He must have had something, for no period was so rich in graduates who afterward made their marks in the world. His personal character was the greatest thing about him. It impressed itself on all the students he taught.

Newton Bateman was born in poverty at Fairton, New Jersey, July 27, 1822. His father, Bergen Bateman, was a weaver and a cripple; his mother, Ruth Brown, one of those rare spirits who breed noble sons. The family, with five children, of which Newton was the youngest, emigrated to Illinois in 1833 in a covered wagon. Twenty miles from Jacksonville, the mother died of Asiatic cholera, and was hastily buried in an unmarked grave, which the panic-stricken neighbors obliterated, and for which her son searched later in vain.

The widower settled in Jacksonville, home of Illinois College, of which Edward Beecher was president, where the children worked for the common support. When thirteen years old Newton listened to his first commencement, and vowed he would one day stand on that very platform and deliver an oration. Four years later he entered the college, and in 1843 realized that boyish dream. He had struggled through by almost unbelievable industry and economy, living at one period in a hollow tree, and subsisting on mush and milk, at an expense of eleven cents a week.

He decided on the ministry as a career and Lane Theological Seminary as the place to study, of which Lyman Beecher, "that incomparable preacher and teacher, that veritable Christian Son of Thunder," as Bateman saw him, was president. He set out on foot, a peddler's pack on his back, selling notions and earning his way. At Indianapolis he paused to visit at the home of Henry Ward Beecher, by previous arrangement with his classmate, Henry's brother Thomas.

"It has been my privilege to have personal acquaintance with all the sons and daughters of Lyman Beecher but two," said Bateman in a chapel talk, "and I thus briefly designate them: Catherine, essayist and philanthropist; Edward, philosopher and scholar; Henry, preacher and orator; Harriet, author; George, the model pastor; Charles, exquisite literary finish and beauty; Thomas, originality, insight and genius."

At the end of his first year at Lane, he suffered a physical breakdown, and took to the road again, selling Lyman's Historical Charts. He opened a school in St. Louis, temporarily, as he thought, but it turned him from the ministry. He became principal of the Jacksonville schools, and married Sarah Dayton. The administration of education became his life work. Bateman School, the most attractive educational building in Jacksonville, preserves his memory there.

He organized the State Teachers Association, helped found and edit *The Illinois Teacher,* and was State Superintendent of Public Instruction, a new office, of which he was the third incumbent. He served a total of fourteen years, being elected seven times, and defeated once. On the death of his first wife he married Annie N. Tyler, a teacher in the Jacksonville Female Academy.

It was while serving as State Superintendent that he met and became intimately acquainted with Lincoln. His room in the Statehouse adjoined that set aside for the Republican candidate, and Lincoln, with the uneducated man's exaggerated respect for learning, found relief in chats with the little schoolmaster. Bateman's service in public office was distinguished. His seven reports are educational classics. He felt strongly about the war, and shared the Northern hatred toward the secessionists. At the 1863 meeting of the Teachers Association he made an impassioned speech, saying, "I believe Jeff Davis ought to be hanged on a gallows higher than Haman's, as his crime is greater."

At the end of his efficient and distinguished career as Superintendent of Public Instruction, Bateman was called to the presidency of Knox, which had suffered in prestige by the departure of Gulliver and his Eastern trained professors.

Newton Bateman came to Knox in 1875. Selden Gale, Chauncey Colton and Flavel Bascom, pioneers long identified with the college, were on the committee that called him. He was under the circumstances the best selection that could be made at that time. True, he had no experience with or in Eastern colleges. He was educated in a college similar in standards and ideals to Knox, but that might have been an advantage. He understood from his own gruelling experience what it meant to secure an education in a poorly equipped struggling college, and to pay his way by his own efforts as did many of his pupils at Knox.

The college equipment consisted of the same buildings that had greeted President Blanchard thirty years previous, "East and West Bricks," "Old Main" and the Seminary. During his administration the first effort was made to add to them. An observatory was built, with a six-inch equatorial made by Alvin Clark's own hand. A gymnasium was erected, of wood, it is true, but serving until the modern structure of brick took its place. "West Bricks" was torn down to make way for Alumni Hall, originally intended to furnish meeting places for the two literary societies, and a chapel for the college. The chapel is now the college theatre—a development which would have astounded the founders—and the remaining space was transformed into lecture rooms when the literary societies were consigned to the limbo of things outgrown.

Doctor Bateman was a little man, physically, inclined to be stocky, but he gave the effect of great dignity coupled with a genial benignity, which was heightened by his dress. He wore the long frock coat, buttoned to his chin, affected by the clergy a hundred years ago. When his hair and beard whitened and formed a halo around his head, he looked like a steel portrait from some old volume of sermons. His literary style was inclined to be florid, but he had good descriptive powers, and his chapel talks were interesting.

During the Bateman period came Maria H. Whiting to be matron, as it was then called, of the Seminary, instead of the more stylish "dean of women" which prevails today. As custodian of hundreds of girls, objects of solicitous attentions from male undergraduates, she was loved and hated by generations of students, and many were the shifts and devices invented to get around her rather strict chaperonage. She built up the Seminary not only by her wise judgment and influence, but by her material substance, leaving all her savings to build a wing to the main edifice, now known as Whiting Hall.

The chair of English was in charge of Melville Best Anderson, known to fame as the translator of Victor Hugo's masterly estimate of Shakespeare, *Paul and Virginia,* the *Divine Comedy,* and other classics, and a regular contributor to *The Dial,* the principal literary periodical of the West. When Anderson was lured to Leland Stanford, he was succeeded by Jeremiah Whipple Jenks, who had won his Ph.D. at Halle in a time when a German degree meant something to American colleges. His specialty was political economy, which he taught with such judicial impartiality the undergraduates never learned what his politics were, but he was also professor of English literature. He went to Cornell later, but his great public work was investigating the "trusts" for Theodore Roosevelt. He wrote many books, and acted as financial expert successively for the German Republic, Mexico, Nicaragua, and China.

Jenks was succeeded, as far as English was concerned, by William Edward Simonds, Ph.D. Strassburg, a fine literary scholar, a stimulating and appreciative teacher, who later became dean of the college until his retirement in 1930. The chair of political economy was filled and well filled by John Pearsons Cushing, also a post-graduate of a German school (Ph.D. Leipsic). Thus within a short period the college came under the influence of three able instructors who had imbibed something of German culture. The public schools, it will be recalled, had been graded according to ideas gathered by George Churchill during his visit to Germany, so there was considerable justification for Madame Blanc's observation that Galesburg reminded her of the little German university towns before the annexation of Prussia.

Another noteworthy accession was Malvina M. Bennett as instructor in elocution at the very period when the Western colleges were going in strong for competitions in oratory on a large scale. At one time the colleges of ten Western States were combined in a league, the winners of the "inter-collegiates" representing their States in the "interstate." This movement was inaugurated by three Knox students, George A. Lawrence, Frank I. Moulton, and Henry M. Read, the first two later trustees and the last a professor of Knox College. Under Miss Bennett's tutelage the college was the winner of five of the State contests, and four of these triumphed in the interstate. Among these successful ones were Edgar A. Bancroft, Minister to Japan, John H. Finley, one of the editors of *The New York Times,* and Otto Harbach, Broadway librettist. These contests, as already foreshadowed, were high spots in college life. Hundreds of rooters accompanied the teams, and it is evidence of how interests have been reversed that though the meets were accompanied by athletic competitions between the colleges, the enthusiasm centered in the oratorical contests. This picturesque phase of college life has wholly vanished.

Bateman was responsible for one innovation about which there are two opinions today, the teaching in colleges of military science and tactics, by which is meant compulsory drill under officers detailed from the United States army. The passage of the bill authorizing this move was due to the initiative of Bateman, who secured the influence of Robert Lincoln, then Secretary of War and son of his old friend, and the two senators from Illinois, Oglesby and Cullom. The War Department jumped at so obvious a method of nourishing the military spirit, so apt to languish in times of peace. The student paid for his uniform, the government

[ 388 ]

furnished arms, and attendance was compulsory, unless excused. Disbelief in militarism was not a valid excuse.

Knox was the only small college to be included in the first ten institutions to which the service was extended. In 1899 it was withdrawn from all but State universities. During the World War, interest in things military flamed up again, and compulsory drill was re-established, this time in the form of the Reserve Officers Training Corps, and as such it exists in many institutions, but campus opinion is setting strongly against it, a number of colleges have modified the rule making it compulsory, and others have abandoned it. The training of a soldier seems contrary to the whole purpose and spirit of a college, and it is to be hoped that enlightened public opinion will ultimately abolish this subtle method of fomenting wars.

There was still a close relation between town and college in the 1880's, though they were less mutually dependent than in the early years. One link between the two which modern progress has broken was the practice of early students "boarding round.". There were no men's dormitories, no fraternity houses, and no college commons. Even well-to-do families were willing to take such desirable boarders, and they were treated as members of the family; they came from similar homes. In some instances they did chores for their board, and their presence in the house and at meals kept families in touch with college gossip, and maintained interest in college affairs. Students living in the antediluvian "West Bricks" took their meals at the Seminary, as did others rooming at houses in the neighborhood.

The social program of the college was exceedingly simple, in sharp contrast with the complex extra-curricular activities today, and afforded little to distract the mind from studies, and the numerous prayer meetings. Each term there was a class party, escorts being drawn by lot to save the faces of girls with no sex appeal; the Christian Associations gave a "getting acquainted" reception at the beginning of the first term, the college year ending with the president's reception commencement week. These might be said to comprise the legitimate social functions. Fraternities, long forbidden, began to creep out from their sub-rosa existence and rent lofts on Main Street for headquarters, where they gave dances, frowned on by the authorities, and which girls living at the Seminary were forbidden to attend.

The college was composed of earnest young men and women, mostly from farms, to whom education meant great sacrifices, and living in a city no larger than Galesburg a new social experience. They dressed more formally than is the negligent custom today; there was no such thing as sports clothes, sweaters would have been dishabille even on the campus, had the students possessed or heard of such a garment. There was not a dress coat, or even a dinner jacket visible. The seniors wore long frock coats—known as preachers' coats or Prince Alberts—the appointed costume for commencement, and also the uniform of the professors. Some of the seniors adopted the "plug" hat as a distinctive head gear.

Most of the students were extremely religious. This fact leavened the whole college fabric. The "Y's" were strong and active. Robert Speer made evangelical visits, and pledged young men and women to the missionary field. Numbers of them attended the Moody summer conferences at Northfield. The faculty was fundamentally orthodox, placing Christian communion higher than mere pursuit of knowledge. Chapel was compulsory, but church attendance was not insisted on as strenuously as in early years, though in theory at least the college felt spiritually responsible for the beliefs of the students. The venerable president maintained that no instructor, however great his intellectual attainments, could teach at Knox if there was the slightest doubt about his orthodoxy.

A conscientious student would attend on Sunday six meetings; gospel service at nine, church at ten-thirty, Sunday-school at noon, Y. M. C. A. at four, young people's meeting at six, and church at seven. In addition there was the Wednesday night prayer meeting, and the Friday night gathering of the college Y's.

The college, while Christian, was non-sectarian. It had outgrown and lived down the denominational differences which afflicted its existence from Kellogg to Gulliver. Gulliver had given
the trustees and the town the first glimpse of a cultural intellectual
institution, as a separate entity, apart from an instrument of religious propaganda. The time was rapidly approaching when colleges could look for support to educational foundations free from
sectarian bias, instead of to one of the denominations. The suggestion had been urged repeatedly during the college's entire history, that it should be put under the wing of one denomination.
Even Gulliver adduced that as a possibility when he was advising
the trustees to find the additional $5000 income he needed to keep
the staff he had assembled, so strong was the belief that only under the ægis of one particular form of religion could a college
flourish. It was still good policy to stress the Christian side of
an institution. Few parents would have trusted their children
to it otherwise. The majority favored one that was safe within
the folds of its own denomination. But the trend was steadily toward a more liberal view, and the separation of education from
the inculcation of any particular religious belief. In Gulliver's
time the board of trustees was more than half clergymen. Their
representation slowly decreased as their influence on affairs, particularly education, waned with the progress of modern thought.
In 1934 the board did not number a single minister; today it has but
one. Lawyers and business men constitute the majority of its
personnel.

This matter of dominance of religion in the college, any college, is important in connection with its intellectual growth.
Knox was cradled in religion, and for more than half its life religious controversy clouded the main issue. Even in the fifties,
when the great schism raged, there were undergraduates with
sufficient perspicacity to see that such matters did not concern a
college. But colleges were a long time working out from under
doctrinal control. Down to Bateman's time it was customary for
the president in his annual report to give the number of Christians

in the college. Bateman was the end of the old school. The four presidents since were certainly Christians in the modern sense, but they realized that a college must have something besides denominational orthodoxy to become a successful educational institution. The history of American thought is found in the history of this college. It moved faster in some places than it did in Galesburg, but it moved in the same direction, and covered the same ground.

The teaching was excellent because of the devotion of a few able men. They lacked modern equipment, and were unfamiliar with modern methods, but they knew their subjects, were earnest, and managed to impart something to all who were willing to learn. The system was patriarchal, too little was left to the initiative of the students, the faculty lacked young men, whose viewpoint would be nearer that of the students, the relation was that of teacher and pupil, of governor and governed, rather than that of two parties engaged in the pursuit of truth. And the same could be said of every college in the Middle West, practically of every college in the country.

### III

#### CULTURE

It is difficult to appraise the intellectual stature of a community except by taking note of its interest in literature, art, music, and other humanities, an intelligent attitude toward which is the mark of culture. In the period roughly indicated as the Eighteen Eighties, but which includes virtually the last quarter of the last century, it seems probable that books were more highly esteemed than in the same community today.

The reason is that there were fewer distractions to occupy leisure time. The principal recreations were simple social gatherings, from the county fair to a meeting of the Hawthorne Club or a dance at Lake George, lectures, concerts, buggy riding, and conversation. The conversation, as has been recorded by several visitors, was intelligent; the society provincial, but good. There was then no such flood of reading matter, good, bad, and indifferent as we have today. The town was not up in current literature. The books it read were the old standard classics. The belief still prevailed that novels, even the greatest, were not serious reading. Even a third-rate religious book ranked higher than a first-rate work of fiction.

Not that the people as a whole read books, or read anything. They were but a short remove from the time when there were no books, and no evening light to read them by. They worked hard all day, were glad to go to bed when it was too dark to see. Wealth brought leisure, later hours, more evening, and kerosene a better light, and those people who read at all read rather good books, and the trash they read did not hurt them. For most people still the evening paper was the extent of their reading, and then down to "the store" for a chat with a few cronies, or to the pool room, or the White Elephant, or to stand on the corner, while the more devout were attending one of their numerous prayer meetings, and the more literate one of the many clubs dedicated to art, music, and literature, or listening to a lecture.

The college library, today so well stocked and well housed, was nothing to boast about—a collection of badly arranged books without catalogue, in a small dusty room. The townspeople never saw it, and few of the students. There were a few good private libraries, and at least one book fancier, who showed with pride his first editions and tooled leather bindings. Most of them considered an encyclopedia all the library needed for a home.

In the public library there were now about 9000 volumes, largely fiction, some of it trash. There were few reference books. The library was open daily from two to nine P.M. All the standard authors were represented on its shelves by complete sets, Scott, Cooper, Dickens, George Eliot, Thackeray, Harriet Beecher Stowe, Jane Austin, Hugo (in translation), Hawthorne, Stockton. A large department was captioned "Juvenile"—Oliver Optic, Horatio Alger, Jr., Mayne Reid, Ballantyne, Harry Castlemon,

J. T. Trowbridge, Martha Finley ("Elsie" books), Pansy, Susan Coolidge, Louisa M. Alcott. The books were much used, and most of them had been re-bound by Colville Brothers in sober black cloth. But the new books were slow in penetrating the public library; its dependence was on the storehouses of the past.

There were few problem books in those days. Some parents and teachers doubted whether *The Scarlet Letter* and *Adam Bede* were proper books for the young, and Tolstoy's *Anna Karenina,* which was not in the library, created something of a furore. The more realistic French writers were taboo. Plain pornography, such as the paper-bound novels of Albert Ross, was passed furtively from hand to hand.

In the high school pupils were thoroughly drilled on specific selected works believed to be literature. *Evangeline, The Lady of the Lake,* or *Hamlet* was read in class line by line, and every hidden meaning, figure of speech, or poetic analogy analyzed and discussed until the students fairly learned them by heart. Thus occurred an embarrassing incident. The Shakespeare used was Hudson's edition, expurgated to protect the morals of high-school students from the facts of life. The worldly old Polonius was commissioning Hamlet to inquire discreetly into the possibly gay life of his son, Laertes, in Paris,

"I saw him enter such and such a house of sale."

What was a "house of sale"? The next line had been excised by Hudson, and no one could explain the phrase until a student, who had an unexpurgated edition, read the next line—"evidently a brothel." There was a painful silence; some of the boys snickered; others evidently did not know what the word meant. The teacher recovered first, and with heightened color said, "We will now go on."

Physiology was taught in both school and college as if the two sexes were identical, and lacked reproductive functions. As a disgusted senior remarked, "You can go clear through Knox College and never learn that babies are not found under gooseberry bushes." An expectant mother was a disgraceful spectacle, followed by whispered comment. Childbirth was never discussed, either in school or society. Children imbibed no beautiful associations with maternity. The obscene passages in the Bible were always skipped in the Sunday-school classes.

Once a year the boys of the high-school building were assembled in a session for males only. The natural inference would be today that it heralded a talk on sex hygiene, but no, the lecture was a stern admonition against fouling the public privy, and writing on the fences with chalk words now found in current novels. The Puritans who warred against slavery, intemperance, Sabbath breaking, with beating of tom-toms, evaded the subject of sex completely. Whatever a child learned was from contemporaries, and it was years before most of them got the matter straight in their minds.

Religious books had great popularity. Margaret Deland's *John Ward, Preacher,* caused something of a sensation. Modern readers may need to be reminded that it was the story of a minister who lost his faith. A prominent Knox graduate had just gone through a similar experience. Ministers preached sermons on the moral of the book. A little later *Robert Elsmere* by Mrs. Humphrey Ward, on the same theme, created an even bigger wave of discussion. David Swing was being tried at Chicago for heresy, though his belief would today be sound orthodoxy. Robert Ingersoll, as mild a skeptic as this country has produced, was going about the country lecturing on "The Mistakes of Moses," and the fear and hatred he excited is unbelievable today, though his argument was little more than had been maintained by Mary Ellen Ferris in her courageous commencement debate twenty years previous.

Some years earlier Elizabeth Stuart Phelps had written *The Gates Ajar,* which was welcomed with open arms by the religious element, and *The Greatest Thing in the World,* by a Scotchman named Henry Drummond, seemed to give a philosophical basis for religious belief.

The sentimental religious books of Mrs. A. D. T. Whitney, and the even more sugary "Pansy" books, were excessively popular, but nothing equalled the vogue of the amazing "Elsie" books. Martha Finley wrote a story about a priggish young Christian named Elsie Dinsmore, who had an overgrown conscience and a wordly father, and the struggles between the two were heroic. The climax was reached when Elsie refused her father's request to play a secular piece on Sunday. When she declined with the air of an early Christian martyr, her father told her sternly that filial obedience was at least as important as Sabbath observance, and that she could sit on the piano stool until she was ready to comply, which she did until she fell off in a swoon. Faith triumphed in the end, and the book made such a hit among the devout members of Epworth League and Christian Endeavor that it was followed by a long series, describing Elsie's progress through girlhood, womanhood, marriage, children, grandchildren, winding up with *Elsie in Heaven*.

From time to time book agents "made" the town, unfolding a display of sample bindings richly gilt, and left on parlor tables copies of such compilations as *The Royal Path of Life, Mother, Home and Heaven, The Lives and Graves of the Presidents, Gaskell's Compendium,* U. S. Grant's *Personal Memoirs,* and Greely's *Arctic Experiences.* More elaborate books were sold in monthly parts, at fifty cents a part, to be bound up when complete, an expensive method of acquiring a worthless book. *The Child's Bible* and *Science for All,* one of the earliest popularizers, were sold thus. In nearly every home were found Will Carleton's bucolic poems, *Farm Ballads, Farm Legends,* and *Farm Festivals.* Every one was familiar with "Betsey and I Are Out," "Over the Hills to the Poorhouse," and "Bessie's Three Lovers." Copies of the complete poetical works of Tennyson, in plush or ooze calf, lay self-consciously on parlor tables, and on the walls hung a yard of New England literature, neatly framed, a row of portraits on one long strip, Holmes, Emerson, Whittier, Longfellow, Bryant, and Lowell. Walt Whitman and Herman Melville were unknown.

The magazines of the fifties, *Ballou's, Peterson's, Godey's Lady's Book,* had given place to the more literary *Century, Harper's,* and *Scribner's,* bought each month at Grose & Stire's or Fahnestock & Fuller's, the two bookstores. Three Knox graduates, Samuel Mc-Clure, John Phillips, and Albert Brady, started a new kind of magazine in New York, and *McClure's* and *Munsey's* superseded *Century* and *Scribner's* with Galesburg magazine readers. The local newspaper was an evening sheet, but in the morning they read *The Chicago News,* later *The Chicago Record,* probably the best paper west of *The New York Sun* at that time, with William E. Curtis as roving correspondent, Eugene Field writing his "Sharps and Flats," George Ade his "Stories of the Street and Town," and John McCutcheon drawing some of the best cartoons of the period, those of the second Cleveland campaign in particular.

The new professor of economics at Knox College, John Cushing, used to gather an appreciative audience on his lawn Sunday morning and read aloud the now famous "Fables in Slang" which appeared in Ade's column Saturdays. Alfred Townsend's "Chimmie Fadden" was another character popular with this knowing group, as later was Finley Peter Dunne, with his spoofs at the Spanish-American War.

These years were brightened by the large number of periodicals edited for children, for which there is no counterpart today. Printing was cheap, good writers worked for small sums, subscriptions paid the cost, and there was no necessity for advertising —which scarcely existed—so large circulations were not essential. A magazine could flourish with a few thousand readers, and many did. The two outstanding publications were *St. Nicholas* and *The Youth's Companion.*

*St. Nicholas* was a merger of several earlier publications, *Our Young Folks* and *The Little Corporal* among them. Under the conductorship of Mary Mapes Dodge it attained high moral standards, for she watched over her readers like an anxious mother hen, and would not allow firearms to be advertised in it—the Flobert rifle for boys was just beginning to be sold. It inculcated love of nature, bird-life, new things then. The Agassiz Association, which anticipated the Boy Scout movement, was one of its departments and organized schoolboys into chapters to break open rocks, collect and study wild flowers, fossils, and butterflies. Despite censorship, its stories were sufficiently red-blooded—some of them good reading today—Noah Brooks, Elijah Kellogg, Frank R. Stockton, Edward Eggleston, William O. Stoddard, Rossiter Johnson, and J. T. Trowbridge—whose "Darius Green and his Flying Machine" was a popular Friday afternoon piece—wrote serials for it, and girl readers were delighted with Susan Coolidge, Mrs. Oliphant, Louisa M. Alcott, Lucretia P. Hale, Saxe Holm, Helen H. Jackson.

*The Youth's Companion,* somewhat more mature, was a famous institution. It included among its contributors some of the juvenile writers mentioned above. Its editor was Hezekiah Butterworth, and his short editorials on current topics were the best things of their kind. But, as *St. Nicholas* sent its readers into field and woods to study nature, *The Companion* sent them out as amateur salesmen. Every fall subscribers received an enormous premium list containing pictures and descriptions of everything a child could possibly want, which sent them scurrying to their friends to solicit subscriptions. Skates, magic lanterns, scroll saws, dolls, paint boxes, microscopes were offered for a certain number of "new names, postage and packing extra," the "extra" covering a large part of the cost. It was one of the most successful promotion plans of that day, and built up the largest circulation of any magazine then existing.

*Wide Awake* was something like *St. Nicholas,* but not so good. Its material was largely reprint, and its pictures stock woodcuts. The illustrations of *St. Nicholas* were one of its charms. *Wide Awake* ran a mystery serial by George MacDonald, "A Double Story," with an impressive moral for the young. There was even a magazine for infants, *The Nursery,* beautifully printed in great primer type with illustrations in outline, like a modern child's book. These publications were absorbed by numerous children, and their influence is incalculable.

There were others not so welcome to parents and teachers, *Golden Days* and *The Argosy,* printed on newspaper stock, more lurid in their contents, little above the abhorred nickel libraries, with serials by Oliver Optic and Horatio Alger, Jr. The predecessors of the "pulps" of today were *The Fireside Companion* and *Saturday Night* for adults. The first four pages of a thrilling new serial were thrown over picket fences of the town in the belief, generally justified, that curiosity as to how the story came out would make a sale for the succeeding numbers.

New writers were coming up, and the more advanced were aware of them. Howells was introducing realism into American fiction. This was the era of the advent of Kipling, Stevenson— *McClure's Magazine* was introducing him to the country—Barrie and Henry James. Life in prairie towns was getting into books. *Stories of a Western Town,* by Octave Thanet (Mary French), describing Davenport, Iowa, might have been about Galesburg. The town and college produced writers of their own. Clark E. Carr published *The Illini,* his reminiscences of Illinois politicians. Carl Sandburg, who was to put the prairies into poems, was studying at Lombard College; Edgar Lee Masters—his imaginary town of Spoon River was Lewiston on that river—and Otto Abels Harbach—whose lyrics were to be sung by countless Broadwayites, author of "Madame Sherry," "No, No, Nanette," and other musical comedies—students at Knox; George Fitch, who put the word "Siwash" into college slang, was a pupil in the public schools, and Don Marquis (Archy and Mehitable) did not attend Knox until 1904.

The list of Galesburg authors could be greatly extended, though not with names of equal note. At least fifty have written published books. A large proportion of these are textbooks, explained by the number of professors in the two colleges. One such was *Civic Biology,* by George W. Hunter, the work with which John Scopes defied the Tennessee law against teaching the theory of evolution, that brought on the famous trial and enlisted the championship of William Jennings Bryan for the prosecution.

An old jingle known to many generations of children,

"Little drops of water,
Little grains of sand,"

was by Julia Fletcher Carney, an early settler. Ralph Waldo Trine's *In Tune with the Infinite* and *What Millions Are Seeking* have found an enormous audience among those who fancy such philosophy; John Finley's *The French in the Heart of America* grew out of his lectures at the Sorbonne in Paris. *The True Story of Paul Revere,* by Charles Ferris Gettemy, grandson of Silvanus Ferris, was a mildly debunking account, the first of what has become something of an obsession with many writers of history and biography. A study of Galesburg according to the newer methods of anthropology was put out in 1896 by Arthur W. Dunn, a descendant of a pioneer and graduate of Knox College. A delightful writer on natural science specializing in entomology is James G. Needham, professor, now emeritus, of Cornell University. And Edward Hurley, one of the many bright and gifted Irish boys who grew up in Galesburg after the coming of their fathers to help build the railroad, is the author of *The New Merchant Marine.*

When Grose & Stire's bookstore became Stromberg & Tenney's, the new books were displayed and made available. Herbert Stuart Stone, son of the successful publisher of *The Chicago News,* and Ingalls Kimball brought out *The Chap-Book,* first of the little magazines, of which *The Lark* is a famous example, and copies sold in Galesburg brought new ideas in both literature and printing. One result was the organization of the Cadmus Club, a group of twelve book-lovers, who began a series of publications in the modern spirit, including an annual almanac. Stromberg & Tenney set aside a corner in their store where the latest books could be browsed over, and dedicated it to the new book club, as a sort of informal meeting place for the local bibliophiles, like the "Saints and Sinners" at McClurg's in Chicago. Under the impetus of John H. Finley, who became president of Knox College in the early nineties, and who designed the club bookplate and title pages for Cadmus Club publications, the organization flourished for several years and gave the town a miniature replica of New York's famous Grolier Club.

Of art there was only a trace. It was not until the World's Fair at Chicago that stay-at-home Westerners saw real pictures, and even then the hit of the Loan Exhibition was Gari Melcher's excessively sentimental "Breaking Home Ties," in the spirit of the chromos which adorned Galesburg walls.

John V. N. Standish, peppery professor of natural science at Lombard University, quarrelled with that institution and left all his property to Knox—which gesture was washed out when Lombard merged with Knox. His passion was horticulture, and he stirred up the town to some appreciation of beauty in its streets and parks. He organized a horticultural society, and did much to improve the town planting. His taste ran to specimens rather than mass planting, but was a long ways ahead of anything the town had hitherto seen. His own grounds, dotted with many rare examples of shrubs and trees, are now the site of the Seymour Library, the most beautiful building at Knox.

Music was an ancient tradition. It began with community singing in the first days of the colony. The early Galesburgers all sang, heartily and rousingly, and not always hymns. When Knox Conservatory got into its stride under William Bentley's supervision—and he was a real musician—the town had concerts, oratorios, cantatas, with well trained voices from that school helped out by guest singers from Chicago and elsewhere. The college lecture courses included one musical number each season, and Rubenstein, Madame Carrena, Godowsky, Fannie Bloomfield Zeisler, Clara Louise Kellogg and other stars of that period played and sang. Some families made the trip to Chicago for a week of opera.

The so-called popular songs were brought to the town by travelling musical comedies and burlesque shows, not very frequently, as there was no real theatre between the burning of the old opera house and the opening of the new Auditorium. By the nineties, however, Galesburg was as familiar with "There'll be a hot time in the old town tonight," "A bicycle built for two," "Sweet Marie" and "The Bowery" as other communities. But the popular music of the town in the eighties was something quite different from either the classical music of Professor Bentley's concerts or the topical songs of the day.

In 1875 there appeared the first of an extraordinary series of hymns which in cities like Galesburg, with their large content of earnest religious young people, their Epworth Leagues and Christian Endeavors, attained a popularity equalled only by the more worldly ditties in communities less saturated with worship. *Gospel Hymns and Sacred Songs,* edited by P. P. Bliss and Ira D. Sankey, held sway for twenty years. Both these men were musical adjuncts to the evangelical work of Dwight L. Moody, who was the logical successor of Charles Finney, whose great revival had set George Washington Gale thinking about founding a religious colony in the West to train prairie-bred Finneys. The hymns were an innovation in sacred music. They had all the "go" of the popular songs which people whistled and sang and bands and orchestras played. They became standard for Sunday-schools, young people's meetings, and Y. M. C. A., which means that every religiously inclined young man and woman heard them over and over, and practically every young person heard them part of the time, for few escaped Sunday-school entirely.

They were not especially good either as to words or music, but their catchiness and their lighter and more cheerful tone, against the grimness of the old hymns of the good Doctor Watts, the Wesley brothers and their ilk, made them popular with young people, for it was the first joyous note that religious worship had yet offered them. Thus in the eighties there floated from nearly every church window the strains of "Wonderful words of life,"

"Beulah Land," "Hold the fort," "Pull for the shore," "The ninety and nine" and "Rescue the perishing." The airs were whistled on Main Street, and sung at social gatherings in the home. On the rack of nearly every square piano and Estey Organ the six successive numbers were displayed as fast as they were published, and family and visitors wound up the social evening with a good sing. These lively hymns, once the spontaneous expression of a religious feeling divesting itself of the blood and hell-fire of the older dispensation, have now almost entirely disappeared from hymnology.

The town imbibed some of its intellectual subsistence from lectures, for the college literary societies continued to give their courses alternate years, and with the aid of the indefatigable Major Pond, most of the platform stars turned up in Galesburg, speaking at the opera house until that burned, and afterward at the Old First Church. George Kennan—pioneer of those investigators who today go over, take a look at Russia, and come back and tell us about it—gave a harrowing account of the horrors of exile to Siberia under the Tsarist regime. Bill Nye, columnist of *The Laramie Boomerang,* whose quaint comments were clipped and reprinted all over the country—for there were no syndicates to cash in on this profitable field (the newspaper syndicate was invented by S. S. McClure)—and James Whitcomb Riley gave an entertainment of mingled humor and sentiment. Matthew Arnold, the venerable English scholar, son of the famous headmaster of Rugby, delivered a lecture on the merits of science compared with literature as a source of culture, which provoked much discussion among the intelligentsia of the town.

Such were some of the intellectual resources of Galesburg during the administration of Doctor Bateman. A few made what was then the supreme gesture of a trip to Europe, and talked about it for years. Some of the professors used such trips as material for chapel lectures. In 1887 the college was fifty years old. The occasion was celebrated with a series of programs in a huge wooden wigwam, erected by the students working in gangs by classes, school being dismissed for the purpose. It marked not only the end of the first half century of the college, but almost the beginning of the new era in education, which was to come so shortly in the early nineties with the advent of a new and different type of president.

## IV

### BROADER HORIZONS

Along in the early eighties there came to Knox from the city of Ottawa, Illinois, a student who had finished first at the Ottawa High School, and who early showed both the ability and the willingness to work. He had not much means, and performed all kinds of tasks to pay his college expenses; household and outdoor "chores," taking care of a horse, a cow, and a garden, setting type in the local printing office, cataloguing the chaotic college library, and then putting his catalog in type and printing it; canvassing for names for the city directory, anything in short that he could find to do. The firm where he learned the printer's trade and for which he edited the city directory were those same Colville Brothers whose business life coincided with so long a stretch of the history of the town.

Despite the fact that his hours were busy ones, he did his college work so well he finished with valedictory honors, besides having won the "local," the "intercollegiate" and the "interstate" oratorical competitions, and minor prizes as well. He found time to take so active a part in the work of his literary society that he was made its president; he was college librarian, contributed to college publications, and improvised burlesques on classic themes which were produced in the open meetings or "miscellanies" with great success. Nor did he neglect athletics, for he played on such college teams as then existed. Moreover, he was socially popular, for in that democratic environment his unaristocratic employments were the rule rather than the exception, and certainly did not interfere with participation in such social life as the college afforded. At Knox he met the woman who became his wife, a charming and cultivated schoolmate, so that he might be considered a complete example of the product of a co-educational college.

From Knox this young man went to Johns Hopkins, where he specialized in economics, became the friend and assistant of Professor Richard T. Ely, with whom he was associated in the writing of *Taxation in American Cities.* His summers were spent at Chautauqua, that center of religion and learning, where he edited its *Herald,* and lectured upon economic subjects. In 1890 he became secretary of the State Charities Aid Association of New York.

Meanwhile, the college was looking for a new head. The oft-refused resignation of Doctor Bateman was at length accepted, the Doctor placed on an emeritus basis with light teaching duties, and the presidency tendered to the young secretary of the Charities Aid Association, John Huston Finley. He was at that time twenty-nine years old, the youngest man to fill the presidential chair of an established college.

The arrival of Finley marked the beginning of a new era for Knox. Now was begun the modernizing, the abandoning of what Burgess had called the "hayseed" methods. The process had been started by Gulliver with his group of young men fresh from Amherst and other Eastern institutions, but the time was not ripe for it in the West. The trustees and the town were not prepared to go the pace, and under Bateman the college had settled back, after its brief interregnum under Professor Hurd, to jog along comfortably in the channels to which it had grown accustomed.

Finley brought to Knox not merely familiarity with newer educational methods; he had acquaintance with men which was to serve the college in good stead. For it can be said without injustice to his other achievements, that his chief contribution was to make the college known. He had what amounts to genius for the restrained but effective publicity of associating the thing advertised with well-known names. He studied the records and found that the bill chartering the college had been passed by the legislature on the fifteenth of February, and established that date as Founders' Day, and persuaded national figures to participate in its commemoration. He instituted the celebration of the anniversary of the Lincoln-Douglas debate, one of the most crucial and far-reaching events in our national history, and again Presidents, cabinet ministers and captains of industry added the prestige of their presence.

These two celebrations were mainly occasions for inviting the attendance of prominent men and associating the college with their name and fame. Thus the college became known throughout the country. In the course of its history Galesburg has been visited by seven Presidents. Lincoln, of course, was not yet President when he came for the debate, and Grant's visit was during his campaign for that office. Hayes was there with Sherman not long after the close of the war to review a gathering of his veterans. Benjamin Harrison came to lay the corner-stone of the Alumni Hall, but McKinley, Taft and Theodore Roosevelt came through the influence of Finley, who knew how to capitalize his wide acquaintance, and word an invitation so that it would be accepted.

The town of Cummington, Massachusetts, where William Cullen Bryant was born in 1794, celebrated the hundredth anniversary of his birth. And Edwin R. Brown, orator of the Cummington memorial meeting, lived at Elmwood, fifteen miles from Galesburg, where Lorado Taft's bronze tribute to the "Pioneer Woman" stands in the tiny public square; and the venerable John Howard Bryant, the only living brother of the poet, associated with the early history of Galesburg, was still living on his great farm at Princeton, forty miles away. So Bryant's advent into the world was celebrated in some respects more completely at Galesburg than at Cummington. All the literati of the Middle West, and most of the leading writers of the country were invited. There were few with whom Finley had not already established some connection. Many of them came. Others wrote letters which were read at the exercises. John Bryant brought an old faded diary, kept by his mother, for the year 1794, in which one could read this calm entry:

Monday 3 Stormy: wind N. E. churned, unwell. Seven at night a son born; Mother and Mrs. Shaw here.

Another innovation along similar lines, but more constructive as far as the cultural purpose of the college was concerned, was inviting lectures by distinguished authorities. Richard T. Ely (economics), Frederic Turner and Harry P. Judson (history), Frederick Starr (anthropology). Finley added new subjects to the curriculum, and new men to teach them, men of character and personality who had already distinguished themselves at Eastern universities.

In this administration biology, physics, philosophy and chemistry were recognized by distinct professorships. The matron at Whiting Hall was succeeded by a dean of women, medical examiners and advisers were appointed for the college, and a move was made in the direction of organized athletics. These things put the college in line with modern institutions, created favorable repute abroad, and influenced cautious Herr Baedeker to list Knox among a few small colleges of the first rank, where it assuredly belonged.

Even more constructive, and certainly more revolutionary was the recognition extended to social life as a part of the culture imparted by a college. Whiting Hall, which had existed for years as a sort of zenana, where female students were carefully guarded and male visitors were permitted, or one might say tolerated, under certain conditions, began to assume the air of a hospitable home. The rooms were arranged for a less chilly reception. It was realized that young men and women, bound to meet in after years, might just as well become accustomed to the amenities of social intercourse, and the inevitable meetings of college life be given a recognition which had hitherto been denied. The deans were women of wide social experience, and a new atmosphere prevailed in the old brown building on the park which would have surprised and delighted students from an earlier era.

Finley made his innovations without ruffling any feathers. He found himself at the head of a faculty of the "old school" nearly every one of whom had assisted at his education. Some of these men had made a great contribution to the upbuilding of the college. They welcomed and co-operated with their former pupil, and he was personally popular with both professors and students.

He was the typical Illinois farm boy with the added polish of Eastern universities. His native speech consciously or unconsciously took on the cultivated accent of the men with whom he associated. His training had made him an effective speaker, the grounding imparted by Miss Bennett crystallizing in an individual manner of his own. He was an enthusiastic walker, and this hobby remains one of his outlets. Every year on his birthday he has marched around Manhattan Island, like Joshua around Jericho, and New York capitulates even as Galesburg.

He had energy, imagination, a genius for making friends, a flair for publicity, an instinct for appropriateness, recognition of merit in his associates. His reports are full of sympathetic and understanding mention of good work done by members of the faculty. It was inevitable that such a man would not remain indefinitely. He resigned to accept the chair of politics at Princeton in 1899. During his seven years he accomplished as much, did the college as much good as any previous president in a longer term.

During these last years of the century, most of the old guard, the professors who had carried the teaching burden for fifty years and had become with time institutions in themselves, passed from the college walls, either by death or retirement. With the death of George Churchill, the retirement of Milton Comstock, and the death of Newton Bateman, and not long after the death of Albert Hurd, passed the old regime that had done an honored and necessary work.

Finley's administration, much as it did to carry to the country at large a new conception of the college, did not bring in much money. His years were those of the depression which began with the end of the Chicago Fair and lasted until the close of the century. He was succeeded by a man whose greatest contribution was to supply the means for the physical upbuilding of the college, so long overdue. Up till now the buildings which constituted the college, with the exception of Alumni Hall and the observatory, were those that had existed from the time of Jonathan Blanchard. Buildings of course do not make a college; Mark Hopkins and his log with a student sitting on one end will occur to mind. But the college needed buildings, not only to carry on the work it was already doing, but to introduce new methods of study and new subjects which had become part of a college education.

The old dispensation under which the president of a college must be a minister, ended practically with Gulliver, but Bateman belonged in spirit to that conception of a college president—even more than Gulliver. The president who succeeded Finley, although technically a doctor of divinity, was much more a man of affairs than any clergyman who preceded him. Most surprisingly, he was in touch with sources from which college endowments are supplied.

Thomas McClelland was a Scotchman, born in County Derry, Ireland. He graduated from Oberlin College, and studied at Oberlin Theological Seminary, as well as at Union and Andover seminaries, but did not remain a preacher. Instead he taught philosophy at a small college in the West, and became president of Pacific University in Oregon. He was genial, friendly, unaggressive, but shrewd and well balanced, thrifty, diplomatic, persevering in plans formed and usually successful in maturing them. He had some of the instincts of a business man, for before coming to Galesburg he had built and financed a small railroad in Iowa, which he later sold to the Burlington, and which might have been one of the "cat's tails" about which John Murray Forbes speaks so feelingly.

Andrew Carnegie made McClelland a member of the board of the Carnegie Foundation. Naturally Knox College was placed on the list of institutions to share in the retirement allowances to professors; for some time it was the only college in Illinois so favored. Through this connection came a gift of $50,000 in 1908. A similar amount was received at the same time from the General Education Board, with which Maecenas of good colleges McClelland was also in sympathetic relation.

The work of securing needed endowment was abetted by alumni, assisted by the prestige of the college itself, but the fact remains that McClelland was the Moses who struck the rock of public benefactions, and some $260,000 gushed forth in the endowment campaign of 1908 and 1909. Such manifestations of interest in the destiny of Knox stirred private benefactions. The quarrel of Doctor Standish with Lombard and the reversion of his estate to Knox has been mentioned. The memory of George Davis, for many years treasurer of the college, was perpetuated by the gift of a science hall from his daughter and her husband. But in some respects the most interesting were the gifts of two brothers named Seymour, prosperous Illinois farmers, neither of whom attended Knox for more than a short time, who gave two distinctive and much needed buildings, the men's dormitory, Seymour Hall, and the delightful Seymour Library. Because of the singular fact of two such gifts from men of the same name, the buildings are distinguished by the full names of their sponsors, the dormitory from Lyman K., and the library in memory of Henry M.—for it was his wife who actually gave it.

Thus the cluster of buildings on the campus grew, and began to take on the ensemble of a modern college. The fraternities, under impetus of cordial recognition from the college authorities in place of the old-time hostility, multiplied in numbers, and built attractive houses in the streets surrounding the college yard.

Increased endowment and new buildings were the landmarks of McClelland's administration. He was not as a president a typical executive. Firm on matters of principle, he was inclined to leave details of college administration and purely academic problems to the faculty, and some were inclined to criticize a lack of aggressive leadership. Nor was he good "show window" stuff. He was not an impressive speaker, did not appear to good advantage at alumni dinners and other public gatherings, and was perhaps not appreciated by the graduates of the college at his true worth. Still, three noteworthy milestones of college progress were set up during his administration: First, the official recognition of Knox as one of five colleges west of the Alleghanies to be placed in Class One; second, its selection by Harvard University as the foremost college of Illinois to be placed on the Harvard Exchange; third, the installation of Phi Beta Kappa.

McClelland's work at Knox was ended by failing health, and he died not long after relinquishing the office. He had served seventeen years, longer than any predecessor but Bateman. He was succeeded by another Scotchman, but there was no other point of resemblance between them.

James Lukens McConaughy was one of the early products of a new profession, that of college president. Instead of being pitchforked into the chair from a church or college faculty, he had deliberately prepared himself for what has become the most distinguished post in the field of education, that of president of an up-and-coming modern college. He brought to Knox scientific management.

McConaughy was born in New York City, and prepared for college at Mt. Hermon preparatory school at Northfield, built by Dwight Moody with profits from Bliss and Sankey's *Gospel Hymns and Sacred Songs*. He graduated from Yale, specialized in education at Bowdoin where he took his master's degree, and was professor of education at Dartmouth when called to the college at Galesburg.

He came to Knox in 1918. He was young, with the confidence of youth, of engaging personality, great social gifts, an eager curiosity about intellectual matters, an omnivorous reader, and remarkably well informed on the current thought of the day, not only in education but in all matters pertaining to human progress. His singularly disarming and modest demeanor was deceptive, for he could be and was a man of purpose, decision and firmness. The members of his faculty, who complained of lack of leadership from McClelland, murmured at what they called the arbitrary attitude of their new president. McConaughy moved rapidly, on a predetermined plan, and with the eagerness for action that had much to do with his success.

Knox needed a shake-up. It was getting into a rut, failing to adjust itself to changing needs and objectives. McConaughy stirred it up. He decided quickly, too quickly some thought, but the outcome was nearly always good. He revised the curriculum, gave a new vitality to campus life, and wiped out before the end of his too short term all traces of the old prairie college which had served so long and well, a modernization begun with the advent of Finley.

So convincing was his personality, coupled with the rightness of his ideas, that when, in response to a flattering call from Wesleyan at Middletown, Connecticut, McConaughy resigned, even his critics were aware of a sense of loss. They had just begun to appreciate him. The trustees were inclined to be a little resentful. The resignation was tendered in the middle of the school year, and McConaughy offered to remain until commencement, but his resignation was accepted to take effect at once. Here is the time when, in the opinion of at least one alumnus, the trustees should have met and bettered Wesleyan's offer, as some of them certainly would have done if a similar emergency had confronted them in their own private business. Since McConaughy went to Wesleyan, that institution has been showered with millions of endowment, not as a result of its president's solicitation, but merely as a by-product of his vigorous administration of the college.

However, Seymour (Lyman K.) Hall, and Seymour (Henry M.) Library were built during his reign, though the impetus started under the previous administration, and an endowment campaign brought $750,000 (in pledges at least) to the coffers of the college.

President McConaughy was succeeded by Albert Britt. Although Illinois born and a graduate of Knox—the second alumnus to become president—he brought to the college and Galesburg the atmosphere of literary New York. He had spent his adult life in that city, as an editor of various magazines, had acquired a flexible and forcible literary style, was an accomplished and ready speaker, and perhaps made a better public appearance than any man since Finley.

He was not so widely acquainted with the leading men of the country as Finley, not so fruitful in securing funds as McClelland, not so experienced in the technical direction of education as McConaughy, but he stimulated the college in other ways, especially in extra-curricular activities, which flourished brilliantly, particularly athletics, for Britt was at one time editor of *Outing* and had a deep interest in outdoor sports. True, this athletic spirit anti-climaxed in the football season of 1935, when the Knox eleven lost every game it played, but that remarkable record brought it more headlines than a season of victory would have achieved.

Under his administration the college took on a sophistication, a modernness in its attiutde toward life, characteristic of the institutions along the Atlantic seaboard. It can be honestly said that these were brilliant years in the history of Knox.

Britt has remarkable self-control, never loses his temper, and is calm, judicial and impartial in a crisis. He never shirks a responsibility or fails to execute a duty, however disagreeable. He was called upon to exercise these qualities to an unusual degree, for during his administration the financial depression occurred in which Knox, and other institutions more heavily endowed, had to introduce stringent measures to reduce expenses, including putting the teaching staff on reduced salaries, and advancing the retirement of some of the professors, exactly as business was doing in its own domain. In this emergency he acted with fairness but firmly, sharing in the drastic cuts, and carrying on with cheerful enthusiasm.

His relations with the students were admirable. He was thoroughly liked, and was able to enter into their interests with unusual sympathy. He developed the responsibility of the students for their own discipline to such an extent that there were few infractions of orderly behavior during his administration. When such occurred, his policy was to treat each man individually, to save the student for the college, rather than to enforce a college rule.

The most significant public undertaking during Britt's incumbency was the consolidation of Lombard University and Knox College. This old school, founded in 1851 by Universalists, as Illinois Liberal Institute, burned in 1852 and rebuilt with money from Benjamin Lombard, had had a prosperous career, but the depression had affected it seriously, and it was felt by both sides that one college of first rank was enough for that locality. The negotiations were conducted by Britt, assisted by two members of his faculty, with such tact and diplomacy that the arrangement arrived at was acceptable to Lombard without impairing the prestige of Knox.

The restoration of Old Main, deteriorating from old age, was undertaken in the last years of Britt's administration, but this was due more to private initiative than official action by the board of trustees or its president. The repairs necessary to the restoration of the exterior have been made, owing to the tireless energy of Mrs. Philip Sidney Post, a graduate of the college, who as Janet Greig was dean of women and brought to Whiting Hall much of the agreeable social atmosphere which marked the nineties. She is today the only woman trustee of the college.

It was Mrs. Post also who secured for Old Main early official recognition of the fact that it is the only existing building associated with the Lincoln-Douglas debates. In August, 1935, a bill was passed to provide for "the preservation of American historical sites, buildings, objects and antiquities of national significance," and one of the first designations made by the board, which is under the jurisdiction of the Secretary of the Interior, and is headed by Doctor Herman C. Bumpus, formerly president of Tufts College, was the historic building on Knox campus around which cluster so many memories. While the building would have been thus recognized on its merits in due course, it is owing to Mrs. Post's promptness and assiduity that the honor comes in time to give a fillip to the celebration of the centenary of the college and city in 1937.

In 1936 President Britt resigned, after eleven years of service, and Carter Davidson, of Carleton College, was elected in his stead. The history of his incumbency is at the present moment an unwritten page of college history.

# 13

## The Twentieth Century

### I

#### CATCHING UP WITH THE PRESENT

The foregoing narrative begins with a close-up of the town as it is today, cuts back to its birth on an unbroken prairie, and brings the story of the town down to the closing years of the last century, and that of the college to the present. We have seen these settlers, emigrants from various towns in Maine, Vermont, Massachusetts, but chiefly from New York—older towns, but not so old as to have forgotten their own pioneer impulse—loading their families and goods in covered wagons and hiking to an appointed spot on a remote and lonely prairie, and there solemnly undertaking the founding of a city.

So virgin was the land on which they planted their settlement, it had never known the handiwork of man, nor scarcely the tread of human foot. There were none of the vestiges of Indian occupancy, camps, trails, burial mounds, common enough in other parts of the region. The prior settlers, the Southerners, had shunned the prairies and clung to the woods. Galesburg began its life in a fresh new world. Its site had no previous human history. Its starting point was zero. It was, the devout settlers believed, a gift from God.

We have seen the town assembled, the colonists living meanwhile in their temporary camp of Log City; we have watched it gradually emerge, find itself as a community. A small group of men and women working together, actuated by the natural impulse to survive, thrive, get on, and express themselves in such social life as their narrow creed permitted—burdened with the self-appointed task of setting up a church and establishing a college—did in fact create a village that became a city, a railroad center, a place on the map, listed in gazetteers, a political unit of the United States.

Its early days were grim and inhibited. There was no warmth, no joy of living, in its creed. It missed much of the picturesque life we associate with pioneer settlements. There was none of the rowdy melodrama, irresponsibility, rough sports and merry-making that animate the life of frontier towns, such as their more genial neighbors, the Hoosiers, enjoyed. The Galesburgers were serious and sober-minded people, and conscientiously avoided pleasure as sinful. It was this town's misfortune never to have sown its wild oats.

People are the ingredients of a town. Their work, ambitions, errors, shortcomings, sins, collectively, compose its history, but the town is an entity, with a life of its own. Behind the individual urge is the community urge, the impulse to make the best of itself as a town, reach for civic benefits, grab them if necessary, sometimes ruthlessly, to lift the community to the eminence all cities covet. For that struggle the Yankees were better equipped, harder, shrewder, than their easy-going opponents, the Hoosiers. When pioneer conditions brought opportunities within their grasp, they fought for them, and took them. Arriving last, they outstripped the other settlements in their territory.

The Hoosiers may have wondered if there was not some inconsistency between the Yankees' everlasting preaching against drinking, slavery and all ungodliness, and their maneuvers to despoil them of the railroad and the county seat, but if so they said nothing. They could hardly afford to stand on ethical grounds. They had started the hostilities and fought as unscrupulously as their opponents. It was all a part of the rough-and-tumble give-and-take of a new country, and in time was forgotten.

The railroad (we are still speaking of the Burlington, though there was now the Santa Fé) brought great prosperity in its wake, but it stripped the town of its detachment and rendered its internal affairs more or less subservient to the economic life of the nation. No longer was it able to depend solely on its own unaided efforts as in the years when commercial transactions could be begun and completed within the boundaries of the town. It was slowly sucked into the stream of national consciousness, sharing not only the good and bad times, but the mental images of its fellow countrymen. The panic of 1837 came to it as an echo from a far-off world. The panic of 1929 penetrated to the core of its being.

Toward the end of the century the comic opera war with Spain was fought to help the circulation of the Hearst newspapers, and produced its quota of Gilbert and Sullivan heroes, among them Dewey and Hobson, and possibly the romantic leader of the Rough Riders. It did not touch Galesburg. Its local militia, Company C, I. N. G., was not invited to join, and the town remained coldly aloof. But it learned the new slogans, "expansion" and "imperialism," and heard talk of its little brown brother, the Filipino. The Far West was now practically closed to settlement; the "movers" no longer trundled through the town and down the Monmouth Road, and some of the romance was departing from the prairies.

But it thrilled to William Allen White's ringing editorial, "What's the matter with Kansas?" ("What's the matter with——" was popular slang in those days.) That struck a responsive chord in the hearts of Western towns. Emporia was just such a place as Galesburg. Bryan with his "crown of thorns" and "cross of gold" came even nearer. He was a student at the neighboring Illinois college, had won a prize at an interstate oratorical contest where a Knox man was a competitor, but the town would have nothing of "sixteen to one"; it was still unalterably Republican, as it had been Liberty, free soil, abolition and Whig.

Bobbed hair swept the country and became epidemic, and Galesburg girls invaded the barbershop as later they were to invade the bar, following the impulse which made fads and fancies national. The bicycle found riders in nearly every family, and brought new problems, ethical and sartorial. Thanks to the local brick industry, Galesburg had the paved streets for it. With a good theatre, touring musical comedies "made" the town, and taught it the newest gags and latest popular songs. Ragtime brought the craze for strange dance steps, tango, maxixe, bunny hug, turkey trot. Most of the Puritan inhibitions, which had hung over the pioneer village, were dissipated by the turn of the century, except among the fundamentalist minority. No one remembered the town had fought a fifteen-year battle over a point of church government.

Of more substantial benefit was Andrew Carnegie's determination to get rid of his money. The imposing public library is one memorial to the canny Scot, and gifts to the college, particularly the faculty retirement pensions, are others. Far reaching in its effect on the methods of Main Street was the rise of advertising to a major commercial force, along with mass distribution of goods. Artificial refrigeration brought vegetables and fruits out of season. The new science of publicity built up idols or revamped old ones, as Ivy Lee touched up Miss Tarbell's John D. Rockefeller to look like something wholly different. The World War, the outburst of prosperity, the ensuing depression, were taken by and affected this town exactly as they did countless other cities. Its history was now one with that of the nation.

It followed feverishly the steps that led us to war, read of the sinking of the *Lusitania,* was roused by the stories of U-boat outrages, maddened by alleged German atrocities, and was herded and stampeded into war by propaganda along with the rest of the nation. It went through the throes of enlistment, draft, farewells to departing troops, bought Liberty Bonds, spent fuelless nights and meatless, wheatless days, knit and sewed for the Red Cross, saved its peachstones, hoarded its tinfoil. After demobilization, it welcomed its recruits home with bands and speeches, published a big book with their names and portraits, lists of gold star mothers, stay-at-home magnates who sold bonds and society matrons who rolled bandages, and forgot them all as promptly as elsewhere. By sheer luck it escaped the melancholy memorial that stands in the parks of many Western cities, as fifty years before it side-stepped the soldiers' and sailors' monument that perpetuates the memory of the Civil War.

During the era of unbridled speculation it invested its savings, was nicked by one pyramided holding company a quarter of a million dollars, paid income taxes, and bought cars, furniture and jewelry on the installment plan. The farmers fed more corn to more hogs and bought more land at mounting prices, until when the crash came, no known crop could be raised at a profit on what the land cost. The dam built by the founding fathers against the inroads of what they considered sin, weakening little by little through the years, gave way entirely and Galesburg youth, including the six hundred at the college, joined the mad dance of freedom and license, painted its lips and nails, put off its clothes, parked its corsets, carried hip flasks to dances, and necked in its flivvers along with millions of youth the country over.

The town went on relief; in one year a million dollars was distributed by AAA to farmers in Knox County; the city rose from the depression with morale intact and showing few marks of its submergence, as did most agricultural towns of Illinois. As already related in the windshield view at the opening of this chronicle, the motor car is bringing back prosperity by making Galesburg the market town of a fifty-mile radius, because the purchasing committee located it at the geographical center of the Military Tract, and the railroad improved its strategic position. But standardization, one of the great changes that have come over our national life, affecting Galesburg and all towns, will bear a more particular examination.

# THE TWENTIETH CENTURY

## II

### STANDARDIZATION OF AMERICA

Let George W. American step into his Buick, step on the gas, and set out to see his country, crossing from coast to coast, as so many of his fellow citizens are doing. If his objective is scenery, he will see much that will delight him. He will cross broad prairies that are gigantic patchwork quilts of wheat and corn fields; he will look off over great lakes like inland seas; he will climb snow-capped mountains, traverse real deserts and observe great rivers, some of them flowing at the bottom of titanic canyons.

But if instead of nature it is civilization that interests him, he will find little to surprise him in the American scene unless he is surprised that so big a country can have so many likenesses. He will not meet a strange American or hear an unfamiliar idiom. He will find the towns and villages in their classes strangely alike, little to choose between Fitchburg, Mass., Elmira, N. Y., Massillon, Ohio, Aurora, Ill., Council Bluffs, Iowa, and Waco, Texas. The same Main Street facade, chain stores, movie theatres, filling stations, government-built post offices, with the same vistas of people down the counter in the drug stores sucking up sundaes, the same groups of children on the street licking Eskimo pie. He will drive up Main Street between rows of cars parked bias to the curb, regulated by the same traffic lights, bawled out by policemen using the same words.

He will cross from State to State unaware he has changed his commonwealth except for the painted signboard "State Line" almost hidden by the huddle of bulletins and poster boards advertising motor cars, tires, gas, tourists' "overnite" rests and hot-dog filling stations. At the threshold of each town he will be warned by the authorities to observe the speed laws and welcomed by Rotary to its luncheon at twelve noon every Tuesday at the National Hotel. The hotel (there is a Biltmore model in nearly every sizeable city now) will serve him with the same luncheon he ate yesterday two hundred miles back in another State. The menu card has been brought to such a pitch of standardized perfection he could slip it in his pocket and order from it the rest of the tour. If he buys the local paper to while away the meal, he will think he is reading the home town sheet, for here are Walter Lippmann, Walter Winchell, General Johnson, Mrs. Roosevelt, Mickey Mouse, Caspar Milquetoast, and Dorothy Dix; only the weather report seems to be local.

The inhabitants of these United States have become more nearly like-minded than any other group in the world. Our country has made its greatest growth since means of intercommunication became common and plentiful. The railroad and the motor car have made the country smaller. People get about and see how other people live and adjust their lives accordingly. England still has its Yorkshire farmers who have never seen London, France its Breton peasants whose "farthest footsteps never strayed beyond the village of their birth," but the inhabitants of this country are brought into contact with each other like the ingredients of a well-mixed salad. The result is an apparatus to make over newcomers into the standardized pattern. Facility of intercourse together with a certain intolerance toward non-conforming dress, action, thought, impel us to adjust ourselves to mass formation like soldiers at the command "Right dress."

Newspapers which began as independent, individual local organs, have been growing more and more like each other as do married couples who spend a lifetime together and unconsciously assimilate each other's traits and mannerisms. The syndicates distribute comic strips, canned editorials, features and photographs, imparting a family resemblance to newspapers published in widely separated cities. Concentration of many papers under one management means that every device for increasing circulation is exchanged and adopted by all. They are alike not only in physical appearance but in policy.

Magazines, especially women's magazines, with their enormous circulations averaging two million or so each, disseminate constructive suggestions about the whole problem of living—food, furnishing, dress, and the upbringing of children, and they too bear a strange likeness to one another and borrow each other's tricks. The movie and the radio distribute eye and ear suggestions to millions nightly. The chain stores greet us on every high street from Maine to California, with the same red-and-gold fronts, the same window dressing, the same arrangement of goods inside. Apartment houses, or duplicate cottages, order the daily lives of millions of families, with dressing table, kitchen sink, and bathtub in identical positions so that life must be lived on the same ground plan.

It has been said that nowhere are there so many people in so large a territory engaged in unrestricted free trade with one another. It might be added that nowhere are there so many people surrounded by the same paraphernalia, doing the same thing in the same way at the same time as in this territory. They flock like sheep to the local movie palace on Saturday night, the same theatre with the same façade and the same film, a unit in a country-wide chain; they turn out punctually in their flivvers Sunday mornings with the same lack of destination; and now the radio with its regimented time-table has them all listening to Major Bowes at the appointed hour like Islam at the call of Muezzin.

Standardization is an omnibus word with many meanings. The standardization of material things is a convenience in an age in which so many material things seem necessary to perform the function of living. No one quarrels with the idea of having all electric light outlets of the same caliber and thread so that any lamp fits any socket. But with us standardization has gone farther than that. The human unit has been standardized so that a family from Springfield, Mass., will fit into a community in Springfield, Ohio, as neatly as an incandescent lamp fits into a socket. There are really two forces at work to force us into the

American pattern. One is that spirit of intolerance which frowns on all efforts to be different from the common run. The other is the spirit of emulation, a disposition to do what others do, keep up with one's crowd, or down with it if necessary.

This generalization, which is as full of holes as most generalizations, is nevertheless a picture of one set of influences working upon the average American, native or imported, to round off sharp corners and shape him into something conforming to the general pattern. It sounds irresistible, but the net result is actually not as bad as it sounds.

## III

### THE HUMAN CONTENT

If our imaginary cross-country tourist concludes that this is all there is to his country, he would be wrong. It is not the one long Main Street it seems. The superficial likenesses are amazing, but there are still to be found in such environments people whose lives escape the dye-stamping process, who inherit their individuality from a frontier still near; salty characters with vision, humor, philosophy, the David Harums, Abe Martins, David Graysons.

The newspaper man already mentioned, whose passion was geology, belonged to this blessed brotherhood. He died in harness at the age of eighty-two. For fifty-five years he chronicled the daily history of his fellow citizens, and was universally beloved. As often as his work permitted he escaped to a world as remote from newsgathering as could be imagined, and in that field made a modest success. There is something epic about such a life, with no outstanding dramatic incident, but radiating a quiet influence that raises it from the humdrum and commonplace. He it was who first showed the writer of these lines the wonders of a geode. With a tap of his hammer he broke a seemingly commonplace boulder, and lo, the inside was one gleaming mass of sparkling jewels. At the heart of many commonplace and conventional communities may be found shining crystals of pure quartz.

The manager of the local telephone line goes home at the end of a day at the office to a workshop in the basement of his home, equipped with power lathe, precision tools for processing metal, grinding lenses, machining parts. He is an amateur astronomer. The workshop is but a means to an end. Here he is building a six-inch equatorial telescope, the foundation already set in masonry in his garden. Nightly he joins the two thousand amateur star-gazers, who have already made discoveries professional astronomers treat with respect.

Another, who teaches manual training at the high school, has a large house on one of the good streets. One can go from room to room without finding a piece of furniture that was not made by his hands. It is fine, beautiful work, panels, carving, inlays in the best tradition of cabinet making, sometimes inspired by Chippendale or Fyffe, sometimes his own pleasing designs. It represents twenty years of spare time work. Measured by dollars, judging by prices in New York for hand-made pieces, the collection might be worth twenty or thirty thousand. Measured as a means of expression, of creation, it has a greater value than that. In this one small town are so many inspired by the same urge to create, that a craftsman's guild meets regularly. Its members stimulate each other by exhibiting their prowess in wood, metal, mother of pearl, brass, glass, and other honest material.

There is something in us that demands contact with elemental forces—earth, sky, wind, sun. There is a philosophy that comes from nearness to the land, tilling the soil, caring for animals, coping directly and at first hand with nature. Outdoor men, farmers, cowboys, shepherds, sailors, hunters, engineers, have it. I have often felt it in my boyhood in the farmers that I knew, strong, quiet, thoughtful men. The earth does things to you— the smell of freshly turned sod, the sun on the back of your neck, running water, the tremendous systole and diastole of nature, giving each month of the round a significance; in the big city they are but names on a calendar.

The Greeks put the idea neatly in the legend of Antæus, whose strength was renewed by contact with Mother Earth. Only by getting him off his feet could Hercules overcome him. The small town is still linked to the soil. It has more affinity with the country than with the city. Its people are still aware of the procession of the seasons, seedtime and harvest, sunrise and sunset, the night and its stars.

But the best element of a city like Galesburg is the people who inhabit it. The statement is made boldly, with full knowledge that this aspect is the one oftenest seized upon for ridicule—their dullness, banality, narrow lives and interests. Modern writers, gluttons for realism, love to depict a small town as the acme of boredom, if not a sink of iniquity. Sinclair Lewis set the fashion with *Main Street* and *Work of Art.* Thyra Samter Winslow was entertainingly malicious in *My Own, My Native Land.* Phil Stong in *Village Tale,* and James Couzens in *The Last Adam,* have dwelt on the sinister side of small town life, the dirty stories around the stove at the general store, the furtive amours in haystacks, sadism, abnormality. Such things make a story. They imply facing the facts of human nature. But they are in a strict sense not true. There are such phases of life, even in Galesburg, but they are phases. To dwell on them distorts the picture. Even in Sodom, N. Y., life is not as bad as James Cain thinks or even James Farrell. It is easily possible to match each sordid, perverted, lecherous old man in a New England village or prairie town with another equally true, drawn from the same community, of noble life, devotion to an ideal, or cheerful philosophy. Nor are queer characters, eccentric personalities, people slightly daft, indigenous to small cities. High visibility makes "ornery" traits stand out.

The indictments of the realists are not true, except as they are true of the human race. They average about the same everywhere. Inhabitants of small towns are no better and no worse than those of big cities, or open country, but in the small town you know them as friends, neighbors, acquaintances, over a long span of years, lifetimes often, and they know you—a sobering thought. You do not need to pretend. You can be yourself.

One is aware of the continuing stream of life. Mankind is seen as a whole, in all of its relations, instead of such detached segments as impinge on one's consciousness among the milling crowds of a great city. You may behold the span of five generations, births, marriages, deaths, the vagaries of heredity, the changing fortunes in human lives. I recall in my boyhood a stern bearded man, son of the founder of the town. I knew his son and his grandson; I know that grandson's grandson—five generations, and such experience may be repeated with other family lines. The lives of such dynasties constitute books, books read with a touch of nostalgia by detached, floating city dwellers whose roots are in some such community as Galesburg.

There is as much romance, adventure, drama, tragedy, in any small town as among a similar sized group in a large city. For one to whom the human animal is the most interesting in the world there is unfailing entertainment, and food for thought, in the changing panorama. What is often disparaged as the gossip of small communities is its most vital quality, interest in human history. After all, what is the difference between country-wide concern in the matrimonial adventures of the five-and-ten princess, Barbara Hutton, or the struggle for possession of Gloria Vanderbilt and her check-book, and the same curiosity, tempered in this case by friendly interest, regarding the marriage of Mame Littleton of our town, whose birth notice we read it seems just the other day, whose father and mother are our friends and neighbors, whose grandfather we looked up to with awe as one of "the rude forefathers of the hamlet"? The country correspondence in the weekly newspaper comes in for much "joshing" with its grist of seemingly trivial social affairs, but it is not a whit more trivial than the society column of a metropolitan newspaper.

Neighborliness! That is the touchstone of the small town. Our common, ingrained humanity finds expression and overleaps mere social distinctions. The girl in the Western Union office rejoices audibly over the good news we are telegraphing, and condoles with us over a misfortune. She goes to our Sunday-school. The carpenter and painter take a friendly interest in their work, with none of that slapdash indifference of city artisans, here today and gone tomorrow, and they do odd jobs for you not countenanced by their unions.

The old postman sits down in your porch to look over this week's *Time* before leaving it, and tells you he is sorry there is no letter from Betty this week—Betty being your married daughter who lives in Texas. The postman has known her from babyhood, when she used to sit on the gatepost waiting for the mail. Now she has daughters of her own. One is surrounded by this warm, friendly, genuine interest that is neither prying nor curiosity, which does not fail in times of trouble. It is the one thing country folk miss in large cities.

The neighborliness of the town is an honest tradition from pioneer days when the early settlers "changed work" and helped one another with bees and house raisings, as is done still among farmers at threshing time. The mutual exchanges of a simple social life, from porch to porch, over the back fence, the casual daily meetings on Main Street, still go on, but they are paralleled now by social functions which differ little from the same festivities in large cities.

Such aspects may not be strictly history, but they have a pertinence in describing a city, for a city is primarily a device for living, and the character of the life possible there is a part of the description. It has taken a hundred years to produce the municipality known as Galesburg. Was it worth while? Is Galesburg a good town as towns go? No one knows yet whether a hundred years is young or old for a city, whether a century represents a small or large fraction of its life. It may be an infant, or it may be middle-aged. If it is still young and lusty, then the first hundred years have been devoted to growing up. It has reached the beginning of its usefulness, come of age. That is a provocative thought, and imposes tremendous responsibility upon those who have the fortunes of the city in their keeping. It may well be asked, what of the future?

## IV

### GALESBURG, OF ALL PLACES

The test of a city, after its economic existence is provided for and it has demonstrated its ability to earn its living, is the kind of life it affords its inhabitants. Galesburg was a planned city. It was located in this particular spot for a specific purpose, and this study is concerned with how far that purpose was realized, and what has been the result.

The purpose was not primarily to create a desirable place to live in the modern sense, but the more self-denying and disinterested one of establishing an educational institution to train young men to preach the gospel with a farming community around it to give it setting and support. That quaint objective has long since disappeared, but it is possible that a town founded under such auspices has acquired as a by-product some quality of gracious living. Apart from its colorful history, which is a part of the history of the Middle West, the description of the city as it is today is incomplete until it has been asked whether the town has anything out of common to distinguish it. Is it a good place to live?

Whether or not so large a measure of godliness as marked its early years was good for it, or whether, as more likely, the college is responsible, Galesburg had and still has undeniable amenity and charm. It has worked itself out from under the weight of Calvinism that depressed its earlier years, but the college continues to contribute its leaven of culture. To a small city a college is a desirable adjunct, and Galesburg is a sort of Western version of Amherst or Dartmouth, a New England college town shorn of its hills. Various visitors, some of them noted, have commented on a certain atmosphere perhaps not usually encountered in middle Western towns. In 1894, when Knox College celebrated the hundredth birthday of William Cullen Bryant (with the venerable John Howard Bryant from near-by Princeton participating) Eugene Field sent his regrets with a characteristic letter.

"I am sorry," he says, "that I cannot be with you at the Bryant celebration. I should like to testify by my presence to my reverence and love for the old poet. *Diis aliter videtur.* There are exacting home duties; things must be written; a delicate little baby daughter must be watched; the wolf must be kept from the door. Many years have elapsed since my home was among your people. They have been eventful years with me, yet at no time in all that period have I ceased to think affectionately and tenderly of the old associates and the old scenes. And it has given me great regret indeed that I have not been able to demonstrate in some practical way how large an obligation I feel that I am under to Knox, by no means the least beloved of my numerous *almæ matres.* It would be particularly pleasant to renew old friendships under the auspices of that reunion which you are about to celebrate. Bryant was so loyal a lover, so enthusiastic a student, and so accurate a reader and interpreter of nature, that I find it easy to associate him with beautiful Galesburg, its embowered homes, its venerable, hospitable trees, its shady walks and driveways, its billowy lanes, its exuberant gardens, and its charming vistas. He would have loved that academic spot; he would have loved the people, too, for he would have found them gracious, appreciative, and sympathetic in all those high and ennobling lines he always pursued."

In 1895 Edward Bok printed in his *Ladies' Home Journal* an editorial on the smaller towns of the country under the title, "Where American life really exists," in the course of which he said:

"Only at rare intervals have we such a careful and discriminating visitor as was Madame Blanc—perhaps one of the brightest women in the French Republic today—who after her thorough

American tour of a year ago, declared that the most cultivated social coterie which she found anywhere in America was in Galesburg, Illinois. 'Galesburg,' says some one in surprise, 'of all places.'"

Madame Blanc, her real name was Therese Bentzon, was the editor of the *Revue des Deux Mondes*. She came here for the purpose of studying the condition of women in America, which included the, to French women, startling innovation of co-education, and for that purpose visited Galesburg and Knox College. She devoted much space to Galesburg, for the town fascinated her, and she has left a delightful picture of it at the close of the century, which inspired Bok's editorial:

"We visit the town," she says, "which is charming with its shady avenues and its verdant boulevards. It covers a vast extent, trees and gardens occupying much of the space. Green trees surround the principal buildings. There are a few mercantile streets, but they are quietly busy as befits a town where trade is only a secondary matter, which has never cared for anything but religion and learning. The elegant quarter is filled with very pretty middle-class houses, mostly of painted wood, but of every architectural style. Lawns encircle them; they seem to be scattered over a meadow. The entire town is scrupulously neat. . . .

"Am invited to several houses in the town, where I find the best of company—women simple, and at the same time well-informed, talking on all subjects and asking intelligent questions. Evidently contact with the college is a constant stimulus, and the society of the professors a precious resource. Some have travelled, but they are not possessed by that feverish desire for change which I have remarked elsewhere, nor is there any trace of pretense or affectation—which is restful. The diversity of religious denominations in this little town, which is so devout as a whole, is singular. . . ."

If it has lost some of its concern with religion and learning, the almost demure devoutness which arrested the attention of Madame Blanc, it has turned at least some of the released energy to measures for common good. The church is no longer the focus of community life. There was a time when every inhabitant was not only a member of the church, but the same church. Today its churches must compete not only with a new skepticism, but with greater distractions. Radio keeps people home; the car takes them elsewhere. Much of the church going of an earlier era was fostered by lack of anywhere else to go. The college circle is still concerned with things of the mind, but it does not embrace the scope of the town, and it too has lost its concern with religion as the step-sister of education. And there are numerous other groups, interlocking and overlapping, which unite the town along various lines and interests, good works, amusement, some occupied with what they conceive to be culture.

Carl Sandburg is Galesburg's only native born poet. He sprang from that Swedish stock which gives the town its ingrained Scandinavian touch. Though a graduate of Lombard, Knox can (and does) claim him, through the merger of the two colleges. Other poets go back to Julia Fletcher (Carney) who in 1845 wrote an immortal verse, "Little drops of water." John Huston Finley finds time in sheer excess of virtuosity from several fields in which he is eminent to write some excellent poems. Born in Illinois, he lived in the town as student and president of the college. Edgar Lee Masters, though a student at Knox, was born in Kansas and grew up in Lewiston on the banks of that winding Spoon River that gave its name to his bitter anthology. But Sandburg belongs to the prairie. He is its authentic voice. His words pour forth with the sprawling fecundity of these fertile lands, silos and grain elevators, windmills, and piebald hogs, far horizons and sunsets of burnished gold. Almost any of his verses would serve as an appropriate pendant to this chronicle of the old Military Bounty Tract. For example he says in "The Prairie":

"I am the prairie, mother of men, waiting.
They are mine, the threshing crews eating breakfast, the farm boys
  driving steers to the cattle pens.

They are mine, the crowds of people at a Fourth of July picnic, listening to a lawyer read the Declaration of Independence, watching the pinwheels and Roman candles at night, the young men and women two by two hunting the bypaths and kissing bridges.

They are mine, the horses looking over the fence in the frost of late October, saying good morning to the horses hauling wagons of rutabaga to market.

They are mine, the old zigzag rail fences, the new barb wire."

# *Bibliography*

IMMEDIATE SOURCES, HISTORY OF
GALESBURG AND KNOX COLLEGE

## I. BOOKS

*Abraham Lincoln, the Prairie Years,* by Carl Sandburg, New York, 1926.

*Album of Knox County,* 1886.

*Annals and Recollections of Oneida County* (Rome, N. Y.), 1896.

*Bryant Centennial, a Book about a Day,* edited by Earnest Elmo Calkins, 1894.

*Condition of Women in America,* by Thèrése Bentzon (Madame Blanc), translated by H. A. Alger, Boston, 1895.

*Diary of Orville Browning,* 2 vols., Springfield (Ill.), 1933.

*Galesburg Public Schools, their History and Work,* 1840–1911, by William Lucas Steele, Galesburg, 1911.

Historical Collections of New York State, 1841.

*Historical Encyclopedia of Illinois,* edited by Newton Bateman and Paul Selby, containing history of Knox County and Galesburg by W. Selden Gale and George Candee Gale, Chicago, 1899.

*History of Henry County,* Kett & Co., Chicago, 1877.

*History of Knox County,* by Charles W. Chapman & Co., Chicago, 1878.

*History of Knox County,* by Albert J. Perry, 2 vols., Chicago, 1912.

*History of Oneida County* (N. Y.), by Samuel W. Durant.

*The Illini,* by Clark E. Carr, Chicago, 1904.

*John Murray Forbes, an American Railroad Builder,* by Henry Greenleaf Pearson, Boston, 1911.

*Knox County Atlas,* 1870; same 1903.

*Memoir of Silvanus Ferris,* by Charles Ferris Gettemy, Boston, 1935.

*Our County and its People* (Oneida County), by Daniel E. Wager, 1896.

[ 435 ]

# BIBLIOGRAPHY

*The Pioneers of Utica, New York,* by M. M. Bagg, Utica, 1877.

*Reminiscences of an American Scholar,* by John W. Burgess, New York, 1934.

*Seventy-Five Significant Years,* 1837–1912, by Martha Farnham Webster, Galesburg, 1912.

*Stories of Old Siwash,* by George H. Fitch, Boston, 1911.

## II. PAMPHLETS

*Address before Knox County Historical Society,* by Erastus S. Willcox, 1906.

*Bishop Hill,* by Michael A. Mikkelson, Johns Hopkins Political and Scientific Studies, series 10, 1892.

*Centennial Annals of Knox County, Illinois,* 1818–1918, arranged by Ella Park Lawrence, Galesburg, n. d.

*Exercises commemorating the Founding of Knox College,* Galesburg, 1894.

*Galesburg, its Rise and Progress,* holiday issue of *Republican-Register,* 1888.

*Galesburg Sketches,* Lee W. Pratt, editor, Galesburg, 1897.

*Historical Discourse commemorative of the Settlement of Galesburg,* by Flavel Bascom; and a Statistical Paper, by Frederick T. Perkins, Galesburg, 1866.

*History of Galesburg,* by Charles J. Sellon; contains a reprint of George W. Gale's "Brief History of Knox College," 1845; Galesburg, 1857.

*Hon. O. H. Browning and his Relations with Knox College and the C. B. & Q. Railroad,* compiled by Frederick R. Jelliff, Galesburg, 1933.

*Knox College, by Whom Founded and Endowed;* a review of a pamphlet entitled "Rights of Congregationalists in Knox College"; by J. W. Bailey, Chicago, 1860.

*Manual of the Central Congregational Church, Galesburg, Illinois,* Galesburg, 1895.

*Organization, Charter and By-Laws and Rules and Regulations, of Knox College, Illinois,* Galesburg, 1874.

*Past and Present of Knox College,* by Earnest Elmo Calkins, three

[ 436 ]

papers in University Magazine bound in a pamphlet, New York, 1894.

*Report of the Board of Education of the City of Galesburg for 1903–1907,* Galesburg, 1907.

*Report of Knox College presented to the General Association of Illinois,* May 24, 1861, Quincy, 1861.

*Richard Gale, Yeoman of Watertown in the Massachusetts Bay Colony, 1614–1678,* compiled by Edward Chenery Gale, Minneapolis, 1932.

*Rights of Congregationalists in Knox College;* being a report of a committee of Investigation of the General Association of Illinois, Chicago, 1859.

*Semi-Centennial Celebration of the Organization of the First Church of Christ of Galesburg, Illinois,* Feb. 25–27, 1887, Galesburg, 1887.

*Social Structure of a Western Town* (Galesburg, Illinois), by Arthur W. Dunn, Galesburg, 1897.

*Story of the Founding,* exercises dedicating George Davis Science Hall, by Ray M. Arnold, Galesburg, 1912.

*Students' Farewell,* issued by the former members of Old Knox, by E. M. Bruner, C. H. Bryant, Charles Marsh, G. P. Chappel, E. C. D. Robbins, W. Edwin Phelps, A. L. Riggs, Geo. H. Beecher, H. C. Foote, Galesburg, 1857.

Whitesboro Centennial Address, 1885.

## III. MANUSCRIPTS

"Autobiography of the Reverend George Washington Gale," 1855.

"Early History of the C. B. & Q.," John Griffin Thompson, thesis, U. of C., 1904.

"Historical Reminiscences," by William G. Stone, Whitesboro, N. Y.

"Journal of Jerusha Brewster Farnham," 1837.

"Journal of J. E. Wetmore," 1836.

Minutes of Trustees' Meetings, Knox College.

"Municipal History of Galesburg," Fred R. Jelliff, 1933.

"Reminiscences of Old Settlers," mainly papers read before Knox County Historical Society: Clark E. Carr, Edward P. Williams, Mrs. M. M. Piatt, Edward P. Chambers, Mrs. Henry Willcox, Mrs. Charles A. Hinckley, Mary Farnham Perkins, Ella Ferris

# BIBLIOGRAPHY

Arnold, George Churchill, Aaron Kellogg, Hiram Mars, Martha
Farnham Webster, Samuel Greenleaf Holyoke, Henry Grosscup,
Mary E. Gettemy.
"The Rôle of the Osage Orange Hedge in the occupation of the Great
Plains," by Mary Louise Rice, Galesburg, 1936.
United States Census, 1830 and 1840.


## IV. NEWSPAPERS AND PERIODICALS

"Annals of Our Village," Mary Allen West, *Our Home Monthly,* 15
papers beginning October, 1873.
*Galesburg Free Democrat,* 1851–1858.
*Galesburg Republican-Register,* founded 1872, now *Register-Mail.*
"How Galesburg Grew," Mary Allen West, *Republican-Register,* July
29 and August 5, 1873.
*Knoxville Journal,* 1849–1854.
*Knox County Republican,* 1856–1895.
*Oquawka Spectator,* 1848–1908.


## V. GENERAL

*America and Her Commentators,* with a critical sketch of travel in
the United States, by Henry T. Tuckerman, New York, 1864.
*America in the Forties,* by Ole Munch Raeder, Minneapolis, 1929.
*American Social History,* as recorded by British Travellers, by Allan
Nevins, New York, 1928.
*Amos Williams and Early Danville, Illinois,* compiled by his de-
scendants, Danville, Ill., 1935.
*The Anti-Savery Impulse,* by Gilbert H. Barnes, New York, 1934.
*The Aristocratic Journey,* by Mrs. Basil Hall (1827–28), New York,
1931.
*A Complete History of Illinois from 1673 to 1873,* by Alexander
Davidson and Bernard Stuvé, Springfield, 1874.
*Das Illustrirte Mississippithal,* by Henry Lewis, Leipzig and Firenze,
1854–7.
*Discovery and Conquest of the Northwest,* by Rufus Blanchard,
Wheaton, Ill., 1879.

[ 438 ]

# BIBLIOGRAPHY

*Domestic Manners of the Americans,* by Mrs. Trollope, 2 vols., London, 1832.

*Emigrants' Guide to the Western States of America,* by John Regan, Edinburgh, 1862.

*The English Traveller in America,* by Jane Louise Mesick, New York, 1922.

*Epic of America,* James Truslow Adams, Boston, 1932.

*Fergus Historical Series,* Nos. 1 to 35 (35 historical pamphlets bound in 5 vols.), Chicago, 1876 to 1903.

*A Gazetteer of Illinois,* by John Mason Peck, Philadelphia, 1837.

*Golden Tales of the Prairie States,* compiled by May Lamberton Becker, New York, 1932.

*History of Illinois, 1818–1847,* by Governor Thomas Ford, Chicago, 1854.

*History of Illinois, to accompany an Historical Map of the State,* by Rufus Blanchard, Chicago, 1883.

*History of Travel in America,* by Seymour Dunbar, 4 vols., Indianapolis, 1915.

*The Illinois Central Railroad and Its Colonization Work,* by Paul W. Gates (Harvard Economic Studies No. 42), Cambridge, 1934.

*Illinois College, a Centennial History, 1829–1929,* by Charles Henry Rammelkamp, New Haven, 1928.

*Illinois in the Fifties, or a Decade of Development, 1851–1860,* by Charles B. Johnson, Champaign, Ill., 1918.

*Illinois As It Is, its History, Geography, Statistics, etc.,* by Fred Gerhard, Chicago and Philadelphia, 1857.

*Illinois in 1818,* by Solon Justus Buck, Chicago, 1918.

*Illinois State Historical—Collections, Transactions and Journal,* Springfield, Ill.

*Illinois and the West,* by Abner D. Jones, Boston and Phila., 1838.

*Illinois in 1837,* S. A. Mitchell, Philadelphia, 1837.

*Incidents and Events in the Life of Gurdon Saltonstall Hubbard,* by his nephew, Henry E. Hamilton (Chicago), 1888.

*Incidents of a Journey from Pennsylvania to Wisconsin Territory in 1837,* by Gen. William R. Smith, Chicago, 1927.

*Journal of a Trip to Michigan in 1841,* by L. B. Swan, Rochester, 1904.

*Jubilee—a Prairie College,* by Roma Louise Shively, Elmwood, Ill., 1935.

[ 439 ]

# BIBLIOGRAPHY

*Memorable Days in America,* being a Journal of a Tour, including accounts of Mr. Birkbeck's Settlement in the Illinois, by W. Faux, London, 1823.

*Life in Prairie Land,* by Eliza W. Farnham, New York, 1846.

*The Life of Jonathan Baldwin Turner,* by his daughter, Mary Turner Carriel, Jacksonville, 1911.

*Narrative of the Riots at Alton in connection with the death of Rev. Elijah P. Lovejoy,* by Rev. Edward Beecher, Alton, 1838.

*A New Home—Who'll Follow? or Glimpses of Western Life,* by Mrs. Mary Clavers (pseud.) an actual settler, New York, 1839.

*A New Guide for Emigrants to the West,* by John Mason Peck, Boston, 1837.

*Notes on the Western States,* by James Hall, Phila., 1838.

*Pictures of Illinois One Hundred Years Ago,* ed. by Milo Milton Quaife, Chicago, 1908.

*The Pioneer History of Illinois,* 1673 to 1818, by John Reynolds, Belleville, 1852.

*The Prairie Province of Illinois,* by Edith M. Poggi, Urbana, 1934.

"Proceedings of the Illinois Anti-Slavery Convention held at Upper Alton, Oct. 26–28, 1837." An "Extra" of *The Alton Observer,* Alton, 1838.

*The Rambler in North America,* 1832–1833, by Charles J. Latrobe, 2 vols., London, 1835.

*Records of the Olden Time, or Fifty Years on the Prairies,* by Spencer Ellsworth, Lacon, Ill., 1880.

*Reminiscences of Pioneer Life in the Mississippi Valley,* by J. W. Spencer, Davenport, Iowa, 1872.

*Reminiscences of Early Life in Illinois,* by Christiana Holmes Tillson (Amherst, Mass., 1872). Reprinted in 1899 in The Lakeside Classics series with the title *A Woman's Story of Pioneer Illinois.*

*Retrospect of Western Travel,* by Harriet Martineau, 3 vols., London and New York, 1838.

*Rise of American Civilization,* by Charles and Mary Beard, New York, 1927.

*The Settlement of Illinois from 1830 to 1850,* by William V. Pooley, Madison, 1908.

*Sketches of America, a Narrative of a Journey of 5000 miles in the*

# BIBLIOGRAPHY

*Eastern and Western States of America,* by Henry B. Fearon, London, 1818.

*Society in America,* by Harriet Martineau, London, 1837.

*Stark County (Ill.) and its Pioneers,* by Mrs. E. H. Shallenberger, Cambridge, Ill., 1876.

*Summer Rambles in the West,* by Mrs. Ellet, New York, 1853.

*Three Years in North America,* 2 vols., by James Stuart, Edinburgh, 1833.

*A Tour through North America,* by Patrick Shirreff, Edinburgh, 1835.

*Travels in the Interior of North America,* by Maximilian, Prince of Wied, 1834.

*A Trip through Indiana in 1840, the Diary of John Parsons,* by Kate M. Rabb, editor, New York, 1920.

*Two Years' Residence in the Settlement on the English Prairie in the Illinois Country,* London, 1822.

*View of the Valley of the Mississippi; or the Emigrant's and Traveller's Guide to the West,* by Robert Baird; second ed., Phila., 1834.

*Weld-Grimke Papers, Letters of Theodore Dwight Weld,* New York, 1934.

*The Western Gazetteer or Emigrant's Directory,* by Samuel R. Brown, Auburn, N. Y., 1817.

*A Winter in the West,* by Charles Hoffman, 2 vols., New York, 1835.

# Index

Ade, George, 397
Adelphi Society: organized, 131; resigned, 187
Advertising: early, 355; patent medicine, 356
Agassiz, Louis, 266
Agriculture, 120; Galesburg founders were farmers, 7; condition of farmers, 15–17; farm machinery, 18; bar-share plow used to break prairie, 152; revolutionized by self-scouring steel plow invented by H. H. May, 153; farm routine today, 18
Akron, Ohio, 87
Alumni Hall, 386
American pattern, 425
Amusements, 161, 241, 327; circus, 244; contests in music, 246; dancing, 328; dancing frowned on, 252; Dunn's Hall used for entertainment, 242; Fair and Agricultural Association, 247; firemen's tournaments, 248; formal balls, 328; games with apparatus forbidden, 162; German or cotillion, 329; National Horse Show and Equestrian Fair, 249; nomadic entertainments, 243; panoramas, 243; state reunions, 247; tableaux, 253; theatre, 329; theatrical entertainment, 164; performances rare, 162; wolf drive, 162
Anderson, Melville Best, professor of literature, 387
Angle, Paul, Lincoln authority, 98
Arcades on Main Street, 146
Architecture, without distinction, 113
Arnold, Matthew, 132, 403
Art, 256; collection at Bishop Hill, 231
Atlantic Cable, laying of, celebrated, 247
Auditorium, 329
Avery, Cyrus and Robert, inventors of spiral stalk cutter, 154

Bacon, Leonard, pioneer choir leader, 165
Bailey, John W., Gale's successor on faculty, 194
Bancroft, Edgar A., minister to Japan, 388
Band of Hope, 331
Bank: Farmers and Mechanics, 21; First, started by James Dunn, 239; Reed's, second in Galesburg, 239
Baptists secure lot through duplicity, 260
Bascom, Flavel, trustee, 191, 385; sketch of, 186
Bateman, Newton: classmate of Charles Beecher, 181; friend of Lincoln, 384; vote exceeds Lincoln's, 298; death of, 408

Beatty, Zaccheus, editor, 349, 360
Beecher, Charles, 385; teaches rhetoric at Knox, 180
Beecher, Edward, 4, 195, 385; sketch of, 180; resigns from Illinois College, 181; Burgess' opinion of, 179; invades Trustees' meeting, 185; makes public statement, 191; rebuked by Selden Gale, 191; delivers address in Chicago, 192; characteristic anecdotes of, 181–182; popularity in Galesburg, 194; inauguration of Gulliver, 376
Beecher, Eugene, son of Edward, 182
Beecher, George, 385
Beecher, Harriet (Stowe), 385
Beecher, Henry Ward, 385; raises money for Edward's church, 194
Beecher, Lyman, 36, 138, 195; "Christian Son of Thunder," 384
Beecher, Thomas, 385
Beechers at Knox, 182
Bees, 96; keeping of, neglected, 126
Bennett, Malvina M., 408; instructor of elocution, 388
Bentzon, Therese (Madame Blanc), 267
Bergen, Mother, entertains Lincoln, 284
Berrien, J. M., 215
Bible Society anticipates the Gideons, 168
Bickerdyke, Mother: nurses soldiers, 303; sustained by General Grant, 304
Biggs, Iram, editor, sketch of, 363
Birkbeck's English colony at Albion, 101
Bishop Hill, 6, 102, 229; colony founded by Eric Jansson, 230; Jonas Olson finds a location, 230; speculates with colony funds, 232; peculiar agricultural methods, 230; exotic architecture, 231; art collection, 231; colony ravaged by cholera, 232; Jansson murdered, 232; Swedes move to Galesburg, 233
Black Hawk War, 300; unjustified, 83
Blanc, Madame (Therese Bentzon), 267, 388; visits Galesburg, 431; description of Professor Hurd's home, 268
Blanchard, Jonathan: president of Knox College, 133, 136, 139, 170, 207, 215, 386; aids escape of slave, 223; appearance of, 143; a good president, 179; sketch of, 137; becomes Congregationalist, 172; defends himself, 186; long sermons of, 140; opinion of his contribution to Knox College, 190; resigns presidency, 187; persuaded to remain another year, 190; backed by business men, 184; attacks secret societies, 258; says "Civil War fomented

# INDEX

by Masons," 323; attacks Judge Craig and Free Masonry, 321; preaches against agricultural fairs, 249; tries to stop Sunday trains, 220; secures Albert Hurd, 264

Bliss, P. P., 402

Bok, Edward, editorial on Galesburg, 431

Book agents, 396

Books in the Fifties, 254—*American Atlas, Boston Common, Cyclopedia of Modern Travel, Dred, Edith or the Quaker's Daughter, Every Lady's Counselor and Lawyer, Gospel Fruits or Bible Christianity, How to Write, Journey to Italy, Kate Weston or To Will or To Do, Letters of Madame de Sevigne, Lilly Bell or the Lost Child, Little Dorrit, Mabel or Heart Histories, Missionary Heroes and Martyrs, Modern Travel, Peace or the Stolen Will, Plain Home Talk and Medical Common Sense, Rozella of Laconia, Spurgeon's Sermons, Tale of Our Own Times, The Family Doctor, The New World, Turkey and the Turks, Waverley Novels*

Books read in school, 341

Books, religious, popularity of, 395

Bowes, Major, 424

Brady, Albert Burt, 397

Brick Church organized, 179

Britt, Albert, 33; becomes Knox president, 413; Lombard University consolidated with Knox, 414

Brooks, John M., engineer, 212

Broom corn, 125; introduced by Swedes at Bishop Hill, 231; brooms made at Knox College, 236

Brothel, 350

Brown, Edwin R., 406

Brown, George W., 297; invents corn planter, 154

Brown, John, memorial service for, 247

Browning, Orville H.: elected trustee, 172; supports Gale, 184; hostile to Beecher, 185, 188; journey to Galesburg, 202; appointed railroad attorney, 215; replies to Beecher, 193

Brown's Hotel, 351

Bruner, Francis, 188

Bryant, John Howard, 123, 215, 406

Bryant, William Cullen, birth celebrated at Galesburg, 406

Bucklin, James, Canal engineer, 200

Bumpus, Doctor Herman C., 415

Bunce, Doctor, 184, 187; pioneer doctor, 207

Burgess, John William, 179; joins Knox faculty, 377; resigns, 380; "Reminiscences of an American Scholar," 377

Burlington ferry, 204

Burlington Route, 3, 5, 6, 8, 212, 214, 215, 418; branches called "cats' tails," 216; mileage, 217; pay car, arrival of, 353; western terminus at Burlington, 203

Business: habits, changes in, 147; hours, 351; letters, copied in press, 150; factories small in 1850, 236; retail establishments, 1850, 235

Business setting of Galesburg, 348

Butter, 13

Cadmus Club, 400

Cain, James, 427

Cairo, Ill., 102, 198, 200; satirized by Dickens, 101

Caledonia Hall, 329, 350

Candles, 116

Capital and labor, 119

Carnegie, Andrew, gives Public Library, 420

Carney, Julia Fletcher, 400, 433

Carr, Clark Ezra, 362, 399; appointed postmaster by Lincoln, 298; books by, 300; helps secure Santa Fé, 369; Minister to Denmark, 299; postmaster, has trouble with Swedish names, 234; sketch of, 299

Carr, Clark M., collects money to pay railroad surveyors, 209

Casey, Bill, fugitive slave, 223

Catholics, 353

Cedar Fork as a sewer, 103, 346

Central Military Tract, 215

Central Military Tract Railroad, 208, 214

Central Primary School, 260, 339, 343

Chain stores, 345

Chambers, Matthew, 69; business methods of, 151; sketch of, 119; trustee of Knox College, 108

Chambers, Smith, becomes supervisor, 315

Chambers' store, 116

Chappell, Leonard, starts oil mill, 113

Chappell, Robert, 350

Charles, George A., official surveyor of Knox Co., 63

Chase, Bishop, and Jubilee College, 101

Chicago, 54

Chicago & Northwestern Railroad, 210

Chicago, Rock Island & Pacific Railroad, 209

Christmas: not celebrated, 88; first celebration of, 353

Churches, 26, 260; St. Patrick's Catholic, 241

Churchill, George: principal of Academy, 381, 388; sketch of, 262; surveys for railroad, 209; creates Galesburg school system, 271; death of, 408

Churchill, Norman, 354; baits Presbytery, 171

Circleville, Ohio, 87

Circuit riders, 80

City, test of a, 430

City water, 335

Civil War, 325; bounties voted to soldiers, 301; ends religious controversy, 195; "fomented by Masons," says Blanchard, 323; McKinley Kantor's *Long Remember*, 307; Mother Bickerdyke nurses soldiers, 303; preliminary clashes, 82; Sanitary Fair held in Colton's store, 303; Sherman's life saved by William Patch, 302

Clark, George Rogers, expedition of, 81

Clothing, how settlers dressed, 96

[ 444 ]

# INDEX

Colton, Chauncey Sill, 210, 354, 385; contributes for school building, 142; gives first schoolhouse, 112; promotes railroad, 207; saves the railroad, 213; railroad director, 209; sketch of, 116
Colton, Gad: first manufacturer, 114; sketch of, 119
Colton's foundry, 145
Colton's store, 107, 116, 145; first at Log City, 118; first building in Galesburg, 118
Colville, Robert, 362, 404; manufacturer of account books, 149
Comstock, Milton, 381; retirement of, 408; sketch of, 262
Conger, Hugh, first blacksmith, 111
Controversial pamphlets, 193
Cooking, pioneer, 95
Corn, 125; and pork staple diet, 95
Cosmetics, 347
Cotton grown in Military Tract, 96
Country correspondence in weekly newspapers, 428
County, Knox, 309
County seat removal: lawyers inconvenienced by courthouse at Knoxville, 311; casts its shadow, 313; local fight swallowed by Civil War, 314; Selden Gale leads fight to move county seat, 311; reapportions Galesburg, 314; secures five Galesburg supervisors, 315; his maneuvers, 313; George Charles heads Knoxville forces, 311; deadlock, 315; fraud, 317; Galesburg's inducements, 316; Galesburg wins second election, 319; issue tried in Circuit Court, 318; Supreme Court confirms lower court finding, 319; new courthouse delayed, 319; opera house used for courtroom, 320; courthouse commenced, 320; courthouse cornerstone laid by Free Masons, 321; Blanchard flays Craig, 321
Couzens, James, 427
Craig, Judge, attacked by Blanchard, 321
Cross, John, slave runner, 221
Curriculum revised by McConaughy, 412
Currier & Ives prints, 335
Curtis, Harvey: president of Knox College, 373; opinion of Blanchard, 195
Curtis, William Staunton, 373; president of Knox College, 195
Cushing, John Pearsons, political economy, 387

Davidson, Carter, becomes Knox president, 415
Davis, George, Science Hall, 410
Davis, Jefferson, Bateman's opinion of, 385
Davis, Southwick, 188
Dean of women established at Knox, 407
Denny, John, family founded Seattle, 205
Deere, John, 154; wealthy plow maker, 380
Diversified crops, 127
Dixon, Ill., 101
Doctors, 353
Douglass, Fred, famous Negro orator, 247

Douglas, Stephen A., 202; monument at Brandon, Vt., 266; well known in Knox County, 277; welcome to Galesburg, 286
Dressmaking, 166
Drug stores, old-time, 347
Duncan, Joseph, 203; Governor of Illinois, 110; backs Canal, 200
Dunn, Ann, 136
Dunn, Arthur W., 400
Dunn, James, started first bank in Galesburg, 239

"East Bricks," 134
Editors and readers, personal relation between, 356
Education, founders not interested in, 269; select schools, 270
Election Day, description of, 317
Electric lighting, 367
"Elsie" books, 396
Ely, Richard T., economist, 405, 407
Emerich, Henry, editor, sketch of, 363
Emigrants Guide, 206
Erie Canal, 52, 73, 198; opened, 77; buried, 199
Erosion of soil, 124
Expurgated texts in high school, 394

Fabrics worn, 147
Farnham, Eli, 354
Farnham, Jerusha, on Civil War, 302
Farrell, James, 427
Farrell, Will, social leader, 329
Female Reform Society combats licentiousness, 167
Fences, 120; osage orange hedge, 121; Virginia rail, 120; barbed wire, 122
Ferris, George Washington Gale, inventor of Ferris Wheel, 160
Ferris, Henry, 63, 116, 207, 354; leaves Missouri account slavery, 226; versatility of, 159
Ferris, Mary Ellen, 343; debates literal interpretation of Bible, 258; becomes head of high school, 259
Ferris, Nathan Olmsted, 122, 141, 207; jack of all trades, 156; imports first sheep, 126; takes popcorn to England, 157; dies in California, 158
Ferris, Silvanus, 134, 184, 206; chief land salesman, 108; joins Gale colony, 56; erects sawmill on Henderson Creek, 91; second marriage, 160
Ferris, Silvanus Western, 141, 156
Ferris, William, 206, 354; first iceman and milkman, 238; introduces ice cream to Middle West, 158; wine making, 158
Field, Eugene, 218, 397; protégé of Professor Burgess, 379; opinion of Galesburg, 431
Finch, Caleb, 354
Finley, John Huston: president of Knox College, 33, 388, 400, 404, 433; establishes Founders Day, 406; wide acquaintance with men, 405
Finney, Charles Grandison, 35, 138, 402
Fire alarm, Old First Church bell used for, 240

[ 445 ]

Fitch, George, 29, 399
Floats in political processions, 278–279
Food: abundant in 1850's, 251; Gargantuan bill of fare, 251; prepared in kitchen, 336
Footwear, 147
Forbes, J. Murray, financier, 210, 216, 409
Ford, Governor Thomas, 78
Fort Armstrong, 199
Fort Massac, 90
Fourth of July celebration, 252
Fraker, Mother, refuses hospitality, 75
Fraker's Grove, 55
Fraternities, 30
Free Masonry attacked by Blanchard, 138, 321
Frémont, candidate for President, 276
Frost, John, 38; joins Gale in founding Oneida Institute, 42
Frost, Joseph P., establishes Frost foundry, 154
Frost's foundry, 237
Fruit, 16
Fugitive Slave Act, 276
Furnace versus oil burner, 338

Gale, George Candee, 109
Gale, George Washington, 35, 70, 130, 134, 206, 266; appearance of, 143; biography, 37–40; plan for Knox College, 45; life in Illinois, 178; Oberlin visited by, 60; trustee, 108; insists church be Presbyterian, 169; resigns from church with Presbyterians, 171; attacks Blanchard, 187; enters suit against College, 178; and Blanchard resign, 187; railroad director, 209; writes his memoirs, 175; attitude toward his children, 177; his interest in literature, 176; his opinion of other denominations, 174; baptizes two Baptists, 174; his sincerity, 173; death of, 196
Gale, George W., Jr., lack of education, 270
Gale, Selden, 109, 172, 206, 315, 385; elected trustee, 196; varied occupations of, 151; publishes Galesburg Newsletter, 208; railroad director, 209; rebukes Beecher, 191; elected trustee, 196
Galena, lead country, 101
Galesburg, 130; approach to, 3; founders, description of, 66–67; location of, 2; laid out, 104; lands acquired by Society, 64; distinguished for white houses, 113; 1850 population, 206; "nigger stealing town," 203; State legislature unfriendly to, 314; city charter, 275; becomes railroad town, 218; benefited by railroad, 197; celebrates laying of Atlantic Cable, 247; scene of Lincoln-Douglas debate, 278; public-school system lags in early years, 269; description of, as today, 3–14
Galva, 200; origin of name, 232
Gas introduced, 366
Gay, Lusher, 103
George, John Wesley, farming history, 15

Gilbert, Thomas, 49; aids escape of slave, 222
Gnothautii: organized, 131; resigned, 187
Golconda, 90
Gospel Hymns, 333, 402
Grand Army of Republic, 305; dominates politics, 325
Grant, Innes, 354; first professor modern languages, 130
Grant, General U. S., 200; sustains Mother Bickerdyke, 304
Greeley, Horace, 276
Green, Beriah, 44
Grimes, J. W., Governor of Iowa, joins Colton to promote railroad, 210
Groscup, Peter, buys Log City site, 98
Grubb, S. W., 349, 360
Gulliver, John Putnam, 405; interview with Lincoln, 375; president of Knox College, 374; inauguration, 376; church roll-call abolished by Armenian student, 381; no financier, 381; ringing farewell letter to trustees, 382–383
Gumm, Jacob, Baptist elder, 260; log cabin used for courthouse, 313

Hampton, Ben Bowles, buys Evening Mail, 363
Hansford, Charles, points out site of Galesburg, 59
Harbach, Otto, 388, 399
Hats, 147
Hay, 124
Hay barn, largest in state, 238
Hay, John, deprecates changing Warsaw's name, 205
Henderson Grove, 62, 76
Hesselquist, T. N., established first Swedish newspaper in America, 233
High School, 340; few students go to college, 344
Hired girls, 334, 337
History in terms of light, 366
Hitchcock, Henry, handwriting of, 219
Hogs, principal livestock, 123
Holyoke, James, becomes supervisor, 315
Holyoke, William: joins Gale colony, 89; organizes first anti-slavery society, 224
Hoosier clapboards, 93
Hoosiers, 76, 418; description of, 78; mainly Methodists and Baptists, 260; quaint customs, 166
Hope Cemetery, 4
Hopkins, Mark, 379
Horse and buggy era, 237
Horsford, Eben Norton, 266
House furnishing in the 1880's, 335
Housekeeping, drudgery of, in 1880's, 338
Hunter, George W., author of Civil Biology (Scopes's textbook), 399
Hurd, Albert, 264, 349, 381; sketch of, 265; establishes Library Association, 255; death of, 408
Hurlburt, Ralph, trustee, 108
Hurley, Edward, 6, 400
Hutton, Barbara, 428

Ice cream, 13
Ice made by William Ferris, 238

# INDEX

Ickes, Mrs., graduate of Knox College, 362
Illinois admitted to Union, 83
Illinois Central Railroad, 105, 210
Illinois College, 384; founded, 84; introduces osage orange hedge, 121
*Illinois Teacher* founded by Newton Bateman, 385
Indiana admitted to Union, 83
Ingersoll, Robert C., 143; his impudent speech, 298; skepticism, 395
Internal Improvements Act, 106, 110; 200, 217; not planned to enter Knox County, 202; peters out, 201
Irish, 326; introduced by railroad construction, 20; quarter, 6

Jackson panic, 106
Jacksonville, abolition town, 226
Jansson, Eric: founder of Bishop Hill, 6, 229; murdered, 232
Jayhawkers, 348
Jelliff, Frederick Reuben: pioneer and veteran newspaper man, 361; makes a hobby of geology, 362
Jenks, Jeremiah Whipple, political economy, 387
Jervis, Timothy, 49
Jews, 326
Johns Hopkins, 405
Jordan, David Starr, 261
Joy, James F., 210, 214
Jubilee College founded, 84
Judson, Harry P., 407

Kaskaskia, ancient capital of Illinois, 81
Kellogg, Hiram Huntington, president of Knox, 47, 129, 144, 170; goes to Europe for funds, 132; imports first sheep, 126; resigns, 133
Knox, General Henry, 109
Knox, James, 184; guest at Lincoln dinner, 284; introduces Lincoln, 290
Knox, John, 109
Knox College, 129, 334; Baedeker's comment, 33; circular and plan, 45; difficulty of obtaining charter, 110; charter granted, 111; gets a setback, 107; age of, 32; first building erected, 112; Old Main completed, 184; erected from railroad profits, 214; made Federal historical monument, 415; Academy, 112; Female Seminary, 129, 246; name changed from Prairie College to Knox Manual Labor College, 109; College Farm, 63; Adelphi Society organized, 131; "Founded by anti-Masons," 139; resident elocutionist, 246; campus, 63; dominance of religion, 391; farmers' children attend, 21; influence on town, 27; only small college to have military drill, 389; park sold to city, 321; social program, 1880's, 389; 1937, 29; Lombard University consolidated with, 414; "West Bricks" and "East Bricks," 134
Knox County: description of, 312; history of, 296
*Knoxiana*, 131

Knoxville, 59; unfriendly to Galesburg, 202; bitterness against Galesburg grows, 310; delights to harry Galesburg, 229; opposes railroad for Galesburg, 203; Hoosier county seat, 103; builds courthouse, 313; county seat fight, 309

Labor unions, 26
Lake Michigan and Illinois Canal, 200
*Lamplighter, The*, 366
Land titles, 61
Lane Theological Seminary, 138, 384
Lanphere, George: democrat, 208; Mrs., entertains Douglas, 288
La Salle & Rock Island Railroad, 208
Lawyers, 240
Lecturers, 255–256; Henry Ward Beecher, Parke Benjamin, Thomas Hart Benton, Elihu Burrit, Cassius Marcellus Clay, Ralph Waldo Emerson, Parke Godwin, John B. Gough, Horace Greeley, John P. Hale, J. G. Holland, Horace Mann, Bill Nye, Theodore Parker, Wendell Phillips, George D. Prentice, H. J. Raymond, John G. Saxe, Carl Schurz, Benjamin Shillaber, T. DeWitt Talmadge, Bayard Taylor, Mortimer Thompson, J. G. Wilson, E. L. Youmans; George Kennan, 403
Lewis, Sinclair, 427
Liberty Party, 274
Liberty Pole, 235
Library, College, 393
Library, Public, 393; established by Albert Hurd, 255; Young Men's Literary and Library Assn., 267; system, 349
Licking Summit, 87
Lighting, 365; electric, 367; gas introduced, 366
Likemindedness of inhabitants of U. S., 423
Lincoln, Abraham, 121, 136, 385; Paul Angle, 98; home town—New Salem, 98; votes for Internal Improvements Act, 201; votes for Knox College charter, 111; defends slave girl, 223; Harrison elector, 274; billed as speaker at Galesburg, 276; first suggested for President by Rufus Miles, 296; first visit to Galesburg, 296; personal friend of President Bateman, 384; Sandburg, Carl, quotation, 285; New Boston, surveyed by, 216
Lincoln-Douglas Debate, 277; deep feeling of people, 280; Lincoln arrives at Galesburg, 281; Lincoln presented with banners by young women, 285; "Knox College for Lincoln," 289; James Knox introduces Lincoln, 290; Douglas welcome to Galesburg, 286; Douglas receives silk banner, 286; George W. Brown drives 4-horse float, 282; discrepancies in stories about, 283, 292; whisky-selling story, 291; repartee between speakers, 291; Lincoln's voice, 293; James Paden's recollection, 292; partisanship of hearers,

# INDEX

287; Ida Tarbell, quotation from, 295; Edward Beecher's opinion of Lincoln's speech, 295; "Uncle Billy" Camp calls on Lincoln and Douglas, 294
Liquor, 23; not sold on Main Street, 351; Band of Hope pledge, 331; corn whisky bootlegged from Hendersonville, 159; drinking in Galesburg, 331; early license fees, 80; old-fashioned grog shops, 369; temperance versus liberalism, 370; vote against license, 275; whisky served at house-raisings, 81; women vote Galesburg dry, 371
Little America, 304
Livery stables, 353
Lodges, 24
Log cabins: how constructed, 92; how furnished, 94
Log City, 91, 417
Lombard University, 6; founded, 261; consolidated with Knox, 414
Losey, Nehemiah, 130, 187, 354; graduate of Middlebury, 266; first postmaster, 146; first professor of mathematics, 100; first surveyor, 104; trustee, 108
Lovejoy, Elijah, murdered at Alton, 224
Lovejoy, Owen, swears opposition to slavery, 227
Lumber, difficulty of securing, 114

McCall, Ida, 343
McClelland, Thomas, 83; president of Knox College, 409; advantages acquired for Knox by, 411
McClure, Samuel S., 397
McConaughy, James Lukens, 33; becomes Knox president, 411; character of, 412
McGuffey, William, Readers, 343
McKendree College founded, 84
McMurtry, William, Lt. Gov., 202; president of railroad, 209
Mack, Max J., 348; able mayor, 333
Magazines, Ballou's, Godey's Lady's Book, Frank Leslie's, Home Magazine, Household Words, Great Republic, Knickerbocker, Ladies' Home Magazine, Peterson's, Putnam's, The Little Pilgrim, The Prairie Farmer, Yankee Notions, 254; Evangelist, 165; Independent, 165, 376; St. Nicholas, 397; Union Signal, 331; Wide Awake, 398; Youth's Companion, 397; Northwestern Christian Advocate, 192; Argosy, Fireside Companion, Golden Days, Saturday Night, 399; Harper's Magazine, 377; Police Gazette, 347
Main Street, 3, 5; definition of, 11; index of town life, 348; standardization of, 422; stores undergo great changes, 345
Mann, Horace, visits Galesburg, 271
Manual labor colleges: Gale believed he invented, 41; popular with legislators, 111
Maquon, 104
Marquis, Don, 399
Martin, Gershom, 358; scandalizes town, 359

Martineau, Harriet, description of Chicago, 54
Masters, Edgar Lee, 104, 399, 433
Matthew, E. D., objects to assessment for streets, 365
May, Harvey Henry, inventor of self-scouring steel plow, 153
Melopæan, 235
Mendota, 210
Merrill, Charles, 350
Metropolitan Block, 350
Mexican War, 300
Michigan and Illinois Canal, 205; opposed by Hoosiers, 84
Michigan Central Railroad, 208, 212
Michigan Southern Railroad, 212
Miles, Rufus, first suggested Lincoln for President, 296
Military Bounty Tract, 61, 199, 201, 205, 421; description of, 70
Military drill introduced into colleges by Bateman, 388
Mills, Colonel Isaac, 68; tries to abandon boat party, 88; dies from effect of boat trip, 90
Missouri Compromise, 277
Mistletoe puzzles emigrants, 88
Monroe's Readers, 343
Motor cars, changes wrought by, 10
Motor traffic competing with railroads, 9
Mount Holyoke College, 48
Music, 401; old songs: Angels Ever Bright and Fair; Ben Bolt; Denmark; Duncan Grey; Esther the Beautiful Queen; Glover's Beautiful Birds; Hehl's Sweet Home; I'm Alone, All Alone; John Anderson, My Jo; Lament of the Irish Emigrant; Lost Birdlings; On the Field of Glory; Rest, Spirit, Rest; Root's Flower Queen; Schiller's Song of the Bells; Some Things Love Me; Star of Bethlehem; Strike the Cymbals; Barring of the Door; The Blind Boy; The Death of Warren; The Dying Christian; The Haymakers; The Hebrew Girl's Lament; The Last Rose of Summer; The Spot Where I Was Born, 257
Contests in, 246
Gospel Hymns, 402; popular songs, 402

National Guard established, 306
Needham, James G., 400
Negro melodies, 305
Negroes, 326; memorial service for John Brown, 247; not natural pioneers, 224; quarter, 6
Neighborliness, 429
New Portage, 87
New Salem, 117; Lincoln's home town, 98
Newspaper, first Swedish, in America, 233
Newspapers, tend to resemble one another, 423
Newspapers: Burlington Telegraph, 204; Chicago Record, 380; Evening Mail, 363; Free Democrat, 192, 234, 247, 253, 258, 271, 276, 296, 298, 357;

# INDEX

*Free Press*, 357; *Gazetteer*, 357; *Hemlandet*, 233; *Intelligencer*, 357; *Knox Republican*, 281, 298, 309, 310, 357; *Knox County Chronicle*, 358, 363; *Knoxville Journal*, 321; *Macomb Bystander*, 363; *National Era*, 361; *Newsletter*, 208, 357, 359; *New York Express*, 165; *New York Observer*, 165; *New York Sun*, 358; *New York Tribune*, 165; *Northwestern Gazetteer*, 357; *Oquawka Spectator*, 204; *Plaindealer*, 363, 364; *Press and People*, 358, 359; *Quincy Daily Republican*, 192; *Register*, 360; *Republican*, 357; *Republican-Register*, 349, 359, 360, 361; *Western Freeman*, 357
Niagara Ferry at Lewiston, 74
"Nigger in the woodpile," origin of, 227
Northern Cross Railroad, 205, 207, 211, 215
Northerners and Southerners, difference between, in Illinois, 79
Northwest territory, 1, 197
"Number Seventeen," 135

*Oak Leaf*, 131
Offices of professional men, 347
Ohio Canal, 73, 85
Ohio River malaria fatal to boat party, 89
Old First Church: organized, 99; begun in 1841, 141; bell used for fire alarm, 240; arbiter of civil differences, 144; first Knox commencement held there, 142; dedicated, 145; Presbyterians withdraw, 171; becomes Central Church, 3; public exhibitions held at, 164; hiding place for slaves, 226; becomes Old First Church, 171
Old Main, 4; completed, 184; description of, 182–183; erected from railroad profits, 214; distinguished by Lincoln, 295; restoration initiated by Janet Greig Post, 414; Federal historical monument, 415
"Old Siwash," origin of term, 29
Oneida Institute, 37; system of instruction, 42; religious fervor, 43; cradle of Knox College, 44
One-price system introduced, 349
Opera House used for courtroom, 320
Oquawka, Ill., 123, 198, 199, 202, 205; description of, 203; gets a railroad, 216
Oratorical contests, 388
Ordinance of 1787, 82
Osage orange day, 122
Osage orange hedge, Illinois College introduces, 121; Turner, Jonathan W., 121
Owen, Parnach, trustee, 108

Package goods, 345
Paine, Thomas, *Age of Reason*, 176
Panics of 1837 and 1929, 419
"Pansy" books, 396
Parker, Lucius, pastor during controversy, 170
Patch, William, saves Gen. Sherman's life, 302

Patriotism inculcated by school books, 342
Paving brick, 13
Peck, John Mason, 51; founder of Shurtleff College, 52
Peoria and Oquawka Railroad, 202, 209, 215, 280
Peoria Lake, 199
Perpendicular industries, 236
Petroleum known as "burning fluid," 235
Phelps, Sophronia, rebukes Southern ministers, 89
Phillips, John S., 397
Phrenological Society, 257
Plays—East Lynne, St. Elmo, The Lady of Lyons, Uncle Tom's Cabin, 330
Plunder Store, 239, 370
Political poetry, 297
Politics: dominated by G. A. R., 325; "Mud elected Douglas," 296; Wide Awakes, 297
Pond, Major, 403
"Poor whites," 79
Popcorn, 157
Portsmouth end of Ohio Canal, 88
Post, Janet Greig, 414
Post, Philip Sydney, 362
Prairie College, 63, 68
Prairie fires, how fought, 122
Prairie schooners, Conestoga and Yankee wagons, 71
Privies, outdoor, 339
Prudential Committee, 49
Public Square, 3; a mud puddle, 234; offered for railroad station, 208; for courthouse, 316
"Pukes," name for Missourians, 81
Purchasing Committee, 57
Puritan tradition dying, 332

Quincy, 205

Railroad promotion, 8
"Railroad Week," 9
Rapp's colony at New Harmony, 101
Reading in the 1880's, 341
Refreshments, 330
"Reindeer," first locomotive to enter Galesburg, 215
Religion, 98; effect on early records, 100; harrowing to young, 166; Knox students extremely religious, 390
Reserve Officers Training Corps, 373
Richardson, Susan, 295; fugitive slave, 221; known as "Aunt Sukey," 223
Riley, James Whitcomb, 403
Rogers groups, 335
Routes to Illinois, 73
Rustication, 136

Sale, Chic, 339
Salter, William Mackintire, 378
Sanborn, David, 215
Sanburn, John Gould, of Knoxville, 96; trustee, 108
Sandburg, Carl, 399, 433; Lincoln quotation, 285; "The Prairie," 435
Sanderson, Henry, 136; entertains Lincoln, 283

# INDEX

Sanderson, Levi, 130; landlord of Galesburg House, 143
Sankey, Ira D., 402
Santa Fé Railroad, 3, 6, 8, 369
Sauk Trail, 53, 198
Scholarships a handicap, 131
School books, 254; songs, 340
Secret societies attacked by Jonathan Blanchard, 258; displaced by Rotary, 24; lodges in Galesburg, 25
Sections, how determined, 65
Selden, Harriet, wife of George W. Gale, 39
Service clubs, 24
Settlers, disappearance of their descendants, 22
Seymour, Mary Ives, establishes salon, 377
Seymour Hall, 410
Seymour Library, 410
Shaker colony on the Wabash, 101
Shawneetown, 90
Sherman, General, life saved by William Patch, 302
Shurtleff College, founded, 84
Simmons, Thomas, 58; trustee, 108
Simonds, William Edward, literature, 387
Singing schools, 113
Slavery: a bitter issue, 81; Anti-Slavery Society, first, organized by William Holyoke, 224; Jonathan Blanchard aids escape of slave, 223; Canada sanctuary for fugitive slaves, 225; Bill Casey, fugitive slave, 223; John Cross, slave runner, 221; early vote against, 275; Fugitive Slave Act, 276; Galesburg conflicts with Knoxville, 222; Thomas Gilbert aids escape of slave, 222; Illinois surrounded by, 77; jail delivery at Quincy, 225; Abraham Lincoln defends slave girl, 223; Elijah Lovejoy murdered at Alton, 224; Owen Lovejoy swears opposition to, 227; national law severe, 228; Susan Richardson, fugitive, 221; Underground Railroad, 227-228; Nehemiah West aids escape of slave, 223
"Slues" (Sloughs), 72
Small-town compensations, 426; folkways, 327
Smith, John C.: originator of boat party, 85; dies from effect of boat trip, 90
Smith, Stephe R., 229; sketch of, 359
Soap making, 115
Social classes, 19-22
Social life: middle class, 333; New Year's calls, 330; upper, middle and lower classes, 327
Society, lands acquired by, 64
Sorghum, 126
Southerners and Northerners, difference between, in Illinois, 79
Speaking Friday afternoons, 341
Spencer, Platt R., penmanship, 343
Spoon River, 199; origin of name, 104
Standish, Professor John V. N.: quarrels with Lombard, 401; leaves property to Knox College, 261

Starr, Frederick, 407
Stong, Phil, 427
Straw vote, 277
Streets: named, 63; in bad state, 364
Students' Farewell, libellous under-graduate magazine, 188
"Suckers," name for Illinoisians, 81
Sullivan, Mark, Our Times, 338
Sunday travel, 72
Swedes, 326; only six in Galesburg, 1847, 229; large numbers from Bishop Hill move to Galesburg, 233; "Swedish Roll" for distributing mail, 234; Swedish quarter, 6
Swift, Erastus, trustee, 108
Swing, David, heretic, 395

Taft, Lorado, sculptor, 406
Tappan, Arthur and Lewis, philanthropists, 42
Tarbell, Ida M., 295, 420
Telephone, 368
Tenant farmers, 17
Tenney, Maud and Helen, first women to receive men's degrees, 380
Textbooks, 343
"Tippecanoe and Tyler, too," 274
Tompkins, Samuel, 58
Town planning unknown to settlers, 104
Townships in Illinois, how determined, 65
Transportation, 9, 123; railroad "callers," 218; essential to Galesburg, 201; early roads Indian trails, 198; wooden turnpikes, 199; stage coach between Peoria and Galesburg, 199; stage driver's opinion of Galesburg, 163; first railway in Illinois, 201; first engine lost, 201; wild-cat trains, 218; pay car, arrival of, gala event, 218, 352; trolley cars, 367
Trine, Ralph Waldo, 400
Trustees, first board, 68
Turner, Frederic, 407
Turner, Jonathan W., Osage orange hedge, 121
Twilight of Pioneers, 354

Uncle Tom's Cabin, 361; inspired by Theodore Dwight Weld, 43
Underground Railroad, 227; origin of term, 228
Union Hotel fire, 380
Universalists, 261
University of Virginia, 112; Gale visits, 40

Vandalia, old capital of Illinois, 110
Vanderbilt, Gloria, 428
Van Horne, Lady, 285
Victoria, Queen: declares slaves safe in Canada, 225; receives Olmsted Ferris, 157

Water supply, 368
Waters, John, 47, 58, 170; trustee, 108; turns against Gale, 189
Webster, Daniel, 211
Wedding, riotous, 332

# INDEX

Weld, Theodore Dwight, 43, 138; leads Lane rebels to join Oberlin, 44; *Uncle Tom's Cabin* inspired by, 43
West, John, 141
West, Mary Allen, 331; spurs action on Liquor clause, 369
West, Nehemiah, 49, 64; aids escape of slave, 223; recognizes hand of Providence, 59; first on the ground, 74; handy man of settlement, 84; erects log cabins for newcomers, 91; clerk of church, 145; trustee, 108
Western New York, 42
Whigs not allowed to vote, 274
Whitesboro, N. Y., 42
Whiting, Maria H., matron of Seminary, 387
Whiting Hall, 4, 387; acquires social amenity, 407

Whitney, Mrs. A. D. T., 396
Willard, Silas: promotes railroad, 207; saves the railroad, 213; railroad director, 209
Willcox, Erastus Swift, 139; opinion of religious strictness, 166; sketch of, 263
Williston, John Payson, gives money for West Bricks, 134
Winslow, Thyra Samter, 427
Wright, George, trustee, 108
Wyman, Jeffries, 266

Yankee peddlers, Southern suspicion of, 79
Yankees, name applied to New Yorkers, 78

Zoar, 87

[ 451 ]

*Prairie State Books*

---

1988

Mr. Dooley in Peace and in War
*Finley Peter Dunne*

Life in Prairie Land
*Eliza W. Farnham*

Carl Sandburg
*Harry Golden*

The Sangamon
*Edgar Lee Masters*

American Years
*Harold Sinclair*

The Jungle
*Upton Sinclair*


1989

Twenty Years at Hull-House
*Jane Addams*

They Broke the Prairie
*Earnest Elmo Calkins*

The Illinois
*James Gray*

The Valley of Shadows:
Sangamon Sketches
*Francis Grierson*

The Precipice
*Elia W. Peattie*